THE
FOOTBALL GROUNDS
OF EUROPE

THE
FOOTBALL
GROUNDS
OF EUROPE

SIMON INGLIS

WILLOW BOOKS
Collins
8 Grafton Street, London W1
1990

Willow Books
William Collins Sons & Co Ltd
London · Glasgow · Sydney · Auckland
Toronto · Johannesburg

First published 1990
© Simon Inglis 1990

Photograph on page 1 of Hampden Park, Glasgow courtesy of Allsport
Photograph on page 3 of VVV Venlo, Holland courtesy of Groundwork

A CIP catalogue record for this book is available from the British Library

ISBN 0 00 218305 6

Set in Sabon by Butler & Tanner Ltd, Frome, Somerset
Printed and bound in Spain by Cronion S.A., Barcelona

CONTENTS

ACKNOWLEDGEMENTS

When I set out on my first groundhopping odyssey around England and Wales in the summer of 1981, I little realised how many of my fellow human beings were similarly and hopelessly besotted with the character and allure of football grounds. But for their enthusiasm, knowledge and support, I would never have contemplated a second journey, which started in Budapest in October 1987 and ended in Turin twenty-two months later. Along the way I was guided and sustained by more people than I could possibly mention. Some, however, helped beyond the call of duty and friendship. Andreas Herren of FIFA, to whom fate led me in a Zurich cinema, gave me invaluable support throughout my researches. He also gave me an official tie, which was nice. Bob Vaughan was both a tower of strength and a Tower of Babel (though he admits to a certain weakness in Serbo-Croat).

My thanks also to Mike Hammond, editor of the 1988–9 *European Football Yearbook*, and Keir Radnedge, editor of *World Soccer*, both of whom let me into the secrets of their address books. Clino D'Eletto in Italy showed me his brilliant collection of postcards and kept reminding me I had the best job in the world, while M'hammed Phaytan at Progressive Tours of London kept me moving with a steady flow of tickets and time-tables.

For extra assistance with travel I am deeply indebted to the following: Deutsche Bundesbahn, Lufthansa, Malev Hungarian Airlines, Netherlands Railways, Norwegian State Railways, Olympia Airways, RENFE Spanish Railways, Swiss Federal Railways and *Business Traveller Magazine*. Harold Inglis totted it all up and Photocraft of Hampstead printed the holiday snaps.

At Collins Willow I am indebted to Gwenan Morgan for her dogged picture research, Judy Gordon for her patience and design, Barbara Dixon for her eagle-eyed editing and Michael Doggart for his continuing faith in me. And for putting up with another bloody book, my heartfelt gratitude to Jackie.

In order of chapter headings, the following have been most helpful:-

Italy: Tony Damascelli, Adriano Botta and all the staff at the twelve Italia'90 offices, Serena Macbeth, Brian Glanville and Citalia (London). **Albania:** Bill Bland (London Albanian Society), Skifter Këlliçi. **Belgium:** Bruno Govers (*Foot Magazine*), Serge Van Hoof. **Czechoslovakia:** Jiri Janicek. **Denmark:** Fritz Ahlstrøm, Finn Nørkjær. **East Germany:** Colin McPherson, Sacher Stolz (*Sportecho*). **England:** Bob Fuller, Sports Pages Bookshop, Football Association, British Olympic Association. **Finland:** Pekka Hurme, Finnish Sports Library. **France:** Philippe Tournon, Jan Buitenga, Patrick Boudreault, Jasper Spodul. **Greece:** Lou Economopoulos, Marie-Louise Ferla. **Holland:** Jan Herman de Bruin, Dr Herman Lubsen. **Hungary:** Susan Margitta, Erika Pollak, George Tabori and Judit Hock (Welcomepress), Klára Adams (Hungarian Book Agency). **Iceland:** Páll Júliusson, Joanna Clinton-Davies. **Luxembourg:** Lyn Smith, Howard Davies. **Malta:** Father Hilary, C.Lops. **Northern Ireland:** Malcolm Brodie, Eric White. **Poland:** Arek Ociepka, Miroslav Golek, Stanislaw Szkaradek. **Portugal:** Manuel Aleixo, Antonio Fajardo, Samuel Garcez. **Republic of Ireland:** Stephen Burke. **Soviet Union:** Prof. James Riordan. **Spain:** Andrea Johnstone, Gerard and Daphne Lane, Sam and Mario Garegnani, Dr Garry Marvin, Inma Felip, Douglas Williamson. **Sweden:** Anna DeSilva, Tomas Glanell, Bo Persson. **Turkey:** Övül Tezişler, Ergun Hiçyilmaz, Ertürk Osman. **West Germany:** John Pegram. **Yugoslavia:** Sava Popović, Yugoslav National Tourist Board (London).

INTRODUCTION

This book is the result of a Grand Tour of Europe, a tour in which I travelled some 51,000 miles and visited over 150 football grounds in 33 countries.

To a real fan it is hardly necessary to explain the allure of a football ground, or indeed the central role it plays within the game. Football is not like theatre or cinema, where eyes are focused upon the screen and all else is in darkness. A football ground – its stands, its terracing, its floodlights, its crowd, its noise, even its smell – is as much part of the event as the match itself. A 'home' ground really is like a 'home' to many supporters; a place of familiarity where, as part of the spectacle, one assumes a role no less important to one's club than the players. After all, the players and managers come and go over the years, but the allegiance of a dedicated supporter can and often does span a lifetime.

Italy 1990 and the daddy of all stadiums.

The football ground, that place of pilgrimage, is the one tangible constant which binds the fan to his or her club. Even if the stands change, even if one changes position from the terraces to the seats, or from the seats to a private box, the ground harbours the soul of the club. And however many matches one attends, the ground – an enclosed environment, a den of escape – always acts as a magnet.

Losing one's 'home' ground, for whatever reason, is a painful business, and one we shall encounter several times on our Grand Tour. Clubs or municipalities abandon their overcrowded, inner-city grounds in favour of modern, out-of-town super stadiums, often to find the old magic has faded irretrievably.

Yet modern thinking still considers the inner-city ground to be a dead duck, strangled by surrounding developments and lack of car-parking facilities. But this is not necessarily the case, as the experience of Hamburg suggests, where St Pauli's quite basic ground has attracted higher attendances than HSV's remote super-stadium.

In Spain and Italy some of the best stadiums are those hemmed in by their urban surrounds. A more central location than Real Madrid's Bernabeu Stadium is hard to find, while the likes of Genoa and Monaco have made a positive virtue out of their limited land resources. Football clubs are community assets, and thrive best when they are physically part of the community. With sensitivity and imagination, their grounds can act as a focus, rather than an irritant.

In the post-Heysel, post-Hillsborough age, there is a danger of reducing the study of football grounds to a mere scientific exercise in which safety and commercial factors become paramount and stadiums are stripped of their vitality. It is easy to forget why so many ordinary people want to attend football matches in the first place.

The challenge of the 1990s is to preserve the very best elements of football's traditional atmosphere, while at the same time adapting the stadium to the realities of the current climate. Hopefully the descriptions of some fine stadiums in this book will lead to a wider awareness of the design innovations already effected in Europe.

At the same time we must recognise that football grounds can never be entirely safe. Homo sapiens being the unpredictable, unreliable animal that he is, it is just as important to re-educate the fan, the policeman and the steward, as it is to redesign the stadiums.

Equally, the threat of hooliganism in Europe, as rampant in Holland, Italy and Greece as it ever was in its English heyday, must not be used as an excuse to transform stadiums into fortresses. The English tried that route and it resulted in the deaths of ninety-five innocent fans at Hillsborough in April 1989. The police acted on the assumption that the crushed and dying were hooligans, simply because they were football supporters herded into pens. Instead they were just ordinary people, caught in a trap of the hooligans' making.

In the long term, the best defence against violence lies not with fences and barbed wire but with attacking the problem at its roots, and these lie way beyond the boundaries of football grounds.

In the short term, FIFA, the world's football authority, took the lead by deciding, in July 1989, that individually numbered seats should be installed at those stadiums staging international matches under its jurisdiction – that is, World Cup qualifiers. Any standing areas still remaining after 1992 will not be usable for such matches. UEFA, the European authority, followed suit soon after FIFA's declaration by setting up its own committee to oversee the gradual phasing in of all-seater stadiums for club grounds.

Some may call this an inappropriate response to isolated incidents. Why should the likes of Iceland, a country with no record of crowd trouble, be forced to suffer for the ills of Athens and Amsterdam? Where is the proof that seats are inherently safer than properly stewarded terraces?

No-one can answer these questions to everyone's satisfaction, except to say that if the only tickets or places available at a venue are for numbered seats, overcrowding will be eradicated and crowd control (for safety as well as for security) will become a much easier task.

Terrace regulars may deride this line of thinking, but its logic is irrefutable. Which is why this book may, ultimately, turn out to be a farewell tribute to the football ground as we have known it for most of the twentieth century.

If there are any messages in this book they are broadly as follows:

That there can be no hard and fast rules about stadiums. What is right for Bari may be wholly inappropriate for Basle.

That often the most successful stadiums (e.g. Bochum and Utrecht) have the least spectacular architecture. Dazzling roofs (e.g. as at Munich and Split) are all very well, but they cost a fortune to construct and then earn nothing in return.

That more senior stadiums are being adapted to hold fewer people at higher prices (e.g. Rangers and Anderlecht), and that this process, allied to the possible formation of a European League after 1992, will force more supporters to watch games on television, or follow lower division teams instead. Fortunately, however, 'small' is already becoming increasingly beautiful, and successful (e.g. Mechelen and Xamax). Certainly the idea that in the twenty-first century football might be played in grounds empty apart from television cameras is a nonsense. So too is the belief that football grounds should aspire to become havens of corporate entertainment. Professional football without a live, committed and involved audience would be a charade.

That the concept of the stadium as a leisure centre (and not just as a sports centre) will sweep the Continent if the planned Eurodrome at Arnhem is a success. The technology already exists for sliding roofs, retractable stages, moving stands, and false floors raised above pitches. Income from Madonna rather than Maradona will influence the shape of stadiums to come, and

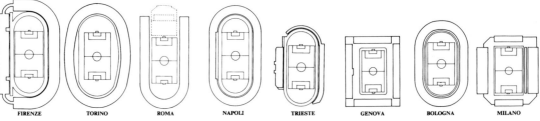

| FIRENZE | TORINO | ROMA | NAPOLI | TRIESTE | GENOVA | BOLOGNA | MILANO |

Italy's 1934 World Cup venues neatly summarise the most common formats used for stadiums: rectangular (known in Europe as English-style), elliptical (the most expensive to build), straight sides and semi-circular ends (cheaper and mostly pre Second World War).

in time an acceptable artificial pitch may even be perfected. (The chances of decent half-time refreshment for the fans are, however, as remote as ever.)

That in future, very few European countries are likely to have the chance to stage the World Cup Finals if the competition remains at its present bloated size of twenty-four finalists.

FIFA's minimum terms of reference for the World Cup now require all-seater stadiums (with individual numbered seats, not benches); a minimum capacity of 80,000, three-quarters covered, for stadiums holding the opening ceremony and Final; and at least a 40,000 capacity, with cover of the main seated area, for the remaining matches.

Italy's lavish response to these demands is detailed in the opening chapter. But where else in Europe can cope with a World Cup? After the United States stages the 1994 Finals, France will be strong favourites for 1998 (having embarked upon a major refurbishment programme for the 1984 European Championships). Switzerland will make a rival bid, but as our tour of that country suggests, the effort might prove a massive waste of resources. The same could be said of several other countries, England included.

That leaves West Germany (1974 hosts), Spain (1982) and the Soviet Union (Olympic hosts in 1980) as the only UEFA members left with a sufficient number of potentially suitable grounds.

Either the World Cup gets smaller, therefore, or it becomes the property of a small elite of nations.

All that is for the future. For the time being, we start our tour with the twelve richly varied Italian venues chosen for the 1990 Finals.

Apart from a vaguely planned route map, the stadiums are featured in no particular order throughout this book.

No doubt I will have disappointed many readers by omitting one ground or another; my choice largely depended on each ground's historical or architectural interest, the importance of its resident club or the fact that it has staged a World Cup or European Championship match.

For those readers disappointed not to find more about British grounds, I can only humbly point them in the direction of my earlier book, *Football Grounds of Great Britain*, also published by Collins Willow.

Finally, the text of this book was prepared before the tide of revolution swept through Eastern Europe in late 1989, affecting particularly the status of Berlin's Olympic Stadium. It is hoped a future edition of the book for the 1994 World Cup will not only take these events into account, but also extend the great Ground Tour to more distant shores.

Simon Inglis
London
October 1989

World Cup 1930–90

	Hosts	Finalists	Games	Venues	Total attendance	Average attendance
1930	Uruguay	13	18	3	434,500	24,139
1934	Italy	16	17	8	395,000	23,235
1938	France	15	18	10	483,000	26,833
1950	Brazil	13	22	6	1,337,000	60,772
1954	Switzerland	16	34	6	943,000	36,270
1958	Sweden	16	34	12	868,000	24,800
1962	Chile	16	32	4	776,000	24,250
1966	England	16	32	8	1,614,677	50,458
1970	Mexico	16	32	6	1,673,975	52,312
1974	West Germany	16	38	9	1,774,022	46,685
1978	Argentina	16	38	6	1,610,215	42,374
1982	Spain	24	52	17	1,766,277	33,967
1986	Mexico	24	52	12	2,285,498	43,952
1990	Italy	24	52	12		

ITALY

MILAN

STADIO GIUSEPPE MEAZZA

If first impressions are the most important, then how could the 1990 World Cup possibly fail to mesmerise us all?

For behold the new Giuseppe Meazza Stadium in San Siro, Milan; a gargantuan concrete, steel and glass temple to the great god of *'calcio'*, where on 8 June 1990 the fourteenth World Cup will open, and with it, a new chapter in the history of stadium design.

Of course every World Cup has produced a stadium or two of beauty or sophistication – Florence in 1934, Bordeaux in 1938, the Maracana in 1950, Gothenburg in 1958, the Aztec in 1970, Düsseldorf in 1974 and the Nou Camp in 1982. But in Italy, once a cradle of architecture, now a guardian of modern style, we expect the best, and in Milan, that most European of all Italian cities, we have found it. As we knew we should.

Milan, after all, possesses the money, the imagination and the drive; it also happens to have a football-fanatical mayor and two of the best club sides of the late 1980s.

If the saying is true that the typical Milanese holds his heart in his hands, one can be fairly sure that stamped upon it would be one of two names: **AC Milan** or **Internazionale**. And if, because of their prowess, the city of Milan merits the title 'Football Capital of Europe', it is an honour the Milanese will be careful not to flaunt too brazenly. They will just try to do that little bit better.

In the section on page 16 we shall describe how Internazionale, or Inter (never Inter Milan, as they are often mistakenly called), came to arrive at San Siro in 1947. In this section, we go back to the origins of the club which built San Siro in the first place, AC Milan.

The English form of their name, Milan (instead of the Italian 'Milano'), tells us of their roots. They were formed in 1899 by an Englishman, Alfred Edwards, as the Milan Cricket and Football Club, and first played on a pitch laid inside the Trotter – a horse-racing track – which was situated where construction of the city's monumental Central Station would begin in 1912. Little is known of this first ground, except that the players, six of them British, had to change into their playing clothes in a nearby hospital. Milan won their first championship while at the Trotter, at a time when only five northern clubs competed and Genoa usually won.

Milan's second ground, Campo dell'Acquabella (where Piazzale Susa is now), was mainly composed of earth banking and was opened in March 1903 with a game v. Juventus. Three years later, after winning a second championship (as plain Milan FC), the club moved a few blocks away to a ground tucked between a laundry and the walls of a cemetery, on Via Fratelli Bronzetti, and celebrated its inauguration on 7 January 1906, not only by winning the city's first ever local derby (v. Unione Sportiva Milanese) but also by rigging up the first goal nets ever used in Italy (fourteen years after their introduction in England).

It was while based at the Campo di Via Bronzetti that Milan won their third championship, in 1907, which was followed a year later by the split which led to the formation of their rivals and current co-tenants at San Siro, Internazionale.

San Siro in 1934 – an English-style ground for a club with an English name.

Milan's next move came just before the First World War, when they teamed up with cycling interests at the Campo Sportivo Milanese, opened on 31 March 1914 with a friendly v. Phoenix FC of Karlsruhe. Known better as the Velodromo Sempione (it was on the corner of Corso Sempione and Via Arona), the ground held around 16,000 and staged two internationals – v. France in January 1920 (Italy won 9–4!), and v. Austria, in January 1922.

By that time, however, Milan had moved on to their fifth ground, on Viale Lombardia. This was inaugurated on 1 February 1920 v. Legnano, and went on to host six games of the *Azzurri*, or Blues (as Italy's national team is known), the first being v. Switzerland on 6 March 1921. Sometimes called Campo Milan, the ground held 20,000 and boasted what was possibly Italy's first ever reinforced concrete grandstand (which in the late 1950s was reported to have survived as part of a tennis club, built later on the site).

But still the ground was neither large nor comfortable enough, so in August 1925 Milan started preparing for their final move, to San Siro, a district which is today on the western outskirts of Milan, and therefore must have seemed at the time even more remote. Behind the move was Milan's wealthy president, Piero Pirelli of the tyre company, who formed a society to buy the 37,000 sq. metre site and fund 5 million lire worth of construction over a period of thirteen months.

Unlike the majority of new Italian stadiums built during the Fascist period, San Siro was rectangular in plan (that is, for football only). It had a concrete, covered main stand, seating 9000, on the west side, with modern facilities underneath and a four-room apartment for the use of the Milan trainer, Mr Burgess, and his family. Opposite this stand was a rectangular open terrace holding 10,000 on concrete benches, while at each

end there was an open stand seating 3000 in a similar fashion. In front of all three open stands was a lower level, called the parterre (a French term used commonly at Italian grounds, meaning the stalls in a theatre), and this held a further 10,000 standing places.

Thus the club with the English name now owned a ground with a rather English flavour, yet one which was to prove easy to expand, stage by stage. For despite all the changes which have occurred over the last sixty or more years at San Siro, the surprising fact is that until 1989 most of the original parterre remained intact, and that underneath all the improvements to the main stand, its basic shell also survived. San Siro has never been completely rebuilt. It has merely been added to.

The new 35,000 capacity Stadio Calcistico San Siro opened its doors on 19 September 1926 with a friendly v. Inter (which the visitors had the nerve to win 6–3), and despite its modernity, the main criticism to be heard from Milan fans was that the stadium was too big!

They were wrong, of course. San Siro immediately assumed the prestigious and lucrative role of Italy's foremost international venue. The first of many games was on 20 February 1927, v. Czechoslovakia (watched by 28,000), and between then and the opening of the Olympic Stadium in Rome in 1953, the *Azzurri* used San Siro more than any other venue. It also staged two matches in the 1934 World Cup: Germany v. Sweden and Italy's semi-final v. Austria, which attracted a record crowd of 40,000 to San Siro.

The stadium first thought to be too large was actually proving to be too small, because even though throughout the 1930s Milan FC achieved little success in Serie A (Division One) of the newly formed national league, the income from rising gates and especially internationals persuaded the

ITALY

Milan Comune (municipality) to purchase the stadium from the club in 1935 and take its development one stage further.

The first San Siro improvement programme started in September 1937. Both uncovered end stands were enlarged and each corner filled in with terraced seating, work which yielded substantial dividends when, on 13 May 1939, another record crowd of 55,000 saw Italy draw 2–2 with their old enemy, the English. An even larger crowd of 65,000 was reported for San Siro's next international, this time against Italy's new allies, Germany, on 5 May 1940.

Milan FC had, meanwhile, been ordered by the Fascist government to adopt the Italian title, AC Milano, in 1938 – actually some years after other clubs with anglicised names had been brought into line – but no sooner had Mussolini ended his days hanging ignominiously from his ankles in a Milan square, than the club promptly reverted to their English name (although they kept the AC tag – Associazione Calcio – instead of FC).

Their neighbours Inter also made an important switch after the war, by finally departing their historic, but inadequate home at the Arena (see page 16) and moving in with Milan in 1947. Thus began probably the most celebrated and successful ground-sharing arrangement in Europe.

(Unlike the twin-club cities of Rome, Turin and Genoa, the two clubs in Milan cannot easily be separated in terms of either their playing record or the social profile of their fans. As with Liverpool and Everton, it is quite common for supporters of both sides to coexist in one family, and it is often only the personalities of the ruling presidents, or the star players which truly mark the clubs apart.)

By the early 1950s Milan and Inter were fighting it out with Juventus at the top of Serie A. Milan grabbed the *scudetto* (championship) in 1951, one point ahead of Inter; in 1953 and 1954 Inter took the honours, only for Milan to strike back in 1955.

What could the Comune do but answer ticket demand by expanding San Siro once again (especially as Rome was about to embark upon its own major stadium project). As early as 1947 plans were drawn up for a three-tiered stadium holding 150,000, but by the time the scheme was finally put into action, in June 1954, the figure had dropped to a more sensible 100,000 on two tiers.

It was a formidable plan, nevertheless. Conceived by engineer Ferruccio Calzolari and architect Armando Ronca, it left the lower tier almost entirely intact, but by removing the main stand roof and wrapping the whole stadium in an outer web of concrete supports, a second tier was to be cantilevered over the lower level on all four sides.

The most innovative element of the plan was the design of access routes to the upper levels. In addition to conventional stairways under the stands, Calzolari and Ronca devised a system of layered ramps, which hugged the stadium's outer walls and led, in a clockwise direction, from ground level to various entry points around the upper tier. To reach, for example, the upper northern end of the stadium, one would find a numbered ramp starting midway along the west side and climb gradually around the outside of the bowl until finding the correct vomitory.

Each of the nineteen ramps was 200 metres in length, 3 metres wide, and rose to a height of nearly 20 metres above ground level. It meant a long, slow climb up a gradient of 1 in 10, but there were also stairwells within the stands (and, later, lifts for the old and infirm).

The advantages of the ramp system were several. Mainly, it was compact, leaving San Siro's surrounding precincts free for car parking and circumambulation. It should be noted, however, that there has never been room to expand San Siro on its east side, because the stadium backs onto the grandstand of the city's main Trotter track – remember, Milan played on the old one between 1899–1903 – and this is almost as popular as the football ground itself (and certainly used more regularly).

But the major impact of the ramps was to give San Siro an unmistakable identity. Its striated exterior, rounded corners and cavernous interior gave it the appearance of a striped can of sardines with the lid removed. It was certainly perfect for viewing football, and although it never quite held the promised 100,000 – despite being hailed as the Stadio dei Centomila (how the Italians love to exaggerate figures) – the eventual capacity of around 82,000 made it at least on par with Italy's other recently completed major venue, the Olympic Stadium in Rome.

San Siro was reopened to the public on 29 June 1955 with a friendly between the Italian champions Milan and their then world-famous Hungarian counterparts, Honved of Budapest. Once more, it could have been argued that the stadium was too big – only 45,000 came to the opening –

The new, unmistakable San Siro in 1955, ramps and all, with the Trotter immediately behind.

but subsequent matches and, again, the first international nearly a year later on 25 April 1956, v. Brazil, attracted bumper crowds of over 80,000.

San Siro's only real weakness was its lack of cover. True, at least 20,000 of the seats derived shelter from the overhang of the upper tier, but in Milan's wet and misty winters this was never enough. (The new upper tier, incidentally, was nicknamed the *'giraffa'* by San Siro regulars, because it rose so high over the proceedings, while the lower tier was called the *'elefante'*.)

Of the two resident clubs, Milan seemed particularly to revel in their new surroundings. They won the *scudetto* in their first season at the revamped stadium, in 1956–7, and have since notched up a further five League titles, four Cup wins, the European Cup Winners' Cup twice, and three European Cups (in 1963, 1969 and 1989). Inter have not been far behind. Since 1956 they have won the championship on six occasions, the Cup twice, and the European Cup in 1964. Only the city of Turin has a better record at League level in the postwar period, but Milan is far ahead in European competitions.

After the remodelling in the mid-1950s, San Siro changed very little over the years, but in 1979 it was given a new name, that of Giuseppe Meazza.

Because the stadium was one of the best in Europe, such an honour was not to be conferred lightly. But Meazza really was special. Both a gifted, intuitive footballer and a notorious, handsome rake, he was the idol of a generation. Fascist leaders hated him for his off-the-field behaviour, but the crowds, male and female, adored him. With his athletic frame (though he could be quite a lazy player), his black, slicked-down hair and his winning smile, he made his debut for Inter in 1927 at the age of seventeen and went on to make 453 League appearances, scoring 272 goals in the process. And though there was pressure on the national coach, Vittorio Pozzo, not to select him, Meazza made 53 appearances (winning two World Cup winners' medals, in 1934 and 1938) and scored 33 times for the *Azzurri*. Only Gigi Riva of Cagliari scored more goals, but Meazza's were invariably memorable, especially the bicycle kicks which became his forte.

The fans called him 'the phenomenal Peppino', but also, much to his distaste, '*Balilla*'. This was the term given to the sharply dressed, macho youths who were supposed to represent the epitome of Fascist manhood. Meazza, the gambling womaniser, was anything but. In fact, to show its disapproval of him, the regime once went

GROUNDWORK

Amid all the changes, the parterre survives.

so far as to honour the entire *Azzurri* team except for Meazza, on the spurious grounds that as a bachelor he was ineligible for the award in question. Snubs like this only served to heighten his popularity, as that of Mussolini waned.

After thirteen seasons playing with Inter at the Arena, Meazza spent two years at San Siro with Milan, before four final seasons at Juventus, Varese, Atalanta and, finally, back at Inter during the 1946–7 season. His later life was colourful and restless, and when he died, aged 69, in August 1979, a suggestion from a Milanese journalist that the San Siro Stadium be renamed after him was enthusiastically adopted.

And so to the late 1980s, which found the city at the top of the footballing world, thanks to Milan president Silvio Berlusconi's millions, the Dutch trio of Gullit, Rijkaard and Van Basten, and the fact that after Milan won the championship in 1988, Inter followed suit in 1989 while Milan concentrated on winning the European Cup. Thus San Siro had both its teams in the European Cup for 1989–90, *and* a World Cup to look forward to at the end of the season.

The Giuseppe Meazza Stadium, was, however, about to overshadow them all – literally.

Truth to tell, by 1987 the stadium was in a

San Siro Mark 3, showing how the corner towers support the third tier and roof girders.

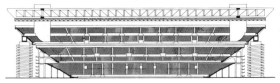

poor state of repair. What had been modern and remarkable in the mid-1950s was outdated and even uncomfortable by the late 1980s, as was indicated by the lack of European finals staged at San Siro (only two altogether – the European Cup Finals of 1965 and 1970).

Regrettably, the city's football fans had also developed a reputation for hooliganism, especially those of Milan who congregate in the parterre behind one of the goals – the so-called Lion's Den, from where a thunderflash was thrown at Roma's goalkeeper Franco Tancredi in December 1987, an attack which nearly cost him his life. Outside the stadium in 1989 a Roma fan died after a fight, again involving Milan supporters.

So World Cup or not, the Giuseppe Meazza Stadium had to be upgraded, and in such a way as not to disrupt either of the two clubs' fixtures. This was partly because Milan had no other suitable stadium for use during the rebuilding programme (unlike Rome), but also due to the fact that each club pays the Comune 7 per cent of its total gate receipts – which can sometimes amount to a rent of £90,000 per match (more than most clubs pay in a year).

The first priority under FIFA World Cup guidelines was to make the stadium all-seated, with individual numbered places. By doing this, however, the San Siro capacity would be cut to 67,000, too few to cope with the demand for club matches and, just as importantly, too few to meet FIFA's minimum requirement of 80,000 for the opening ceremony of the 1990 tournament. Milan therefore was left with no choice but to enlarge the stadium, for this was an event which the city *had* to stage if it were to maintain its role as the de facto football capital of Europe – given that the political capital, Rome, had the Final for itself.

(Even so, to adapt the cliché 'Milan earns while Rome spends', the Milanese felt they had earned the right to stage the Final not only because of their standing in football but also because of their willingness to invest heavily in improved facilities. Rome, on the other hand, had few honours to its name and was endlessly arguing about the costs of its own stadium reconstruction.)

But how could San Siro be enlarged without destroying its trademark, as it were, the existing series of ramps? The solution reached by architects Ragazzi and Hoffer was to construct eleven, freestanding cylindrical towers on three sides of the stadium – the fourth, east side, backing on the

GROUNDWORK

San Siro's new roof structure goes up. The yellow crane was later sold to a Japanese shipbuilder.

Trotter, not having sufficient space for expansion – these towers to support a third tier capable of seating approximately 18,000 extra spectators, thus creating an all-seated total capacity of 83,107 – sufficient for FIFA, for future UEFA finals, and of course for both Milan and Inter.

The next stage was to roof the stadium, since FIFA regulations for the opening match also require that at least two-thirds of the capacity be covered. Again, the solution lay with the cylindrical towers. Of the eleven to be built, the four taller corner towers would support a grid of eight enormous steel roof girders, forming a rectangular opening to correspond almost exactly with the dimensions of the pitch below.

So far, so ambitious. But also so expensive.

In March 1987 it was announced that the Italian government would grant the Milan Comune 48 billion lire (£22 million) towards its costs for the World Cup (the same as Naples but less than for Rome, Genoa or Bari). Yet by mid-1989 the estimated final costs had doubled to well over 100 billion lire.

But even if this was not the most expensive

programme of works undertaken for the World Cup, it was almost certainly the most spectacular. Indeed the scale of the operation can hardly be imagined. Statistics only hint at its enormity. The main load-bearing girders, for example, weigh 1050 tonnes each. They have the second longest span in the world – 205 metres – and it took four, nail-biting hours for two enormous yellow cranes to hoist them into place on top of the corner towers, a manoeuvre watched on the ground by a crowd of over 4000 spectators plus millions more on television.

Each of the eleven cylindrical towers is layered with yet more ramps, 300 metres in length from top to bottom, so that in conjunction with the stadium's existing ramps the effect is a dizzying one of lines upon lines, diagonals against spirals, like an op-art painting.

Inside the stadium, the new roof hovers above one's head like a solar orbiting module waiting for its launch. Covered with translucent, vaulted Plexiglass panels, it casts intricate shadows across the pitch (not so welcome), while enclosing the triple tiers like a mammoth greenhouse. The

15

ITALY

ITALIA '90

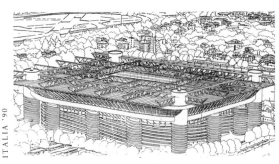

The stadium has landed! San Siro reaches new heights
of towering technology.

rectangle of sky in the centre only accentuates its scale, so that the opening seems somehow smaller than the pitch below.

Down at ground level there have been other equally important, if not quite as breathtaking developments. Apart from a new pitch, a moat has been built in front of the main stand, seats installed on the parterre, and under all the stands the facilities for the public, press and VIPs have been completely overhauled. Until 1990 the San Siro stadium had been a great place to watch football but not much fun at half-time. Now at least the facilities exist, even if the crowded aisles don't always let you reach them.

New lights have been suspended from the roof, a video board installed at the rear of the east side (where a third tier has not been built because of the Trotter), and of course the surrounding precincts, car parks and roads have all been resurfaced and, in some cases, redesigned.

Not all the stadium's environs have changed however, particularly those to the north, where one still finds a delightfully traditional hippodrome, much larger than the Trotter, surrounded by leafy avenues and sprawling, luxurious stables which might have come straight out of an English country manor. Passing through these clippety-cloppety lanes, which smell of sweet straw and turf, it is hard to believe that the twenty-first century profile of the Giuseppe Meazza Stadium lies so close at hand.

But then the contrast would be pretty marked wherever the stadium was located, for there simply is no other stadium in Europe like the one in San Siro, just as there is no footballing city quite like Milan.

And although our journey around the football grounds of Europe has begun here, in terms of awe-inspiring architecture the story might almost end here too, with our gazing up at the towers and girders of San Siro, wondering what on earth they will think of next.

MILAN

ARENA

In total contrast to San Siro, the oldest venue in the world ever to have staged first-class football is the Arena in Milan. That is not to say it was designed for football, because it was built some sixty years before the modern game would emerge from English public schools, and over a century before the Milan club **Internazionale** would start to use it for their more important matches. Nevertheless, we may safely state that apart from bullrings in Spain, the Arena is the earliest surviving example of a European stadium built since the fall of the Roman Empire.

The Arena was a product of the early nineteenth-century occupation of Milan, when French revolutionary zeal saw the implementation not only of Napoleonic laws but also of grandiose prin-

ciples of urban planning. Conceived as part of the formal park of Sempione, on the north side of Milan's enormous Sforzesco Castle, the Arena was designed by Luigi Canonica as a single-tiered elliptical stadium, in pure neoclassical style, and inaugurated by Napoleon himself in 1807. It was used mainly for military exercises and horse racing, but there were also mock naval battles, staged when the pitch area was artificially flooded. Napoleon obviously hoped to emulate the extravagant displays staged at Rome's Colosseum, some sixteen centuries earlier, and if he didn't go so far as to throw Christians in with lions, his forces did use part of the Arena as a prison.

Only in the late nineteenth century, when a 500 metre athletics track was laid, would modern sport as we know it be introduced at the Arena. Football followed a decade or so later after the formation, in March 1908, of the FC Internazionale Milano, by Italian and Swiss players who apparently resented the dominant British influence at Milan FC.

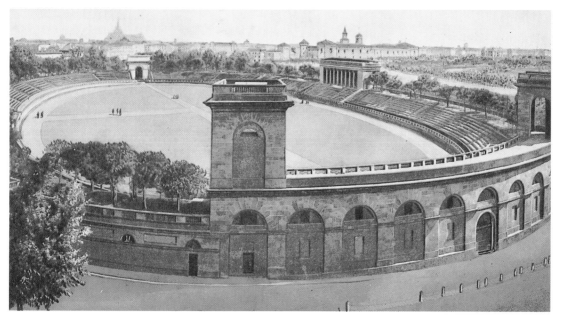

Milan's Arena, the oldest venue in the world ever to have staged first-class football.

Inter's first games had been on an open, stony ground called Campo Ticinese, in a working-class quarter of southwest Milan, near where the Genova Station is now situated. But on occasions the Comune did allow them to use the Arena, which at least had a decent pitch and was more centrally located.

On 15 May 1910 the Arena made history by staging the first ever match of the Italian national team – the *Azzurri* – when, appropriately, France were the visitors in front of a 4000 crowd.

Then, in 1912 Inter moved from Ticinese to a ground just east of the city centre, on Via Goldoni. A female founder member of the club performed the opening ceremony, cracking open a bottle of champagne against a door. Maybe she used too much force because the small wooden stand soon started to fall down. Yet while rivals Milan FC moved into their impressive new stadium at San Siro in 1926, Via Goldoni continued to serve Inter until June 1930, when one of the stands really did collapse, during a vital match v. Genova (fortunately without fatalities). This was at the end of Italy's first national league season, the league having come about as a result of the Fascist government's reorganisation of Italian football. Another consequence of Fascist intervention was that Internazionale, whose name was deemed to have dangerous Marxist connotations, were given the new title of Ambrosiana-Inter, after Sant'-Ambrogio, patron saint of Milan. (Milan's local dialect is similarly called Ambrosiani.)

As Italy's first League Champions, and with attendances rising fast, Ambrosiana-Inter took up more or less continual residency at the Arena from 1930 onwards, and for the next decade crowds of up to 30,000 crammed into the stadium or perched in the surrounding trees to watch Giuseppe Meazza and his *nerazzurri* (black and blues) win two championships, one Cup, and invariably out-perform their San Siro neighbours.

The Arena was also a popular athletics venue. Thirteen world records were broken there between 1926–73. But as an international football venue it was used only twice between the wars, its last full match being in November 1935 v. Hungary. Inter stayed on however, and during the Second World War an echo of the Napoleonic era was felt when the Nazis shot eight Milanese partisans inside the Arena (a plaque recalls their memory).

After the war Ambrosiana-Inter returned to their former title, Internazionale, and soon found they had outgrown the old stadium. It was last used by the club in season 1946–7 (apart from one friendly v. Brazil, staged in 1960), and Inter have shared San Siro Stadium with Milan ever since.

17

The Arena has, for its part, become a rather sleepy relic.

Apart from the addition of a synthetic track and floodlights on eight short masts, the Corinthian columns of the main viewing area, the Doric gateways in each corner, the marble terraces and Napoleon's echoing reception room ... little has altered. Nowadays it is used mainly for women's and youth football, community sports, and the occasional game of American football, or rock concert.

But for the vast majority of visiting passers-by, the Arena is simply a monument of indeterminate origin, age and quality; handsome, rather overgrown, but hardly worth stopping for in a city rich with so many other treasures.

TURIN

STADIO NUOVO COMUNALE

Before almost every World Cup there have been scare stories about this or that stadium not being ready in time for the big kick-off. The 1930 World Cup began before the main Centenario Stadium was complete. In 1950 fans arrived at the Maracana to find it a building site. The same occurred at some Spanish stadiums in 1982.

With only a year to go it seemed that this too might be the fate of Turin's new stadium, being built in the northern district of Cascina Continassa. But whatever its state of advancement on 10 June 1990, when it is due to stage the first of five World Cup matches, one thing is for sure. Turin's New Comunale Stadium is already destined to be one of the most beautiful in Europe.

Apart from the World Cup (when 67,411 of its 71,609 seats will be used), the New Comunale Stadium is to host the games of both Turin clubs, **Juventus** and **Torino**, whose former home, the **Stadio Comunale**, was deemed to be unsuitable for modernisation (see page 20).

Whether this was a wise decision or not, only time, and no doubt the city of Turin's accountants, will tell. When plans were first drawn up for the new stadium in 1987 (by architects Hutter and Cordero, in collaboration with engineers Majowiecki and Ossola), the estimated costs were 60 billion lire (roughly £28 million) – a highly optimistic assessment, it would seem, judging by the enormous scale of the project. But at least 43.6 billion lire of that total was going to be met by a government grant.

That money came late, so that work began on the 35 hectare greenfield site only in mid-1988, with just two years to go before the World Cup. Within a year the costs had spiralled to approximately 140 billion lire (albeit including added infrastructure such as an overground rail link to the stadium) and, in best Italian tradition, the political bickering began. The Turin Comune (run by a coalition of five parties) could not agree, the mayoress (a Euro MP and Torino supporter) said no more money was available, while the building contractors were said to be demanding an extra 20 billion lire to speed things up. They also allegedly claimed that once the work was completed, they would have the rights to sell advertising within the stadium (whereas anyone with the slightest knowledge of World Cups knows that there is as much chance of FIFA signing away income from stadium advertising as there is of Maradona signing for a club in the Albanian Second Division).

Construction work continued throughout this dispute, nevertheless, and as the stadium's dramatic profile steadily rose up against the Piedmont skyline, there was always the sneaking hope that if all else failed, one man in Turin would be able to rescue the whole project.

That man, of course, is Gianni Agnelli, one of the wealthiest men in Italy and the power behind the Fiat car company, which employs 50,000 workers in Turin alone and since 1923 has provided the wherewithal for Juventus to maintain its claim to be Italy's top club – no easy task since the recent successes of Milan's mighty pair of monied clubs.

Certainly the new Turin stadium is an arena befitting Agnelli's expensive hobby-horse.

In common with Bari's new stadium – the only other completely new installation for 1990 (see page 45) – Turin's is on the American model, with car parking (for 4000 vehicles) and wide, open approach roads on all four sides. There is also a direct rail link to encourage more people to leave their cars behind.

Like Bari, an artificial mound around the bowl

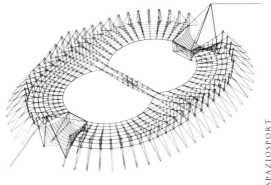

Turin's unique stadium roof in model stage
(left) and computerised form (above).
Will it turn out to be the ruin of Turin?

has been created, on what was already a sloping site, so that only the uppermost third tier is actually visible above ground. This was done to reduce the stadium's impact on its otherwise flat surroundings, but it also makes access to the seating quite simple, via a radial system of ramps leading either down to the middle or lower tiers or up to the third. Cut into the mound behind each goal there are further, wide entrance routes leading down to the pitch (which is sunk 10 metres below ground level), and on the east side, again forming part of the mound, there is an ancillary block for use as a commercial development, to help pay back some of the stadium's crippling costs.

But by far the most captivating feature is the stadium's roof. Its main structural element is a ring of fifty-six steel double masts, rooted around the perimeter and leaning back from the pitch. Each mast supports steel tensioning cables, doubled and tied together like a rope ladder, and it is these cables which support the canopy.

This is no ordinary cable tensioned roof, however. Firstly, the roof material itself is a light aluminium and synthetic composite, with thin translucent strips dividing its surface into sections. These sections were literally hauled up into position like a marquee, the fifty-six cables acting as guy ropes, being tied down to a series of huge concrete anchor blocks which circle the outer mound.

Secondly, directly over the halfway line, two lines of tension cables actually cross over the pitch from one side of the roof to the other, like draw strings. This is certainly unique at a football stadium, but whether it will enhance the design

remains to be seen – the major worry being the shadows cast down by the cables onto the playing surface (a problem encountered at the Aztec Stadium during the 1986 World Cup, when a cluster of loudspeakers was suspended over the centre spot, with irritating results). (On the other hand, for a harmless spot of pre-match entertainment Turin could always import a batch of English goalkeepers, to see who can punt the ball over the cables.)

The third interesting feature of the roof is that it is split in two halves, with a gap behind each goal. The gap is not uncovered, however. Rather, there is a tall, inverted V-shaped steel support which leans back behind the opening and bears more tension cables, this time supporting a translucent Teflon canopy. Underneath this, there is a break in the uppermost tier (not in the two lower ones), to make room for video information boards

Midfield action at Turin, August 1989.

and perhaps, at a future date, a stage for use during concerts. The gap should also serve to provide ventilation of the pitch.

Turin's new stadium at Continassa is, overall, a fascinating combination of ideas, materials and shapes, rather like a finely tuned musical instrument, in which each element hinges upon another and is tied together by its strings.

Whether this delicate instrument can be tuned in time, or will remain in tune with local needs, remains to be seen. Turin has yet to face the music, and the conductor wants his money.

TURIN
STADIO COMUNALE

Without wishing to seem a kill-joy, one cannot help but ask, was it entirely necessary to build a new stadium in Turin?

True the old Comunale Stadium was hardly attractive, nor in an especially convenient place for road access. But it was certainly not beyond redemption, anymore than, for example, the stadiums at Bologna or Florence. Its main drawback was the fact that if, as is required by FIFA regulations, individual seats had been installed throughout, its capacity of 49,491 – already severely reduced for safety reasons from the original 70,000 – would have been cut still further. To compensate, since there is little room to build a third tier around the perimeter (as has been done at Palermo and Bologna), the only solution would have been to remove the track and excavate down to form an extra lower tier (as was done at Florence or, more substantially, at Porto).

If this method was ever considered, it was rejected. Turin decided on a new stadium, and now it is having to pay for that decision. On the other hand, Juventus know all about the dangers of old stadiums. In May 1985 thirty-nine of their fans died in one, in Brussels.

Despite their youthful name **Juventus FC** are actually the older of the two Turin clubs, hence their affectionate nickname, 'La Vecchia Signora' – the old lady. They were formed by students in 1897 and adopted their famous black and white striped kit in 1906, after a member returned from England bearing a Notts County shirt. They first played at the Velodromo Umberto I (named after the late king), but in 1920 moved to their own ground, on Corso Marsiglia (which no longer exists), in the north of the city. Also known as Campo Juventus, this quite substantial ground staged two internationals, v. France in March 1925 and v. Ireland in March 1926.

After the Italian championship had been reorganised into a national league in 1929, the Zebras (as they are also known) quickly established their supremacy, and they had already won a hat-trick of titles when the city of Turin unveiled a stadium truly fit for its gallant new champions – the one we now know as the Stadio Comunale.

One of several constructed under the Fascist regime, especially in the run-up to the 1934 World Cup, the new stadium was officially titled the Stadio Municipale 'Benito Mussolini', and yet despite bearing the Duce's name, it exhibited little of the ideological symbolism or pomposity which tainted so much officially sponsored architecture of the period (the PNF Stadium in Rome, for example, see page 50). In fact in several respects Raffaello Fagnoni's design for Turin closely resembled that of the Prater Stadium in Vienna, completed in 1931 and, ironically, the product of Europe's most radical Socialist administration.

Built almost entirely out of reinforced concrete in just 180 days (a slight contrast with the new stadium's schedule – but then, in 1933 they were building for the Duce), the Stadio Municipale had three levels. A parterre, which, as at Florence and Bologna, was a flat concourse around the six-lane running track, was used for standing and for access to a series of bridge-stairways leading up to a raised tier of terraced seating.

Over the west side, curving around the bowl, was a concrete, cantilevered roof, which although not as sensuous as Nervi's at Florence (built a year earlier) certainly appeared sleekly confident, with a double row of supporting columns at the rear.

On the outside, the perimeter wall was the picture of 1930s' modernity: a lower floor of concrete grills and plain openings, an upper floor of glass screens and concrete vertical supports. It was exactly the kind of modernism which must have seemed exhilarating in 1933 yet now appears distinctly cold and utilitarian.

Surplus to requirements – Fagnoni's Stadio Municipale and tower (left) in its prime.

In the northeast corner, next to the *'antistadio'* or training ground (whose own covered stand backs onto the main stadium), stood the stadium's one sore point, or rather, sore thumb. This was the freestanding concrete tower which had 'Stadio Mussolini' painted in bold letters down its side. If this tower was somehow meant to symbolise the character of Fascist Italy, it certainly succeeded. It was about as impressive as a coal-bunker, it looked half-finished, and yet you could hardly ignore it.

Inauguration of this fine stadium with its awkward tower took place in the Duce's presence on 14 May 1933, with the Italian student games. Juventus moved in soon after, and then on 11 February 1934 a packed 54,000 crowd saw the first international, Italy v. Austria. Austria returned to the stadium in May to face France in the World Cup. Switzerland v. Czechoslovakia followed a few days later.

Juve, meanwhile, carried on winning the *scudetto* until they had amassed five titles in a row,

before Bologna broke their run in 1936.

But it would not be long before honours galore would return to the banks of the Po, this time courtesy of the Zebras' rivals, **Torino**.

Nicknamed the *'granata'* (pomegranates) because of their distinctive red shirts, Torino had formed in 1906, when a breakaway group from Juventus merged with another local club, FC Torinese (who were themselves linked with the first club ever to form in Italy, FC Internazionale – no relation of the Milan team).

(When it comes eventually to choosing a proper title for the new Turin stadium at Cascina Continassa, one of the favourites names to go forward will be that of Vittorio Pozzo. Pozzo was a founder member of Torino who later coached Italy to two World Cup titles in 1934 and 1938, before demonstrating his considerable talent as a journalist for *La Stampa* newspaper.)

Torino played only 1 kilometre west of the new Stadio Mussolini, at their own ground on **Via Filadelfia**. Built with money donated by Count

21

ITALY

Cinzano, it opened on 17 April 1927 with an international v. Portugal. Only 6000 attended, but at its peak Filadelfia often held 40,000.

Surrounded as the ground was by working-class tenement blocks, it was hardly surprising that Torino's image was always that much more down-to-earth than Juve's. Unlike the Stadio Mussolini, Filadelfia was designed purely for football, with three sides of open, concrete terracing and one covered stand, behind which was a walled-in training ground. A proud but simple gateway in the club's colours led in from the street.

Yet it was at humble Filadelfia that the *granata* would match their neighbours' achievements of the 1930s by winning the Double in 1943, followed by four championships in a row between 1945–9. But then on 4 March 1949 it all came to the most horrific end, when the team was wiped out in a plane crash on the hilltop of Superga, just outside Turin. Torino would never be the same again.

Inside Filadelfia's ivy-covered main stand you can still see two plaques commemorating the victims of Superga, both sent from Buenos Aires clubs, River Plate and Racing (because of the close affinities between Argentina and Italy). But you can no longer see any competitive football at the ground. Torino abandoned Filadelfia in 1960 and moved to the much larger Stadio Comunale (as the Stadio Mussolini was renamed after the war).

But even if there were a game at Filadelfia you would still not be able to see it properly. The main stand is propped up with scaffolding, while the terracing, though in remarkably good condition after all these years, is fenced off.

Filadelfia is by no means finished however. Awash with sentiment as the fortieth anniversary of Superga approached in 1989, Torino repurchased the ground from the Comune and use it now for training. And although they will never

GROUNDWORK

Memorial at the old Stadio Comunale in honour of Italy's World Cup triumphs (1934 and 1938) and Olympic Gold (1936).

restore it for first-team games – especially not with the new stadium in existence – ownership of the hallowed land seems to be enough for the time being. A link with the past.

Which brings us to the fate of the old Stadio Comunale. Time has not been kind to this ground either. Barely changed since the war, apart from the addition of eight floodlight pylons in 1961 and a synthetic running track – now quite faded, it hardly seems a grand enough stage for Juventus, the holders of a record number of twenty-two Italian championships and the only club in Europe to have won each of the three main European competitions.

What will happen to the old stadium after it is abandoned, if all goes according to plan, in 1990, no-one knows. A sports museum perhaps? A centre for students? With the Comune's mounting debts out at Cascina Continassa, the likelihood is that it will remain a rotting hulk for many years to come, unless, that is, Juventus follow Torino's example and buy up their old stamping ground. On second thoughts, maybe Signor Agnelli had better keep his money for the new stadium. Such a magnificent stage is going to need a magnificent set of players to fill it up.

Filadelfia –
back in the family.

GROUNDWORK

GENOA
STADIO LUIGI FERRARIS

If ever there was an inner-city football ground with site problems it was this one: no parking space, no room to expand – upwards or outwards, a river bed and main road on one side, a prison on another, housing on the third side and, just to complicate matters, a listed fourteenth-century villa pressing up against the fourth.

And yet this being Genoa, there really is nowhere else for a stadium to go.

Squeezed between the seafront and the mountains, Genoa is a planner's nightmare; a congested, claustrophobic city which, from its straggling industrialised coastline, spreads inland, up hillsides and along valleys, wherever space will allow and roads can reach. Even if the Comune (municipality) had been able to find available space for a new stadium, the likelihood is that they would have had to issue fans with helicopters and hiking boots to reach it.

Instead they have opted to make the best of a difficult situation, and the best is what they have achieved. The rebuilt Luigi Ferraris Stadium is a glowing example of the modern stadium as an urban art form, and despite suffering from serious design hiccoughs along the way, the finished product is worthy of the highest praise (and, it is to be hoped, imitation). Viewing distances are short, there is no running track, and the stands close in on the pitch to create an environment which, in the best traditions of football, is a sealed-in world of its own.

As some of the following chapters will show, there are modern stadiums like Dortmund, Bilbao and Utrecht which achieve the same effect, yet none do it in such a contemporary guise as the Luigi Ferraris Stadium.

Genoa, along with Turin, was actually the birthplace of modern football in Italy, if only because as the country's most commercial port it was naturally susceptible to the influence of foreign customs. Thus in 1893 a group of English businessmen founded the Genoa Cricket and Athletic Club, which fielded Italy's first ever football team and won six of the first seven championships between 1898–1904 (albeit in competition with only a handful of northern clubs). In later years

Genoa in the 1950s. The Villa Musso Piantelli is just behind the open double decker (far side).

ITALY

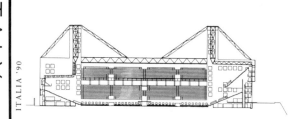

Gregotti's square deal for the new Luigi Ferraris Stadium. Compare this design with Nîmes (see page 107).

the Fascists forced the club to drop their anglicised name in favour of the Italian 'Genova', but since the Second World War, as **Genoa 1893**, they have shunted up and down between the divisions with little to celebrate.

The ground they moved to from their first pitch in San Gottardo, in March 1910, has also changed names. It was initially known as the Campo Sportivo, or Campo Marassi, after the district in which it lies, on the east bank of the Bisagno River. With its pitch originally at right angles to the present layout, it had one wooden stand with a pointed gable over the centre, built alongside the prison in 1915, and shallow banks on three sides. The Campo Marassi staged several internationals between 1912–28 and was then rebuilt as the Stadio Comunale and inaugurated on 1 January 1928 with a match between Italy and Switzerland, watched by 28,000. Construction work continued, so that when Brazil and Spain played there during the 1934 World Cup the ground's capacity had risen substantially to 51,000. By then it had also adopted the name of Luigi Ferraris, an engineer and former Genoa centre-half who was killed in action during the First World War.

Around the same time on an adjacent Marassi pitch (long since built over) another team was playing. This was Andrea Doria, formed in 1895 and named after a sixteenth-century Genovese admiral (whose impressive *palazzo* lies just behind the Principe Railway Station). In 1927 Andrea Doria (the team, not the admiral) joined up with Sampierdarense, from the port district of Sampierdarena, to form Dominante, which, after three year of failing to live up to the name, retitled itself Liguria. Sampierdarense then broke away again, reached Serie A in 1934, changed back to calling themselves Liguria in 1937, until finally, in August 1946, the whole tangle was resolved when they and Andrea Doria finally tied the knot to form

Unione Calcio Sampierdarenese-Doria, better known to all and sundry as **Sampdoria**.

The Stadio Comunale which they now shared with Genoa 1893, meanwhile, acquired a new look. Cantilevered roof extensions were added to each wing of the main stand. Behind these extensions, spiral walkways were erected to give access to the upper levels of both open end terraces.

The final section to be improved was the east side when, in 1951, an uncovered, reinforced concrete double-decker stand was built, with standing terraces on the upper level, and its rear wall only a few metres away from postwar housing blocks and the old Villa Musso Piantelli.

But although the stadium now held 55,773, of which 40,000 were seated, it was never ideal. Rather, it had been cobbled together piecemeal and with little finesse. In that respect at least, Genoa 1893 had stayed close to their English traditions.

When eventually in 1986–7 preparations began for the World Cup, the Comune had little choice. Since so much of the stadium needed attention, the most cost-effective solution was to start again.

Problem number one was this: one way to improve the stadium's lack of space was to cover up the Bisagno riverbed, which ran parallel to a busy road skirting the back of the main stand. This new space would contain extra car parking and a temporary press centre for 1990. However, some conservationists protested against this course of action on the grounds that the Bisagno was a natural feature which should be left alone. Everyone else saw it for what it was – a miserable, polluted trickle flowing through an ugly, dried-up valley.

Problem number two: how could a stadium in such a confined location be completely rebuilt in the space of three years, without any disruption to the weekly fixtures of two popular clubs, and without carving up the pitch?

Problem number three: how was it possible to provide a reasonable level of comfort in such a small space and yet retain a viable capacity – say 44,000 – for league football and the World Cup?

The man presented with the unenviable task of overcoming these obstacles was a Milan architect, Vittorio Gregotti. Gregotti came to stadiums relatively late in his distinguished career. First he won the competition to remodel Barcelona's Montjuïc Stadium for the 1992 Olympics (see page 200), then came the commission for Genoa, followed shortly after by one for Nîmes in southern France (see page 107). As it transpired, this last project, the Stades des Costières, was the first to be completed, in February 1989, but then Gregotti was working on a greenfield site and on a smaller scale. Genoa, by comparison, was a much tougher challenge, as he would soon discover.

As at Nîmes, Gregotti opted for a stadium based around four corner blocks, linked by four rectangular stands. These blocks, painted in distinctive 'Pompeii Red' (one of Gregotti's favourite shades), house ramps leading up to the second deck of each stand, ramps which are revealed through large openings in the external walls, as if a zebra-crossing had been tucked inside a red box.

On top of each block is a square tower, and this supports diagonally fixed white steel girders which bear the load of the stands' flat roofs. Silhouetted against the sky or against the rising hills of Manin to the north, the geometric minimalism is remarkably forceful.

Still outside the stadium, the arches and main entrance of the old façade have been preserved, but set in a box-like Pompeii Red frame which, in typical Gregotti style, is pierced by a grid of square openings. The square motif is repeated inside the stadium, in the form of openings on each corner block, not placed for viewing the match but for shedding light on the ramps and refreshment areas. In doing this, Gregotti has, probably unwittingly, provided a delightful Post-Modern echo of the corner galleries which formerly made such an impression at Bilbao's San Mamés Stadium in Spain (see page 224).

Work on the first phase of Gregotti's design began in July 1987, when the old stands were literally sliced down the middle, so that the main stand and one half of each end terrace could be restructured. This not only halved the available capacity for the 1987–8 season (and therefore cut revenue also), but created enormous logistical problems, not least being the two clubs' loss of facilities and the inevitable damage done to the playing surface throughout the building.

But more seriously, there were disagreements about the specifications. Gregotti had originally planned for an all-seated capacity of 40,000, with a pitch width of 65 metres. The Comune decided it wanted more seats and, to comply with FIFA's World Cup standards, a pitch width of 68 metres.

There could be no arguing with FIFA, but adding to the capacity was more difficult. Still,

Halfway to paradise – Genoa in mid 1987.

two extra rows were added at the rear of the main stand's upper tier, and in September 1988 the newly finished half of the stadium was opened to the public.

But though they came, as it were, to praise Caesar, they ended up by burying him. Especially those sitting on the new upper tier, who found to their irritation that they could not see the nearest touchline, just the linesman's head as he bobbed up and down the line.

On the lower tier, the spectators in the first few rows in each far corner couldn't see the pitch at all from certain angles. This was because toughened glass screens, installed in place of security fencing (as at several other World Cup venues also), proved to be impenetrably reflective when looking towards the far goal.

Overnight, Genoa's half-finished ground was dubbed the 'Stadio per non vedenti' – the Stadium of the Blind, and the recriminations began. Some fans reckoned the terracing was too steep, that the fixed seats were difficult to squeeze past, and that the roofs offered too little protection against the wind and rain. One report even claimed wildly that from some sections of the ground you couldn't even see the goalposts.

For his part, Gregotti admitted mistakes had been made. After being forced to make provision for two extra rows, his office, it transpired, had not made the correct readjustments to the rake (or slope) of the concrete stepping.

But many of the criticisms, the architect complained, were down to the Comune. It was they who wanted more seats. It was the Comune who had stipulated the use of glass screens, whereas Gregotti had wanted an all-round moat (which would have reduced the capacity further, because

25

ITALY

LUIGI GHIRRI

September 1988 – half the stadium is complete, but marred by sight problems and an over-reflective screen.

moats take up more space). It was the Comune who had opted for fixed seats, because tip-up seats are more easily vandalised.

But it was no more than the usual storm in an Italian tea cup – those daily sports papers have to be filled, after all. And the solutions turned out, after careful study, to be relatively straight-forward. Indeed, it could be said that the stadium is better for the subsequent readjustments than it would have been had the original design been adhered to. Nor was the cost of these adjustments exactly crippling. The stadium's original budget was 45 billion lire (about £21 million), whereas the final cost, as estimated in mid-1989, was expected to reach 55 to 60 billion, a rise of some 22 to 25 per cent. For a stadium which has been vir-tually rebuilt from scratch, that is a mere ripple in the ocean compared with the overspending at other

venues for 1990, such as Milan, Rome, Naples and Florence (which might explain the uproar over Genoa – it created a useful diversion from more serious miscalculations perpetrated elsewhere).

Here is how the Stadium of the Blind regained its sight.

In the main stand's upper tier, the concrete stepping was heightened by just 50 centimetres and the configuration of seats altered. In the lower tier the height of the seats was varied, to create a slightly curving rake. Tip-up seats were also installed, as had been the original intention, but on metal frames which provide a barrier for the person behind to lean on (a system also used on Milan's new third tier).

In addition to these modifications, during the summer of 1989 the pitch was raised by 90 centi-metres – no great problem since a new pitch was already on the agenda. The only drawback was that with a higher pitch, sight lines for the two lowest rows were consequently worsened. According to FIFA regulations, however, tickets for these rows would not have been sold for the World Cup anyway, because they are less than 1 metre above pitch level and would therefore be obscured by advertisement hoardings (which are, of course, worth far more to FIFA than the income from a few hundred tickets).

To reduce the reflection problems, the screens behind the goals were removed and moats dug, while those 200 or so seats affected in the main stand wings were also taken off the market.

But how could the Comune compensate for this loss of seats?

Once the completed west side was opened in September 1988, warts and all, demolition began on the opposite half, and it was on the east side that the solution was found. Previously, the height of the stands was restricted by the presence of the Villa Musso Piantelli; the Comune solved this problem in November 1988 by the simple expedient of buying the villa and therefore freeing itself to build another few metres higher. The east side was thus raised to accommodate not two, but three tiers, thereby increasing the projected overall capacity to approximately 44,600.

New dressing rooms have been included underneath the east side, connected to the main stand by a tunnel under the pitch (to give journalists direct access from the press box to the players' area). Under the north stand there is further space to be used as a sports centre for the public.

As the stadium reached completion in December 1989, having been out of action for just one month during the playing season, only minor criticisms remained. Firstly, underneath each seat in the upper tier of the main stand were small holes, placed there to increase the amount of light falling onto the concourse area beneath. Unfortunately the fans thought these were intended for litter disposal, an error not greatly appreciated by those gathered below. The holes have now been filled in.

Secondly, when a woman living directly behind one of the stands looked out at the finished stadium and saw red – Pompeii Red to be exact – she complained to the Comune that the view would devalue her flat. Other residents on the higher floors also complained, not because of the colour but because their previously unobstructed

LUIGI GHIRRI

Simply red, simply stunning – Gregotti's Post-Modern approach has instilled new dynamism into the stadium as an urban art form.

view of the pitch was now completely blocked.

But one of the most heartfelt regrets was that the completed stadium, having been finished in two phases, would never look completely new. It had not taken long for the scribblers of Genoa to violate those virginal red walls.

Gregotti once told *Panorama* magazine, 'The fan is a momentary contingent. The stadium is there to last in time, longer than the whistles of the public.'

But he was wrong, and not just because the graffiti has proved to be more than momentary.

The fan is the whole *raison d'etre* of a stadium. He is the stadium's single most important constant, without whom the structure has no meaning. Which is why, in the architect's defence, stadiums like Genoa's, which challenge so powerfully our preconceived notions and raise our expectations, can also serve to advance the game and give it renewed life.

For this reason, it is to be hoped that, despite all the problems he encountered in Genoa, Signor Gregotti will not give up on football quite yet.

VERONA

STADIO BENTEGODI

It is stately, it is perfectly proportioned, it attracts tourists from all over the world and provides perfect all-round vision for 25,000 spectators. But that's enough about Verona's Roman Arena.

Nineteen centuries after the Arena was built, Verona now has another worthy stadium – the Stadio Bentegodi, home of **Hellas-Verona**, a club with a classical connection of its own. The Hellas part of the title derives from a team formed by scholars in 1903. Their Greek teacher suggested the name, while the boys chose to play in yellow and blue, the traditional colours of Verona.

Hellas played their first official match in 1906 and three years later based themselves at the original Campo Bentegodi, which was really a drill ground, situated on land between what is now Via Bentegodi and Via Bertoni, a few blocks south of the Arena. Marcantonio Bentegodi had been a wealthy benefactor who, before his death, set up a foundation to encourage sport in the city. (Even now, apart from the current stadium, there are several sports clubs named after him.)

For reasons obscure, Hellas did not always see eye to eye with the administrators of the Campo Bentegodi, and just before Italy's entry to the First World War in May 1915 they were told to leave.

This they did, building for themselves a new ground just outside the medieval city gates of Porta Palio, next to a canal and close to the site of the present stadium. Porta Palio was opened on 15 November 1915, and although cosy enough, it was not destined to become the club's long-term home. After the war they adopted the title Hellas-Verona, and in August 1928 merged with two other local clubs, Bentegodi and Scaligera, to form AC Verona, using the original Bentegodi ground as their base.

The new club spent most of the ensuing four decades in Serie B. In 1959 they readopted the earlier title of Hellas-Verona, and four years later, this time of their own accord, left one Bentegodi Stadium for another. (The old site is now occupied by a pensions office.)

The new Stadio Bentegodi lay a few kilometres westwards, in the outlying Borgo Milano district, and was inaugurated on 8 September 1963 with a Cup tie v. Mantova. It was then a very plain, open bowl consisting of three tiers and encased on the outside by utilitarian glass curtain-walling – modern, economical, but hardly inspiring.

The lower level, or parterre, was sunk 2 metres into the ground and was reached through a series of tunnels from the outer concourse. Above the parterre was a narrow middle tier of only four rows, and above this a third tier of fifteen rows, providing an overall capacity of 42,500, all-seated. It was not much to look at, and until they won their first championship in 1985, nor, in truth, were Hellas-Verona.

But the stadium does have one remarkable quality. Verona is situated in the middle of the Padana Plain, which has always been susceptible to dense fogs throughout the autumn and winter (which might explain why Juliet had such trouble finding Romeo here). And yet amazingly, since the stadium was opened only one match has ever had to be postponed due to fog. Why this should be so, no-one has the foggiest idea.

The stadium's prospects have certainly been brighter since Verona's selection as a World Cup venue, especially given the fact that it had previously staged only one international, v. Czechoslovakia, on 7 April 1984.

A second game followed more recently, v. Uruguay, in April 1989, by which time the Bentegodi was able to boast a new pitch (installed with hot-water undersoil heating by a company from Finland), and a new look.

A section shows Verona's new upper tier and roof.

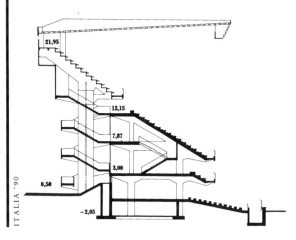

21,95

12,15

7,87

3,00

0,50

−2,05

ITALIA '90

GROUNDWORK

Verona 1988 – the added outer ring clearly visible (left).

Verona 1989 – few frills but low bills.

The most significant part of its refurbishment programme for the World Cup was the extension of the third tier by a further twelve rows. This has been achieved in a similar fashion to the extensions at Palermo and Bologna – that is by encircling the existing stadium with a freestanding structure – although at Verona the outer supporting columns, seventy-two in all, are in reinforced concrete rather than steel. Adding the extra tier would have greatly enlarged the capacity, but the installation of individual seats (green at the sides, yellow and blue at each end) has, in effect, meant that the total has risen only slightly, to 43,700 for 1990.

At least Verona fans can now count on protection from the elements. Before the recent work only a small number, mainly those in the middle tier, were sheltered. The erection of a light metal cantilevered roof now covers all but the parterre. It does not, however, house all the floodlights, as is the growing trend with elliptically shaped roofs. Instead, four new masts, 43 metres high, have been erected on the surrounding concourse.

Behind the main, west stand the World Cup press centre is destined to become a table-tennis hall (ping pong being a popular sport in the city).

Beyond this is a small stadium, being converted to hold 5000 spectators, where the lower division club Chievo played until recently. To the south and east are regular blocks of postwar housing, while behind the north curve is a modern indoor basketball hall, set amid car parks which hold 8000 vehicles.

All very orderly and admirable, of course, and for sure, apart from adding to the comfort of Verona's *jalloblu* (yellow-blue) supporters, the improvements for 1990 have also, happily, made the stadium more appealing in appearance, both inside and out. But the Stadio Bentegodi remains an essentially functional stadium, with few frills or focal points.

To this the gentlemen of Verona have the best possible response. They now have a covered stadium perfectly equipped to deal with their needs, and it cost them a mere 21 billion lire, only 4 billion over the initial budget. Compare that with the sums spent at slightly smaller venues like Bologna and Palermo and it represents an astute piece of business. And if it is the sort of venue which is hard to criticise, yet hard to love, give it, like the Arena, another nineteen centuries and who knows what future tourists will make of it.

UDINE

STADIO FRIULI

Trust the people of Friuli to build a stadium unlike any other. This distinct northern region, nudging

the borders with Austria and Yugoslavia, has its own ethnic roots, its own language, its own prejudices (as anti-semitic outbursts among the fans suggested in 1989) and, in its capital of 100,000 inhabitants, Udine, a stadium which would be the envy of cities three times its size (such as nearby Trieste, which staged one game in the 1934 World Cup but whose stadium is now outdated and whose team, Triestina, currently languishes in the Italian Third Division, Serie C. And now those little upstarts in Udine are to grab the limelight!).

Udinese, the Stadio Friuli's resident club, know all about Serie C, since they have spent more time in it than in the top flight. Formed as a gymnastics club in 1896, they rose to second spot in Serie A in 1955 and have been up and down since, without major honours and having attracted the most headlines for their sensational £3 million signing of the Brazilian folk-hero Zico in 1983.

Udinese's first proper ground was the Campo Polisportivo, inaugurated in September 1924 with a match v. Italian champions Pro Vercelli. It was later named after Luigi Moretti, who owned both the ground and the city's famous brewery, next door. Situated just west of Udine's delightful city centre, and still used for training, the Stadio Moretti held around 20,000 and served Udinese until 1976, a portentous year for the whole region.

The municipality had almost finished building the new Friuli stadium, a few kilometres north-west of the city, when on 6 May an earthquake struck. Over a thousand people were killed, many more were rendered homeless, and the Stadio Moretti, which was itself damaged, was immedi-

ately converted into a first-aid post for the injured.

United by their grief and suffering, for the people of Udine the opening of the Friuli Stadium came as a mixed blessing. First there was a rugby match, during which a thunderstorm erupted and one spectator died when lightning struck his umbrella. Then, several days later, on 20 September 1976, as Udinese took on Seregno in a Serie C game, another earth tremor shook the stadium. Mercifully no further damage was caused, and the Friuli Stadium became a rallying point for the shaken community, while at the same time capturing the admiration of the Italian people, for whom a stadium without style is no stadium at all.

What attracted everyone's attention was the Friuli's unique, reinforced concrete arch which supports the roof over the main, west stand. The brainchild of engineer Giuliano Parmegiani and architect Lorenzo Giacomuzzi Moore (who have overseen the recent improvements for 1990), the arch was conceived as an echo of the undulating hills around the city. Both dramatic and functional, it spans 160 metres and is, in section, a hollow rectangle with walls only 20 centimetres deep. One can walk up through its echoing interior

GIULIANO PARMEGIANI

Unmistakably Udine – arch, floodlights and video board.

to the apex, where porthole windows look out onto the pitch, 30 metres below. Floodlighting and closed-circuit television cameras are housed along the front, while exactly in the centre of the arch, scratched on the floor, is a workman's scrawl which commemorates the arch's completion, on 31 October 1974, at 12.30pm.

Sheltered under the roof are 11,600 seats and, under a small, secondary cantilevered cover in the south corner, a viewing platform for the handicapped has been added for the World Cup. A plaque below the central VIP section recalls those Udinese players who died in the First World War.

The remaining three sides of the stadium are open and were built up in three phases between 1976–82, to raise the total capacity from its original 16,000 to 47,616 (38,965 seated). For the World Cup, however, individual grey and pale green seats have been installed throughout, thereby reducing the total to 38,685. After the competition, when FIFA technical requirements no longer apply, this will rise to 42,133.

As the most recently built stadium of the twelve World Cup venues, the Friuli needed the least amount of work for 1990. Nevertheless, 9 billion lire (£4.2 million) had to be spent, which was 30 per cent more than the stadium had cost to build originally. Another 10 billion lire was invested in new press and VIP facilities behind the main stand, expanded car parks (to hold 4670 vehicles), a tunnel linking the dressing rooms with a training pitch, improved access roads, and the hire of a Japanese 'Video Cosmo' board, like a giant's television set.

No doubt many of the fans would have liked some of the money to have been spent on providing roofs over the uncovered seats, especially since Udine is said to be the wettest city in Italy. But therein lies the major drawback of the main stand's unique design. How could one possibly add extra roofing without detracting from the spectacular sweep of the arch?

Aesthetics aside, one positive, practical consequence of the arch's presence is that, combined with the curving roof it acts like a megaphone in amplifying the sound of the crowd. Also, because the arch bears floodlighting, the stadium needs only two floodlight pylons. These are red, triangular, steel masts, which face reverentially towards the arch almost as if *it* were the focal point – the stage – while the pitch were merely the orchestra pit.

Inside the arch, someone is watching you.

Behind the floodlights and the east side of the stadium is the circular Palasport Carnera, an indoor sports hall named after local boxer Primo Carnera, the world heavyweight champion in 1933. Beyond this is the village-like district of Rizzi, whose church spire can be seen (and its bells heard ringing) from the stadium.

Before the World Cup the Friuli had already tasted international football, its first match involving the *Azzurri* being on 17 November 1979 v. Switzerland, a country with which Friulans enjoy close cultural ties, not least in certain aspects of their regional tongue. A good chance to hear what this sounds like comes before many a game at the Friuli Stadium when, accompanied by the marching band of the region's Alpini soldiers (who sport natty feathers in their caps), the Udinese fans sing the traditional refrain, 'O ci biel ciscjiel a Udin' – 'Oh what a beautiful castle in Udine'. As long as the rain holds off, the stadium isn't too bad either.

Under the arch, extra cover for the disabled.

ITALY

BOLOGNA

STADIO DALL'ARA

In 1925 **Bologna FC** had just become the first club to break the northern domination of the national championship when work began on the city's new municipal stadium. It was among the first of a substantial crop of stadiums to be built under the Fascist dictatorship, and together with Nervi's stadium, 90 kilometres south in Florence (see page 36), was also among the finest. But while Nervi's work contributed towards a new era in stadium design, Bologna's Stadio Littoriale (as the Dall'Ara Stadium was first known) was a quintessential example of the historical genre. Even its name, commonly given to Italian stadiums of the period, had a spurious link with antiquity. In Ancient Rome the *littori* were those officers who,

as a symbol of their legal power, bore in front of them the fasces, a bundle of rods bound up with an axe in the middle (whence the Fascists derived both their name and Party symbol).

Inaugurated on 29 May 1927 with an international v. Spain, Bologna's Littoriale was, as at Florence, a single-tiered stadium with a flat concourse, or parterre, at pitch level, from which a series of stairways led up to the seating. Like Florence, only the west side was covered, and on the opposite side stood a Marathon Tower. But there the comparison ended.

The architect of the Stadio Littoriale, Costanzini, used classical Roman models for his design and external decoration, but that is not to denigrate the stadium. After all, the Romans had tackled, and overcome, many of the inherent problems of stadium design, nearly 2000 years before modern man came to face the issue. Furthermore, the Stadio Littoriale was, and still is, in perfect harmony with its surroundings which,

CABICAR

Rosso bolognese – the rich brickwork of the Dall'Ara Stadium and pool blends harmoniously with its warm surrounds. In the foreground is the '*antistadio*', while alongside the tower, then winding up the hill, is the world's longest portico.

as we shall see later, are quite charming.

With a capacity of approximately 50,100 (33,570 seated), the stadium was enclosed by a two-storey wall of arched windows and doorways, clad in the characteristic brick of the city, *rosso bolognese* – a rich, terra cotta brick which, together with the clay tiles commonly used in the region, lend Bologna's cityscape an all-encompassing warm glow. (Ironically the city has long been known as *Bologna La Rossa*, for its leftist political leanings.)

On the west side of the stadium there was a flat, propped roof over the main stand, immediately behind which were tennis courts, a tall, red-brick, indoor swimming pool, and next to this, in the northwest corner of the site, a rectangular open-air swimming pool with rounded-off corners and seating on all four sides, like a mini-stadium.

Seen as a whole, these three buildings constituted as solid and purposeful a group of sports building as anything built in the 1920s, while the use of decorative red brick echoed grounds of the same period, such as Ibrox Park in Glasgow, Villa Park in Birmingham, and even Fenway Park, the baseball stadium in Boston, USA.

On its east side, the Littoriale Stadium was dominated by an imposing, though actually rather clumsily proportioned, six-storey Marathon Tower – a hodgepodge of arches, windows and balconies. Bologna has several fine medieval brick towers, but the Marathon Tower was designed more as a platform for Fascist propaganda than as an aid for sporting events. Along the street frontage were wall-mountings for flags and fasces, with a first-floor balcony providing an ideal spot for reviewing passing parades. After Mussolini had subdued the mighty forces of Abyssinia in 1936, a statue of Vittoria (Victory) was placed upon the tower roof. She, however, suffered greatly during the Second World War, when trigger-happy German troops used her as target practice, and it has recently cost Bologna FC's sponsors 80 million lire to restore her in time for the 1990 World Cup.

The Marathon Tower's other major embellishment has not survived. On a marble plinth facing the pitch and framed by the tall archway of the tower's second level, stood a bronze statue of Mussolini, in heroic pose on horseback. When the real Duce was finally dismounted in July 1943, the statue was melted down and, appropriately, used to cast likenesses of two of

Il Duce at the Littoriale. The floodlights were for political rallies rather than football. Note the pitch-level parterre.

the partisans who had fought to unseat him.

One unique feature which did survive the war is the Portico di San Luca, the world's longest covered walkway, which runs past the east stand, on either side of the Marathon Tower. Bologna has 14 kilometres of such porticoes and arcades altogether, but this particular one, completed in 1732 and 4 kilometres in length, has a rather special function. After skirting the stadium perimeter it continues southwards a short distance before wending its way, like a slow train, up the gently rising green hillside which lies behind the stadium's south curve. Eventually, 660 arches from its starting point in the city, it reaches the Sanctuary of San Luca, clearly visible on the summit, where there is a Byzantine image of the Madonna, reverentially preserved and believed by many to have talismanic powers. But after the wartime bombing of Bologna it was the portico itself which offered the better protection. Home-

Two faiths – the Marathon Tower and portico.

GROUNDWORK

33

GROUNDWORK

Bologna steels itself for the World Cup. As at Verona, the only way to expand was outwards.

less families took up lodgings along its length, one family per arch.

One set of people in Bologna, however, have good cause to curse the portico, and that is the Bologna FC or *rossoblu* (red-blue) football team. As part of their training routine, twice a week they have to run up its punishing incline to the top of the hill. But then Bologna's players have had to be fitter than most in recent years, for another reason related to the stadium's design.

In Italy it is common for each major stadium to be linked to a nearby training ground, called the '*antistadio*'. While the main stand at Bologna was being refurbished for the World Cup, the only changing rooms available were in the antistadio, which was reached via a 200-metre tunnel running under both the stadium's north curve and the adjacent busy main road, the Via Andrea Costa. Thus both teams had to use up a vital six or seven minutes of each fifteen-minute half-time break simply getting to and from the dressing rooms.

While some readers stop to calculate how long it would take them to walk 200 metres in studded boots, we shall return to the archives. After its opening in 1927 the Littoriale Stadium became one of the focal points of Italian football in the prewar period. In 1929 Bologna won their second championship, followed by the Mitropa Cup (a forerunner of the European Cup) in both 1932 and 1934, and then, having finally broken Juventus's five-season stranglehold on the *scudetto*, they won another four League titles before the end of the Second World War. Apart from several further internationals, the Littoriale also hosted two games in the 1934 World Cup, Sweden v. Argentina and Austria v. Hungary.

After the war the stadium was renamed Stadio Comunale, and for the next two decades the *rossoblu* drifted along in mid-table, until in 1963–4 one of the greatest controversies in Italian football history occurred. Bologna were challenging for the title when they were docked three points after accusations of drug-taking among the players. The club appealed – perhaps it was all that running up to San Luca which made them seem so super-fit – the points were restored, and Bologna thus finished the season level on points with Inter. Bologna won the subsequent play-off in Rome (since neither goal-average nor goal-difference is used to determine placings in Italy), but their celebrations were tinged with sadness over the death, just three days earlier, of their club president of twenty-four years, Renato Dall'Ara. An immensely popular man whose period of office, unusually, straddled both the Fascist and postwar periods, he was finally honoured when the stadium was named after him in June 1983.

By then, however, the place was in a sorry state, as indeed were the team. Relegated in 1982 for the first time in their history, they plunged straight down to Serie C the year after. Seldom had such a great Italian club sunk so low, and it was feared that if money could not be found to repair the stadium it would have to be closed. Refurbishment plans were, nevertheless, drawn up in 1984 after Bologna had bounced back to Serie B, and it was these plans which were put into action when, three years later, Bologna was selected to stage four games of the 1990 World Cup. There was talk of building a new stadium out of town, but this was deemed to be too expensive. Even so, the final bill of 55 billion lire was some 23 billion over the government's original grant and was met by stiff opposition within the city, especially after two workmen were killed during the building operations.

Modernising and expanding the stadium was always likely to be a contentious issue. Not only was there a need to harmonise any improvements with the existing historic brickwork, tower, and adjoining sports facilities, but the views of San Luca and the portico had also to be preserved.

Several of the improvements were quite straightforward. For example, by removing the parterre, and, by way of compensation, creating new vomitories for access to the lower rows, sufficient room was created around the pitch to install both a moat (instead of the tall railings which formerly ringed the parterre), and a new eight-lane synthetic track. (The pitch hardly needed attention. One stadium official described it as 'like an English lawn'.)

Although they will not serve during the World Cup, both swimming pools were completely over-hauled at the same time, while on the tennis courts behind the main stand a lightweight metal-frame covered in white, synthetic fibre provided an airy open space for the World Cup press squad. Similar quick-to-assemble structures are in use at several other Italian venues, but the one in Bologna was the first to be completed, and after the tournament it will provide cover for the tennis courts.

The most sensitive part of the operation was the extension of the stadium. As at Palermo and Verona, this was achieved by erecting a new framework on 120 steel columns around the entire perimeter wall, to support an extra tier of seating. The original external brickwork has, as a result, been smothered in a web of steel. Of course this is hardly ideal, but it has to be said that at Bologna the final result is not at all jarring, mainly owing to the use of light blue, turquoise, white and

yellow paint on the steelwork, a combination which throws the red brick into sharp contrast.

From inside the Dall'Ara Stadium, the 'join' between the original tier and the recent addition is almost impossible to detect. In numerical terms, it added 9000 places, which, when combined with the areas already installed with individual seats, gives the Dall'Ara Stadium a final all-seated capacity of 40,782, of which 38,000 will be used for the World Cup.

With a shining, regilded Vittoria back in her place atop the tower, the brickwork all scrubbed and repointed, a new cantilevered roof over the main stand, a new track, new scoreboard, new seats, new lights and, as a result, a renewed sense of purpose about the stadium, Bologna's period of depression at the beginning of the 1980s seems all but forgotten. By 1988 the team was back in Serie A, and by mid-1989, despite all the political rows about spending, the stadium refurbishment was well-advanced of several of the other Italian World Cup venues. Maybe the Madonna up on San Luca was having an effect after all.

June 1989 – the roof and upper tier are complete, the parterre gone. Note the glass screens.

ITALY

GROUNDWORK

ITALY

FLORENCE

STADIO COMUNALE

The Florentines first started playing a form of football some four centuries ago during the Renaissance. Their favourite pitch was the Piazza di Santa Croce, where the retainers of Florence's richest families would routinely beat the living daylights out of each other in pursuit of a large leather ball. (The name given to this ritualised game, and still applied now for soccer, is '*calcio*'. The Italians are thus the only nation in the world to use a term which does not derive directly from the English word 'football'.)

To the delight of tourists, '*calcio fiorentino*' is still played as vigorously as ever, while the modern game perfected by Victorian Englishmen has an altogether different stage, a few kilometres east of the old city centre, on a green expanse of ground known as the Campo di Marte.

One corner of this area is taken up by the Stadio Comunale, a structure as important in the development of twentieth-century stadium design as the old version of *calcio* is to the story of the game itself.

For it was at the Stadio Comunale that a 'great leap forward' in stadium design occurred. Built between 1930–2, it was the work of one of Italy's most respected technician-architects, Pier Luigi Nervi, who had the audacity to demonstrate that modern stadiums did not have to resemble Roman temples, pseudo-classical palaces, nor even disguise their function behind curtains of brick or stone. Nervi tore up the rule book, wholeheartedly embraced the newly fashionable material of reinforced concrete, and by marrying his own vision with modern techniques he produced a stadium which was both calculated and graceful.

And although Nervi would not work on

BAL/RIBA

Forget the Ancient Romans – Nervi's cantilevered roof at Florence was a breakthrough in style and technique.

another stadium until 1957, when he began the Flaminio Stadium in Rome (see page 50), after Florence in 1932 stadium design would never be the same; Nervi's influence was to be seen in stadiums built all over Europe and South America right up until the 1970s.

Two events led to Nervi being commissioned by the Comune (municipality). Firstly, as had occurred in several other Italian cities, the local Fascist leadership had ordered, in 1926, the merger of the city's two senior football clubs, Libertas and Club Sportivo Firenze. The new **AC Fiorentina**, it was hoped, would build a team to challenge neighbouring rivals, Livorno and Pisa, and ultimately give Florence a team worthy of the national league (established in 1929). This was a period of great public works in Italy; Mussolini was at the height of his popularity, cities all over Italy were building or planning new stadiums and, as every history student learns, the trains ran on time. Meanwhile, Fiorentina's small and basic ground on Via Bellini, in the northwest of the city, was clearly running out of time.

The second impetus came from the decision to stage the 1934 World Cup in Italy, and although this was before the age of worldwide football coverage, the Fascist regime was no less concerned to show off its achievements than Hitler would be at the 1936 Olympics. Furthermore, Mussolini had yet to clamp down on the country's several talented modern architects (some of whom would later die in German concentration camps).

Nervi was, nevertheless, the first Italian to apply modern architectonics to the design of a stadium, and apart from Turin's Stadio Municipale, completed one year after the Stadio Comunale, Italy's seven other World Cup venues for 1934 would all follow traditional or historical models.

Named originally the Stadio Comunale Giovanni Berta, after a local Fascist leader, Nervi's stadium was completed in the summer of 1932 and initially held 32,000. In plan it was shaped like a letter 'D', not in honour of the Duce, as was joked in Florence, but to accommodate a 220 metre sprint track, which ran in front of the main stand and then on to the stadium gates, where it formed an entry point for marathon runners. Therein, however, lay the stadium's weakest point. Instead of the seating tiers on either side of the main stand curving round the track to link up with the two end curves, as is usual, because of the extra-long straight they continued parallel to

BAL/RIBA

Nervi's spirals still give cause for delight. Contrast his Marathon Tower with Bologna's.

the touchlines some 50 metres beyond each goal line. Only then, out on a limb, did a narrow corner of terracing link up with the end stands. Thus the corners provided a splendid view of the start and finish of the sprint track, but a most uncomfortable view onto the football pitch.

The rest of the stadium was, however, a *tour de force*. Viewed from the outside, the concrete supports of the bowl were left exposed to reveal their sculptural, almost organic form. Along the east side, three widely sweeping helicoid stairways led to the upper gallery. These spirals were perhaps Nervi's most daring innovations, if only because he had no models on which to base them and was dependent entirely upon his own calculations. That they remain intact, and still give cause for delight, is testimony enough to both his skill and artistry. (Nervi actually planned five such stairways, but lack of funds meant that two, one at each end, were not built. Rather more prosaic steel versions of the originals were erected, finally, during the preparations for 1990.)

Dominating the centre of the east side was the 55 metre tall, slender Torre di Maratona, which sprang from a platform slightly cantilevered over

ITALIA '90

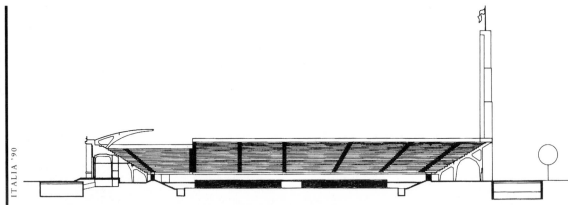

New depths at the Stadio Comunale – notice that the pitch has been excavated below ground level, a moat dug, and on either side of the stadium underground car parks built.

the lower seating tier. More streamlined than any of its predecessors – at Amsterdam and Montevideo for example, its smooth, concrete sides displayed fasces, while its rounded front edge, panelled in glass, perhaps served as a model for Helsinki's Olympic Stadium tower, completed six years later.

Arguably the tower is too slight to have the impact Nervi probably intended, and the same may be said of the main entrance to the Tribuna Centrale or main, west stand, whose understated frontage with a central portico of protruding pilasters is in marked contrast to the exciting elevations on the other three sides. The German architect Erich Mendelsohn, writing in 1933, thought Nervi's façade bordered on dullness. With one's mind 'keyed up to the vigour of form' already in evidence in other parts of the exterior, the frontage appeared 'half-heartedly timid'. Restraints may have been placed upon Nervi's final design, it is true, but Mendelsohn's criticism still holds true, even if the issue is regrettably difficult to judge because an intrusive concrete wall now isolates the entrance from the main approach road.

The main stand's interior induces no such disappointment. Undoubtedly Nervi's *pièce de résistance*, the roof is as breathtakingly graceful now as it was revolutionary in 1932. Its supporting trusses are inclined so far back and so high up in the stand that unless one is looking side on, the slender concrete canopy appears to be miraculously cantilevered. No other roof had ever been so technically daring, and it would not be

long before imitations and refined versions would pop up all over Europe and South America.

Finally, there was a flat, lower concourse, or parterre, all around the stadium, divided from the track by iron railings and linked to the first rows of seats, a couple of metres above, by a series of bridge-like stairways. In practice as many as 5000 fans would line the railings to view matches.

Under the main stand the concourse widened out to house a glass-walled cafe, which served as a popular, lively meeting point before and after matches.

AC Fiorentina had just completed their first season in Serie A when the Stadio Comunale Giovanni Berta opened for their use in September 1932. On 7 May 1933 the first international was held, v. Czechoslovakia, and since the 1934 World Cup, when Florence staged three games (Belgium v. Germany and Italy v. Spain, followed by a replay), the stadium has become the fifth most used international venue in Italy.

After the war Berta's name was dropped, as were the Fascist emblems on the tower, and in 1953 four floodlight pylons were erected, then in 1968 the Comunale staged the European Championships' semi-final, England v. Yugoslavia (when a crowd of only 21,834 saw Alan Mullery become the first English international ever to be sent off).

A year later, two unfortunate modifications were made following Fiorentina's second championship win in 1968–9 (the first had come thirteen years earlier). Wooden terracing was laid over sections of the parterre, which raised the potential capacity to 66,344. This was later reduced to a

Before reconstruction – the awkward D-shape is clear, as are those awful roof extensions.

more practical limit of 49,000 and the terracing was ripped up by disgruntled fans during a stormy game in 1980.

But even less inexcusable was the erection of flat roof extensions, each with two ugly white steel pillars for support, on either wing of Nervi's original canopy. Thus the pure lines of the stand's front and side elevations were completely destroyed, as inaptly and ineptly as if a petrol can had been bolted onto the bonnet of a Porsche.

Happily these awful appendages (added before the stadium became a listed monument in 1982) were dismantled during the restoration of the Stadio Comunale for the 1990 World Cup, and replaced by more sympathetic steel cantilevered extensions which echo exactly the curvature of the original roof. But even though there are panels of Plexiglass between the old and new roof sections, in order to distinguish the original roof's identity, the net effect has been to increase the number of covered seats by only 678, from 8522 to 9200. One wonders, therefore, whether it was really worth compromising the original design for such little gain.

In every other respect the 66 billion lire (£30 million) refurbishment programme – over double the original government grant – has improved the stadium considerably. Briefly, the changes have been as follows:

Outside, at each end of the stadium, two ramps now lead to small underground car parks for officials and VIPs. These are in addition to 9200 spaces already within the Campo di Marte area.

All existing concrete surfaces have been refaced. Concrete technology in 1930 was still at a relatively early stage, while Nervi worked to very strict financial limits and had to face all the terracing in cheap cement.

The areas under the main stand and leading onto the parterre have all been revamped to create more facilities for the public. For example, under the east, or Maratona Stand there will be an underground, covered swimming pool plus changing rooms for an athletics track, which is to be built behind the north curve.

The need for a new track arises from the fact that the original track inside the stadium was removed in order to lower the pitch by 2.4 metres.

This was to enable a new, albeit shallow, tier of terracing to be built, leading down from the parterre. The railings which used to line the parterre have been removed and thus its intended function – as a promenade rather than a viewing platform – has been restored. (The original concrete bridge-stairways leading up to the seats have all been replaced by steel versions.)

As in all World Cup stadiums, individual seats have been installed throughout, so that although the new lower tier added to the potential capacity, the final total is much the same as before, at 49,033 (limited to 44,781 for World Cup matches).

For security, a ring of 360 glass screens, as installed also at Rome, Genoa and several other Italian venues, has been erected in front of the new lower tier (rather than obtrusive fencing), at a total cost of 288 million lire (approximately £135,000). The Comunale Stadium must also be one of the few grounds in the world to have water hydrants positioned behind each goal. These are not, as you would imagine, for pitch irrigation – hardly necessary with the new Cell-System pitch installed – but for connecting to high-pressure hoses to be used for crowd control.

Had it not been for the stadium's importance as a historical monument, there can be little doubt that it would have been torn down as an outdated, unsuitable venue for the modern game. Even now, after all the modifications, some inherent design problems subsist, poor visibility from the corners and a lack of cover being the most serious.

And yet it remains such an inspiring stadium. The hills of Fiesole still provide a verdant backdrop beyond the north curve (the Fiorentina end). The east elevation, with its tower and three spiral stairways, is as delicately poised and balanced as ever. Moreover, since the renovation work much of the previous, ugly clutter around the base has been removed, allowing us to see, once more, how it was that Nervi broke the mould; imperfectly maybe, but with sufficient verve to suggest that functionalism need not be devoid of style, nor modernism devoid of character. Paul Bonatz would develop the argument with his small concrete cantilevered stand at Stuttgart in 1933 (see page 261), to be joined by further advances at Turin, Arsenal, Oviedo, Feyenoord, Helsinki and Bordeaux before the decade was out. Thanks to Nervi, and not before time, the game of the twentieth century was at last to be played in stadiums of the twentieth century.

CAGLIARI

STADIO SANT'ELIA

When the capital of Sardinia was selected as a venue for the World Cup, many non-Italian football fans might have asked themselves, 'Cagliari ... weren't they a famous team once?' They were indeed, largely thanks to Italy's top-scoring striker, Luigi 'Gigi' Riva, who joined Cagliari in 1963, led them to Serie A the following year (for the first time in their history), and in 1970 spearheaded the club's one and only championship triumph. It was those years of hope and glory which led to the construction of the new Sant'Elia Stadium, and, as is so often the case, once Cagliari had moved in they were never able to repeat their success. By the time selection for the World Cup came around, the team was down in the depths of the Third Division, Serie C.

In truth, until Riva's apotheosis, Cagliari were a pretty modest, provincial outfit, on an island which had always seemed a step or two behind the rest of Italy. They formed in 1920 and in 1923 settled on a dirt pitch on Via Pola (still in use, and visible en route from the airport, on the corner of Via Pola and Viale Trieste). Then in 1952 the club moved across town to the southeastern outskirts of Cagliari, on the edge of the vast *stagni* (swamps) and salt-pans which dominate the coastline. Their new Stadio Amsicora, named after an ancient Sardinian leader, held 16,000 and had a pair of uncovered concrete stands, with two unterraced ends around a sandy track. But it was never more than basic, and despite staging one international, v. Switzerland in December 1967, Amsicora served Cagliari for only eighteen years. (It is now used by the city's championship-winning hockey club, and a minor football outfit, La Palma.)

Amsicora's replacement was built a short distance away and only 200 metres from the shores of the Gulf of Angeli, in the undeveloped district of Sant'Elia.

To the astonishment of all Italy, Cagliari won

the championship in June 1970. They then played their first match at the new stadium on 2 September 1970, a Cup tie v. Massese, although the official inauguration took place a fortnight later when St.Etienne were beaten 3–0 in Cagliari's first European Cup tie. A crowd of 60,000 squeezed into the stadium that night – yes alright, '*come sardine*' (like sardines – the expression is the same on the island as it is in English), and the night sky glowed with floodlights and local pride.

Sant'Elia was a typically modern Latin stadium: elliptical, with two levels of concrete bench seating, one tier slightly cantilevered over the other to provide a modicum of shelter. There was no roof and few facilities in its simple, unadorned concourse area, which lay under the ring of forked concrete struts which supported the bowl.

Although built relatively recently, continual exposure to the salty sea breezes meant that the concrete exterior and terracing needed considerable refacing when it came to prepare for the World Cup. A new pitch was also a priority. Cagliari thus played their first twelve matches of the 1988–9 season back at Amsicora, which had a safety limit imposed of just 7500. Far from being a financial disaster, the switch proved to be just

the filip Cagliari needed in their efforts to escape from Serie C. Crowds of well over 7500 packed into the old stadium – yes, yes, '*come sardine*' – before the team returned to Sant'Elia in March 1989 and went on to win promotion in front of crowds up to 25–35,000 in their final games – remarkable by Serie C standards.

Further work in 1989–90 included installing individual seats – thereby reducing the capacity to 42,855 (41,000 for the World Cup), erecting a roof over the main, west side, laying a new synthetic running track, and supplementing the existing four floodlight pylons with four additional masts. Replacing the original four pylons with larger, heavier ones was out of the question because the geological base on which the stadium is located would not have sustained the weight. (When first built in 1970, 1000 piles, 15 to 20 metres deep, had to be sunk in order to stabilise the foundations.)

Having eight floodlight mountings is unusual enough, but Sant'Elia's roof is also out of the ordinary. Instead of using concrete or steel supports, architect Adriano Rossi chose to use laminated wooden beams instead, on the grounds that the material would prove more elastic in the stiff sea breezes and more resistant to salt corrosion,

GROUNDWORK

Sant'Elia before the roof went up, with the Castello on a distant hilltop.

41

not to mention adding a softer, warmer touch to the stadium. A glow of a different sort was noticed in September 1989. Turf brought in from Rome was found to be infested by millions of glow worms, which turned Sant'Elia's pitch into a sorry, bumpy mess, made playable for Cagliari only by heavy sanding.

Sant'Elia's exposed environs have, meanwhile, been much improved in the run-up to 1990. On the seafront and on the opposite east side, years of dumping had created an unwholesome terrain of rubble and garbage, now cleared for car parks. Behind the south curve are the grimly isolated high-rise apartment blocks of the Borgo Sant'Elia, next to which the hill of Sant'Elia is topped by a military installation, looking out over the gulf. Behind the north curve is a circular Palazzo dello Sport, while to the northwest, on another high point in the distance, is the Castello, or Castle district, the heart of medieval Cagliari.

Inside, the stadium is quite uniform, with few details to arrest the eye. The balcony walls are in pale red brick, the east section for VIPs is dressed in a speckled marble called granito, and under the concourse are brick walls which form a wind break against the prevailing winds, blowing in from the sea and making the air at pitch level much cooler than on the exposed upper tier.

Sant'Elia's modernisation was relatively inexpensive by Italian World Cup standards – about 24 billion lire (£11 million), only marginally over budget. But for Cagliari's *rossoblu* (red-blue) fans, who celebrated promotion to Serie B in 1989, building costs were far less important than the club's return to the footballing limelight after years in the doldrums – out of Serie A since 1983 and no international match at Sant'Elia since its one and only game, v. Spain on 20 February 1971. Ironically 'Gigi' Riva missed playing in that one, but he'll be there in the stands in 1990, just as he has been at Sant'Elia on many occasions since his retirement. With the VIP section having a new roof, however, this will be the first time he has been truly overshadowed.

PALERMO

STADIO DELLA FAVORITA

Although the mountains of Sicily are most commonly associated with banditry, the fate most likely to befall you on Palermo's Monte Pellegrino would be to have your breath taken away. Towering 2000 feet above the port, Pellegrino provides a marvellous vantage point over Favorita Park, a large rectangular plot of green, 3 kilometres west of the city centre. The Bourbons named the park Favorita, apparently after one of their royal number, but nowadays the area is firmly in the hands of the people. Apart from the football stadium, there is an athletics stadium next door (explaining why, unusually for Italy, the football venue has no track), a hippodrome, a swimming pool and a tennis club, all laid out invitingly at the foot of the steeply rising rockface of Pellegrino. Given a pair of powerful binoculars, and providing you didn't suffer from vertigo, you would never have to pay to watch sport in Palermo again.

Unione Sportiva Palermo trace their origins back to 1898, when Anglo Panormitan FC were formed under the direction of the local British consul. The first colours were red and blue, but after the shirts had been washed a few times they ended up as pink and black. Palermo have thus been the *rosanero* ever since (apart, that is, between 1937–43, when a change of strip was ordered by those dowdy Fascists, who maybe considered pink to be unmanly).

Having settled on their colours, finding a permanent ground proved more difficult. Nine grounds were used during the club's formative years, most of them dotted around what was then the western limits of the city, before the current stadium was built still further out, on the edge of the Favorita Park.

Called originally the Stadio del Littorio (a name used ad nauseam for stadiums built during the Fascist period – for explanation see Bologna, page 32), it had stands on two sides only, one of which on the main, south side (facing Monte Pellegrino) boasted a particularly advanced, reinforced concrete roof, at least as daringly cantilevered as was Nervi's in Florence (completed in the same year), if not quite as stylish – or well publicised.

In the inaugural match on 24 January 1932, Palermo celebrated with a 5–1 win over Atalanta, and went on to win promotion to Serie A for the

La Favorita pictured from Pellegrino, before reconstruction and the tragedy of August 1989.

first time. By 1936 they were back in Serie B, and the following year the stadium was renamed after a local Fascist, Michele Marrone. After the war it became the Stadio Comunale, although amongst the fans La Favorita remains, of course, the favourite name.

During Palermo's second spell in Serie A, between 1948–54, both end terraces were built up, so that by the time Palermo staged its first – and until 1990, its only – full international, v. Switzerland on 28 December 1952, the capacity had risen to 40,000.

There then followed two dizzy decades during which Palermo were promoted to Serie A only to be relegated soon after, on no less than six occasions. In 1986 they went out of business completely, but since reforming in 1987 have fought their way back to Serie C from the regional depths of Serie C2 (the equivalent of a Fourth Division).

The next major development at the stadium occurred in 1984, when a second tier was begun, raised on a steel frame outside the original structure. This increased the capacity to 44,860, but

it was not accompanied by the creation of any supplementary facilities for the public. In fact, had it not been for the political necessity of including Sicily in the World Cup programme, it is doubtful whether such a basic stadium would ever have been selected.

There were several deficiencies to be overcome. Firstly, the facilities within the main stand had to be completely modernised. Only the original central façade was to be left, with new hi-tech, glass-fronted blocks built on either side and a new, extended roof erected to cover the 12,100 seater stand. Great care was taken to ensure that the new design would not in any way clash with the scenic surroundings. Natural colours and a low profile were essential for a building which most passers-by would view with Monte Pellegrino as its backdrop.

Inside the stadium all the existing concrete surfaces had to be refaced and, astonishingly, the south curve had to be completely rebuilt after it was found to have had no foundations. Individual seats were then installed throughout. Since this

43

ITALY

would have meant a loss of capacity to below the required FIFA levels, the second tier was extended, as in 1984, by a quickly assembled steel framework circling three sides of the stadium and linking up on the south side with the newly converted main stand. Even with this extra ring, however, La Favorita was still the smallest of the twelve venues, with a total all-seated capacity of 36,630, although for Palermo's matches this will rise to 40,500 after 1990 (unless, that is, the city's Supervisory Committee, which monitored the effect of the stadium's redesign on the environment, succeeds in its demand that the extra third ring should be dismantled after the World Cup. There is about as much chance of this happening as a local Mafia XI playing the Drug Squad in a charity match).

While all these improvements were being effected, the *rosanero* found themselves forced to play at the nearest suitable stadium, which happened to be in Trapani, almost 100 kilometres west of Palermo. Not surprisingly, gates dropped dramatically to around 3000, and so, in addition to the total bill of around 40 billion lire (£18.5 million – nearly double the original budget), the municipality had also to pay Palermo compensation for their loss of revenue.

But there was far, far worse to come. On 30 August 1989, just one day after a team of FIFA officials had visited Favorita in order to check on progress, disaster struck. As a team of men were working on the half-finished roof structure, one of the large cantilever supports fell down onto the seated area below. Four workmen were killed instantly, a fifth died a week later of his injuries.

On the day after the tragedy, while the funerals were being held and all Palermo was rife with rumours and recriminations, another seven of the roof beams fell in at the south end of the main stand. Fortunately no-one was hurt this time, if only because the site had been closed by order of the local magistrate, but the scale of the collapse immediately put Palermo's position as a World Cup venue into serious jeopardy.

And yet how could the Italian organisers deny Palermo, after so much suffering in the cause of the competition? To take the World Cup away from hard-pressed Sicily at that moment would have been a grave political and psychological blow, not to mention an insult to the relatives of those who died.

FIFA's response was sympathetic. As long as the rest of the stadium was ready, Palermo could

Favorita as the architects intended, designed to blend in with its dramatic backdrop.

ITALIA '90

stage its schedule of three World Cup games, roof or no roof. After all, how often does it ever rain in Sicily during July? Nor would sun be a problem, since the games were each scheduled to be played either at five o'clock or nine o'clock in the evening.

As it transpired, work on Favorita was halted for only eight days, while a team of technical experts investigated three possible causes of the collapse: a design fault in the original plans, possible defects in the materials used, or faulty construction methods by the building contractors. Rumours of sabotage and Mafia vendettas were not taken too seriously, but at the time of going to press none of the inquiry's conclusions were known.

What we can say for sure is that Favorita, for all its ills, has become a vastly improved venue.

Apart from the overall unity which the refurbishment has achieved, the stadium has a new Cell-System pitch (a popular Swiss installation which incorporates advanced, integrated irrigation and drainage systems), an electronic scoreboard, improved all round facilities for VIPs and the press (to be used after the World Cup as part of a public leisure centre), and a landscaped, palm-tree lined precinct around the perimeter, which was previously encircled by an ugly concrete fence.

That was there, apparently, to stop gatecrashers. But it didn't stop one Sicilian who, in September 1976, tried to enter the stadium without paying, by hang-gliding down from Monte Pellegrino and landing on the pitch in the middle of a Cup tie v. Fiorentina. Or was he just trying to offer Palermo his services as a new winger?

44

BARI

STADIO NUOVO

We say Stadio Nuovo, but the betting is that a poll to be conducted to find a proper name for the new stadium in Bari will come out in favour of the title Stadio San Nicola – Saint Nicholas Stadium. This is because the saint's remains are preserved in Bari, having supposedly been filched from Myra (now in Turkey), by sailors in the eleventh century. Most people know Saint Nicholas, of course, as Santa Claus.

But whatever its eventual name, Santa Claus himself could hardly have delivered a more fabulous gift to this attractive, businesslike coastal city on the heel of Italy – a stadium which puts Bari at the forefront of European sport, even if the local club, the *Galletti* (Roosters), are best known for their frequent flitting up-and-down between the divisions.

FC Bari formed in 1908 but soon split into two factions, Ideale and Liberty. In 1928, however, the Fascists – seeking order in all things and especially the prohibition of anglicised names – ordered the two to merge under the title of **Bari AS** (Associazione Sportiva). But it would be another six years before the city's first major stadium would be ready.

Dedicated to the Italian 'victory' of the First World War (an event hyped by the Fascists in a vain attempt to establish the nation's fighting spirit), the Stadio della Vittoria cost 2 million lire – a sum raised almost entirely by public subscriptions. For this sacrifice the people of Bari were rewarded when Mussolini came to inaugurate the stadium on 6 September 1934, on the occasion of the National Fascist Youth Championships. Bari AS moved in three months later, their first match being a Serie B encounter v. Comense (now Como) on 16 December 1934.

The 30,000 capacity Vittoria Stadium was a typical design of the Fascist era, with an open, elliptical tier around a running track, a concrete half-cantilevered roof over the west side, and on the east side a concrete framework, never completed, called the Torre Maratona (demolished in the early 1960s). It was, in effect, a cheaper version of the new stadium in Bologna.

The setting was splendid however, that is if

Bari's former home, the Stadio della Vittoria – a cheaper version of Bologna.

one ignored the adjacent gasworks. Like a traffic roundabout surrounded by roads (as the Rome Colosseum is today), the stadium was approached along a wide road leading from the sea wall of Bari's Gran Porto. Across the perimeter road to the north lay the city's exhibition grounds, the Fiera del Levante.

In late 1943 the Vittoria Stadium became a symbol of defeat, as first the pitch and roof were damaged by German bombs, then the Allied Southern Command arrived and turned the stadium into a rest area for the troops. One of the British army officers stationed there was the future Manchester United manager, Matt Busby, who in July 1944 organised a British team to take on a Bari XI.

After the war, under the name of Stadio Comunale, the stadium was expanded with an extra tier, and at last witnessed victory for Italy in each of the *Azzurri's* four internationals there, the first being on 14 December 1947, v. Czechoslovakia, the last in February 1988, v. the USSR. By that time the stadium's days were already numbered. Although it had once held a record crowd of nearly 43,000 (for a Serie A game v. Roma in September 1969), its concrete structure was in very poor condition and the capacity had been limited to 34,000.

Thus for the 1990 World Cup it was decided to start afresh on a greenfield site, a few kilometres west on the edges of the outer suburb of Carbonara. Commissioned for the project was Renzo Piano, one of Italy's most prolific and charismatic architects, best known for his design (with Richard Rogers) of the Pompidou Centre in Paris.

45

ITALY

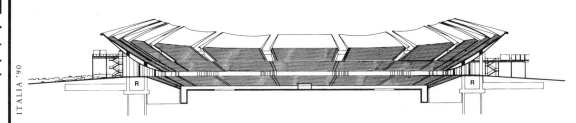

Beauty and practicality at Bari. As at Turin, a mound created around the perimeter, plus the sinking of the pitch below ground level, reduces the stadium's profile on the landscape and makes for easier access from the concourse to all three tiers. An underground roadway (R) for VIPs and emergency vehicles circles the stadium and provides players and officials with an easy route to the dressing rooms under the lower tier (next to the moat).

But his stadium for Bari shares little of the urban, hi-tech style of that famous building. It is instead a predominantly reinforced concrete structure designed to stand in proud isolation on an open, 50 hectare rural site.

Several features distinguish it as a stadium of immense beauty and practicality, much of which is due to Piano's collaboration with Joseph Zucker, an Austrian architect who had previously worked on stadiums in Iran.

The pitch itself is only 1 metre below ground level, but it seems deeper because a gently sloping artificial hill was formed around the stadium, to create a green, 60 metre deep buffer zone (as at Turin's new stadium). Branching out across this zone is a radial system of access paths, which not only safely funnel crowds in from the surrounding car parks (which hold nearly 10,000 vehicles), but is intended to provide a psychologically calming environment. We shall see ...

One admirable feature is the tunnel ring road which runs under the stadium perimeter and keeps team coaches, police cars, ambulances and so on completely separate from the pedestrian precincts above. No other stadium in Europe offers such excellent, all-round communications.

The stadium itself has a pronounced bowl shape, consisting of two tiers, capped by a slightly arched cantilevered roof composed of translucent Teflon panels. This covers 70 per cent of the 60,000 seats, of which 56,874 will be used for Bari's five World Cup matches (including the third and fourth place play-off).

Viewed from a distance the stadium has an immense, sculptural impact on the landscape. It is as if a spaceship had dropped onto a landing pad, and then a series of gangways lowered down to the ground from its smooth underside. Once the crowd had entered, one imagines these stairs sliding back into place and the whole, sleek saucer spinning off into the heavens.

Close to, the main impression is one of lightness and air, a stadium in which the voids are as important as the solids. The actual finish of the concrete is also, unusually, of a very high standard. This was partly because each reinforced concrete unit is of a slightly different shape (to create the undulating profile of the roof) and therefore had to be cast on site, like the pieces of a jigsaw puzzle, using the minutest calculations.

Not surprisingly Bari's new stadium was neither easy nor cheap to build. It took eighteen months alone to gain planning consent from the vacillating Ministry of Public Works, to buy the farmland, and then to agree with conservationists on the preservation of an ancient settlement discovered during ground clearance, just behind the north curve. From the original government grant of 55 billion lire agreed in March 1987 (though not paid until several months later), by mid-1989 the final cost had risen to nearer 125 billion (approximately £58 million), of which 80 billion lire was for the stadium, the rest for supporting infrastructure (roads, press centre and so on).

For a city of 360,000 inhabitants, and with a football team which, since 1958, has been promoted to Serie A five times but never survived there longer than three seasons, to spend so much on a 60,000 capacity stadium represents an enormous gamble. To realise fully the stadium's appreciable assets, therefore, the city will have to start attracting major European finals, internationals, and athletics events at least as important as the Mediterranean Games. The *Galletti*

MICHELANGELO BELVISO

Bari in early-1989. The pitch is laid, and the ancient settlement (bottom right) accommodated.

themselves could help by roosting awhile in the top flight. Otherwise, once the spotlight of the 1990 World Cup has faded, Renzo Piano's symphony of design could easily end up as a hollow tune which soon goes out of fashion. Such a brave undertaking deserves more.

NAPLES

STADIO SAN PAOLO

To many northern Italians the city of Naples – reckoned to be dirty, overcrowded and backward – lies beyond the pale. To southerners who know different, success on the football field represents one, some would say the best, possible riposte to such prejudice. It would be impossible, because of this, to describe San Paolo merely in terms of its bricks and mortar. Without its fanatical *tifosi* it is, or at least was before 1990, just another large, rather featureless concrete bowl. But on match days it is almost as thunderous and pulsating a crater as is the famed volcano of Vesuvius, which looms over Naples so menacingly. Indeed the stadium is said to vibrate in such

an unnerving way that residents of nearby flats have reported household objects breaking when a Napoli goal is celebrated. Tests subsequently conducted to check the stadium's stability have, we can happily report, found it to be quite safe; it did, after all, survive the appalling earthquake of November 1980, and not even Napoli's fans could rival 7 points on the Richter scale. They have, besides, a reputation for leaving the stands when the mood takes them and venting their emotions on the pitch instead (which has led to the stadium being closed on several occasions).

It would also be impossible to describe the stadium without reference to *him*. If the Stadio San Paolo has not formally been renamed San Diego, there is little doubt that it has become, de facto, the temple of Maradona. For until his £5 million signing in 1984, the light-blues of Napoli had had relatively little to celebrate – in 1962 and 1976 they won the Italian Cup (a competition which

47

ITALY

enjoys scant regard), and there had been several near misses in the championship. Moreover, apart from Cagliari's triumph in 1970, no southern team had ever won the *scudetto*, while Naples itself barely figured on the international scene until 1960. The north-south divide was as sharply defined in football as it ever was in economic terms.

The game initially came to Naples courtesy of English sailors, who helped establish the first club, Naples FC, in 1904. Eight years later dissident members formed a rival club, Internazionale Napoli, only to rejoin forces in 1922 under the name of Internaples. This club was then reconstituted as Napoli in 1926, and based itself at the 45,000 capacity Stadio Giorgio Ascarelli (named after the club's first president), an open stadium with straight sides and semi-circular ends, situated a few blocks east of the current central station. The *Azzurri* ventured down here only twice before the Second World War. In fact their game v. Switzerland in February 1932 was the first Italian international ever played south of Rome. The Stadio Ascarelli then staged two games in the 1934 World Cup – Hungary v. Egypt and the sparsely attended third-place play-off, Germany v. Austria. German influence surfaced a few years later when a change of name to Stadio Partenopeo was ordered (Partenopeo was the ancient name for Naples). This was because as a Jew, Giorgio Ascarelli was an embarrassment to a regime increasingly bound by Nazi prejudices. The stadium staged one further international, v. France, in December 1938 (the last in Naples for twenty-two years), before it was destroyed in bombing raids during the Second World War.

Napoli's next ground, in the hilltop district of

Vomero, on the northwestern edge of the city, had also been affected by the war. The Germans used it as a staging post for prisoners, and when the Neapolitans finally turned on their former allies in September 1943, four days of German reprisals left thousands of civilians dead, some of their bodies being dumped on ground behind Vomero's north terrace. Once the Germans had retreated, Napoli's players returned to find the pitch littered with bullets and so badly scorched by petrol that falling over in a tackle was an experience much to be avoided.

Vomero became Napoli's regular home in 1944. It held around 20,000 and had two, uncovered stands, with wooden terracing at each end. But with residential developments encircling the ground and Vomero developing an unsavoury reputation for pitch invasions and riots among the supporters, in April 1957 the municipality began building a new stadium a few kilometres westwards, in the outlying district of Fuorigrotta. (Vomero is now a peaceful, well used community sports centre known as the Stadio Collana, named after one of its former directors.)

Napoli's third home was called the San Paolo – or Saint Paul's Stadium – (on the advice of the local archbishop). Designed by Carlo Cocchia, it was a streamlined open bowl cradled by fifty-six concrete uprights, with two superimposed tiers and a capacity of 85,012. Officially it was all-seated, but in practice so many fans stood up on the upper level that barriers were installed. Napoli v. Juventus opened the stadium on 6 December 1959, but the official inauguration took place a month later on 6 January 1960, with an international v. Switzerland.

Thereafter, San Paolo changed very little, and nor did the fans, whose number rose to an incredible average of 70,000 per match but whose weakness for invading the pitch was only partly checked by the presence of fences and a moat.

But the stadium did put Naples firmly on the international football map, by staging the 1968 European Championships' semi-final, USSR v. Italy (won by Italy on the toss of a coin), four games in the 1980 European Championships, and, significantly, almost as many internationals as Milan during the period 1960–89. Yet despite having a stadium to rival those in the north, and for many years a millionaire president (the shipping magnate Achille Lauro), Napoli still had few honours to show for their efforts. They needed

Vomero – Napoli's base from 1944–59 and scene of some notorious crowd disorders.

GROUNDWORK

ALAIN SCHROEDER

The classic concrete bowl of San Paolo before refurbishment began for the World Cup.

a messiah, and in Maradona their prayers were answered. When Napoli subsequently achieved the Double under his leadership in 1987, six decades of pent-up frustration and passion erupted throughout southern Italy. 'Guerra' the Napoli players shout as one, before they leave their dressing room. Now, at last, they had 'vittoria' too.

And, of course, a World Cup for which to prepare. Directed by Fabrizio Cocchia, son of San Paolo's original architect, the first phase of reconstruction began shortly after the Double celebrations and concentrated on the stadium's acute lack of facilities. This was remedied by building a raised concourse around the exterior, to house toilets, meeting rooms, refreshment bars and technical installations for the press, VIPs and public.

Inside the stadium, new dressing rooms have been constructed under the track and warm-up areas on the west side, a tricky operation which in turn required improvements to the 4 metre deep moat.

The original plan had been to remove the moat and the running track, lower the pitch and extend the lower tier downwards (as at Florence), thereby increasing the capacity by 10,000. But this idea was dropped because, apart from the cost, it

would have required Napoli to play elsewhere – and there simply is nowhere else to put 70,000 season-ticket holders safely. Instead therefore, it was decided to retain the moat, lay a new Tartan track – since apart from Bari, southern Italy has no other major athletics venue – and more importantly, alter the rake of the existing lower tier (which had always been too shallow), to improve the angle of viewing.

By doing this, and by astute management of the upper tier, the overall capacity has been kept to around 86,000, despite the installation of individual seats throughout. For the World Cup, however, only 74,090 seats will be occupied.

Finally there was the erection of a canopy to provide cover for 80 per cent of the seats. Supported on twenty-eight square steel masts ranged around the stadium perimeter, it is composed of translucent panels, folded and pointed like a concertina, but interspersed with a raised vaulted section over each cantilevered steel beam. The back of the roof has been left open to allow ventilation, to maintain some of the stadium's original airiness, and to keep in view the Astroni hills to the north and the prominent Cape of Posillipo, which overlooks the Bay of Naples, a kilometre south of the stadium.

49

As Napoli's roof went up, so did the costs. But who would dare oppose spending on *calcio*?

But no amount of new construction could ever improve the stadium's best feature – the Neapolitan supporters themselves. There is, for example, the old man who throws salt onto the pitch before each game, to bring good luck. Another regular dresses like a Mexican and patrols the running track, blithely crashing cymbals together. For truly important games, the team's lucky mascot, *'ciuco'* (a small donkey), is brought out on parade, and it has been known for a magician to be brought in to cast a lucky spell over the stadium.

Nor are the players immune from ritual. Set in a wall by the tunnel, to be kissed or touched by any player who feels the need, there is a ceramic tile depicting the Madonna.

The Naples Comune has been doing a great deal of praying and pleading itself. In this, one of Europe's poorest cities, it was faced with a rise in refurbishment costs at the stadium from around 35 billion lire (£16 million) in 1987 to well above the 100 billion mark by mid-1989. No amount of magic was going to make that bill disappear, or, it seemed, to win any relief from government coffers in Rome. Meanwhile those long-suffering residents in the flats surrounding the stadium had to endure six days a week of construction noise plus a seventh day of rumbling homage to Maradona (or rumbling anger when he did not turn up for games).

Few other Neapolitans will complain however. They will expect the Comune to muddle through the crisis in its usual manner – a pinch of salt, the 'hand of God', a lot of shouting in the corridors of power ... what else can it do with so little money and such an expensive obsession?

ROME

STADIO FLAMINIO

This is a tale of two stadiums: one which staged the 1934 World Cup Final, the other, built later on the same site, which hosted the football tournament of the 1960 Olympics.

There was first a stadium on the Flaminio site (situated between the Villa Flaminia and the western slopes of Parioli – Rome's smartest district) in 1911. Called the Stadio Nazionale, it never actually staged an international match, and was subsequently abandoned during the First World War.

Then came the Fascists' 'March on Rome' in 1922 and, since no dictatorship can possibly survive without building at least one stadium of epic proportions, in 1927 reconstruction of the Nazionale began.

Yet despite its suitably vainglorious title of **Stadio del Partido Nacional Fascista**, the new stadium was not, as one would have expected, built in the ancient Roman mould (as at the Colosseum, for example), but in the Hellenic tradition. That is to say it was U-shaped, with stands on three sides only. Over the west side was a small, propped concrete roof, while both side stands extended 30 metres beyond the south goal line and, at their extremities, overlooked an open-air swimming pool which lay 20 metres behind the goal. The southern boundary of this unusual stadium was then sealed off by a grandiose screen wall, punctuated with columns, each one capped by a strutting, sporting figure in the sort of heroic pose in which the Fascists seemed to delight.

Another unusual facet of the PNF Stadium, as it was known, was that unlike most stadiums built during the Fascist period (San Siro apart), it had no running track. And yet astonishingly, the pitch dimensions did not conform with international standards.

Despite this, the PNF Stadium's official inauguration took place on 25 March 1928 with an international, a 32,500 crowd seeing Italy beat Hungary 4–3. Significantly, this was the first time the *Azzurri* – essentially a northern Italian XI – had ever played in the capital, or indeed south of Bologna. Moreover, until that game, only two players from Roman clubs had ever been selected.

But Rome would soon catch up, and the PNF Stadium went on to stage another dozen internationals over the next twelve years, including three matches during the 1934 World Cup: Italy v. USA; the semi-final, Germany v. Czechoslovakia; and the final, Italy v. Czechoslovakia on 10 June 1934, when 50,000 patriots celebrated a 2–1 home victory in front of a beaming Duce.

By then a fourth side of terracing had been added, between the swimming pool and the south goal, while underneath the stands were the offices of the Italian Olympic Committee (CONI) and the government sports federation, plus various gymnasiums and a covered swimming pool. These facilities, together with an athletics track and tennis club laid out behind the north curve, made the stadium a favourite gathering point for the sporting-conscious elite of Mussolini's Rome. (Among its prewar regulars was Paul Gallico's fictional adventurer, Hiram Holliday, who polished up his fencing at the stadium gym before taking on the Fascist, Del Tevere, in a duel.)

Apart from internationals, the PNF Stadium also became the home of Rome's oldest and most privileged club side, **Lazio**.

Taking their name from the region around Rome, Lazio had formed in 1900 and played their first games in the Piazza d'Armi, a military parade ground in the Quartiere Prati. In 1906 they moved to a ground near Villa Borghese, called Parco dei Daini, but were forced to leave in 1913 after a stray ball landed on the carriage of the prefect's wife, leading to the club's immediate eviction. The park area still exists, by Via Pietro Raimondi.

Lazio's next home was at Farnesina, roughly where the Stadio dei Marmi is now, next door to the current Olympic Stadium (see page 54). But it was too distant from the centre, so within a few

The PNF Stadium in 1934. The dome of St Peter's is just visible on the horizon.

The flamboyant gateway to the PNF Stadium screened an open-air pool behind the goal.

months Lazio started afresh at the foot of the Parioli heights, a short distance northwest of the Stadio Nazionale. Called the Rondinella and opened in November 1914, this new ground would serve Lazio until their move to the PNF Stadium in May 1931.

In 1940, nine years after this move, they were joined at the PNF, somewhat reluctantly, by their deadly rivals, Roma. **AS Roma** were a product of the rationalisation of Italian football during the early Fascist years. They formed in 1927 by the merger of four clubs: Roman, Alba, Fortitudo and Pro Roma, none of whom had an adequate ground. For two years, therefore, the new club played at the Motovelodromo, an ugly venue with a concrete racetrack, stuck out in the southeast suburbs, until in November 1929, during the inaugural season of the national league, Roma were able to move into a ground of their own, in the heartland of their urban, proletarian support in south Rome.

And what a ground it was, too.

Situated on Via Zabaglia at the foot of Testac-

The Parioli heights overlook Flaminio as Lazio and Roma settle in for 1989–90.

GROUNDWORK

cio Hill, close to the Tiber, Campo Testaccio cost 1.5 million lire to build – a phenomenal amount for that period, and was constructed almost entirely out of wood. There was one covered stand and three sides of open terracing, formed by wooden boards painted alternately in the club colours of red and yellow. Because of this, when empty the Campo Testaccio positively exuded character and identity. When full, the ground was said to roar like thunder, as 20,000 *tifosi* stamped rhythmically on the boards. Testaccio Hill itself was invariably milling with people, straining for a view, while behind one goal the home supporters were close enough to breathe down the visiting goalkeeper's neck.

Hardly surprisingly, in eleven years at Testaccio the *giallorossi* (red-yellows) lost only twenty-six home games, before they finally had to accept that the much-loved ground was no longer big enough nor safe enough for continued use. Their last game there was on 30 June 1940 (shortly after Mussolini took Italy into the Second World War), and the following season they kicked off at the PNF Stadium, as co-tenants with Lazio. Some older Roma fans would say that the club has been homeless ever since.

No trace of Campo Testaccio remains, and sooner than anyone imagined the same became true of the PNF Stadium. It staged its last international on 14 April 1940, v. Romania, and after the war, renamed first as the Stadio Nazionale and then, after the Superga aircrash in 1949 (see page 22), as the Stadio Torino, it went slowly into decline. Tainted by Fascist connections (as indeed, rightly or wrongly, Lazio have been for many years) and rendered obsolete by its design, the writing was finally on the wall when work began on Rome's new Olympic Stadium in the early 1950s. Once that was complete in 1953 (see page 54), Roma and Lazio moved out of the Stadio Torino, and four years later the bulldozers moved in.

But it was soon replaced, for on the very same site a new stadium arose, and this time the design was much more enduring. It was, in fact, the first stadium Pier Luigi Nervi had worked on since his revolutionary Comunale Stadium in Florence opened in 1932 (see page 36).

Aided by his son Antonio and using his own building company (Nervi and Bartoli), Nervi created on the site a stadium of quite striking simplicity, in a modern style which still remains

Thirty years on, Nervi's Flaminio Stadium and Palazzetto (top right) are still a delight. Mussolini's white obelisk by the Olympic Stadium can just be seen in the distance above the main stand.

fresh over thirty years on. With an original capacity of 55,000 (24,300 seated), it was essentially an open concrete bowl, higher on the east side than at the ends, with two standing areas filling the semi-circular space between each goal and the curving seating tier. A concrete vaulted roof covered 8000 seats on the west side, with intriguing small circles of glass set within each vault to add light. Skilfully integrated under the stands was a covered swimming pool.

(Directly north of the stadium, Nervi also designed an exquisite, dome-shaped Palazzetto dello Sport, an indoor sports arena which provides further evidence of Nervi's inspired use of an otherwise drab material, reinforced concrete.)

The Flaminio Stadium, named after the district, staged its first match on 13 March 1959, an amateur international between Italy and Holland. The following year it was used for the semi-finals and final of the Olympic soccer tournament, Yugoslavia taking the gold against Denmark on 10 September 1960.

But the Flaminio has always played second fiddle to the Olympic Stadium, despite the fact that when Lazio have been in Serie B and transferred its matches to the smaller venue, its closer quarters and lack of running track have undoubtedly provided a better atmosphere.

In recent years, the Flaminio's most sustained period of senior footballing action came in 1989–90, when both Lazio and Roma were forced to play their games there during reconstruction work at the Olympic Stadium. CONI, which owns both stadiums, immediately cut the Flaminio's capacity to 31,630 – less than half the Olympic total – and put up tall netting to protect the players from missiles, even in front of the main stand – such is the state of anxiety which pervades the modern Italian game. But if that is the price one has to pay to get close to the touchlines in the current climate maybe the Flaminio is best staying out of the limelight after all.

ROME

STADIO OLIMPICO

However much the people of Milan or Turin might resent it, all roads for the 1990 World Cup lead to Rome, and to the final on 8 July at the Olympic Stadium. But slow, often impenetrable roads they have been, and in the three years preceding the competition, the 'eternal city' echoed as much to the eternal clamour of bureaucrats and fraud investigators as it did to the clatter of construction work at the stadium.

Only in Rome, where the seat of power resides, could it have taken so long to extract decisions from the decision makers, leading some critics to wonder if the city actually wanted the World Cup Final on its doorstep.

Only in Rome, surely, could it have been suddenly decided, in a half-reconstructed stadium, after nearly five years of planning and with just twelve months to go before the finals, to completely rebuild the main stand.

And yet Rome had to be ready, or face eternal humiliation, and there is nothing which stirs up a Roman bureaucrat more than the possibility of a loss of face (unless, of course, it be the search for a scapegoat).

In truth, before 1990 the Olympic Stadium was never, per se, a structure of particular merit. But its location has always been quite superb, and quite in keeping with the Romans' apparent propensity for building stadiums at the foot of hills (as we saw in the previous section with Testaccio and the PNF Stadium).

Situated in the northwest of the city, some 3 kilometres due north of the Vatican and 1.5 kilometres west of the Flaminio Stadium, the Olympic Stadium nestles at the foot of Monte Mario. Seventy years ago this area was said to have been unwelcoming, infested and subject to flooding from the river. Then the land level was raised and handed over to the Military Academy for exercises and shooting practice, until in 1928 the architect Enrico Del Debbio was entrusted with the task of creating a sports complex on the site. This was to be known as the Foro Mussolini – a place of homage to Il Duce and a hothouse of Fascist

From the north side of Monte Mario, the Olympic Stadium as it looked for the 1960 Games.

physical endeavour. For the placing of a stadium at the heart of this complex, Del Debbio chose a natural dip in the land, so that its structure would not impinge too greatly upon views either up to or down from Monte Mario. The new stadium was to be called the Stadio dei Cipressi, the Stadium of the Cypress Trees.

But even under a Fascist dictatorship the bureaucrats of Rome still managed to hold up the works – remember, the city was already building the PNF Stadium not far away – and by the time the Second World War broke out the Cipressi was little more than a shallow bowl, a mere shadow of the modern 100,000 capacity Colosseum which the Duce had asked for.

The surrounding Foro Mussolini was much more advanced, however.

Crossing a new bridge over the Tiber, one first encountered a tall white obelisk, dedicated to Mussolini. This led onto the Piazzale dell'Impero, a gleaming white, marble walkway decorated with mosaics of sporting scenes. At the end of this, in front of the southeast corner of the Cipressi Stadium, was a circular, tree-lined opening, with the surprisingly understated, abstract Fountain of the Sphere in the centre.

All of this survives today, and despite the unease one may feel about its original sponsors, it cannot be denied that the juxtaposition of marble, mosaics and cypress trees, set against the verdant backdrop of Monte Mario, has an undeniable charm (except on match days, that is, when the whole area becomes strewn with litter).

The same cannot be said of the Stadio dei Marmi (marble), a training stadium built between the obelisk and the Cipressi's east side, which looks as if it had come straight out of a kitsch Hollywood epic on Ancient Rome. One almost expects to see a toga-clad Victor Mature emerge from the trees and call out, 'Hi Julius! Fancy a quick jog round the track before the game at the Colosseum Superbowl tonight? And you, Brutus?'

The Stadio dei Marmi has low terracing ringed by fifty-four sculpted figures of muscle-bound athletes, one of whom, a naked footballer, appears none too happy with the prospect of kicking a stone ball with his bare feet.

But at least this ridiculous pseudo-classical stadium is well used. It now has a synthetic track, and forms part of the Academy of Physical Education, a solid building immediately next to the obelisk. Other installations in the Foro Mussolini

The Stadio dei Marmi – Fascist kitsch and marble terracing, with Monte Mario beyond.

include tennis courts (lined with more sculptures), a swimming pool, the large headquarters of CONI (the Italian Olympic Committee) and, to the north, the Ministry of Foreign Affairs.

It had been the Duce's intention that this area would play a part in an international exhibition scheduled for 1942, or even host the 1944 Olympics. But of course neither event took place, and during the Second World War the words 'Foro Mussolini' took on a rather different twist. *'Foro'* means hole as well as forum, and with the Italians having to face crippling shortages, the last hole on the ever-tightening belt became known sardonically as the 'Foro Mussolini'.

Following the war, the Cipressi Stadium's administrators, CONI (who receive their income from the state pools operation, Totocalcio) commissioned plans from architect Annibale Vitellozzi for completing the project, and after the usual political wrangles and then nearly two and a half years of construction, the new stadium was finally inaugurated on 17 May 1953. The famous Hungarians of the day were invited to the opening, and they fully justified their reputation with an exhilarating 3–0 win against the *Azzurri* in front of a packed crowd of 80,000 spectators.

We say 80,000, but some sources gave the capacity as 90,000, and the stadium was even called, rather optimistically, the Stadio dei Centomila (100,000), a tag also applied to the revamped San Siro two years later. But the official title was always Stadio Olimpico, while the area around it was renamed the Foro Italico. (Mussolini's name is still visible on the obelisk, however, and this remains the Duce's only sur-

ITALY

GROUNDWORK

The lights are down at the Olympic Stadium, but who would have thought they'd be so huge?

viving memorial. If nothing else, it provides a prominent meeting point for fans before a game.)

Apart from staging the 1960 Olympic Games and becoming the new home for both clubs in the capital, **AS Roma** and **Lazio** (who moved over from the Stadio Torino – see previous section), the Olympic Stadium immediately assumed the role of national football stadium. Before 1953, Milan had staged more than twice as many internationals as Rome. But after 1953 the imbalance shifted in favour of the capital, which also pulled rank when the European Championships came to Italy in both 1968 and 1980. It has, in addition, hosted two European Cup Finals, in 1977 (Liverpool v. Borussia Mönchengladbach) and 1984 (Liverpool v. AS Roma).

Apart from that hooligan-plagued last match (when Lazio fans gave weapons to the English in order to beat the *giallorossi* mob), the Olympic Stadium was usually a pleasure to visit. Monte Mario starts its ascent within a few metres of the rear of the main, west stand, and stretches round to the south of the stadium, with the fifteenth-century Villa Madama a noble presence halfway up the hill. If one ascended the winding lanes behind the stadium, one could even see most of the pitch (no longer possible since a roof was added in 1990). There was another superb vantage point, a tree-covered knoll rising up behind the north curve, but this was always fenced off from

the public, for obvious reasons.

The actual structure was a completely open, elongated oval, which from the cypress-lined concourse had a clinically modern frontage of concrete balconies and green railings. It could be said, unkindly, that it resembled a multi-storey car park, but in fact it had to be quite sparse so as not to diminish its surroundings.

Inside the stadium there was little to catch the eye, apart from a line of glass-fronted television and radio cabins cantilevered over the rear of the main, Monte Mario side. The marble terracing on this side, incidentally, was said to have been taken from the same Travertino quarry used for the Colosseum, eighteen centuries earlier.

Besides being rather unexciting, the stadium interior did have one major drawback. Both end terraces, the Curva Nord and Curva Sud, were so far behind each goal that the nearest spectators could get was nearly 50 metres from the goal line, a distance of almost half a pitch's length, while those on the rearmost seats of each curve were over 200 metres away from the far goal.

When it came to preparing for the World Cup, in January 1985, the elimination of this design fault was one of several major restructuring proposals put forward by CONI for official approval.

CONI's plan was as follows. The stadium already held 80,000, including 15,000 standing places, but had to be enlarged to hold at least 80,000 individual seats (in order to meet FIFA requirements for the World Cup Final). So, while bringing the two new curves nearer to the pitch, they would also be made taller than the originals, to accommodate 24,600 at each end. The east, or Tevere Stand (Tiber Stand), would be extended at the rear (by building outside the existing boundary – as at Bologna and Palermo) to add 6900 places. A similar number would be added to the Monte Mario Stand opposite, except that these would have to be added by building over the existing access road which ran between the stand and the hillside.

To comply further with FIFA regulations, which require at least two-thirds cover for World Cup Final venues, a roof was also to be built, supported by cables slung from eight pillars erected outside the perimeter.

CONI's plans were approved by the World Cup organisers in June 1985, and all seemed fine. But then, as even Mussolini had found, getting a stadium finished in Rome was no simple matter. It was not until February 1987 that the local Comune (municipality) finally deigned to give CONI the go-ahead, and not until March of the following year that the Italian government authorised subsidies to each of the twelve venues.

The Olympic Stadium was to receive 56 billion lire (£26 million) from the government towards the total estimated costs of 90 billion lire. (This figure included extra reconstruction around the stadium and the vital improvement of road links between the stadium and a vast new communications centre being built by the state television company, RAI, a few kilometres away.)

Only in May 1988 and with less than two years to go before the big kick-off, did work begin on the almost total reconstruction of one of Europe's biggest stadiums.

Would Rome make it in time?

By February 1989 the Tevere side was completed, followed a few months later by both new end curves and a moat encircling the entire running track. This moat was lined on both sides by toughened glass security screens – an innovation for 1990 which will be closely monitored by several countries.

All things considered, progress was pretty impressive. Except that while all this was happening, the original roof design was abandoned. It had been touted as the largest stadium roof in the world. It certainly promised to be one of the most expensive. A little late in the day, therefore, new plans were made for a much simpler, more lightweight cover, cantilevered over the stands on a steel frame and composed of translucent Teflon panels. In many respects it was to be a simpler version of the roof so successfully built over the Prater Stadium in Vienna, but it was hardly a thing of beauty, and given the stadium's location in such scenic surrounds, that was an important consideration.

By the time the new roof plan was unveiled in February 1989 the estimated costs had reached approximately 150 billion lire and investigations had begun into the way in which government tenders for the building work had been awarded.

But there was more. It was then realised that the whole Monte Mario Stand would have to be completely rebuilt, rather than simply extended and refurbished. Apparently, problems with the foundations were discovered, due to water seepage from the adjacent hillside, and it was also realised that the rake of both new end curves

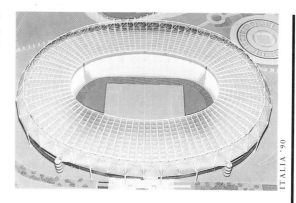

ITALIA '90

Roofing the Olympic Stadium was always likely to be problematic, especially in view of its prominence at the foot of Monte Mario. The solution finally chosen has sixteen external tubular steel pillars and a radial system of translucent vaulted sections. Being in Rome, it will attract the severest scrutiny.

would not correspond with that of the existing stand, thus reducing the potential capacity and making it trickier to add a roof. Why these problems had not been foreseen much earlier became the subject of another investigation, for not only would this late change add perhaps an additional 20 billion lire to the already massively overspent budget, and put considerable pressure on the building schedules, but it also meant Roma and Lazio could not use the stadium throughout season 1989–90. CONI thus had to invest more funds on preparing the Flaminio Stadium for their temporary sojourn, while privately hoping that neither club would do too well that season and therefore their furious season-ticket holders would feel less inclined to pack out a venue whose capacity was less than half that of the Olympic Stadium.

Meanwhile the government was changing for the forty-ninth time since the war, politicians were campaigning for the European elections, and thus no-one in Rome seemed prepared to make any decision, either for or against the granting of more money for the stadium.

But that is the way Rome works, or rather doesn't, and that is why the World Cup organisers warned that if the Olympic Stadium was not finished, they were perfectly within their rights to switch the Final elsewhere, by which they meant Milan.

The threat was sufficient. Rome's stadium may not have been built in a day, but it was at least made ready for the 1990 World Cup Final with more than a day to spare.

ALBANIA

TIRANA

STADIUMI QEMAL STAFA

Isolated (or protected?) from the rest of Europe, East and West, by a hard-line Marxist-Leninist regime, the People's Socialist Republic of Albania may have officially banned religion but it regards football as a very serious matter indeed.

The most surprising thing about the national stadium is that it is named not after Comrade Enver Hoxha – founding father of the republic – in whose honour seemingly everything else in Albania is dedicated, but Qemal Stafa, a writer and founder of the Albanian Communist Party who was killed in May 1942, aged twenty-two, by

No lights and only a six-lane cinder track, but Qemal Stafa would have been proud of it.

ACTION IMAGES

58

the occupying Italian forces in Tirana, the capital. Busts of the bespectacled partisan are displayed in several towns, while the anniversary of his death is commemorated as the Day of the Martyrs.

Construction of the stadium began in 1938 during the reign of the self-appointed King Zog (referred to today as the 'antipeople's regime'). But only months after Zog's Minister of Education laid the first stone, Mussolini's troops invaded the country and the stadium's completion, by young volunteers, was delayed until after liberation in November 1944. Inauguration followed in October 1946 with the Balkan Games, the first international sports event staged in Europe after the war. Albania (known as Shqiperi to the locals) won the football section against Yugoslavia, Bulgaria and Romania.

Apart from international matches and Spartakiáda (mass celebrations of sport and physical fitness, held every five years), three Tirana clubs use the stadium: **Partizani, 17 Nëntori** (17 November being Liberation Day) and **Dinamo**. For matches against less attractive opposition, or when fixtures clash, the nearby, rather neglected 12,000 capacity Dinamo Stadium is also used Since Tirana's population is only 250,000, average gates of around 11,000 are the equivalent of capacity crowds at Munich or Naples. In fact Albania boasts the highest per capita football attendances in Europe (Scotland coming second).

The Qemal Stafa Stadium is one of the most centrally located stadiums in Europe, situated just off the Avenue of Martyrs, a wide thoroughfare which, like most of the city, has virtually no motorised traffic. (There are no private motor cars and even top players arrive at the stadium on bicycles.) All around are leafy Italianate side streets and imposing public buildings such as the State University, the People's Assembly and a new Enver Hoxha Museum.

The stadium's best feature, flanked by hedges and grass slopes, is a white rusticated stone entrance block, with two stairways leading to a balcony, which overlooks a piazza in front of the university. A white, concrete, cantilevered roof on this side provides the only cover. Opposite is a raised open tier of seating, added in 1974, running the length of the pitch. Both semi-circular ends of the ground have open terracing, lined by flags and trees, with a basic electric scoreboard at the north end. In the distance looms the 1600-metre high Dajti mountain.

The VIP entrance – they keep the Red Flags flying there.

Although officially holding 20,000 all seated, as many as 30,000 have been known to squeeze in for big games, and for an unknown reason it is customary for all spectators to rise to their feet as the last minutes of a game approach.

As one would expect in a country where Stalin is still officially revered, the stadium perimeter is lined with such pithy slogans as 'Physical training for work and defence – a duty for all' and 'We implement and practice the directives of the 9th Congress of the Party of Labour of Albania.'

And if the 10th Congress so directs, the Qemal Stafa Stadium will soon have a complete refit: a new main stand and extended terracing to double the existing capacity, floodlights (the first in Albania), and an eight-lane tartan track in place of the existing six-lane cinder track.

In King Zog's time Albania had 15 football pitches. By 1981 it had 3000. Qemal Stafa, no doubt, would have been proud of them all, not merely the one which bears his name.

The people's entrance.

AUSTRIA

VIENNA

WIENER STADION

The Wiener – Viennese – Stadium is known to most foreigners as the Prater Stadium, Prater being to Vienna what Gorky Park is to Moscow or Central Park to New York – a vast open space for the city to breath, to play and, of course, to ride upon that famous Ferris wheel overlooking the not-so-blue Danube.

But the Prater is a pleasure ground with a difference, for in its centre is a major sporting complex, with the national stadium at its heart. A decade or so ago the stadium might not have elicited much comment; it was large, outdated and of no especial merit. But not any longer. A new roof has transformed the Wiener Stadium, which as a result may, once again, hold its head up amongst the great stadiums of Europe.

Its development has been a gradual process. Demands for a national stadium began in 1919, it being clear that the Hohe Warte ground (see page 64) was inadequate. But not until the Austrian Republic's tenth anniversary, in 1928, was the first sod cut, and speculatively at that, since a decision on the stadium's final location had yet to be made. Every sports association in Vienna seemed to take a different view on the matter, until the Prater site finally received the go-ahead in May 1929.

This was the period of 'Red Vienna', when a dynamic socialist-controlled administration invested huge sums in health, housing, education and welfare, and saw the building of a national stadium as an integral part of its ideological programme. Not least, a stadium project would provide employment (at a time when 500,000 Viennese were without jobs), encourage sporting participation, and also perhaps divert attention from more intractable issues, such as the growth of opposition from the right. The Wiener Stadium was, therefore, just one building block in what American observer John Gunther described in 1936 as 'the most exhilarating social monument [of] probably the most successful municipality in the world'.

Nuremberg's stadium designer, Prof Otto Ernst Schweizer, was chosen as architect, and his principles were straightforward. Using the Roman amphitheatre as his model, he created an elliptical, completely open, two-tiered stadium in which reinforced concrete and glass replaced columns and open arches, with access to the terraces via a ground floor corridor and regularly spaced stairways built along the concourses circling each tier. It was simple, efficient and, when opened after twenty-three months of construction, held 60,000 spectators. The opening match was on 11 July 1931, between workers' teams from Vienna and Lower Austria, and in the ensuing days athletics championships were held, followed by the so-called Workers' Olympiad (one of three such events, organised by the Socialist Workers' Sports International; the first was at Frankfurt in 1925, the last at Antwerp in 1937). This being Vienna there followed a concert at the new stadium, with 800 musicians conducted by the nephew of Johann Strauss, master of the waltz. These were golden days also for Austrian football, as Hugo Meisl's Wunderteam provided the nation with football worthy of its splendid new stage.

The party did not last. In 1934 the political pendulum swung violently towards the right. After the Anschluss with Germany in 1938, part of the Wiener Stadium became an army barracks,

VOTAVA

VOTAVA

The Prater's remarkable roof cost £17.5 million and took only ten months to complete.

AUSTRIA

then during the war, while continuing to stage German internationals until 1942 and Viennese League matches until three weeks before VE Day, the stadium also served as a staging post for Austrian Jews en route to the death camps. The Wehrmacht used the stadium too, as a planning base, which made it a regular target for air raids in 1944. In one raid alone it was hit 275 times; one section of the terracing was flattened and the adjacent swimming pool and cycle track were destroyed.

It took only months to restore the stadium however, and in December 1945 Jules Rimet was on hand to see Austria play France in their first postwar home international. As Vienna began to mend its war damage, the 1950s saw a boom in spectator sport, the direct result of which was an expansion of the stadium. In November 1956 the floodlights were inaugurated, for Rapid Vienna's European Cup tie v. Real Madrid, while at the same time work began on a third tier, which, when finished four years later, increased the Prater's capacity to 91,150 – a figure nearly reached in October 1960 when the stadium's record crowd of 90,593 saw Austria's match v. Spain.

Further improvements followed during the 1970s, including the installation of an all-weather running track and individual seats in place of benches, thereby reducing the capacity to 72,000. But the most dramatic development began in December 1985 with the addition, at long last, of a roof. The company chosen for this difficult task – difficult because the existing structure was to remain intact – was Voest-Alpine Hebag of Vienna, and without becoming too immersed in technicalities, here is what they achieved in just under ten months.

The all-sheltering roof is in the form of an ellipsoid ring, in two sections. The outer ring is suspended from a network of 112 A-shaped supports, each 17 metres tall, which circle the exterior. But this outer roof covers only the two uppermost tiers. To cover the lower level, attached to the rim of the outer roof is an inner section, which is itself tensioned above the ground by a 460 metre ellipsoid ring. Both roof sections are formed and linked by a sophisticated system of spokes and jointing, in which hollow beams are knotted together and then injected with high-strength cement (a technique used originally for jumbo jet hangars).

The result is 32,000 sq. metres of finely tensioned roof (compared with, for example, 20,000

sq. metres at Cologne) which, remarkably, is so lightweight that it was able to sit upon the stadium's existing exterior columns. No strengthening was needed at all.

Yet for all its structural wizardry, as one approaches from the Danube side of the Prater, the Wiener Stadium's roof is barely noticeable. All one sees is a pale-green framework sitting high above the outer walls, as if the stadium were a half-empty gasometer. Below, the stadium's original skeleton of concrete pillars is still clearly visible, although since refurbishment the concrete and pale-green cladding have a particularly clean appearance, partly owing to an inclined glazed screen at the very top which not only helps illuminate the upper tiers but also deflects wind and rain away from the walls below.

From inside the stadium the roof seems almost miraculous, especially as its outer ring points upwards while the inner ring dips down towards the pitch, 4 metres lower behind the goals than at the sides. Three hundred lamps mounted on the inner tension ring provide the floodlighting.

So deep, yet so unobtrusive is this pale-grey panelled roof, that for all its scale the Wiener Stadium feels quite intimate. Light floods in from the upper concourse, while the balcony walls and stairways – all part of Schweizer's original design – are spotless, thanks to the sheltering qualities of the roof.

An unusual feature of the Wiener Stadium is its ring of glass-fronted boxes at pitch level, below the lower tier. These are not for wealthy executives, as one might expect, but for offices, gymnasiums, meeting and exhibition rooms, a restaurant, workshops, even a bicycle hire shop. The 1931 Communal Council would approve heartily, as they would also of the Prater's surrounding sports facilities which are used by senior Viennese teams FK Austria, First Vienna and Wiener Sport-Klub, for training purposes.

But the actual stadium, which now holds 62,958 (37,258 seated), is patently under-used. Owing to declining attendances, FK Austria moved their League matches out to the Franz Horr Stadion (see page 64) in 1982, and since 1972 Austrian Cup Finals, unless two Viennese clubs are involved, have generally been two-legged affairs staged on club grounds. Meanwhile the national team sometimes plays at smaller stadiums such as Linz, Graz or Innsbruck.

The Wiener Stadium has, it is true, staged two

European Cup Finals (1964 and 1987, with 1990's final also scheduled), and one Cup Winners' Cup Final, in 1970. There have also been regular athletics meetings, plus, inevitably, visits from the Rolling Stones, Michael Jackson, David Bowie and the Pope.

VIENNA

GERHARD HANAPPI STADION

When Vienna's most illustrious club, **SK Rapid**, first sought to replace their cosy ground in the western suburb of Hütteldorf, they did not have to look far for a designer. Architect Gerhard Hanappi was the perfect choice, having enjoyed a fifteen-year career with Rapid, during which time he scored 113 goals and won a record number of 96 Austrian caps. Between 1954–60 he was voted Austrian player of the year seven times.

Formed as a workers' club in 1899, Rapid had opened their Pfarrwiese (parish meadow) ground in Hütteldorf in 1912, during the first season of the Viennese League. Rapid won the title that year and went on to dominate the League (which only deigned to admit non-Viennese clubs in 1949).

Much-loved Pfarrwiese, also known as Rapid-platz, served the club for sixty-five years, but surrounding residential developments made it awkward to redevelop, so in 1971 work on a new stadium began nearby on the site of a nursery.

But such a stadium deserves more. Created by visionaries, transformed by visionary engineering, what the Prater really needs to bring it alive is another footballing visionary.

In short, another Wunderteam fit for this Wunderstadion.

Pfarrwiese, meanwhile, became a tennis centre.

Christened Weststadion, the new ground was inaugurated on 10 May 1977, Rapid entertaining their arch rivals, FK Austria. With an all-seated capacity of 19,300, it is almost perfect in its modern, simple symmetry. Each side has an identical double-decker, cantilevered stand, cranked slightly in the centre for better viewing. The south or main stand backs onto Keisslergasse and a noisy suburban railway line. Behind the north stand and the open west end are Rapid's training pitches, with the wooded hills of the Wienerwald in the distance, while apartment blocks command an excellent view over the open east end. The floodlights are on tubular masts in each corner.

Rapid's seats are unusual. Their thin meshed construction allows snow to melt and drain away more easily during Vienna's heavy winters, and makes cleaning quicker than for the more common plastic designs. The seats also bear distinctive colours: green, blue, pink and yellow, which simplifies ticket distribution as well as enlivening the stadium's overall appearance.

The new Rapidplatz has two strong links with the past. First there is the famed *Rapid Viertelstunde* – the Rapid Quarter Hour, a sustained period of handclapping which the fans have traditionally used to stir their team's recovery from

The old Rapidplatz ...

... and the new.

lost causes. Second is the stadium's current name. Three years after its opening, Hanappi died of cancer, aged fifty-one, and on 21 February 1981 the Weststadion was dedicated in his honour. His

achievements as a player were already legendary, but as an architect, the stadium's design – so practical, so well geared to football – suggests that he still had much to give to the game.

GROUNDWORK

Midwinter at Favoriten.

VIENNA

FRANZ HORR STADION

That **FK Austria**, the 'Violets', should have a ground at all is a quite recent phenomenon, for they started life in 1911 as Amateure, a team of bourgeois Corinthians; strolling gentlemen to Rapid's artisans, or as one commentator put it, 'Rapid work, Austria play'. Even throughout their glory years of the 1930s, as FK Austria, they played at whichever ground would have them, including the home of their arch-rivals, Rapid (although more often than not it was the Wiener Stadion).

The late 1970s saw the Violets hit a purple patch – four championships in a row and an appearance in the 1978 European Cup Winners' Cup Final. Then in 1982 they decided it was time

to put down roots. This they did at a surprisingly unprepossessing ground in the district of Favoriten, known for its immigrant Bohemian population and nowadays dominated by an urban motorway which slices through the area, leaving the stadium apparently stranded atop a tall, grim embankment. The ground had actually been purchased by the Viennese FA in 1974 and dedicated to its president, the Socialist MP Franz Horr.

FK Austria's arrival saw the construction of two single-tier, cantilevered stands, one all-seated on the north side, the other for standing only, behind the west goal. The east end behind, is merely a grass bank with no terracing, curved around the remains of the old speedway track, while opposite the new north stand is a short, traditional wooden stand with bench seats, next to a longer bank of open bench seats. Immediately behind here lie allotments (one of which was once cultivated by FK Austria's star of the 1930s, the Czech centre-forward and Favoriten resident, Matthias Sindelar).

In such a setting and with a capacity of only 10,670 (4670 seated), the Franz Horr Stadium hardly seems like a hothouse of football. Indeed it would seem quite drab were it not for the garish violet paint which liberally adorns both new stands and much of the fencing. Certainly FK Austria (now called Austria Memphis, after their sponsors) are not entirely at home here, since their offices and training facilities are both still based at the Wiener Stadium, where they continue to play their more important games.

VIENNA

HOHE WARTE

Before the Wiener Stadium opened in 1931, Austria's largest venue was the quite remarkable Hohe Warte, home of **First Vienna FC** (note the English name), a club formed in 1894 by gardeners

from the neighbouring estate of Baron Rothschild. The ground itself, named after the adjacent hilltop observatory, was laid in a hollow formed by the excavations of a tile manufacturer, with the hillside providing an embankment so massive that the ground was probably the largest sports arena in continental Europe (although in England, the Crystal Palace grounds were bigger). It was not the safest, however, because when its largest crowd of 85,000 assembled for Austria v. Italy on 15 April

1923 (thirteen days before Wembley opened in front of at least 126,000), wet weather caused sections of the earth banking to subside. What is certain is that Hohe Warte is at least as lopsided a ground as those of Dukla Prague, Charlton (London) or Padova (Italy).

Apart from the hillside terrace, now heavily overgrown at its summit and with the observatory peeping over the trees behind, the remaining three sides accommodate relatively few spectators.

The north end is merely a tree-topped, steep, grass bank lined with advertisements, while the south end does have some terracing, but curved some distance behind the goal. In a corner of this terrace, at the foot of one floodlight pylon, is a memorial to First Vienna players who died during both World Wars, and to two of the club's favourite sons, Rudi Rockl and Poldi Hofmann.

Hohe Warte's survival as a senior venue is largely due to the existence of a new stand, on the east side. Here, in complete contrast to what one expects after a strenuous climb up the winding,

Hohe Warte's hillside terrace and observatory.

leafy approaches from Heiligenstadt, in the Danube valley, is a stylish, low, single-tier grandstand with a vaulted, cantilevered roof. Completed in 1974, this new stand has 2370 seats, in a total capacity currently limited to only 10,000.

Elsewhere, the ground indicates that a return to the club's roots might not come amiss. There is, to put it bluntly, plenty of weeding work for gardeners all over the terracing.

VIENNA

SPORTKLUB PLATZ

A fine example of how narrowly confined grounds can be adapted to suit modern requirements is the 10,000 capacity home of Vienna's oldest club, **Wiener Sportklub** (formed as a cycling club in 1883), in the western district of Hernals. The Sportklub Platz was opened on church land in 1904, but what we see now dates largely from 1971 onwards, when supporters fought off a merger with Rapid, rolled up their sleeves and helped to build a low, narrow covered stand with 2500 seats along the east side. Floodlights arrived in 1975, and five years later the open terrace at the north end, with a hillside cemetery as its backdrop, was redeveloped, with offices and changing rooms, and just enough room for the players to emerge from a tunnel behind the goalnets. Financially, things have always been tight for Sportklub (not helped by a total lack of major honours since 1959), but there are uprights at the rear of this new terrace to support a roof, should funds ever become available. The west side, consisting of an

even narrower strip of open terracing, is overlooked by neighbouring flats.

Unusually the Sportklub Platz has only two floodlight pylons, in opposite corners, yet the ground's most illuminating feature, especially noteworthy for other small clubs anxious to capitalise on their limited space, is the new 2900 seater stand at the south end. Built in 1984, it has solid blue screen ends and cladding, and rises high above the rest of the ground. But it is more than just a grandstand. The rear half, backing onto Hernalser Hauptstrasse, consists of offices, shops and apartments so that from street level one would hardly guess what lay on the other side.

Sportklub Platz. Note the mesh seating.

BELGIUM

BRUGES

OLYMPIASTADION

It may have an unoriginal name and it may lack character, but the Olympiastadion offers a rare glimpse of that much-touted ideal, ground-sharing.

Built by the municipality and designed by a father and son, Armand and Paul Jonckheere, the Olympiastadion was opened in August 1975 for the use of two of Belgium's oldest clubs, **Club Brugge KV** and **KSV Cercle Brugge**.

Club Brugge formed in 1891 as RFC Brugeois and played first on the Ratteplein (Rat Pitch!), and then at the Albert Dyserynckstadion, better known as the Klokke – an obscure nickname no one can fully explain. This small neighbourhood ground held 16,000 and witnessed many an epic European match between 1967–74. Indeed part of

its main stand had only just been modernised at the time of Club's final departure (which suggests that ground-sharing had not been in the pipeline for long). Though still used by a junior club, the Klokke is now slowly decaying, and if it were not for a blue gateway on Torhoutse Steenweg (still bearing the RFCB crest), it would easily be missed.

Cercle Brugge formed eight years after Club and have never quite caught up. Their homely, green-painted Edgard Desmedt Stadium on Magdalenstraat was less developed than the nearby Klokke, and nowadays is used by Cercle's women's team.

As the lesser club, with average gates of around 5000 – only a third of their rivals' – inevitably Cercle had more to lose by sharing the much larger, concrete and steel Olympiastadion. They did, however, win the Cup in 1985, and in 1986 reached the final again, coincidentally against Club. So, for the first time a Belgian Cup Final was held not at Heysel but at the two clubs' joint stadium. Club won the game, but then they

Broken glass and fading dreams at the Klokke, old home of Club.

The Olympiastadion, Bruges – dull name, irrefutable logic.

usually did. In fact Cercle did not manage to beat Club at the Olympiastadion until November 1988, thirteen years after its inauguration.

Club, on the other hand, have thrived since the move. They immediately won a hat-trick of championships (including the Double in 1977), then a place in the 1978 European Cup Final, v. Liverpool, followed by two more League titles and the Cup, as we have noted, in 1986. Whatever grievances former Klokke regulars felt initially, therefore, this glut of honours proved to be the perfect ameliorative.

At the stadium the two tenants enjoy complete equality. Each pays the city 6.5 per cent of gate receipts, and each has identical office space in opposite corners of the main, west stand. Above the players' tunnel is a space for the club crest of whichever team is at home, while behind the main stand, again for the sake of balance, a few metres from a war memorial taken from Cercle's old ground is a bust of Albert Dyserynck, RFCB president from 1919–31, retrieved from the Klokke.

The stadium interior is similarly even-handed. There are two identical cantilevered stands, one on either side, each with glass screen ends and black, orange and grey seating on the upper tier,

with terracing below. The main stand also has a line of executive boxes at the rear – hence the translucent roof panels to lighten the view – plus a new lofty entrance hall, added in 1986 and financed by the two clubs. In the opposite stand, on the east side, are the offices of the city's sports department.

Both ends are also identical: low, covered, rather traditional-looking terraces – perhaps deliberately to remind supporters of their old haunts – with Cercle's fans taking the north or Kerk end (the church is visible behind), and Club's occupying the south or Bad end. (Bad refers to the swimming baths behind, not to the fans.)

Overall the Olympiastadion holds 29,412, including 7034 seats. Everything here is spotless. Not a bush or railing is out of place, and on three sides are neatly laid out training pitches, like a model army camp. No doubt in time the Olympiastadion will start to feel more like home for supporters of both clubs, for although it may at times seem a clinical sort of stadium, the logic of its existence cannot be faulted ... at least not by any outsider. But then, how easy it is to be rational about ground-sharing when it affects someone else's club.

ANTWERP

BOSUIL STADION

Royal Antwerp FC are Belgium's oldest club, and it would appear they have its oldest stadium. But though the club was formed by Englishmen, in 1880, and given an English name, to step into the Bosuil Stadium, even today, is to be transported back to a Scottish ground of the 1950s. There is the archetypical main stand, Tribune One, with a pointed, central gable on its pitched – and patched – corrugated roof, so like the grandstands designed between 1905–25 by Glasgow engineer Archibald Leitch. The remaining three terraces sweep around the oval track, high and open at the ends, with a propped roof over bench seats at the rear of the side terrace, known as Tribune Two. It could be Hampden, it could be St Mirren or Partick Thistle. For goodness sake, even the goal

posts at Antwerp are square, just as they always used to be in Scotland!

Given the club's origins, it was at least appropriate that Bosuil (which means 'owl' and is the name of the district) was inaugurated on 1 November 1923 with an international v. England in front of 40,000 admiring spectators. Leading up to the stadium was a formal approach way, with tennis courts ranged on either side of a tree-lined, rectangular pond. For its time, Bosuil had every advantage; large terracing, open surrounds, wide approaches, and of course a fine, traditional, if not always successful, club in residence.

There have been four major changes since then. In 1936 the capacity was raised to 50,700 with the addition of extra terracing at both ends and 11,700 seats under a new roof opposite the main stand. Three years later, on the day of a match v. Mechelen, this new roof blew off in a gale, scattering debris across the surrounding training pitches. It was replaced in 1940. Then in 1956, after Antwerp's first and only Cup win, a third tier of

BELGIUM

JOHN VAN DEN EYNDE

Antwerp's Bosuil Stadion – a classic prewar design which might have come straight from Glasgow.

terracing behind both goals was added, this time on tall concrete stilts behind the banking, to add a further 10,000 places. Finally, in October 1961, the floodlights were officially switched on with a friendly v. Benfica.

Competitive European action followed in 1964, when Bosuil staged the European Cup Winners' Cup Final replay, Sporting Lisbon v. MTK of Budapest, watched by only 19,924 (although that was *six* times the attendance for the first game, at Heysel).

Antwerp's newly enlarged Bosuil was filled only once, for Belgium's European Championship semi-final v. West Germany on 14 June 1972. But after the Heysel tragedy in 1985 there came a drastic cutback. Just like Hampden and all the other grand old Scottish grounds, time had most definitely not been kind to Bosuil. Thus the upper level of each terrace was fenced off as being dangerous, and an overall limit of 34,500 (including 12,000 seated) imposed in the remaining areas. But unlike its Scottish look-alikes, since then Bosuil has not been pulled back from the brink.

Nowadays (that is, mid-1989), the stadium is a forbidding hulk. Every surface is stained, while under the stilts at each end there lurks an eerie, dusty gloom. Those terraces still in use are composed of gravel with concrete footings, while cracked slabs on the upper, fenced-off sections reveal gaps showing through to the concrete ramparts far below. It all adds up to a grim nightmare of neglect and shoddy construction – possibly the worst at any senior stadium in Western Europe.

From the ridiculous to the sublime, there is a ray of hope for Antwerp, however. Despite average gates of only around 10,000, the club plans to emulate the town of Arnhem in Holland by building a Eurodome (see page 147). Expected to cost between at least 1 and 2 milliard Belgian francs (£15–30 million), the West German design provides for a hi-tech, all-covered, four-sided stadium holding 44,000. Two of the roofs would slide over the pitch to provide a totally indoor arena, with the possibility of a false floor above the pitch for exhibitions, concerts and other events.

The design is no fantasy, as Arnhem have proved, but funding the project is a different matter altogether. Still, far more interesting for Antwerp to draw castles in the air than face anything so dull as a pile of repair bills.

● In the Kiel district, south of central Antwerp, the **Kielstadion** looks more modern than Bosuil but is actually older. **Beerschot** moved here in 1913 and a wooden stand from that era still survives. But the other three sides of the stadium were rebuilt in 1978 and the main stand then further transformed in 1985 by the awkward addition of executive boxes along the front.

Nowadays the Kielstadion is a colourful, tree-lined, almost sleepy ground, linked to a tennis club (as befits Beerschot's bourgeois image). But it has an illustrious past, for it was here, incredibly, that the Olympic Games were held in 1920. After Stockholm in 1912 it was quite a contrast, but Antwerp's Olympisch Stadion, as it was then called, held a respectable 27,250 (now 22,000) and sported stone arches behind each goal and a new main stand. At the same time there were still trees on the terraces.

Following four years of war, the Games were a joy, even if few nations entered and the organisers

Beerschot's Kielstadion – unlikely scene of the 1920 Olympics.

went bankrupt afterwards.

But the Kielstadion might soon disappear. Beerschot plan a new Utrecht-like stadium, incorporating a cinema and shops. The cost? About half of Antwerp's dream stadium, and some would say twice the likelihood of it being realised.

MECHELEN

ACHTER DE KAZERNE

Halfway between Antwerp and Brussels is the unusually named Achter de Kazerne – Behind the Barracks. It is home to an unusual club too – **KV Mechelen** (FC Malinois in French), who represent the most successful of Europe's growing breed of 'small is beautiful' clubs, like Xamax, Brøndby, Wimbledon and St Pauli.

Mechelen formed in 1904, and first developed the ground in 1953 by building a 3800-seater, cantilevered stand, typical of its period, with concrete beams and glass screen ends (now cluttered rather with private boxes along the rear). Opposite was built a plain, propped flat roof over terracing, and in 1987 both narrow end terraces were roofed. Current capacity is 12,000.

The barracks of the ground's title are still to be seen, behind the south end (which has red and yellow seats on its new upper level), while a graveyard lies beyond the much lower opposite terrace. Mechelen are said to prefer building up a first half lead at the barracks end,

since an agile ghost guards the north goal.

Few people gave Mechelen a ghost of a chance when they entered the European Cup Winners' Cup for the first time in 1987–8, but against all the odds they won it, and soon afterwards announced plans for a 25,000 capacity all-seated stadium on the edge of town. It has yet to be built, and that, in Belgium at least, is about the only predictable part of the Mechelen story.

Another example of small is beautiful – behind the Barracks at Mechelen.

BELGIUM

GROUNDWORK

The view from Heysel's Block Z – crumbling terracing faces the space-age Atomium.

BRUSSELS

STADE DU HEYSEL

Fourteen years after the 'Ibrox disaster' and eighteen days after the 'Bradford fire', the name Heysel became synonymous with the word 'tragedy'.

But the events of 29 May 1985 were more than a tragedy. They were a sign of the times.

It is not this book's intention to analyse the details of that shameful evening, if only because they barely touch upon our main theme, the history and architecture of football stadiums.

But, you ask, quite naturally, did not the design and condition of the stadium contribute to the death of thirty-nine innocent people?

Of course they did, in the same way that when a drunken driver smashes his car into a tree, the state of the road, his car *and* the tree may be said to have contributed to his misfortune. But he still should not have been on the roads. In a similar

vein, discussing the lamentable state of Heysel's terracing and fences should not divert us from the fundamental reason why spectators died there.

They died because a group of young Englishmen, intoxicated by alcohol and xenophobia, attacked people whose only crime, apart from perhaps supporting the opposing team, was to have purchased tickets in an adjoining section of terracing, officially reserved for neutral fans. How careless of them. Did they not see the Union Jacks and swastikas of their assailants from Blocks X and Y, and realise that these people saw Block Z as their rightful *Lebensraum*?

And when the hapless victims panicked and were forced down into the bottom corner of Block Z, only one factor caused the stampede to continue. Not the design of the stadium, nor the state of the terracing, nor the strength of the crush barriers. As the Belgian judge at the trial four years later put it, the thugs were impelled by a 'thirst for violence', a thirst which could not be assuaged even when the retaining wall collapsed and the bodies started piling up.

'How can I forget those people?' the father of one of the victims later recalled. 'I saw them with my own eyes; violent, enraged. I saw them punching, spitting, throwing the passports of the dead and injured into the air to show their contempt.'

No amount of excuses can expiate the guilt of those malevolent young men. Even if the wall had not collapsed, but held firm, people would still have been crushed as they fled from the onslaught.

Even if the dividing barriers between Blocks Y and Z were inadequate, should they have posed an open invitation for violence?

And even if there had been more police and gendarmes in that section of the ground, how much physical abuse should we expect officers of the law to absorb in the course of their duties? Nearly an hour before the fateful stampede in Block Z, fifty policemen had been forced to withdraw from the opposite end after being attacked by Juventus supporters. Twenty-seven officers were injured, many by lumps of concrete torn up and hurled from the terracing, by both sets of supporters.

Ah! So the terraces were crumbling. Indeed they were, in parts, but then they had been for some time, so why had this not happened before at Heysel? And why has it not happened at several other stadiums with terracing in a similar condition – Berne, for example, venue of the 1989 European Cup Winners' Cup?

Consider, for a moment, Heysel's record as a big match venue: apart from 1985 it had staged six other European finals: the European Cup in 1958, 1966 and 1974, plus the European Cup Winners' Cup in 1964, 1976 and 1980. No other stadium in Europe has staged so many (Rotterdam coming closest with six major finals). Heysel also staged the 1972 European Championship Final, when West Germany beat the USSR 3–0.

None of these matches presented any major security problems, whereas now, who in Brussels would disagree with the Belgian Commission of Enquiry's conclusion in July 1985 that, ' . . .it is an error to organise a football match if that event subsequently proves to require 3000 men to maintain law and order'.

It was a grim conclusion to reach after fifty-five trouble-free and colourful years at the national stadium.

Situated in the northwest district of Heysel, the stadium was originally built as the centrepiece of

Belgium's 100th anniversary independence celebrations, and accordingly given the title of Stade du Centenaire. Around it was laid a large Parc des Expositions, with the main exhibitions being held in the truly grand Grands Palais – whose five solid wings with their green rooftop sculptures can still be seen from inside the stadium. And although the facilities have changed greatly over the years, the Heysel Stadium and exhibition complex have largely retained their integrity of design and purpose (more so than several similar interwar developments, Wembley included).

The Stade du Centenaire opened on 23 August 1930 with the World Cycling Championships, but was officially inaugurated three weeks later on 14 September, when, in the presence of Prince Léopold, Belgium won 4–1 against Holland (from whose rule Belgium had declared its independence 100 years earlier).

The next decade saw some spectacular events at the stadium; gymnastic displays, Roman Games, ballet, and hot air ballooning, and after the wooden cycle track went up in smoke during the German occupation, speedway came to Heysel in 1946. There have also been military tattoos, religious gatherings, hockey's European Cup (in 1970), the European Athletics Championships (first in 1950), rugby, motorcycling, boxing, and a return of cycling, several times in the form of the Tour de France, making a detour en route to its climax in the Parc des Princes, Paris. In 1976 Heysel also hosted an elaborate celebration of King Baudouin's twenty-fifth year on the throne.

For football, Heysel became Belgium's Cup Final and leading international venue, while before the war it often played host to two of Brussels' leading clubs, Racing Club and Union St. Gillois. (The nearest club football to Heysel in recent years was when Racing Jet de Bruxelles – since moved 30 kilometres south, to Wavre – played a few seasons during the late 1980s in the small, but very trim 12,000 capacity ground known as Heysel II, next to the stadium's main, west entrance. Compared with its big brother, Heysel II's modern terracing is immaculate, but then RJB seldom ever attracted more than 1500 spectators.)

In 1971 the City of Brussels, which owns Heysel, initiated a four-stage modernisation programme, beginning with the installation of a Tartan all-weather running track, the first of its kind in Belgium. In 1974, to replace seven smaller pylons

ALLSPORT/DAVID CANNON

The pathetic debris of terror on Block Z. Riot shields were not enough.

from the early 1950s, four new 60-metre high floodlight masts were erected, by the same firm who constructed the weird, silvery hulk which dominates the skyline just south of Heysel – the famous Atomium, Brussels' main attraction during its Expo '58, and still a wonder to behold, over thirty years later.

Despite an especially bitter winter, the third stage of modernisation went ahead during season 1978–9, when a plain but deeply overhanging, cantilevered roof was built over the banking on the east side – now called Tribune Two. This has 7553 seats under cover and a further 1746 orange and brown seats in the front section. Heysel now had a seating total of 15,644 – still relatively few by international standards – in a total capacity of 60,000.

Finally, a year later, a Longines electronic scoreboard was positioned along the crown of the north terrace (Blocks X,Y and Z). Unusually shaped, it is 46 metres long but only 4.4 metres high.

We say 'finally', but of course after the events of May 1985 the Heysel story does not and cannot end there. Despite the modernisation programme, Heysel retains its basically traditional layout. The main stand, Tribune One, curved in a slight arc around the west side, has changed little in sixty years. It is still, nevertheless, a noteworthy grandstand, whose deep roof, though propped at the rear, suggests that when it was constructed the age of full cantilevering was not far off. The stand's dressed-stone façade, meanwhile, which looks out over a car park with formal lawns and sculptures, is a fine example of classical proportions given a modern interpretation and lightened by the gen-

erous use of glass. There is a measure of unnecessary pomp in the stone mouldings above the projecting entrance bay, but the overall effect is balanced and harmonious, even if Tribune One's interior is now a touch gloomy and sparse.

If the main stand has aged with a modicum of dignity, the same cannot be said of Heysel's two end terraces. Both are, by modern standards, quite outdated and would certainly not meet the criteria laid down by, for example, Britain's Safety of Sports Grounds Act, introduced in 1975. Their basic composition is compacted shale steps, widely moss-encrusted and with crumbling concrete footings, and crush barriers formed by weathered concrete uprights with tubular steel, often rusting, horizontal bars.

The perimeter fencing, placed just inside the original low, concrete retaining wall, is equally basic and certainly not capable of acting as a crush barrier, while the fateful wall itself is also not designed for heavy load bearing – as was proved.

Similarly, the concrete walls at the uppermost rear of the banking have deteriorated badly. In 1985, it was reported, there were holes in these walls big enough for ticketless supporters to squeeze through.

Most seriously of all, the only access to the terracing is from the back. There is no form of escape at the front, except through three double gates in the perimeter fence, at the foot of each aisle. This, for a terrace holding over 22,000.

Not one of these shortcomings was commented upon by UEFA's inspectors, who were said to have spent less than thirty minutes inspecting Heysel in February 1985, prior to the European Cup Final.

But we say again, none of this, none of this at all

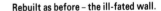

Rebuilt as before – the ill-fated wall.

GROUNDWORK

excuses the behaviour of those reckless Liverpool supporters. They did not act as they did merely to highlight the stadium's inadequacies.

For anyone visiting Heysel in the late 1980s, it was not so much the stadium's condition which elicited surprise – that has been well publicised – so much as the fact that since the tragedy in 1985, so little had changed. Apart from a few new barriers, patches of concrete here and there and the picking out of the aisles with bright green and yellow paint, it was as if nothing untoward had ever happened. Even the ill-fated wall in the corner of Block Z had been rebuilt in its original form.

Just as surprising, there was not a single memorial or reminder of the tragedy, not even the smallest of plaques to honour the thirty-nine victims. If the rest of the football world remembers 29 May 1985, it was as if the authorities at Heysel had determined to wipe it from their memory. As a consequence, visiting that corner of the stadium where the deaths occurred was an eerie experience. It was all so, so ordinary.

Part of the reason why little had been done to improve the terracing is that plans were supposedly afoot to rebuild Heysel completely and thus lay the ghost forever, rather as Glasgow Rangers did by remodelling Ibrox after the disaster there in 1971 (see page 184).

Soon after the 1985 European Cup Final, the Belgian government ordered £12.7 million worth of repairs to the stadium, and in the meantime cut its capacity to 35,000.

But the Belgian FA resisted pressure to rebuild Heysel entirely. That, they said, would be 'like making the English abandon Wembley'. They also argued that big games could be played safely at Heysel, and that it was only the fans who had been at fault. But then the FA themselves were being prosecuted for criminal negligence as a result of the tragedy. (In fact their Secretary General was convicted in May 1989, although his sentence was suspended, and both the Belgian authorities and UEFA, who were unpunished, may yet face massive compensation claims.)

For three years after 1985 there was an impasse, as the FA, the City of Brussels and the government disagreed as to who should pay for the reconstruction, but then in November 1988 the FA announced that Heysel would, after all, be demolished and a new stadium rebuilt on the same site. To be called the King Baudouin Stadium, the proposal was for an all-seated capacity of 45,000, with an integrated shopping complex and 20,000 parking spaces.

But nearly a year after this announcement no detailed plans had been released and, as they say in Belgium, the whole question seemed to have been put *'dans le frigo'*, in other words, on ice.

Whatever the future, and whenever work does start – 1990 was the proposed starting date – one thing is certain. The new stadium must incorporate a memorial of some kind to the thirty-nine dead. The bereaved families deserve no less, even if the authorities in Brussels, and certain sectors of English opinion, would dearly love to sweep the whole sorry business under the carpet of history.

Neo-classical pomp at Heysel's main entrance.

BELGIUM

BRUSSELS

STADE CONSTANT VANDEN STOCK

If there is a more luxurious football stadium in Europe – and we include Monaco in this – then the president of **Anderlecht**, M. Constant Vanden Stock, will want to know where. Because in the last five years the stadium which now bears his name has been rebuilt to the very highest specifications – not with integrated shopping centres or office blocks, but with the comfort of the fans as its highest priority. In short, the new Anderlecht stadium is like a hotel with a pitch in the middle.

You may not agree with Vanden Stock's approach, but you cannot deny the excellence of the result.

But before crossing the threshold, we should note that few people use the name Stade Constant Vanden Stock. No offence to the president – it is simply that for years the stadium has been known as Parc Astrid, after the public park which adjoins the ground on its south side. The name Anderlecht, meanwhile, is that of the surrounding residential district, in the southwest of Brussels, though the club is often referred to as Sporting. Its full title is actually Royal Sporting Club Anderlechtois.

Anderlecht formed in 1908, when Brussels already had five other clubs in the First Division – Daring, Union, Racing Club, Excelsior and Léopold. Having joined the Third Division and laid out their first ground on what is now Rue Demosthène in 1909, the club was promoted in 1913 and moved to Parc Astrid five years later. This ground was originally named Stade Emile Versé, after an early patron of the club.

Until the mid-1930s, while Anderlecht drifted between the First and Second Divisions, the Stade Versé was a simple, tree-lined, open ground with one wooden stand. The turning point came in 1935 when, following Anderlecht's promotion to the First Division, a new, quite substantial two-tiered, reinforced concrete main stand was built with an inclined cantilevered roof and glass screen ends. It was, for its time, one of the most advanced stands in Europe, and was copied at several Belgian grounds, including Mechelen in 1953 (see page 69). But for all its modernity, perhaps the nicest touch was a line of flowers which always adorned the central balcony.

With a bright young team – including Constant Vanden Stock himself – and a revamped stadium, by 1939 Anderlecht had started to outstrip their main Brussels rivals, Daring, and after signing legendary goalscorer Jef Mermans in 1942, they went on to overshadow every other club in Belgium.

Since winning their first League title in 1947 Anderlecht have amassed a further nineteen Championships (including five in succession betwen 1964–8) and six Cups, while the rewards of this success have been continually ploughed back into the development of the stadium. In the early 1950s the open terrace opposite the main stand was covered with another impressive concrete, cantilevered roof, and shortly afterwards, on 6 March 1954, new floodlights were inaugurated with a friendly v. Racing (of Buenos Aires, not Brussels).

Despite these improvements, Parc Astrid, with a capacity of 37,000, was too small to host some of Anderlecht's early exploits in European football. These were switched to Heysel, where a Belgian club record attendance of 64,703 was established for Anderlecht's European Cup tie v. Dundee in 1963 – only nine more spectators than saw Anderlecht put out Real Madrid in the first round (this, at a time when Anderlecht were still only semi-professional). But it was not until 1976 that Anderlecht became Belgium's first European winners, by beating West Ham in the European Cup Winners' Cup Final, coincidentally also at Heysel. They lost the following year's final, but reclaimed the trophy in their third consecutive appearance, in Paris in 1978. Anderlecht later won the UEFA Cup in 1983.

By then Parc Astrid was covered on all four sides and was easily the best ground in Belgium. Over the popular east end terrace – dubbed the O-Side – a propped roof had been erected, corresponding with the height of the adjacent south side roof, while behind and above the west end terrace was built a tall cantilevered stand decked in translucent roof and screen end panels.

None of these four stands from the 1970s has survived into the 1990s.

Such was Constant Vanden Stock's ambition on assuming the club presidency in 1973, that although Parc Astrid was already virtually the de facto national stadium in preference to Heysel, he

GROUNDWORK

Glass screens protect visiting goalkeepers from stray champagne corks at Anderlecht.

felt that it was still no more than adequate for a club of Anderlecht's considerable stature.

Vanden Stock has never been a mere money-bags president. Even without his wealth, as owner of Belgium's largest brewery, Belle Vue, he would still have been a perfect candidate for the job. He first joined Anderlecht at the age of ten, and was a regular during the 1930s until a double fracture ended his career. After the war he served for many years as organiser of the national team and is currently also a vice-president of the Belgian FA. Vanden Stock is to Anderlecht what Santiago Bernabeu once was to Madrid and Spanish football – a wily and astute leader who knows the game from every angle.

Redevelopment of the stadium which now bears his name, rather than that of Emile Versé, began in March 1983, when Anderlecht's games were switched to Heysel and the 1935 main stand came down. In its place, in just six months, arose a 5200-seater stand designed by Brussels architect Michael Boelens (who has also worked for Standard, Gent and Racing Genk). From inside the stadium the new stand appears typical of the modern era – two tiers of orange seats and a plain, almost flat, cantilevered roof with brown ribbed fascia and roof-mounted floodlights. In between the two seating tiers is a row of thirty-one glass-fronted private boxes, the first in Continental Europe (though a familiar sight at English grounds since 1963, when Manchester United first installed boxes). The new stand's street frontage did suggest, however, that Vanden Stock's stadium was not going to be merely functional. It could easily be the offices of a successful medium-sized corporation, with its warm, natural brick, vertical blocks, reflective glass curtain walling and neatly tended shrubberies and greenery.

But this was just the start. In 1985 an almost identical stand went up on the opposite, Parc Astrid side, but with one subtle difference. Instead of individual boxes, the middle section was taken up by a glass-fronted lounge running the length of the stand, incorporating three rows of what Anderlecht term 'Business Seats'. Behind these seats are lounges, restaurants and bars – serving

75

GROUNDWORK

Gateway to a footballing haven – Parc Astrid shows
its corporate face.

not just Belle Vue, incidentally – spaciously arranged and air-conditioned so that although inclined glass panels insulate the occupants from the rest of the stadium, the general environment is extremely pleasant, like that of a modern conference centre in which a football pitch has taken the place of a lecturer's rostrum. If one must watch one's team from behind a sheet of glass, this must surely be the best way to do it. Even the crowd noise from outside is filtered in through loudspeakers and controlled by a volume switch, naturally, so that one's small talk need not be interrupted by anything so disturbing as a goal being scored.

In 1987 the two side stands were linked behind the west goal by a third stand of the same ilk, this one having a continuation of the Business Class section but with terracing on its lower tier. That left the only bastion of the old stadium, the popular O-Side terrace, to be redeveloped, and

that will take until about 1991 to complete, again with a two-tiered stand, giving the finished, all-enclosed stadium a total capacity of 32,000, including 22,000 seats.

Thus it will have taken about eight years to redevelop Parc Astrid, at an estimated total cost of 1,100 million Belgian francs. And who will have paid for all this? Those nice cosy people behind the glass, of course. Their advance payments for private boxes and Business Class seats, in three- and six-year leases respectively, have meant that in theory the whole project will have paid for itself by 1994, a quite remarkable and astute piece of planning.

This is all very well for those who can afford the luxuries, but what about the ordinary supporter? He will not see inside the lush interiors, with their warm, yellow brick walls, marble floors, potted plants and dark yellow carpets patterned with the letters RSCA. Yet his own accommodation, be it seated or standing, has improved as a result of these luxury developments. In fact, one of the most impressive aspects of the Constant Vanden Stock Stadium is the extremely high standard of workmanship all round.

Fortunately, the areas surrounding the ground have not changed. Parc Astrid, the trim, terraced houses, the avenues, the local bars – they are all the same as before, even if the stadium has changed beyond recognition.

Easy as it would be, therefore, to snipe at Anderlecht's assiduous courting of a new breed of spectator, the reality is that those of us who crave the noise, the buzz, and the smell of a vibrant, passionate football crowd will still find it all at Anderlecht, whatever else is going on behind those glass partitions.

LIÈGE

STADE DE SCLESSIN

The place they call 'the burning city', because of its mills, mines, chimneys, and acrid air, is a real football stronghold, with a murky river, the Meuse, coursing through its thumping heart.

On that river, in the midst of two of the largest hooting, snorting, rumbling steelworks, is the

Stade de Sclessin, home of Belgium's second most successful team, **Standard Liège**.

But Standard were no works team emerging from the grime.

They were instead formed in 1898 by students of a Catholic college, while Sclessin, where they moved to in 1909 on joining the Second Division, was then a quite rustic area. True, industry had already cast its shadow on Ougrée, on the opposite bank of the Meuse, and an electric tram did stop right outside Standard's new front door, but otherwise the ground stood in farmland belonging

GROUNDWORK

The air is cleaner, plastic seats and private boxes have moved into Sclessin, but the slag heap still watches over Standard.

to a riverfront chateau, 100 metres beyond the south touchline, while the ground's most noticeable feature was a tall tree, which stood just behind and to one side of the south goal. Until the football authorities ordered its branches to be lopped, it apparently took quite a hammering from wayward strikers.

How quickly the scene was to change, and where better to observe this change than from the summit of a slag heap which has peered over the north end of the ground for over sixty years. When times were hard between the wars, this ragged mountain provided local supporters with the best free view in Belgian football.

We start our vigil from this dusty high spot in 1923, two years after Standard's promotion to the First Division. The club have just bought the ground and, unfortunately for us, they decide to move the pitch 40 metres towards the Meuse, thus providing space to build a bank of terracing at the north end, called the Pourtour (outer edge). Away goes the familiar tree and the farmhouse, while

the chateau now seems lost in its increasingly urban surrounds.

The ground re-opens in 1925 with three uncovered terraces and one small stand seating 2000. Cars park on what had been fields until recently, and smoke and dust fill the air, making the players' eyes smart. But still the ground is a success, and in 1939 a roof goes up over the east terrace. It looks a very modern sort of roof – concrete, curved downwards at the front and almost fully cantilevered, with a double line of columns astride the upper rear gangway.

After the war Standard at last begin to overtake their neighbours, Liégeois (see page 78). They win their first major honour, the Cup, in 1954, and with the profits they expand the main stand. Further extensions in 1956 and 1963 create 7500 seats in an overall capacity of 40,000.

Both end terraces have also grown during this period, and in 1957 floodlights are erected. Through the hazy glow we see that the first floodlit match is v. Racing Club de Paris. Standard are,

77

by now, standard bearers of professionalism in Belgian football, and the man who owns the neighbouring steel mills, Paul Henrard, ploughs money into his team's struggle against Anderlecht's domination. The investment succeeds; between 1958–71, Standard win six championships and two more Cups.

But Scessin is changing. Our vantage point is shrinking as coal mines close and the steel industry declines. The air seems cleaner but there is more traffic, since a bridge behind the ground now links Scessin with Ougrée, across the river. A new road, the Quai Vercour, runs along the Meuse embankment, and it is the terrace at this end which, in 1972, is rebuilt and named the Tribune Vercour. Like several stands in Belgium, the roof has translucent panels, and provides cover for 12,500 standing. The sides and back of the stand are kept open, so allowing riverside breezes to whistle through, while also providing spectators with a panoramic view of two of Liège's three surviving steelworks, Cockerill Ougrée and Cockerill Sambre. Scessin now holds 43,000 and is Belgium's third largest ground, as befits a club which has just won a hat-trick of championships.

Our slag heap is now barely high enough to see the pitch, especially since Standard have added a new scoreboard, but in February 1984 we spot a hubbub in the car park – policemen, reporters, anxious officials. We learn that Standard's captain, Eric Gerets, has been found guilty of bribing the players of Waterschei so that Standard could win the 1981–2 championship. We are used to foul smells in this part of Liège, but this stink beats them all, especially as the men behind the bribes turn out to be Standard's president and UEFA luminary, Roger Petit, and their respected coach, Raymond Goethals. Yet despite the fix,

Standard's seventh title win is allowed to stand, and unlike the dust which forever blows across the ground from our slag heap, the dirt does not stick for long.

In 1985 the depression over Scessin starts to clear, and we witness the construction of a new main stand, almost identical to the one built at Anderlecht two years earlier, though smaller in scale. Not surprisingly it is the work of the same architect, Michael Boelens, and has two tiers of red seats with thirty private boxes in between. Incredibly, it takes only three months to build.

With this new stand, and the installation of benches on the Tribune Vercour's upper tier, Scessin now has 8100 seats in an overall capacity of 30,500. One day, for sure, the new stand will be extended round to the north end, and our view will thus be blocked forever. The covered east terrace will no doubt follow suit – its concrete roof and underbelly have not worn well. In the meantime, we look over a ground of great character, with red fences and barriers, much light and shadow, and the ever-present clatter of the steelworks all around. We barely jump now when the furnaces let off a sudden blast of steam, as if a jumbo jet were taking off nearby. And we hardly remember the last time anyone joined us on the slag heap for a free view of the match.

● Across the Meuse, on a hill above the sprawling Cockerill Sambre steelworks, is the neat, 18,000 capacity ground of the area's third League club, **RFC Seraing**. The **Stade Hubert Freson**'s main feature is a low, cantilevered stand with a translucent, wrap-around roof in a lightweight, tubular steel frame – erected by the same firm that built Anderlecht's former west end stand and several others in Belgium. The steelwork, needless to add, came from Liège.

LIÈGE

STADE JULES GEORGE

In complete contrast to Standard, our final call in Belgium is to the almost rural setting of a wonderfully quirky ground, home of **RFC Liège**, known until 1989 as Liégeois. The stadium's name

has also been recently changed, to Stade Jules George, after a former president, though most people still refer to it as the Stade de Rocourt, the name of the district on the northern outskirts of Liège where it is located.

Three features make it an unusual venue. Firstly, the concrete cycle track – a rarity in itself, nowadays (there is also a shale running track). Secondly, at the west end there is no spectator accommodation, except in a freestanding building overlooking the track. This is the Chalet, a private members' club with 350 Business Seats in a hi-tech, glass-fronted lounge, tacked onto the front of an otherwise traditional old café. Perhaps to emphasise its antiquity, the building now bears the English title of 'Great Old Club'. Close by this odd mixture of old and new is a memorial to O.S.Flesch, promoter of the stadium when it was built in 1920 (although the club formed in 1892).

But the feature which most grabs one's attention is on the two sides of terracing – the open east end, and the covered north side – where serried ranks of white, concrete crush barriers give the impression of an orderly graveyard. Each barrier has three wide legs, like a squashed cricket wicket, and the effect is quite startling. No other major stadium in Europe has crush barriers so white and so chunky.

The fourth, south side of the ground is taken up by the two-tiered, cantilevered main stand, which, like Anderlecht's old west stand, is liberally decked in translucent side and roof panels. Slightly tinted green, these cast a rather sickly light on the seats beneath. On the tier below, immediately above the finishing straight of the cycle track, is a row of seventeen private boxes, while the stand's main entrance, which looks out onto training pitches, has recently been given a hi-tech facelift with glass-enclosed lounges and staircases.

All in all, an intriguing mixture of styles, colours and textures, in a stadium which holds 35,000, including 4850 seats.

GROUNDWORK

Stone Age wickets or Cubist sculptures – the Stade de Rocourt's
unique white crush barriers give one of Europe's few surviving velodrome-cum-football grounds
the appearance of an orderly graveyard.

BULGARIA

SOFIA

STADION VASILIJ LEVSKI

Viewed from the Soviet Army memorial opposite the main entrance, it would be easy to mistake the Vasilij Levski Stadium for any one of the heavy, pseudo-classical institutional buildings which line Sofia's immaculate cobbled streets. That balustrades and pilasters should adorn the façade of the national stadium has double significance, however.

Firstly, it is indicative of the unusual degree (within Eastern Europe at least) to which Sofia has been protected from the worst scourges of modernism, in the city centre especially. Secondly, it suggests that the stadium owes its exterior design to the Soviet-inspired (or inflicted) style

GROUNDWORK

Golden domes and Nervi-style cantilevering at Bulgaria's national stadium.

often caricatured as Stalin's Gothic (but which was actually a mishmash of neoclassical proportions and over-elaborate ornamentation).

Sure enough, the Vasilij Levski Stadium was constructed between 1949–53 at the height of this architectural influence, just before Stalin's successor, Khrushchev, denounced the style in 1954. Levski himself was a nineteenth-century revolutionary who died in 1873 at the age of thirty-six, fighting against the reviled Turkish occupiers. Levski was also reputedly a sportsman. Indeed the pseudonym 'Levski', or 'lion-like', is said to have derived from his prowess as a long-jumper.

Before 1949 the stadium was a 15,000 capacity ground with an earth pitch, used for a while by Levski Sofia (see below). Then the Central Committee for Sport decided to convert it into the national stadium, and the terracing was accordingly built up to accommodate 70,000. Since then this has been reduced to 55,000, all seated.

Entering through the grandiose main entrance, lined with plaques recording world records achieved at the stadium (all of them by Socialist athletes), the rear main seated area is protected by an unexpectedly plain, modern cantilevered roof, cleverly extended from the rear of the classical frontage so that neither style jars. The rest of the stadium is open, with a large electronic scoreboard at each end.

Opposite the main stand, above the open banks of seating, is a line of viewing cabins which is in fact the upper storey of an office block attached to the stadium. Built in 1967, this houses the headquarters of the Bulgarian weekly *Futbol*. Behind it are the floodlights of the adjacent Narodna Armia Stadium, home of CFKA Sredec (see page 82), only 200 metres distant.

The snow-capped Mount Vitosha (2300 metres high) is, as ever in Sofia, a looming presence in the south. One can also see, behind the stadium, the golden domes of the Alexander Nevski Cathedral, the green roofs of the university and the red star over Party headquarters.

No doubt it was the Party which inspired a message above the stadium's press block, reading 'Sport for a peaceful world'. As we shall shortly learn, it is a message not all Bulgarian players have taken to heart.

SOFIA

STADION LEVSKI GERENA

Vitosha are one of the two great powers in Bulgarian football (along with Sredec, see page 82). Formed in 1914 as Levski (after the national hero), the club played formerly at the Rakofski Stadium, now used only for training, and later on the site of the present Vasilij Levski Stadium. When this became the national stadium in 1949, Levski moved to the Dinamo Stadium (now site of the club's swimming pool). Since 1959 they have played at the Levski Gerena Stadium, whose construction was not completed until 1970 (a year after the club merged with Spartak Sofia and were renamed Levski Spartak). Situated in Gerena, a northeastern district of Sofia, the stadium is in the centre of a huge sporting complex run by the Ministry of Internal Affairs (which explains why Vitosha are so dominant).

Not so powerful that they can resist the dictates of the Party's Central Committee, however. After a stormy Cup Final and a brawl in the players' tunnel at the national stadium in 1985, Levski Spartak were officially reorganised and renamed Vitosha (their opponents in that match and main rivals, CSKA, became Sredec). Imagine Western governments trying to take such action against errant clubs!

The Levski Gerena Stadium is all-seated with a capacity of 45,000 (formerly 60,000), and although local derbies might not always fill the stadium

Vitosha – impressive from afar.

GROUNDWORK

81

they are invariably switched to the Vasilij Levski Stadium. (Visiting neutrals should note that on such occasions Vitosha fans take over the south curve of the national stadium, Sredec followers the north.)

On its south side the Levski Gerena Stadium has a concrete cantilevered roof, supported at the rear by thick angular columns set inside a curving, glass-walled concourse; impressive from a distance, but like a shabby bus station close to.

Blue and white plastic seats in striped sections fill the remaining open curves, around a disused sandy running track, with standard utilitarian tower blocks – as familiar in Stockholm as in Sofia – forming a backdrop to the east. To the north rise the Balkan Mountains, and beyond the stand roof, the hazy peak of Mount Vitosha reminds one and all of the club's new identity.

There has been no attempt since 1985 to change the name of the stadium, perhaps because although fans of 'the Blues' cannot argue with the Red Flag of the Central Committee, in private Vitosha will always be Levski to them.

SOFIA

STADION NARODNA ARMIA

The Narodna Armia – People's Army – Stadium is literally a couple of goalkicks away from the Vasilij Levski Stadium, in the middle of Park na Svobodata (Liberty Park), laid out in 1880 by Swiss foresters to commemorate Sofia's liberation from the Turks.

This is the home of Bulgaria's record championship winners, **CFKA Sredec** – the Reds, formed originally in 1948 as September CDV, then quickly renamed CDNA. In an attempt to make this army team the best in the land, if not the most popular – a public relations hurdle all army teams in the Eastern bloc face, there were mergers with Red Banner in 1964 and Septembri in 1969 (the club then became known as CSKA Septemvrijsko Zname).

The current, more evocative title CFKA Sredec was adopted when the club was officially disgraced and then renamed after the June 1985 Cup Final brawl – Sredec being the Slavic name for Sofia before 1500 and meaning 'in the centre'. As at Vitosha however, fans still use the old name, CSKA.

The club's original ground in 1948 was the UNAC Stadium, immediately next to the Vasilij Levski Stadium and now occupied by a cute, mock-classical, open-air ice hockey arena (thus CSKA and Levski were neighbours for a short time). Whereas Levski took eleven years to complete their stadium, the Narodna Armia Stadium was built in just one year, since the army could commandeer all the labour and materials it needed, and it opened in 1957. Current seating capacity is 32,000, although a further 3000 can stand around the track.

In common with the two other main Sofia stadiums there is just one cantilevered roof (a small, upturned, vaulted construction on the east side), which backs onto a short approach road leading through the park to the national stadium. Old flaking, wooden bench seats, painted green, red and white, fill the remaining three open sides, making the modern all-weather athletics track seem all the more pristine.

Lining the upper levels are slogans which reflect the club's military affiliations: 'Order, discipline and organisation' and 'Revolutionary thinking and action.'

Yet the Narodna Armia Stadium has rather a soft edge, the red and white paintwork and its warm terra cotta track being surrounded by a pleasing green swathe of trees and parkland. Order, discipline and organisation are all very well but mother nature usually steals the show.

The People's Army in training.

CYPRUS

After the abandonment some 1400 years ago of the second-century Roman stadium at Kourion, twelve kilometres west of Limassol, the island of Cyprus had no major sports venue until 1902, when the **GSP Stadium** (GSP stands for Cypriot Gymnastics Club), was opened in the capital, Nicosia. A basic, 10,000 capacity ground, built just southwest of the city's Venetian walls (opposite the Ministry of Education), the GSP is still home to **Olympiakos**, but was superseded as Cyprus's main international venue by the **Makarion Athletic Centre**, also in Nicosia, in 1978. (This would have occurred sooner had the Turkish invasion of northern Cyprus in 1974 and the subsequent partition of the capital not interrupted the building programme for two years.)

Named after Archbishop Makarios, the first president of an independent Cyprus in 1960, who died in 1977, the new stadium is a couple of kilometres west of Nicosia and south of the green line which divides the city. It is an extremely plain, open, shallow bowl with an all-weather track, sloping moat and English-style floodlight pylons, and holds 20,000 spectators, mostly on terraced concrete bench seats.

Nicosia's two most successful and popular clubs, **Apoel** and **Omonia** share the Makarion Stadium, which was inaugurated with a friendly between the two rivals on 30 August 1978. In May 1989 the stadium was host to the Olympiad of small countries.

Cyprus's other international football stadium is in the southern port of Limassol. Called the **Tsirion Stadium** (after the man who donated the land), it also has a total capacity of 20,000 and is shared by all four of Limassol's senior clubs: **AEL**, **Aris**, **Apollon** and **Apep**.

Opened on 11 May 1975 with a European Championship qualifier v. England, it is located

Makarion Athletic Centre, Nicosia.

high on a hill above the town, and has identical, multi-gabled, propped roof stands, one on either side, with shallow grass banking behind each goal. But one's eye is particularly drawn beyond the south goal, towards a magnificent view of Limassol and the port below.

Unfortunately visitors might have to wait to sample this view since the Tsirion was suspended indefinitely from international action following attacks by supporters on a referee after a World Cup qualifier in February 1989, in which Scotland scored a winning goal v. Cyprus during much-disputed time added on for stoppages.

Tsirion Stadium, Limassol.

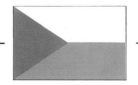

CZECHOSLOVAKIA

PRAGUE

STRAHOV

Prague is a city of many hills, one of which, the Strahov, is the magnificent setting of Czechoslovakia's national stadium. Built originally in 1935 and named after the President, Tomáš Masaryk, who retired that year (the name was dropped after the Communist takeover in 1948), the stadium was substantially refurbished for the European Athletics Championships in 1978. It was then officially named after a prewar athlete and journalist, Evžen Rošicky, who died in a Nazi concentration camp. Most fans refer to it as The Strahov, however.

Situated high above the wooded parklands around the Strahov Monastery and outwardly

The Strahov's upper deck was added in 1978 but cries out for a paint job.

resembling a decaying fortress, one's first impression of the stadium is of concrete masses and peeling paint.

The main stand on the west side is the original prewar post and beam construction, with corner galleries at each end, an uncovered tier of seats at the front, and extra floodlights along the flat, pale blue roof.

Behind the stand the floodlights of the adjacent training stadium are visible. These were the Strahov's original lights before 1978. The newer floodlight pylons lean over the stadium roofs like lacrosse rackets at the ready.

All around the remaining three sides is a continuous covered upper deck, added in 1978, with terraces and yellow crush barriers in front. Perched on the roof at each end are electric scoreboards, both taller than the upper tier itself and standing out against the sky like monoliths.

The upper stands have a distinctly utilitarian feel, with steel column supports, set at a slight angle, orange tip-up bench seats, and on every bit of steelwork, flaking green paint. Repainting the stadium is said to be a never-ending process, but the use of imported high-quality paint would almost certainly solve that problem at a brush stroke (and smarten up the country's other peeling stadiums, too).

The Strahov holds 36,000 – 50,000 before 1978 –

including 12,000 seats; smaller than the nearby Letna Stadium, home of Sparta Prague, where internationals are also held, and modest even for a small country which boasts so many fine sporting figures. Zátopek himself broke several records on the Strahov track.

But most stadiums, great or small, would still be dwarfed by the astonishing arena which is linked via a walkway 100 metres east of the Strahov: the vast 250,000 capacity **Spartakiádní Stadion**, where every four to five years thousands participate in a mass celebration of sport and physical fitness. These Spartakiáda make the opening ceremonies of Olympic Games look like mere sideshows by comparison.

The mainly sand-covered arena is actually the size of four football pitches and is used for tennis and football in between events. The stands, which are of little note, form a huge rectangle into which the entire area of the Strahov Stadium could be comfortably accommodated.

Altogether, therefore, the Strahov hill represents a sporting Acropolis in a city well-blessed with stadiums, from tumbledown ash-covered football grounds to the ultra-modern Štvanice tennis arena, opened in 1986. Prague has long been fêted for its theatres, churches, parks and castles, but for sheer variety and curiosity value its sporting stadiums take some beating, too.

PRAGUE

STADIÓN LETNÁ

Within sight of the Strahov floodlights, the Letná – or Summer – Stadium is one of the finest purpose-built football grounds in Central Europe. **Sparta Prague** are, however, more than just the nation's most successful and popular football club. With an active membership of 4400, they have provided champions in numerous disciplines, most notably tennis. Navrátilová, Mandlíková, Suková and Kodeš all started their careers with Sparta.

As at the Strahov, the black steel exterior of Sparta's stadium – peeling paint and all – is not a pretty sight, which is all the more surprising considering its role in national life. To explain; behind the south side of the stadium runs a main

road called Obránců míru, with the large expanse of Letná Park beyond. It is along this route that the annual May Day parade passes, viewed by the Party bigwigs from a raised platform built into the rear of the stand. Not exactly Red Square but an honour for Sparta all the same.

Known in their first season as King's Vineyard, Sparta started life on this very site in 1893, the same year as their arch rivals, Slavia, formed, also in the Letná area. The original stadium was destroyed in a fire in April 1934, a fire in which some 10,000 sporting trophies were lost. Melted remnants of the inferno are now displayed in the club's current trophy-cum-museum room.

The existing main stand dates back to 1938 but, like the rest of the stadium, was completely redesigned in 1973 by Kyril Mandel (architect also for Sparta's rivals, Dukla, and Prague's tennis and ice hockey stadiums). Mandel obviously understood the needs of football spectators because

CZECHOSLOVAKIA

GROUNDWORK

Mandel's Letná Stadium – lightness and simplicity seldom fail when it comes to designing for football.

every vantage point provides a perfect view.

The stand, filling only the centre section of the west side, has a thin, slanting roof and blue bench seats, and is clearly distinguishable from the newer two-tier additions. These link up with each wing of the main stand and continue along three sides, parallel to the pitch but with angled rows in each corner. Their upper tier of plain wooden bench seats is covered by a flat, half-cantilevered roof with diagonal supports at the rear. The lower tier

is uncovered terracing, except in the northeast corner, where the angle is blocked off by a white concrete wall – actually vertical, but by an optical illusion appearing to slope by 45 degrees – on which is mounted a neon-lit advertisement for Klenoty, a state-run chain of jewellery shops. At night the sign lights up and amounts almost to a distraction.

Although the stands are all-enclosing, each one is so well fenestrated along the rear that light pours into the seated areas. To add to this sense of lightness, along each side is a single spindly row of floodlights supported 2 metres above the roofline, like birds perched on a telegraph wire.

Outside the stadium, the main entrance features a sculpture of a diving goalkeeper, beyond which Prague's castle, Hradčany, and its cathedral, St Vitus, rise up in the distance, with the Strahov visible farther off. To the northeast the lights of Dukla Prague are just visible.

Though large enough to accommodate 42,000 (21,000 seated) the Letná Stadium is an excellent example of how clean, simple lines combined with plenty of light seldom fail to produce a pleasant stadium environment, however tightly enclosed. On the pitch Sparta have dominated Czechoslovak football for some years. Around the pitch they show a lighter touch.

PRAGUE

STADIÓN JULISKA

However well **Dukla Prague** perform, and in the early 1960s they were almost invincible, as an army club they can never be as popular as Sparta or Slavia. Formed in 1948, in 1956 they adopted the name Dukla, after a Carpathian mountain pass where Soviet and Czechoslovak forces won an important battle in 1944.

Their home, the Juliska Stadium, in the military-dominated Dejvice district of northwestern Prague, is quite extraordinary. Holding 28,800, over 11,000 are accommodated on the west side, on a massive bank of seating cut into the side of a hill, quite overpowering the rest of the stadium, which is virtually flat and would otherwise resemble little more than a training field. With its huge slab of red and yellow seats (the club colours)

and its deeply overhanging cantilevered roof, this main stand appears totally out of scale with its surrounds.

Looking sideways from these giddy heights, the hillside overlooks the shallow, terraced northern end and is topped by the houses of such sporting heroes as runner Emil Zátopek and the 1973 Wimbledon champion, Jan Kodeš, before continuing its sloping path down towards the River Vltava.

Opposite the main stand is a small, glass-fronted balcony on stilts over the terrace, part of the club's modern yellow and brown clad headquarters. Behind is a brewery and, in case the army loses sight of its real masters, the unmistakeable pinnacle of the International Hotel, known as the Russian Ritz because of its Stalinist Gothic design.

The southern end of the stadium has no terracing and is overlooked by the gaunt buildings of the club gym, while the narrow floodlight pylons, unusually, are all-white.

'Under the leadership of the Communist Party for the further development of Socialist Sport' reads a slogan written in red and yellow at the back of the main stand. It is not a message much heeded in Prague, where not even the wonderful panorama to be enjoyed from Juliska's hillside stand can tempt more than a few die-hard fans to watch Dukla.

Dukla's stadium of two halves, with some famous neighbours looking down from their hilltop homes.

PRAGUE

STADIÓN VRŠOVICE

Bohemians ČKD and their ground certainly live up to the image their name evokes, but they actually began life as AFK Vršovice (named after the district) in 1905, when Bohemia, with Prague as its capital, was still part of the Austro-Hungarian empire. Only during a tour to Australia in 1926 did they adopt the Bohemians tag, in order to identify more closely with their newly independent homeland. On their return Bohemians took on a nickname, 'Kangaroos', after bringing back two live marsupials from Brisbane.

Less romantically, the Communists retitled the club Železničáři Bohemians in 1949 and Spartak Praha Stalingrad in 1952, until the club eventually won back their former identity after sponsorship by the ČKD machinery works began in 1961. Nowadays, of course, the name Bohemians conjures up the image of an unconventional lifestyle, as personified perhaps by Prague's most dissolute writer, Jaroslav Hašek, creator of *The Good Soldier Švejk*.

Their truly Bohemian ground opened on 19 August 1914, some two weeks after the outbreak of the First World War, and soon became affectionately known as '*d'olíček*' – the dimple – owing to its location in a small hollow. Of all Prague's wonderfully idiosyncratic grounds, it is the one which takes football back closest to its roots, to the backyard of working-class communities. Its cinder pitch was not grassed over until 1951.

The Vršovice Stadium holds 18,000 and has one stand, opened in 1970: a narrow, steeply raked cantilever construction seating 3020, with black girders, green and cream walls at the rear (more peeling paint), and a web of steel barriers inside which seem designed to stop people falling out of their bench seats onto the pitch below.

The remaining three sides are open and completely overlooked by a neighbouring Hussite Church and surrounding blocks of apartments, as if the stadium were in fact a communal back garden. The residents certainly command the best view. The east side terrace, which used to be covered, rises up the hill and is just a couple of metres deep with a high fence behind. The south terrace is of wooden construction, because the club cannot afford steel and concrete.

So compact is *d'olíček* that instead of stanchions to support them, the nets are held up by strings tied to the perimeter fence. Even the floodlights, installed in 1955 before any other Prague club, are on a small scale, barely taller than the surrounding buildings.

With their green and white shirts and their

D'olíček – inadequate but lovable.

87

reputation for pure football – rather like West Ham in London – Bohemians are a neighbourhood club based in a cubbyhole ground; a

ground which is pretty inadequate in most respects but entirely lovable nonetheless. Come to think of it, just like the Good Soldier Švejk himself.

PRAGUE

STADIÓN DR V. VACKA

A suitable case for treatment – the Dr Vacka Stadium.

A kilometre east of Vršovice Stadium, just past the local Party H.Q., we find **Slavia Prague**, formed in 1893 as a club of students and intellectuals, and

until recent years the second most successful club in Czechoslovakia.

Although fondly called Edenu by the locals (after a neighbouring restaurant), as is apparent from its rather shabby appearance, the Dr V.Vacka Stadium harks back to Slavia's golden era of the 1930s (Vacka was mayor of Prague at the time). With a capacity of 42,030, the stadium comprises a basic post and beam main stand, with red facings and bench seats, wooden walls and screen ends, looking out over three open sides of terracing lined with advertisements and party slogans.

Behind the southern or railway end the sound of train announcements from an adjacent station is hard to miss. Beyond the northern end stand uniform blocks of flats lined up in a characterless estate whose streets all bear, perhaps appropriately, Soviet names.

An unkempt black cinder track surrounds the pitch, while the blue, white and red barriers on the terracing appear to have been designed for extremely short supporters. They don't have short memories however. In the wooden stand are 'No Smoking' signs saying 'Nezapomeň na Bradford' – 'Don't forget Bradford'.

BRATISLAVA

STADIÓN TEHELNÉ POLE

As Sparta were pioneers of football in Bohemia, so 1st Čs Šk Bratislava, formed in 1919 and now called **Slovan Bratislava**, were in Slovakia. But the Tehelné pole – or Brick Field – Stadium, named after the district, east of the city centre, was built during one of Slovakia's darkest periods. Stadiums and public works have often served as useful diversions from political repression, and so it was that work on Tehelné pole began on 10 December 1939, nine months after Slovakia's puppet president, Josef Tiso, was installed by the Nazis and Bratislava renamed Pressburg. Over 600 workers

laboured on the 25,000 capacity stadium, which opened on 22 October 1940 with a propagandist match against Hertha Berlin. Two years later the stadium also staged the Third Reich's last ever international, v. Slovakia, on 22 November 1942 (fielding a Pole and an Austrian in a 5–2 win).

Immediately after the Communist takeover in 1948, 1st Čs Šk Bratislava became NV Bratislava and, with the city's giant chemical plant as sponsor, won a hat-trick of championships. In 1969, as Slovan, the club became the first Czechoslovak, and indeed the first Eastern European team to win a major international honour, when they beat Barcelona in the final of the European Cup Winners' Cup. (Ironically, every other Warsaw Pact country boycotted that season's competition after Western European attempts to split the draw, East and West, in protest against the

GROUNDWORK

invasion of Czechoslovakia in August 1968.)

Tehelné pole's current capacity is 50,000, of which 13,000 are seated. The original main stand has blue steel columns, a white roof, glass screen ends and wooden bench seats – a complete contrast to the modern cantilevered stand built opposite between 1975–8 (when Slovan had just achieved a League and Cup double and supplied seven of the 1976 European Championship winning team). Similar to that of the Rheinstadion, Düsseldorf, the roof of this stand is supported by steel cables slung from concrete masts.

Both ends of the ground have open terracing. Behind the electric scoreboard and a line of fir trees hugging the south curve lie the club's ice hockey arena, velodrome and tennis courts. Behind a corner of the terracing is the club's soccer school, established in 1980, while beyond a *Pravda* hoarding on the north curve, until an ice stadium took its place in 1989, there used to be visible the concrete floodlight pillars of the neighbouring Inter athletics stadium. (This barely developed

venue held 25,000 and was used by Slovan's rivals, Inter ZTS.) In the distance lie the Small Carpathian Mountains.

Owing to the political and cultural balancing act which links Czechs with Slovaks, games involving the national team are fairly evenly divided between Tehelné pole and Prague although, as Slovaks never fail to point out, results are far better here. There was one, controversial exception, however. For Czechoslovakia's vital European Championship qualifier v. Romania, in November 1983, although Bratislava was the venue the Czech manager refused to change a winning team and thus selected eleven Czechs. Even after a late goal was disallowed for offside and Czechoslovakia were heading for failure, the manager still kept his two Slovak substitutes on the bench, and at the final whistle a riot erupted. One visiting supporter, it is rumoured, was killed, and it needed six trucks to clear the stadium of bottles afterwards. They were wine bottles, mind you. Beer, apparently, is for Czechs.

Tehelné pole. Along the nearside touchline is a rolled-up pitch cover on wheels.

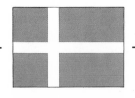

DENMARK

COPENHAGEN

IDRÆTSPARK

The Danes might have been a touch slow to embrace professional football, and it may have taken them a while to launch a serious challenge to their fellow Europeans, but in one respect they were way ahead of other nations. For it was in Copenhagen that some of the first steps towards the concept of a genuinely all-encompassing Idrætspark, or sports park, were taken in 1911. And although never as extensive as those complexes subsequently built in Germany, by the mid-1920s the Idrætspark was one of the most innovative and advanced in Europe.

It was originally laid out on the grounds of the Fælledparken, common land just north of the city, which in the late nineteenth century became popular for team games such as football and hockey. To cater for this interest, in 1908 a mock-classical pavilion was built in the middle of the common, and it was this building which three years later was converted into a delightful grandstand for Denmark's first fully enclosed football ground. Like a Palladian villa, its lower floor was dressed in rusticated stone, and at each wing there was a portico with Doric columns. Between the porticos, a covered balcony held 325 seats for officials and journalists, and there were 3800 uncovered seats in front. By those less privileged fans frequenting other parts of the ground, this seated section soon became known as the 'Expensive Stand'.

Opened on 25 May 1911 with a match between a Copenhagen XI and Sheffield Wednesday, the newly enclosed ground held 12,000, and unusually for its time (outside the British Isles, at least) had no running track. Instead, a separate track was laid behind the ground in 1912, and two years later, on its north side, the solid, rather severe looking Idrætshuset was opened – the first reinforced concrete building in Denmark – with a large indoor sports hall holding 2300 spectators.

By the late-1920s the complex was complete. Between the athletics and football stadiums was a hockey pitch, also used for women's athletics (a rarity in Europe at this time – they were only admitted to the Olympics in 1928), while on the north corner of the Idrætshuset, an indoor swimming pool was built in 1929, paid for from the profits of yet another installation by the athletics track, the Park-Teatret, a cinema and ballroom, opened in 1926.

Concentrating now on the football ground, there were several developments over the years. In 1922 a 4000 capacity terrace was built at the

Boaters and bonnets at a packed Idrætspark in 1914. Frankfurt took the classical pavilion theme a stage further (see page 264).

POLITIKENS PRESSEFOTO

east, or Øster Alle end, a few metres behind the original narrow strip of terracing. Because of its composition, it was called the Cement Stand. It gained a roof in 1925, and though modernised somewhat since then, its essential appearance has altered little.

In 1928 the opposite, Hockeybanen terrace was built up but not covered, and, apart from an electric scoreboard added in the early 1980s, this too has barely changed. Holding 10,500, it consists of wooden steps on a concrete framework, behind which, on the site of the former hockey pitch there is now an indoor ice-hockey and skating rink. Immediately beyond this lies the athletics stadium. Now called the Østerbro Stadion (after the district), this has one basic cantilevered stand, built in 1958 opposite the Idrætshuset, and holds 7000 overall.

Back in the football stadium, opposite the 'Expensive Stand' another quite simple stand, with angled props, was built in 1934, originally all-standing, but now with seats in the central section. Behind it are two training pitches used by the B.93 club, hence the stand is called either the '93 Stand', or, in contrast to its opposite, the 'Cheap Stand'.

Of course, the small but 'Expensive Stand' could not last, especially as the 1950s saw between 15–30,000 arrive at the Idrætspark each Sunday for First Division double-headers. Even so, the stand's replacement could hardly have been more sensational. Based on a design already executed at the Universitario Stadium, Venezuela by a Danish partnership, Christiani-Nielsen (who had also worked on the Maracana Stadium), the new main stand was a towering triple-decker, holding 12,300 seats, with one of the most daring cantilevered roofs ever seen in Europe. Only 6 centimetres deep at its leading edge, the concrete roof arches skywards over the upper tier, revealing its smooth undersurface to all inside the ground.

It certainly deserved to inherit the title 'Expensive', having cost 8 million Danish kroners and taken two years to build, but as is often the case with innovative designs, it has proved entirely inappropriate. In Venezuela, no doubt, such a roof provides perfect shelter from the sun. In the freezing climes of northern Europe, however, it offers about as much protection as a bikini in a snowstorm.

There was one other, crucial mistake. The architects forgot to provide a means for players to get from their dressing rooms down onto the pitch. Since football tends to be marginally more exciting when players are involved, a tall, narrow spiral staircase had to be squeezed into the bowels of the stand. Just what the trainer ordered after ninety sapping minutes.

The first visitors to try out this staircase were England, who celebrated the stand's opening on 2 October 1955, with a 5–1 win over their hosts. Nine days later a Scottish League XI arrived, winning 4–0 against a Copenhagen XI, in the Idrætspark's first ever floodlit match. Undeterred by these defeats, the fans continued to flock to the stadium, and on 30 June 1957 a match v. Sweden attracted Denmark's official record gate of 51,600. (More attended Brazil's visit three years later but not all entered the ground legally.)

Since those heady days, Denmark's stock in world football has risen substantially, while structurally the stadium has hardly changed. Its total capacity is still 48,000 (including 13,500 seated), although this is reduced to 45,000 for evening matches.

There has, however, been one major alteration to the main stand's appearance. In 1985 the Hydro Oil Company asked schools to submit paintings for what was to become one of the world's most prominently displayed examples of children's art. Out of 13,000 entries, one by nine-year-old Michael Jørgensens was chosen, and, enlarged several hundred times, it now fills the whole underside of the roof. Michael's picture shows two red stick men prancing in front of a goal net, on a thickly turfed pitch. The background is, shall we say, a little murky.

To use such a large space thus was undoubtedly a bold gesture on the part of the Idrætspark. But it has to be said that unless you are close at hand on a bright, sunny day, far from enhancing the stand, the picture actually detracts from it. To put it bluntly, it looks a bit of a mess.

On the other hand, if the roof offers precious little protection from the elements, the least it can do is provide an interesting diversion. And if Michael's efforts fail to amuse, one only has to look out from the upper tier, over the athletics stadium, to see in the distance the Øresund, the stretch of water which divides Copenhagen from Sweden, 25 kilometres to the east and distinctly visible on a clear day.

Nearer at hand, underneath the stand, are the headquarters of the Danish Football Union.

Three clubs use the Idrætspark complex. In the

DENMARK

The Idrætspark's triple-decker 'Expensive Stand'. Nowhere is there a more daring display of reinforced concrete cantilevering, and yet nowhere is such a form so inappropriate. Copenhagen's climate is not that of Caracas. Although difficult to discern in this photograph, Michael Jørgensens' mural fills the underside of the roof.

Østerbro Stadion are **B.93** (Boldklubben 1893), not to be confused with **B.1903**, who currently share the main stadium with **KB** (Kjøbenhavns Boldklub), Denmark's oldest and most honoured club. Until the 1950s, B.93 and KB dominated the Danish League, but since then, apart from one Cup win in 1982, B.93 have been very much the underdogs, while KB have managed only four honours since 1953. B.1903 have, in the past, played at their own stadium in Hellerup, a suburb of Copenhagen. Attendances are not high; KB attract the most, perhaps 1200.

Yet for international games, the Idrætspark is still very popular, as was proved when the go-ahead owner of Denmark's first ever professional club, Brøndby (based some 20 kilometres west of the stadium), announced plans to build a new national stadium. His idea of a 60,000 capacity

Danmark Stadion immediately sparked off a political row between those wanting to maintain the traditions of the Idrætspark, and those who saw it as a decaying hulk with no future.

As the row developed, the *Tipsbladet* sports newspaper conducted a poll on the issue, the result being an overwhelming vote of support for the old Idrætspark.

But Brøndby's plans did at least give the Idrætspark's owners a kick up the backside, and now there are plans to remodel the stadium for 1993. Two options are being considered – one of which calls for the pitch to be shifted by 90 degrees. But whichever is chosen, the towering main stand will survive, which means that Michael's painting is, at least, safe for a while yet. How Michael feels about this, now that he is growing up, we can only imagine.

EAST GERMANY

EAST BERLIN

STADION DER WELTJUGEND

Such is the path taken by the Berlin Wall that it almost appears to have been deliberately routed around the Stadion der Weltjugend (World Youth Stadium), which has the Wall on three sides as if in its own special enclave. Clearly visible across the Wall, 1 kilometre away, are the tall lights of West Berlin's Poststadion. While the latter was staging football during the 1936 Olympics, the Weltjugend – then a fairly basic sports ground known as the Polizei (police) or Mitte (middle) Stadium – hosted handball. After the war it was renamed Zentralstadion, and when the present terraces were built up by 'voluntary' labour in the early 1950s it was again retitled, as the Walter Ulbricht Stadium, after East Germany's Communist leader. Never a popular politician, Ulbricht retired in 1971 and two years later, to commemorate the World Youth and Student

Wet at the Weltjugend.

Games, the stadium adopted its present name.

The army club ASK Vorwärts were based here until moved lock, stock and gun barrel to Frankfurt an der Oder in 1971. Internationals were also staged at the ground during the 1950s, but without floodlights and with its terracing and 20,000 bench seats deteriorating, the 48,000 capacity stadium's only importance now is as a neutral venue for Cup Finals, held here since 1975.

EAST BERLIN

FRIEDRICH LUDWIG JAHN SPORTPARK

Friedrich Ludwig Jahn (1778–1852) was the father of mass participation sport, a Prussian gymnast who pioneered fitness programmes as a means of preparing patriotic youngsters for military service and a wholesome life. Now the stadium which bears his name is home to East Germany's most successful club, and also probably its least popular. As Party favourites, **Berliner FC Dynamo** are tainted by their close links with the state security services, which may or may not explain why BFC have won the championship almost every season since 1979, get to sign most of the country's best players, yet still their gates at the 20,000

EAST GERMANY

TONI THONFELD

The masses at play, just as Friedrich Ludwig Jahn would have wished.

capacity, all-seated Sportpark are usually lower than the national average.

The stadium itself, built in 1951 but completely refurbished in 1987, is not surprisingly East Germany's most modern. Apart from a computerised scoreboard and unusual floodlights on tripods, it has a tall, but not full-length, cantilevered main stand which dominates the surroundings. The white panelled underside of the roof is even rather luxurious, like a glossy ceiling. Unfortunately the stand faces west, so although Party officials gain an excellent view of decadent West Berlin – with the three spires of the Friedenskirche prominent on the skyline – they also have to face the afternoon sun.

Opposite the main stand is a cover angled around the track corners, immediately behind which lies the so-called 'Death Strip' of the Berlin Wall, where many discontents have fallen in their attempts to reach the West. (Hertha Berlin's old ground is just beyond the wall to the north.)

● Because of their strong prewar traditions, by far the most popular club in East Berlin, with the ordinary workers at least, is **1.FC Union Berlin**, whose 26,000 capacity **Stadion an der Alten Försterei** really is, as the name suggests, a forest lair. Opened in 1906 on the banks of the River Spree, in the southeast of Berlin, the ground was home to prewar club Union Oberschöneweide and its several factory-sponsored successors until 1.FC's formation in 1966. It has three tall, steep banks of terracing fronted by high security fences (which suggests the fans are not all model citizens) and one low side of bench seats, with no track but also no lights or cover. Though underdeveloped, apparently in the middle of nowhere and hard to reach, it is here, claim many East Berliners, that the city's real footballing heart is to be found.

LEIPZIG

ZENTRALSTADION

Each nation in the Soviet bloc has its showpiece stadium, designed as much for mass rallies as for sport, but in East Germany (as in Poland) this stadium is to be found outside the capital, in the country's second largest city, Leipzig. Begun in 1950, when the bombed ruins of the city were piled up to form the banking (as in Leningrad, Warsaw and several West German cities), the Zentralstadion, or Central Stadium, was finally opened for the 1956 Deutsche Turn und Sportfest. Essentially an open oval-shaped arena, it bears a close resemblance to other postwar Socialist-inspired stadiums, especially the 23rd August Stadium, Bucharest, opened three years earlier.

(Over a hundred smaller East German stadiums were built during the same period as part of the country's Five Year Plan.)

Nowadays the Zentralstadion holds 95,000 all seated, although crowds of up to 110,000 have been recorded, for example when East Germany played their first ever competitive football international, v. Wales in the World Cup, in May 1957. Since then it has been the GDR's prime international venue, also used by neighbouring club Lokomotive Leipzig for important European matches.

Characterised by four, huge banks of floodlights – 144 lamps on each – leaning perilously on double columns braced by steel guy ropes, the stadium, though impressive in scale, is otherwise rather featureless inside.

In order to enjoy the best view of the 'human tableaux' so popular during mass rallies, the VIP's boxed-in section is situated on the west side. From the concourse above this one can scan the Leipzig skyline – three skyscrapers, several spires, and factory chimneys galore, their silhouettes all soft-ened in the polluted haze which seems to bedevil every major East German city. Looking down the tree-covered banking, however, all is natural calm; the Elster River flows alongside the stadium with parkland and extensive training facilities to the north.

On the east side, above the wide tunnel, is a glass-fronted, neoclassical loggia for officials and press. Above this, at the top of the perimeter concourse, is a museum of German sport based, of course, on Socialist historical models (i.e. nothing much good occurred before 1945, so no mention of VfB Leipzig's prewar honours). The museum actually forms the upper storey of a daunting, almost palatial, entrance block, flanked by wide steps with blue railings leading up to the terracing. Heroically posed sporting statues break up the laboured façade, creating the overall impression of a national shrine.

Just behind the south curve, visible over the stadium's crown, stands a clock tower over-looking the adjacent Festwiese, a large square field with turfed terracing which is used for training

Even the floodlights seem to strain for a better view at the Zentralstadion.

EAST GERMANY

and parades and is identical in layout to the Berlin Olympic Stadium's Maifeld. The Leipzig tower is in fact named after a competitor in those 1936

Olympics, the wrestler Werner Seelenbinder, who, as a member of the Communist Party and resistance movement, died in a Nazi concentration camp in 1944.

A fine view of this tower and the Zentralstadion's rising sylvan banks is to be had from across the Festwiese, from the wide Friedrich Ludwig Jahn Allee. It is here we find the heirs of Jahn, at the famous Deutsche Hochschule für Körperkultur, the physical education hothouse which in athletics if not in football has forged East Germany's reputation as one of the world's top sporting nations and made the Zentralstadion opposite just one stopping-off point along a well-trodden road to international acclaim.

LEIPZIG

BRUNO PLACHE STADION

Opposite a large cemetery in the southeast district of Probstheida is the Bruno Plache Stadium, home of **1.FC Lokomotive Leipzig**, the team of the railway workers (in a city with the largest railway station in Europe). Holding 22,500, the stadium has one 2000 seater, prewar grandstand with green screen ends, blue and yellow facings and 'Rauchen Verboten' ('No Smoking') signs everywhere. The remaining three sides around a shale track consist of open, stone-faced terraces, with lights not in the stadium but over the adjacent training pitch

(an indication of the club's priorities, perhaps?). Close by is the Battle of Nations monument, where Napoleon was thwarted in 1813, and Lok fans might erect a similar memorial if their team ever breaks BFC Dynamo's grip on the League championship. Bruno Plache (1908–49) meanwhile has his own memorial on the stadium gates; he was editor of *Roter Sachsensport* (Red Saxony Sport).

● Leipzig's homeliest venue is **Chemie Leipzig's** 22,000 capacity **Georg Schwarz Sportpark**, on the edge of woods in the northwestern Leutzsch district; a tight ground with a tall, very English bank of terracing at one end, and a small old clubhouse opposite the wooden stand. No lights, no modernity, only a few party slogans, but heaps of green and white charm.

Tradition beats progressivism in Leipzig, at Lokomotive (left) and Chemie (right).

HALLE

KURT WABBEL STADION

In the grey, provincial industrial city of Halle, birthplace of Handel, **HFC Chemie** play at a stadium whose main interest lies in its unspoilt, traditional setting and its dour prewar styling. Opened in 1936, it was originally named after the S.A. thug, Horst Wessel, who died after a street brawl in Berlin six years earlier and by skilful propaganda became the martyred hero of the Nazi's rallying song. The stadium bears the hall-mark of National Socialist design – heavy, rough cut stone on its perimeter wall and a ceremonial archway entrance behind one goal. After the war it was renamed the Kurt Wabbel Stadion, after a

Halle-born wrestler and footballer who died in Buchenwald concentration camp in 1944. Chemie Halle inherited the stadium in 1963 from BSG Turbine Halle, added a small cantilevered stand on one side in 1973 and, later, four English-style upright floodlight pylons. Tall tenement buildings overlook the ground, which is otherwise an uncovered oval of terracing holding 27,000.

DRESDEN

DYNAMO STADION

Architecturally, the only noteworthy features of **SG Dynamo Dresden**'s stadium are the floodlight masts. Sloping, triangular in section and rising from tripod bases, they sit like attentive giraffes, guarding what is otherwise a shallow, completely uncovered oval arena.

The Dynamo Stadium started life in 1923 as the Ilgen Kampfbahn (Ilgen was a rich industrialist and local liberal politician), the centrepiece of a typical Weimar Republic sports complex in which a stadium was linked to a swimming pool and surrounded by tennis courts, hockey pitches and training areas. (Similar centres at Frankfurt, Düsseldorf and Cologne, among many, were developed at around the same time.)

The blanket destruction of Dresden by Allied bombers on 13 February 1945 left the stadium a ruin and it was not until 1947 that play resumed in the by then-renamed Rudolf Harbig Stadium (Harbig was a 'progressive' athlete). The present Dynamo club evolved in the period 1949–53 and once they had become a force in Europe, it was decided, in 1972, to use the simpler title, Dynamo Stadium. Otherwise the stadium has one major

distinction – it is by far the best attended venue in East Germany, regularly attracting over 20,000 spectators, more than twice the national average, and capacity crowds of 38,000 for European games. There are 6500 seats.

● Until the late 1960s Dresden's main football venue, used for internationals, was the **Heinz Steyer Stadion**, formerly known as the Ostragehege, home of prewar SC Dresden (for whom Helmut Schön played). While this club dominated the wartime league, Steyer, a former Dresden footballer, was executed by the Nazis in 1944 after spying for partisans in Greece. The stadium is now used only for athletics.

Giraffes on the prowl at Dynamo Dresden.

ENGLAND

While most European countries were only just starting to build their first substantial stadiums in the 1920s, by then the majority of English clubs were already firmly established in the grounds which they still occupy today. With the exception only of Norwich City (whose present ground opened in 1935) not one of England's major clubs has moved to a new ground since 1924.

That is not to say that English football grounds are all archaic, or 'slums', as they have been so often described. In many cases hardly a brick or patch of concrete from the early days has survived, and so high are the standards required by the

British Safety of Sports Grounds Act, passed in 1975, that England's Victorian and Edwardian grounds are often in better condition now than many Continental stadiums built relatively recently.

But it is true that England has learnt little from Europe in terms of stadium design. By the 1950s, for example, while most large nations were already embarking upon their second or even third generation of stadiums, in England the majority of clubs were building the same kind of stands and terraces which had been popular in the 1920s. Cantilevered roofs were tentatively introduced

Wembley – the most famous greyhound stadium in the world.

only thirty years after their first appearance on the Continent. Furthermore, with the exception only of Manchester United and Leeds, in the postwar period no English club ever properly considered their ground as a single architectural entity. Thus development was carried out bit by bit, stand by stand, often by different architects and in clashing styles.

England was not alone in this – some Dutch and Belgian clubs have acted similarly. But it is a mark of the conservatism of English club directors that not since Wembley's construction in 1923 has an architect of any national repute been commissioned to design a football ground from scratch.

Yet despite this, and despite the appalling death tolls at Bradford in 1985 and Hillsborough in 1989, fans all over Europe continue to talk with affection of *'le stade à l'anglaise'* and *'das typisch englische Stadion'*. By that they refer not only to the absence of running tracks, but also to the sense of tradition which permeates English grounds. This is not something which can be dismissed lightly. It is real, and it helps explain why England sustains the largest professional league in Europe and enjoys comparatively high attendances throughout its four divisions. Inner-city stadiums, tightly enclosed, with an identity even for differentiated sections within the ground, create a sense of belonging seldom found in a featureless super-bowl (see, for example, the Hamburg experience, pages 276–7).

The sheer density of grounds within certain areas is also a major English characteristic. London, in particular, though hardly regarded as a serious football city by anyone living north of Birmingham, has eleven professional club venues – more than any other city in Europe. It is also, of course, the home of **Wembley**.

Wem-ber-ley, as the fans pronounce it in their songs, has for many years been a symbol of the malaise within English football. When its chaotic inauguration took place for the Cup Final, on 28 April 1923, it was unquestionably the grandest, largest soccer venue ever built. Sixty years later it was a national disgrace – decaying, uncomfortable and dingy.

Not only that, since 1966 (when it staged the World Cup Final), Wembley has been the exclusive venue for England internationals. Even lesser games have been held there, instead of at provincial venues where a better atmosphere might

result. No other European football association, apart from Scotland, has concentrated its fixtures so entirely upon one stadium. And whereas, for example, four West German, three French and three Spanish club venues have staged European finals, in England only Wembley has been accorded the privilege (four European Cup Finals, in 1963, 1968, 1971 and 1978, and the Cup Winners' Cup Final in 1965), even though there are several English grounds worthy of consideration (especially in view of UEFA's recent choice of relatively basic grounds like Berne, Basle and Lyon).

That imbalance is certain to continue now that Wembley is the only English stadium able to meet FIFA standards for World Cup matches, having undergone a three-year refurbishment programme said to have cost £1 million per month. From a venue once holding 100,000, including 44,000 seats, Wembley now has a capacity of 81,500 all-seated. Four thousand of those seats are in the Olympic Gallery, a balcony suspended from the roof. Meanwhile, below stairs, the stadium's notoriously spartan toilet and refreshment facilities have been gradually upgraded.

Certain inadequacies, however, are unlikely to be solved. Though not as bad as at the Parc des Princes or the Bernabeu, parking is limited and the approach roads are always congested.

Wembley is more than just a football stadium. Apart from Rugby League Cup Finals and an annual American football showpiece, it is used, most profitably, as a major concert venue, and most regularly (three times a week) for greyhound racing. Every year over 65,000 visitors pass through its doors simply to have a guided tour.

But there is one quality Wembley Stadium possesses which can neither be planned nor bought, and that is the stadium's magical atmosphere on big-match days. In the same way that Wimbledon's Centre Court is special in the world of tennis, Wembley is quite unlike any other national football stadium. This may be due partly to the famous twin-towers, partly to the all-enclosing low roof, perhaps even to the eccentric presence of the sand-covered greyhound track. Or maybe it is none of these things but simply Wembley's almost indefinable, inherent Englishness.

In the current, long overdue drive to improve safety and comfort at the football grounds of England, this is one quality which should never be undervalued if the English game is to maintain its popularity thoughout Europe.

FINLAND

HELSINKI

OLYMPIASTADION

Meeting in Berlin in August 1936, the International Olympic Committee awarded the 1940 Games to Tokyo, then a year later withdrew the offer when Japan attacked China. Helsinki stepped eagerly into the breach, having drawn up plans for its own Olympic Stadium in 1927 and broken ground in 1934. Indeed, the IOC President, Count Henri de Baillet-Latour, had himself laid the foundation stone in June 1936.

With the 1940 Olympics to aim for, work proceeded apace, sizeable financial help coming from the sale of consumer items bearing the stadium's logo. Built on a granite bed in woods very close to the city centre, the Olympiastadion originally held 25,000, with wooden terracing added to raise the capacity for the Games to 62,000. Even with this temporary arrangement, the stadium maintained a clean, white, distinctly Scandinavian economy of style. It was unquestionably modern, avoiding all the retrospective pomp of Berlin (1936) and Los Angeles (1932), and even today bears up well to critical post-modern scrutiny.

The architects were Toivo Jantti and Yrjo Lindegren – Lindegren won an Olympic gold arts medal for the design – and the world seemed suitably impressed when the stadium was inaugurated on 12 June 1938. The most talked-about feature was its 72 metre tall white tower, which still marks out the stadium for miles around on the city skyline and has provided wonderful views of Helsinki for over 3 million visitors. Incorporating twenty-two rounded balconies, its design is clearly reminiscent of the tower which dominates Uruguay's Centenario Stadium, built for the 1930 World Cup, which was itself a futuristic interpretation of the tower theme made popular by Jan Wils at his 1928 Olympic Stadium in Amsterdam. (Other prominent stadium towers are

GROUNDWORK

Crisp, white Finnish lines at Helsinki
(left and opposite page).

at Bordeaux, Florence, and La Coruna.

The main stand at Helsinki was, and remains, equally striking. With twelve slim columns topped by conical capitals supporting the deep, over-hanging white concrete roof, it seems highly advanced for 1938. Along the front of the roof are floodlights, added in 1940 (again, very advanced for Europe), part of 434 lamps which ring the upper tier of the stadium bowl. The upper tier itself rises in steps from each wing of the main stand, until reaching a peak in the central section opposite the main stand.

Directly behind the main stand are two adjacent football pitches, each sharing the same terraces and one long, low covered stand. Called Pal-lokentta, this 7000 capacity ground is used for lower division games and in 1955 staged the World Archery Championships.

Of course Helsinki never did get to stage the 1940 Olympics. Although the medals were struck and the Olympic Village was all ready for its guests, with Europe otherwise engaged the IOC had no option but to cancel, three months before the scheduled opening. Helsinki thus had to wait until 1952 for its big moment (since London was promised the Games for 1944, although it, too, had to wait until four years later).

By 1952 the wooden terracing had been replaced by concrete, creating a capacity of 50,000 (40,158 seats), but for the Games an extra 20,000 places were added with temporary stands behind the upper tiers. The most recent major change came in 1955 when the South Curve was remodelled.

Apart from the 1952 Games, best remembered for Zátopek's three gold medals, the Olympia-stadion has witnessed 46 world records and over 1600 events, including American football, boxing, the World Speed Skating Championships, World Bandy Championships, a Billy Graham gathering and, inevitably, a Rolling Stones concert. To-gether with Rome, it is the only stadium to have staged both World and European Championships in athletics and the Olympic Games. It is also the only stadium in the world to be featured on a bank note (the current 10 Finnish markas note).

Football plays its part but has never been the stadium's mainstay, as is demonstrated by the fact that although the record football crowd came for the Olympic final in 1952 (58,553 saw Hungary beat Yugoslavia), the highest gate for a domestic match is 17,293 for a meeting between the sta-dium's resident club, **HJK** (Helsingin Jal-kapalloklubi), and Valkeakosken Haka in 1965.

With so much sporting history bound up in one corner of Helsinki it is heartening to find, in a wing of the main stand, an excellent sports museum. The stadium is, however, an exhibit in itself. Uncluttered, crisp and white, like a majestic ocean liner, it is proof of how the most basic bowl-shaped arena can be enriched by confident simplicity. Alongside Stockholm, Amsterdam and Munich, it is undoubtedly one of the finest con-tributions to twentieth-century architecture the Olympic movement has made.

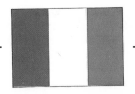

FRANCE

NANTES

STADE DE LA BEAUJOIRE

A stadium as fresh, light and smooth as the region's best Muscadet, the Stade de la Beaujoire is the fruit of a happy blend of ambitious local government backing a successful football club.

Many clubs and cities would have been quite content with a centrally located, floodlit ground like the Marcel Saupin Stadium, which was **FC Nantes**' former abode. With three concrete vaulted roofs and a capacity of 27,000 (12,000 seated), it was modernised as recently as 1963 – the year the 'Canaries', formed only twenty years earlier, reached the First Division (since when they have become France's most consistent domestic outfit, never having been relegated and with six championships to their name). But to attract the 1984 European Championships to this western

coastal city, the tidy, though hemmed-in ground offered no opportunities for development, especially since the River Loire flows within a whisker of its south stand. Very scenic, but most inconvenient.

Hence architect Berdje Agopyan, an assistant of Roger Taillibert's at the Parc des Princes, was called in to create one of Europe's most pleasing football stadiums, beyond the old town centre, on the east bank of Nantes' second river, the Erdre.

A combination of daring design and practical convenience, the Stade de la Beaujoire's sweeping green-grey roof (coloured not only to match the Canaries' colours but also to blend with the surrounding landscape) rises on each side, where there are two tiers, then dips over the single-tiered end terraces, where white concrete roof supports form open bays at the rear. Two ramps feed the upper level of the main west stand (named after Nantes' most famous son, Jules Verne) and thus the stadium resembles a modern version of the Ullevi Stadium, Gothenburg. There is however one design problem – the open end bays expose spectators to chill winds from the river valley, so it is planned to drape wind-resistant mesh across the openings.

Named after the district, La Beaujoire was inaugurated on 8 May 1984 for the visit of Romania, who returned six weeks later for a European Championship match v. Portugal. France also played Belgium here in the competition on 16 June, the only time the 52,467 capacity stadium (32,000 seats) has been filled for football.

La Beaujoire has also become France's second most important rugby venue (after Parc des Princes), which explains the extra turf behind each goal.

Space outside is no problem, either. Beyond the

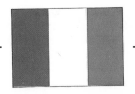

FC de NANTES

Modernised 1963, vacated 1984 - the Marcel Saupin Stadium.

ALLSPORT/TREVOR JONES

La Beaujoire – fresh, light and smooth, though a touch windy.

massive car park (holding 13,000 vehicles) one can see, across the Erdre, France's most advanced club centre for training and educating young footballers, La Jonelière. Meanwhile, second team fixtures, rugby, hockey and archery keep the old Marcel Saupin Stadium free of cobwebs. Past, present and future are all nurtured in Nantes; the Canaries have much to sing about.

BORDEAUX

PARC DE LESCURE

When unveiled on 12 June 1938 for Brazil's World Cup match v. Czechoslovakia – a bruising encounter which led to three sendings-off, two broken limbs and sundry other injuries – the Parc de Lescure (also called the Stade Vélodrome Municipal) was, for all the artlessness on the pitch, quite the most breathtaking stadium in France; as dramatic a break from traditional stadium design as Munich proved to be in 1972. Even now, following a major refurbishment between 1985–6, the home of **Les Girondins de Bordeaux** merits comparison

with the best of modern stadium architecture, having survived half a century of changing styles with consummate ease.

A Parc des Sports was first laid out on former vineyards in Lescure in 1920, in an attempt to promote physical welfare following the First World War. International football made its first appearance in 1922, v. Spain, but it was not until the municipality purchased the land from an old Bordelaise family, the Johnstons (who were actually English and owned a ceramics factory), that planning began for a major stadium. In 1934 two local architects were entrusted with the task, and despite their lack of experience in sport (or perhaps because of it), Jacques D'Welles and Raoul Jourde broke completely new ground with a reinforced concrete structure which skilfully

FRANCE

Parc de Lescure before the cycle track was removed.

fused neoclassicism with contemporary Art Deco (a compromise common to French municipal works during that decade but outside Bordeaux never applied to stadium design).

D'Welles took the oval plan, formed around both athletics and cycle tracks – since at that time cycling, then rugby, were the city's two favourite sports – and built two identical stands on each side. These stands were linked with lower curving roofs at each end, to provide cover all round. Nothing unusual about this, at least not by today's standards, except that the form of the stands was quite revolutionary. Developments in concrete technology allowed all the roofs to be cantilevered, the most adventurous application of such technology at that time, and to add strength to beauty, the roofs were formed in vaulted sections. This ribbed effect – copied in stadiums all over Europe and still used today with more modern materials – may have been an attempt to mirror the arches of Bordeaux's nineteenth-century Pont de Pierre. Or was it an allusion to the waves which brought shipping and wealth to the city?

Certainly, even today, the Parc de Lescure's most stunning interior features are its four viewing bays which form the links between the side roofs and the slightly lower end roofs. Like the bridges of ships, these rounded, glass-fronted bays protrude beyond the wavy roof line to add dash and a sense of movement. The nautical theme is strengthened by large round openings, like portholes, which light the stairways behind, and the floodlight towers, which are actually winched up the gantries by electric motors, like flags up a mast. This is apparently to protect the lights, when not in use, against strong winds.

The stadium's exterior commands equal interest. Venetian-style bridges act as stairways up to the upper tier, which is ringed by open archways. These openings are divided by drainpipes shaped like classical pilasters, while every surface is coated in a cream-coloured stucco, with barriers and railings picked out in maroon.

But there is more, for Parc de Lescure has three grand entrances. On Boulevard Maréchal Leclerc the visitor is greeted by a monumental concrete arch, 23 metres wide and 19 metres high, coffered on the inside in Roman style. Through this unique arch is a courtyard decorated with niches and plaques, which honour the stadium's creators, and four enormous vases decorated with mosaics.

The second entrance, on the stadium's eastern corner, crowded in by small buildings and gardens, is marked by a classic Art Deco Olympic Tower (shades of Amsterdam), whose red luminous mosaics sparkle under floodlight.

North of the stadium lies an adjoining sports complex, also designed by D'Welles, with a track, tennis courts, fronton court (for pelota) and indoor training halls. This leads out to the circular Place Johnston, where a smaller Olympic tower and a semicircle of turnstiles comprise the third entrance. All is in perfect harmony with the neighbouring avenues and town houses.

With a capacity of around 25,000, the Stade Vélodrome Municipal was too small to be considered for the 1984 European Championships and was, in any case, in desperate need of modernisation. Rather than abandon this architectural masterpiece however – and spend vast sums on a politically controversial replacement – it was decided, thankfully, to emulate Toulouse by removing the running and cycle tracks in order to enlarge the stands and terraces. Under the guidance of architect Guy Depuis, great care was taken to restore the structure while at the same time enhancing spectator comfort. For example, despite the great expense due to drainage problems, a security moat was built around the pitch instead of obtrusive high fencing.

The reborn Parc de Lescure now holds 51,460 (26,960 seated), putting Bordeaux on par with the other major venues in France. Without a decent team it would have been hard for the city to justify its outlay of more than 100 million francs, nearly double the original estimate. But the Girondins

The lights are lowered but Bordeaux remains on the crest of a concrete wave.

excelled themselves during the preceding months of political debate, winning the championship in 1984 and 1985, and, once the stadium redevelopment was completed (without disruption to the fixtures), the Cup in 1986, then the Double, plus a semi-final place in the European Cup, in 1987. No supporter could ask for richer rewards, both on and around the pitch.

TOULOUSE

LE STADIUM

While the city of Toulouse is better known for Caravelles and Concordes, **Toulouse FC** was itself the victim of a crash landing, in 1967: Les Violets,

as they are known, went out of existence and transferred all their players to Red Star of Paris (out of the frying pan into the fire, as it transpired, since in 1978 Red Star also collapsed, see page 122); but happily they revived three years later and returned to the First Division in 1982. For this reason alone the condition of the ground has been of only secondary importance in the hearts of TFC supporters.

FRANCE

LA DÉPÊCHE

Le Stadium or '*le petit Wembley*'?

Known as Le Stadium to distinguish it from other Toulouse venues (such as Sept Derniers, home of the famous rugby club Stade Toulousain), construction work started in 1937, the same year as TFC were formed at the more humble Chapou ground of TOEC, a rugby and swimming club. A year later Chapou staged the 1938 World Cup game Romania v. Cuba (who were only there because Mexico withdrew, but still managed a shock 3–3 draw before losing the replay). The ground is now tennis courts and a swimming pool.

Le Stadium, meanwhile, was not completed until 1950 and was then mainly preoccupied with cycling and rugby. The ground record of 39,540 was set in 1951 for a French Rugby Union final, Carmaux v. Tarbes, and three years later 37,471 saw France play Great Britain in a Rugby League World Cup match. Football has never matched those attendance levels.

In common with Bordeaux, Toulouse missed out on the 1984 European Championships because the municipality, under mayor Pierre Baudis, could not fund a major refurbishment of the 29,900 capacity stadium. But encouraged by TFC's return to the First Division in 1982, Baudis' son Dominique, newly elected in his father's place, sanctioned 15 million francs' worth of redevelopment for 1983–4 (as posters all over the city continue to remind the public even today). That money was patently spent on the interior, for the exterior remains drab – a blank outer wall in various shades of beige and ochre; not at all welcoming. Inside, however, there was a major transformation. The cycle track was replaced by extra seats, to increase the capacity to 38,225, now all-seated and mostly under cover. The record gate so far for a soccer game is 35,160, for TFC's UEFA Cup tie v. Moscow Spartak in October 1986.

Perhaps the most striking characteristic of TFC's home is its resemblance to Wembley, albeit on a smaller and more enclosed scale. Apart from cover all round, it also has straight sides and semicircular ends, two towers flanking the main entrance, and private boxes and a press box suspended from the roof. Even the floodlights, six roof-mounted gantries along each side, remind one of England's national stadium.

The setting is rather different however. Le Stadium is built on the Île du Ramier, in the middle of the Garonne River, forming part of a large Parc des Sports whose original white Art-Deco central hall, set in landscaped gardens, can still be seen opposite the stadium, albeit cut off by an intrusive flyover. Close by are exhibition halls, parks and, since this is France, a boulodrome (an indoor hall for the popular game of boules). A real pleasure island, in other words, but, most important of all, a stadium with a club back in business.

NÎMES

STADES DES COSTIÈRES

The Languedoc city of Nîmes was already able to boast Europe's best preserved Roman arena and, on the plain outside the city, an excellent open-air amphitheatre by the Japanese architect Kurokawa. Now, another public arena has arisen, one which provides football with a fresh blueprint for the 1990s.

Taking only fifteen months to construct, the Stade des Costières opened on 15 February 1989 with an 'A' international between France and Holland, and is the new home of **Nîmes Olympique** (who formed in 1937 and previously played at the 15,000 capacity Jean Bouin Stadium). The name Costières refers to one of the region's most popular wines.

For those who know his work, the new stadium is instantly recognisable as the work of Vittorio Gregotti, one of Italy's foremost architects, and although it was the first to be completed, Nîmes was actually his third stadium commission. But whereas at Barcelona's Olympic Stadium (see page 200) Gregotti was revamping an existing structure, and at Genoa (see page 23) rebuilding on an existing site, at Nîmes he was able to start from scratch on a greenfield site.

Like Genoa, Costières is a stadium 'à l'anglaise' – that is, without a track. But there the comparison with England ends, since no English club has ever had the imagination to hire an architect of Gregotti's calibre. And yet the result is quite simple – four rectangular stands, two of them covered, linked by four corner blocks, each with a different function; offices, sports halls and changing rooms, meeting rooms, and even a billiard hall. The stadium is thus in use every day.

Pure Gregotti.

Visually, the stadium is dominated by liberal use of Gregotti's favourite motifs – the square and the grid, the almost clinical use of white surfaces, and the startling orange paving which covers the inclined banks behind each end terrace (although Gregotti wanted to use grass).

Apart from its impact as a thoroughly urban Post-Modern building, Costières has two interesting technical innovations. The open end terraces have collapsible bench seats, so that when larger crowds are expected the benches can be lowered to ground level and stood upon as on ordinary terraces. Thus the stadium's capacity can vary between 18,600 to 26,180.

But the most publicised feature is the perimeter fencing, known as the Cloez System (built in France but, according to an English engineer, invented in Norfolk). This incorporates an electronically-operated series of gates which, at the push of a button, open onto the pitch like a set of dominoes, one after the other. After the Hillsborough disaster in April 1989, the English press and several clubs saw this system as the cure for all their ills – it keeps hooligans off the pitch yet allows people onto it in the event of an emergency.

And indeed it is a beautifully simple idea, but until it can be fully tested in the more demanding circumstances of Liverpool, Rotterdam or Madrid, we should not get too carried away. Fences are still only the last resort, and an ugly one at that, even at Nîmes.

Squaring up (left) and fencing in (below) at Nîmes.

MARSEILLE

STADE VÉLODROME

At first glance the stadium of **Olympique de Marseille** appears a typical 1930s' creation, with two apparently identical concrete stands, uncovered end terraces curved around the lines of an old cycle track, British-style floodlight pylons and a pale peach exterior enriched by a hint of Moorish decoration. But delve deeper and one discovers a stadium and a story as unpredictable as a midnight stroll around the Old Port of Marseille itself.

Olympique formed in 1898 and played at the cramped Huveaune Stadium, where there was barely room between neighbouring buildings and the back of the goals to squeeze in more than a line or two of onlookers.

By the mid-1930s Olympique, or OM for short, were already Cup specialists – four wins and nearly a Double in 1934 – and patently required a stadium more befitting their status. This came about just after OM's second championship in 1937. The Stade Vélodrome – *'pelouse verte, piste rose'* (green pitch, pink track), just like the Parc des Princes – was opened on 13 June of that year, OM hosting Torino of Italy. Italy also played here in the 1938 World Cup, v. Norway and, in the semi-final, v. Brazil.

As the postwar period saw a gradual decline of fortunes, Olympique's often difficult relationship with their municipal landlords reached rock-bottom in 1965. Probably the lowest point came in April when only 434 people saw OM's Second Division match v. Forbach.

Drastic action was called for, but when it came, French football was taken completely by surprise.

OM's saviour that summer, new club president Marcel Leclerc, reckoned that the Stade Vélodrome was costing the club too dearly, and since the municipality would not lower its rental charges, Leclerc took Olympique back to its roots.

Identical stands at Marseille, but spot the difference, and the cycle track in the corners.

Even though the old Stade de l'Huveaune nearby was no better than a rural amateur team might possess, did not meet League standards and its one stand was probably unsafe, in a matter of two weeks Leclerc confounded everyone by hiring an army of workers to spruce it up, rebuild walls and replant the pitch in time for the new season.

Such a superhuman effort invigorated both supporters and players. After one season OM were back in the First Division and back at the Stade Vélodrome. Two championships and two Cup wins followed, including the Double in 1972, an incredible turnaround in just seven years. In 1970, to cater for the growing crowds, the pink cycle track was built over with extra seats and terracing, making it a velodrome in name only, and the floodlights, originally erected in 1963, were updated to become one of the top three installations in Europe.

In July 1980, however, the lights went out. Unpredictable as ever, OM were back in the Second Division and forced into liquidation. Yet once again they were rescued, and once again promoted, in 1984, with an average gate of almost 16,000 – incredible by French Second Division standards.

Further refurbishment took place that year for the European Championships, when a record crowd of 54,848 attended France's semi-final v. Portugal, on 23 June (the other match in Marseille, Portugal v. Spain, surprisingly drew less than half that number). OM's club record is 48,039 for a European Cup match v. Ajax on 20 October 1972.

Nowadays the Stade Vélodrome bears a confident air, largely thanks to the arrival as club president in 1985 of brash young millionaire Bernard Tapie. To update what is basically a quite old-fashioned stadium, the rear half of the main Jean Bouin Stand was converted into sixty private boxes on two levels, inserted between the original roof supports (so that it now looks like a cantilevered roof). Opposite is the Ganay Stand, identical apart from the boxes. At the front of both stands a lower tier of seats was built on frames attached to the original cycle track. Indeed one can clearly see the original track perimeter wall under the framework. The seats installed behind each goal are similarly built over the track, but with a very shallow rake, though at least the wooden floorboards are good for stomping on. Altogether these modifications brought the stadium's capacity down to 45,000 all-seated.

One of the delights of the Stade Vélodrome is its surroundings. Sleek metro trains emerge without warning from a tunnel immediately behind the South Curve, while beyond a clutter of high-rise apartments lie the unspoilt hills of Provence; two worlds in a city of myriad worlds, and it all turns pink at sunset. Behind the North Curve stands an Art-Deco radio tower which was part of the prewar Parc des Expositions.

Back in the stadium's spacious forecourt are memorials to the men in whose honour the stands are named: Jean Bouin, a world-record runner who died for his country in 1914 (there is a Jean Bouin Stadium next to the Parc des Princes in Paris and several others around France), and Gustave Ganay, a champion cyclist who died, aged thirty-four, during a race at the Parc des Princes in 1926. A risky sport, this cycling, for just inside the players' tunnel is another memorial, to one d'Aimé Constant, another famous cyclist who died on the Stade Vélodrome track in June 1963. Mind you, he was sixty-two at the time.

Returning to the present, Bernard Tapie brought to Marseilles not just money and coach Michel Hidalgo (as general manager), but razzmatazz too. Behind the North Curve now stands, on stilts, an 80 sq. metre video board (as at Gothenburg). This shows 'still' shots during the game plus action replays at half- and full-time.

But what makes Marseille different from any other stadium, apart from OM's fanatical supporters, is its post-match entertainment. Starting the minute the players leave the pitch, it lasts about five minutes and the crowd never knows what it will be – fireworks, a laser show, or perhaps a few songs from a top recording star. Whichever, it is always a major event, boosted by a total of fifty-six loudspeakers pumping out 10,000 watts of power around the arena (more than enough for the likes of Michael Jackson and co.). Microphones have been placed on the terraces to allow the supporters' cheers to be amplified through the system – handy for morale if OM are losing – and the stadium even has its own radio station for broadcasting on match days.

In short, the Stade Vélodrome is an old stadium bristling with modern technology, which might not suit the conservatives but certainly brings in the crowds. Yet given OM's chequered past, who would dare be complacent? Thus, a few streets away, Huveaune remains ready and primed for a first-team recall. You never know.

MONACO

STADE LOUIS II

We refer to the home of **AS Monaco** as a 'stadium' only for want of a better word. Quite simply there exists no other sports-orientated structure in the world which packs so much into such a small space, so lavishly and with such ingenuity.

Space has always been a problem in this tiny principality. Although the Association Sportive de Monaco formed in 1924, its football section had no proper home until the first Louis II Stadium was inaugurated on 23 April 1939. This was one block away from the existing stadium, tucked in between the railway line and the harbour wall, with only a few metres to spare for one stand and some narrow terracing. From his palace on top of the adjoining rock face, Louis II (who died in 1949) commanded a perfect view down onto the

pitch (not that he couldn't afford the entrance fee).

Since joining the French League in 1948 and winning promotion five years later, AS Monaco have invariably attracted the smallest following in the First Division – the population is only 27,000, after all – but they thrive on royal patronage (Albert, son of the reigning Prince, has even trained with the team). Five times championship winners (four in their old stadium) and four times Cup winners, AS Monaco have exerted an influence far beyond the normal expectations of a small-town outfit with a small-town stadium.

But where in this crowded enclave could they build a new stadium?

The sun-kissed, tax-free haven of Monaco – Monte Carlo casinos, fast cars et al – may be associated with profligate lifestyles, but land management in the principality has to be positively miserly. With only 195 hectares to its name (approximately 480 acres), how could it be otherwise? Hence only a part of the new Louis II Stadium is actually a stadium. Nothing novel in that, you say, until you discover, literally, the

GAETAN LUCI

Monaco's cliff-top palace overshadowed the old stadium. The new one is a palace itself.

full extent of all its hidden depths.

The key to building Monaco's new stadium lay in the sea, or rather in holding back the sea. Thus in the 1970s, by damming and backfilling the sea bed to a depth of 40 metres – a hugely expensive and complicated fifteen-year process – 22 hectares of land were reclaimed and given the name Fontvieille Village, of which 3 precious hectares were designated for the stadium. Three hectares would barely suffice for a modest-sized venue in a heavily built-up area, but the award-winning Parisian architect Henri Pottier and his four assistants, Messrs Gaudin, Rechsteiner, Boisson and Iori, had to squeeze in far more than a mere pitch with stands. There had to be car parking (for local residents as much as for visitors to the stadium), offices (to provide weekday income) and a host of other sporting facilities for the Monégasque public. Furthermore, since so much of Monaco is visible from the surrounding heights and seafront, the stadium had to be in harmony with its environment from every angle.

Pottier's team started planning in 1979. Construction began two years later, and in January 1985 Prince Rainier, Louis II's grandson and heir, declared this modern masterpiece open. Champagne flowed, money poured in and within months the Cup was on its way to Monaco. Three seaons later the club's fifth championship was won. An impressive record.

Yet the first thing which confounds most visitors, as they arrive at the stadium's main entrance, is that there should be a football ground at all behind the façade; it is, apparently, no more than a collection of shops and offices, albeit ranged attractively in blocks of varying heights with modern, post-modern and traditional forms happily commingling. Inside the main entrance, so pristine are the chrome turnstiles, escalators and ticket booths that one still doubts that a stadium, rather than say, a hotel or conference centre, could lie within.

One's disbelief is further suspended by going, not straight through to the stands, but to a 1750 capacity car park, which occupies the first *four* storeys of half the building, one level below ground, three above. The same levels on the other half of the stadium are taken up by an Olympic-sized swimming complex seating 500, with adjacent bistro, and a multi-purpose sports hall accommodating between 2200–3500 spectators.

On their own these four levels would be a major

On the third floor. Note the lights housed in the roof.

ALLSPORT/DAVID CANNON

asset for any small town, but in Monaco they are only the beginning, for on top of this base, astonishingly, sits the open-air stadium, with its artificial running track and grass pitch actually laid above the concrete roof of the car park. The cultivation of grass on top of buildings is nothing new, but to maintain a pitch in this setting, to the standards required for first-class football, borders upon the incredible. But there the pitch is, in all its green splendour, and if it suffers a few bare patches at all that is more the fault of the salty sea air and the shade from the stand roofs rather than from the lack of a natural substructure.

Once inside the arena – remember, we are now above the swimming pool, car park and sports hall, three storeys or 13 metres above street level – the technical details of the Louis II Stadium are rapidly eclipsed by an appreciation of its physical beauty.

Firstly, three sides of the arena are covered by roofs formed in independent stepped sections. Though tiled in traditional Provençal style on the upper surface, the roof sections are clad underneath with modern ribbed terra cotta panelling. Floodlights are housed neatly in the roof fascia.

Natural light floods in also from the open arches between each roof and stand (as at Bordeaux), and these arches are mirrored by a tall, curving range of nine ornamental arches which cap the fourth, open end (reminiscent of the Los Angeles Coliseum). This end was left deliberately open, not only to provide views of the towering hills close by – the tallest point is nicknamed 'tête de chien' (because it resembles a dog's head) – but to allow the strong mistral wind to ventilate the pitch. The road immediately behind this end of

FRANCE

the complex forms the unmarked border between Monaco and France.

With a total capacity of 20,000, the stands themselves are the least surprising element of the stadium, apart from the bright yellow of the seats. They are interrupted in the corners and along each side by eight massive cylindrical supports, which house within them access routes but also act as foundations for the entire structure (each being sunk deep into the bowels of the sea bed). Prince Rainier of course has his own spacious viewing box – but then he did help pay for the place.

Having said this much we are still only skimming the surface. As Henri Pottier himself suggested, the stadium is not 'object-like' or structured in 'futuristic silhouettes' (as, for example, Munich). Instead, it 'interiorizes' its technology. This in turn allows every part of the complex to be in regular, simultaneous use, the main elements being three pools, the sports hall, several multi-purpose gymnasiums, shops, 9172 sq. metres of office accommodation, a fitness centre and, last but not least, AS Monaco's own club HQ and its Centre de Formation – a college for up to twenty young footballers who actually study and live

in the stadium (their bedroom windows are just below the open arches). All this is in a super-structure designed to withstand earthquakes of up to 7.5 on the Richter Scale, and heated from calories generated by refuse incineration.

So aesthetically pleasing, so clinically spotless, so cleverly conceived and styled is this sporting palace, that the average, hardened, cynical football fan, finding no graffiti, no dirt, and suspecting also that there may be no soul, may dismiss the stadium as little more than a manifestation of immense wealth and privilege. Which it undoubtedly is. But the importance of this complex is that it succeeds in fulfilling all the sporting, social and environmental requirements that any stadium development must nowadays meet if it is to justify public expenditure and win community support.

For this reason, and despite the fact that the Louis II Stadium cost 600 million francs (still less than Munich's Olympic Stadium), it is to Monaco, as well as to the likes of Milan and Barcelona, Utrecht and Nîmes, that the enlightened developers of the late twentieth century flock in order to learn, and invariably gasp in admiration … and envy.

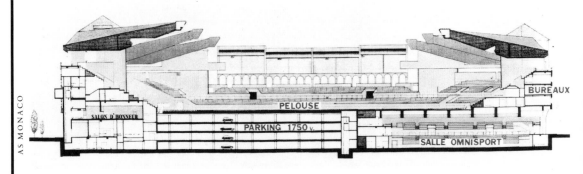

AS MONACO

A cut-away section reveals Monaco's hidden depths with the pitch (pelouse) above the car park.

SAINT ETIENNE

STADE GEOFFROY GUICHARD

When Geoffroy Guichard opened a grocery shop in the old Saint Etienne casino a century or so ago, he not only started what was to become one of France's largest retailing operations – 'Casino' (now comprising over 2000 shops and super-markets), but he also, indirectly, gave birth to a French footballing legend: ASSE, better known as **AS Saint Etienne**.

The Casino shop colours of green and white were adopted when the Association Sportive Casino was formed in 1920, and Les Verts have been making headlines ever since (not always for the right reasons). During their first decade the original corporate identity was cast off under orders from the French Football Federation, and two other clubs were absorbed: Racing Club Stéphanoise and Stade Forézien Universitaire (both remembered in a war memorial in the existing main foyer).

With funds raised by public subscription, the now-expanded club was able to buy land adjacent to a gas and steel works, and employ the Parisian building firm which in 1924 had laid out the Olympic Stadium, Colombes. St Etienne's needs were more modest; they settled for one small wooden stand and a playable pitch on marshy ground. One touchline was overshadowed by a steel foundry whose chimneys belched out brown smoke.

The small ground was opened with great pride nevertheless on 13 September 1931 and dedicated by the club president, Pierre Guichard, to his father, the old grocer. (There is a bust of Geoffroy, who died in 1940 aged seventy-three, in the stadium's main entrance hall.) St Etienne lost the inaugural match against Cannes, 8–3, but within two years had embraced professionalism and by 1938 were in the First Division.

The stadium has undergone three major changes. In 1957, after the first of Les Verts' record ten championship wins, the running track was removed to create a rectangular stadium, described in the club history, *Allez les Verts!* (see bibliography), as *'typiquement britannique'*.

In 1965 ownership of the stadium was assigned from the Guichard family to the municipality for a sum of 135 million old francs (though the family remained closely involved). In a spirit of goodwill the city also paid for the erection of floodlights, first used for a friendly v. the USSR on a foggy night in October 1965. Les Verts put five goals past Lev Yashin, not the sort of gift the famed 'keeper was expecting on his thirty-sixth birthday.

A second major rebuilding programme began after St Etienne's Double triumph in 1968. Both end terraces were covered and, using an identical form of construction – corrugated sheeting over a propped steel frame, the Henri Point Stand (still surviving) was built opposite the main stand (which was then a concrete cantilevered construction whose roof, unusually, had a section scooped away in the centre, as if a giant had taken a bite out of it). The work took a mere six months but, because the stadium is built above old mine

workings, it was necessary to bore 36 metres underground to stabilise the foundations. The stadium could now hold 39,570 fans, and ecstatic fans they were too during St Etienne's record-breaking run of 1967–82, which included two championship hat-tricks (1967–9 and 1974–6), five Cup wins (making four Doubles in eight years!) and a European Cup Final appearance in 1976. And although they added another championship in 1981 and were Cup runners-up in 1981 and 1982, the bubble burst spectacularly in late 1982 after a scandal involving illegal payments to players. By 1984 Les Verts were red-faced, down-hearted members of the Second Division.

Overshadowing this sudden demise was the fact that two years before relegation, practically a whole new stadium went up, in preparation for the 1984 European Championships (even though the stadium at the time, modernised only sixteen years earlier, would have delighted most clubs). The Henri Point Stand, a low, all-seated stand with solid screen ends, was tarted up, but around it were erected three completely new, tall, masterful stands, the work of local architect Jean-Pierre Ganivet. Their height, combined with lightness and colour – achieved by using translucent roof panels and painting all the steelwork green, gave St Etienne's home the unmistakable stamp of a great, custom-built football ground, easily the equal of Dortmund, Lens or Glasgow Rangers.

The three new stands also raised the overall capacity to 48,274 (22,200 seated), a figure subsequently reached only once, during the European Championships, when France played Yugoslavia on 19 June 1984. (The other EC game, Spain v. Romania, five days earlier, attracted only 15,000.) St Etienne's own highest home gate is 47,717, for a Cup tie v. Lille on 11 May 1985 (the same day as the Bradford fire in England).

As at Lens, each stand bears the name of a prominent club man. The main stand's upper section is named after Pierre Faurand, club president from 1952–9. Its main entrance, in green and white with yellow details, is studiously modern if hardly lavish. The south stand – red and yellow seats above a terrace – recalls Jean Snella, who served the club in three spells as player and coach between 1938–67. Behind it are training pitches and a covered ball court.

The identical north stand is named after Charles Paret, a director during Les Verts' purple patch in the 1960s and 1970s. Finally the east or Henri

FRANCE

S.A.M.

Les Verts fill the Henri Point Stand, but the other Greens would look up to the sky in despair.

VILLE DE ST. ETIENNE

The new main entrance (top) and interior, with the ever-present foundry and Casino ads.

Point Stand is dedicated to a senior member of the Casino retail company, who still advertise prominently in the stadium. Thus the old grocery connection persists to this day, as indeed does the belching chimney of the neighbouring foundry, which can still be seen behind the northeast corner floodlight pylon.

St Etienne's environment is not all satanic gloom: much of the city is as green as Les Verts, and across the road from the stadium, next to a high-walled military installation, is a large sports complex including the Henri Lux Athletics Stadium.

But truthfully, one cannot escape the iron and steel clatter which filters into the Geoffroy Guichard Stadium, the very pulse of an industrial city with football stamped on its heart. Whatever else Saint Etienne may have experienced over the past three decades, both highs and lows, theirs is a bright, modern utilitarian stadium whose very design and scale suggests only one thing – business, and football business at that.

LYON

STADE DE GERLAND

Rather like its resident club, **Olympique Lyonnais**, in recent years, the Stade de Gerland was for some time a fine institution badly in need of modernisation. But for the stadium's municipal owners, the problem was how to achieve this while preserving the integrity of what was essentially a grand, but problematic design.

For the Stade de Gerland was the work of one of France's most prominent architects of the early twentieth century, Tony Garnier, and as such had to be adapted with extreme care, however outdated its basic format.

Born in Lyon in 1869, Garnier was a visionary urban planner who dreamt of strictly zoned, reinforced concrete cities without churches, prisons or police stations. Exhibiting his ideas in 1904, in the form of an imaginary Cité Industrielle, he became a leading influence on modern architectural thinking (on Le Corbusier for example), and in 1905 was given a chance to put his views into practice when Lyon's newly elected reformist mayor, Edouard Herriot (later a radical Socialist prime minister), appointed Garnier as city architect. Apart from the stadium, built between 1913–20, he also designed a massive, steel-spanned abattoir (now an exhibition hall), a hospital and the 'Les États-Unis' residential district.

For all his progressivism, Garnier's stadium in the district of Gerland owed a great deal to classical models (as would most stadiums until the 1930s), a sure sign of a man who had spent five years studying in Rome. But the stadium's setting said everything about Garnier's notion of the Industrial City; fenced in and designated as a recreational zone, it was set on flat land, some distance from any neighbouring buildings, with wide streets on all four sides forming a grid. Dominating this plot was a single-tier elongated arena, straight at the sides and with low curved banks at each end. Each side had two modern monumental concrete arches, twice the height of the banking, facing its opposite number across the pitch. The spectator accommodation was concentrated between each arch along the straights of the tracks, for athletics and cycling, while the field was designated for public displays and rallies ('*manifestations populaire*') and rugby rather than football, which was then a minority sport in France. Around the stadium, but still within the perimeter, were other sports facilities – swimming pool, hockey pitches and so on – with a grand entrance flanked, naturally, by two lions.

As an integrated sports complex it was very much the forerunner of similar, though larger German developments of the 1920s, ironically perhaps, since German reparations after 1918 helped complete the Gerland Stadium by 1920. Otherwise the stadium itself provided no cover for spectators and, though aesthetically pleasing, in practical terms it was no more advanced than any of its predecessors such as the White City, London (1908) or the Deutsche Stadium, Berlin (1913).

Gerland played no part in the 1938 World Cup

(despite Lyon's importance as France's second city), and staged little senior football until the formation of Olympique Lyonnais in 1950 (from the bones of a former club, Lyon Olympique Universitaire). In the meantime the cycle track was removed and the end banking raised so that the stadium grew to resemble, in form if not in detail, many a European super-bowl of the 1930s. Two side roofs were built, also. But the greatest changes occurred during the run-up to the European Championships in 1984, when the athletics track was removed and the side stands extended towards the pitch. But how to cover these stands in a modern form without compromising Garnier's arches?

At Berlin's Olympic Stadium the grafting of modern roofs onto the existing base can be said to have failed; at Lyon the operation was a success, though whether Garnier would have concurred is another matter. Suspended from trellis girders, 125 metres long, the new roofs are supported at each end by two vertical columns, rather like a goalpost (as found in Britain at Glasgow Rangers and Aston Villa). At Lyon, however, the vertical supports have been continued upwards to form floodlight columns (as at Norwich and Monza).

Although they do not obscure the arches, the roofs do tend to dwarf them, and yet the dark blue open trellis steelwork seen against the sky does have a certain theatricality of its own. Instead of trying to blend in with the existing structure (as at Berlin), the new roofs at Lyon make their own statement. Both stands are double-deckers, the main side having private boxes slung from the roof.

Garnier's ornate concrete archway frames more modern steelwork.

FRANCE

GROUNDWORK

Lyon's new roofs create a drama of their own in an old theatre.

Rejuvenated Gerland was now able to accommodate 51,680 all-seated and staged two European Championship matches in 1984: Denmark's games v. Yugoslavia and v. Spain. The stadium also staged the 1986 European Cup Winners' Cup Final, Dynamo Kiev v. Atlético Madrid. But it is still not ideal. The open end terraces with their white concrete bench seats are too far from the goal lines, yet there is little scope for further modernisation without completely destroying Garnier's original concept. No doubt in 1920 the Stade de Gerland was highly regarded, but in the 1990s it is an anachronism; too big for a club like Olympique Lyonnais, too unwieldy for modern sports events.

Many of Garnier's ideas from his Cité Industrielle have become common currency in modern urban planning – pedestrianised streets, community centres, multi-level railway stations – but on the evidence of the Stade de Gerland his views on stadium design, we can, and should, consign quite happily to the archives.

STRASBOURG

STADE DE LA MEINAU

Just as one hundred years ago it would have seemed inconceivable that Strasbourg, capital of the much disputed border region of Alsace, should one day house a European parliament, so twenty years ago it would have been unthinkable to stage major international matches at the Stade de la Meinau.

How times have changed.

Michel Hidalgo called Strasbourg's rebuilt stadium 'one of the most beautiful in Europe', but there is more to it than mere good looks. In the same league as Bochum and Utrecht, the new Meinau incorporates virtually all the finest elements of modern football stadium design, even if its resident club, **Racing Club de Strasbourg**, have in recent seasons not always lived up to their slick surroundings.

Laid out originally at the turn of the century on the Jardin Haemmerlé, in the suburb of Meinau, the ground was first used by FC Franconia, and from 1914 by Neudorf, who formed in 1906 and played in a German league until the return of Alsace to French control in 1919. In homage to the Parisian club of the same name, Neudorf then adopted the title Racing Club de Strasbourg.

One wooden stand, erected in 1920, lasted until 1951, only for it to be carted off to the nearby village of Schirmeck, where it is believed still to be in use. Until then Meinau held around 20,000 and was chosen to stage one match in the 1938 World Cup. In an exhausting encounter, Brazil emerged as 6–5 victors over Poland, on a pitch so muddy that the Brazilian Leonidas would have played in stockinged feet had the referee not ordered him to put his boots back on.

Improvements to the pitch, running track and end terraces, plus the erection of a new 2500 seater stand, were completed in 1951 (after Racing's first Cup triumph) and thereby raised the capacity to 30,000. Floodlights were first used for a friendly, v. Kaiserslauten, in April 1959, and in 1970 Racing merged with another local club to form Racing Pierrots Strasbourg-Meinau, a name which not surprisingly failed to catch on and was dropped in 1976.

Planning for Strasbourg's dream stadium could not have begun at a more opportune moment. The municipality decided to go ahead in 1978, and one year later Racing won their first and only championship. Architect François Sauer and engineer André Dahan, employed by the city to oversee the project, set out to remove the athletics track and thus create what they termed a *stade à l'anglaise*, to provide more cover, more seats, and better facilities for the disabled. Not a trace of the old ground was to remain.

The cost of this reconstruction came to 117 million francs over four years, of which more than half came from state and regional funding. Each stand was built in stages, so that Racing's schedule was never disrupted, and official inauguration took place on 17 April 1984, a friendly v. West Germany. Two months later Meinau welcomed near capacity crowds for West Germany v. Portugal and Denmark v. Belgium in the European Championships. The stadium then had provision for 49,982 (13,456 seated), but once the championships were over extra seats were installed on the east terrace to create the current capacity of

La Meinau – one of several reasons why France leads the bidding for the 1998 World Cup.

GROUNDWORK

FRANCE

42,756 (including 16,828 seats and 554 places for the handicapped). Strasbourg has since staged the 1988 European Cup Winners' Cup Final, Mechelen v. Ajax, and in the same year celebrated a visit from the Pope.

Like all practical designs, Meinau's layout is simple. Four identical cantilevered stands are ranged in a slight arc along the touchlines (to aid viewing), with seats at the rear, standing below. Four angled corner sections on the upper level have terracing also, while at the rear of the main, South Stand is a line of private boxes fronted by open balconies, as is the growing trend for such executive installations.

For safety and easy access, a walkway between the perimeter fence and terracing allows full circulation at the front of each stand, plus space for the disabled. Access to the seats is via an all-round first-floor concourse, situated above the ground floor facilities.

These facilities are, in the North Stand, Strasbourg's Centre de Formation, where up to seventeen young footballers can be accommodated, coached and cosseted; in the West Stand, Racing Club's offices, with shrubs and lawns in front providing relief from the concrete facings and tarmac surrounds; and in the East Stand, a restaurant looking out over a tree-lined waterway immediately behind the stadium. This is the Rhin Tortu (the crooked Rhine), leading to the main River Rhine which forms the border with West Germany, a few kilometres eastwards.

Sensitive use of pebble-dash steps and flooring, plus rippled concrete on all facing walls, contrasts neatly with the matt brown of the regularly spaced steel roof supports, while various shades of red, ochre and beige on all barriers, cladding, turnstiles and seats create an understated harmony.

And if the World Cup should return to Strasbourg, as is hoped for 1998, the Brazilians can at least be assured of a firmer footing this time. So can match officials. Meinau's new pitch has, intriguingly, been laid with two narrow tracks of red shale along one half of each touchline, especially for the linesmen. This should cut down on wear of the turf, but in Alsace it is no guarantee against further borderline disputes, at least not when the dreaded offside flag goes up.

GROUNDWORK

As Strasbourg proves, revealing a stadium's structure need not lessen its external impact.

LENS

STADE FÉLIX BOLLAERT

In the heart of the Pas de Calais' mining district, we find that for **Racing Club de Lens**, as for Strasbourg, success on the pitch does not automatically come gift-wrapped with a bright new stadium. Yet, like another former mining stronghold, Gelsenkirchen in West Germany, one also wonders why so little is heard of Lens when it possesses such an admirable stadium.

Formed in 1906, Racing Club's first settled ground, in 1913, was called La Glissoire – the Slide – where the ball had often to be fished out of surrounding marshes and the players bathed in nearby waterpools. But after four years of trench war and heavy shelling – Vimy and Arras are just to the south – the whole of Lens came to resemble La Glissoire. (German prisoners who cleared the ruins were camped where the present stadium stands.)

By 1922 La Glissoire was restored, thanks to 5000 francs' worth of war reparations, but two years later Racing moved into the comparatively luxurious (i.e. mud-free) Municipal Stadium, before turning professional and making the Félix Bollaert Stadium their resting place in June 1934.

Bollaert, a wealthy mine owner who no doubt saw the advantages of channelling his workforce's energies into sport, built this new stadium after seeing another new ground at nearby Bully. In those days 75 per cent of the town worked in the mines, and while this figure has steadily diminished, Racing's recent fortunes have fluctuated wildly, from the limelight of European competition to the depths of the Third Division. Yet despite this, and in a town of only 38,000 inhabitants, a 51,000 capacity stadium of striking proportions has been built. To the outsider it simply does not make sense.

Evidently the Lensoise take their sport very seriously, as other facilities in the area bear out. Also, the stadium was developed with the intention of attracting the 1984 European Championships. Imagine the prestige – a small, depressed mining town staging a major tournament in preference to cities like Bordeaux or Toulouse!

Redevelopment of the formerly elliptical Félix Bollaert Stadium began in 1975 (Racing had just

As at Dortmund and St Etienne, Lens have made tradition a virtue.

reached their second Cup Final) with the construction of a covered terrace immediately behind the west goal. Designed by local architect Martic Mylan, it appears to be a quite conventional structure, albeit of generous proportions with large glass screen ends. But close-to one sees that the roof, supported on three slim pillars, is constructed from blocks of laminated pine, a most unexpected departure from the concrete and steel norm and one which, perhaps because it resembles the interior of a sauna, certainly creates a warmer-than-usual atmosphere. Opened in December 1976, this end of the stadium is named after Henri Trannin, a former director of the club.

When further redevelopment followed in 1983, in preparation for the European Championships, Mylan adopted the same construction methods for the rest of the stadium, resulting in four free-standing but almost identical stands, and a

Laminated pine adds a softer touch to the concrete and steel norm.

FRANCE

GROUNDWORK

The 1934 stand at Lens survives amid its 1984 successor, and both are enhanced.

capacity of 51,000, of which 17,000 are seated. The new Stade Félix Bollaert was inaugurated on 13 June 1984 for the European Championship match between nearby Belgium and Yugoslavia, watched by 45,000, and a second match, West Germany v. Romania, followed four days later.

The east stand, a double-decker with seats on the upper level, is named after Elie Delacourt

(1896–1979), described on a plaque behind the stand simply as a 'supporter'. In one corner is a raised, solid platform for disabled spectators, and in the concourse behind is a detached brick lodge, formerly used as club offices. Exhibition grounds lie beyond.

The north side also has a two-tiered stand. Its lower terrace is dedicated to Anton 'Tony' Marek, a former player whom Lens bought in 1934. The upper seated section is also named after a player, Louis Xercès (1926–80).

Most interesting of all is the main stand, named after Max Lepagnot (1901–82), a mine director and club luminary. Its entranceway resembles that of St Etienne – a glass-fronted block slotted under the sloping upper tier. Yet a few steps into this apparently modern foyer one is faced by warm brickwork, arches, cream cornices and green woodwork; its corridors like cloisters, its vaulted roofs like a church. This is the body of the original 1934 main stand, and how clever, how admirable of the municipality to have taken the trouble to preserve it. A delightful surprise, and full credit is due to the architect for the use, elsewhere in the stadium, of so many different materials to relieve the tedium of bare concrete – red tiles, black rubberised floors, multi-coloured seating, pine roofing and marble plaques.

And all charmingly surrounded by trees.

Well, not all. Underneath the main stand is a tunnel which runs under the Dunkirk-Arras railway line a few metres away, to a training area on the other side of the tracks. From there we see a range of slag heaps, *'triste et noir'*, on the horizon – a reminder of the industry which once gave Lens its wealth and purpose but now lies dormant.

COLOMBES

STADE YVES DU MANOIR

After Antwerp's shoestring efforts in 1920 (see page 69), the French Olympic Committee for 1924 promised an Olympic City on the scale of Versailles, with a 100,000 capacity stadium at its centre. Louis Faure-Dujarric won a competition to design the stadium, but his extravagant classical arena was never built. Postwar Paris could not

justify the expenditure, and in 1922 the city accepted an offer from the amateur sports club **Racing Club de France** for the use and expansion of their 30,000 capacity Yves du Manoir Stadium and its extensive grounds on the former racecourse of Colombes, a municipality just northwest of Paris. (Du Manoir was a member of Racing's rugby team who died in action as a First World War aviator.)

Faure-Dujarric now came up with a somewhat humbler concept which involved raising the stadium's existing terraces and constructing two almost identical stands, the Tribune d'Honneur

GROUNDWORK

Colombes in 1989, with the revamped Tribune d'Honneur on the far side. For forty years this was France's main Cup Final venue.

and the Tribune du Marathon. Together these held 20,000 seats, in a total capacity of 60,000.

Apart from the main Olympic events in 1924, Colombes (as it is usually called), staged ten matches in the football tournament, and after the Games it took over from the Stade Pershing (see page 122) as France's main Cup Final venue, a position it maintained until 1963, apart from five occasions between 1938–44. The record attendance for a Colombes final is 61,722, for Reims v. Racing Club de Paris in 1950 (the latter were the professional football branch of Racing Club de France). For international matches Colombes shared the honours with the Parc des Princes, again until the mid-1960s. Thereafter the old stadium slipped out of the reckoning and almost into terminal decay, until the Tribune d'Honneur was modernised in 1978–9.

Soccer plays only a minor role in its current life. Matra Racing used it for their reserve team matches, while the new all-weather track is well used by the community. But the regular attraction remains, as ever, the rugby games of Racing Club

de France (and even these attract average crowds of only 6000).

The Stade Yves du Manoir is, today, literally a stadium of two halves. Its main entrance is smartly decked in blue and white cladding. Inside, the main Tribune d'Honneur has 10,000 new light blue seats and renovated blue steelwork. All else is in disrepair and has been closed to the public since the Heysel disaster in 1985. The Tribune du Marathon, opposite, is overgrown at the rear, its stained concrete crumbling, its wooden bench seats rotting. Both open end terraces – black shale underfoot and no crush barriers – are similarly forlorn. One end is overlooked by a row of high-rise tower blocks, built on a former Olympic car park. Behind the Tribune d'Honneur is an incongruous Alpine chalet, the stadium's original restaurant.

Yet for all its decay, the old Olympic Stadium still possesses great potential. There are twelve adjacent training pitches and plenty of room for modernisation. In fact, it is said that were Colombes not governed by Communists the stadium might well have been redeveloped as the future Olympic and World Cup centrepiece of Paris.

As it is, politics and stadium construction have always been closely intertwined in France, so the Yves du Manoir seems set for a worthy, but unglamorous future as a community asset which time and fashion has otherwise passed by.

● Also used for the 1924 Olympics, in the Buttes-Chaumont district, was the **Stade Bergeyre**, named after a rugby player who died in the First World War. Owned by one of several now-defunct Paris clubs, Olympique, it staged one Cup Final, CAP v. Le Havre in 1920, but two years after the Olympics

was demolished, forcing Olympique to merge with Red Star (see below).

Three Olympic matches were played at the 25,000 capacity **Stade Pershing**, named after the commander of the American army, which built the stadium as a gift after the First World War. Situated in the Bois de Vincennes, it was opened for the Inter-Allied Games, held between the victorious nations of 1914–18, and apart from hosting five further internationals also staged French Cup Finals between 1921–4. Pershing is now, like Colombes, mainly used as a community sports centre.

PARIS

STADE DE PARIS

Over the years there have been ten professional football clubs in Paris. Recently there has been only two. But some fans would argue that the soul of Parisian football lies not with Paris Saint-Germain or Racing Club in the concrete vaults of the Parc des Princes but in the northern district of St Ouen. There, tucked in amongst the bleak, industrial buildings of the Rue de Dr Bauer, is the small, traditional ground of one of French football's greatest legends, **Red Star**, the third but arguably best-loved club of Paris.

Formed in 1897 by one Jules Rimet and named by the English governess of one of Rimet's associates, Red Star moved to St Ouen in 1910. Built amid allotments and within sight of Montmartre's Sacré-Coeur (before factories blocked the view), the stadium was inaugurated on 23 March 1911 for a friendly international, France v. England. For the next three years St Ouen became France's prime venue, though gates were still no more than 5000 and, hemmed in by gardens and small huts as it was, it remained a modest ground even by the standards of the day. According to Guillaume Hanoteau's stirring history of Red Star (see bibliography), the president of Daring Club, Brussels, was said to have been quite shocked when he visited in 1920. Suitably humbled by his reaction and bolstered by winning the Cup in 1921 and 1922, the club added two new stands and a

running track, unveiled for a match v. Racing Club de France in October 1922. In the presence of Jules Rimet, by then president of the French Football Federation, Red Star also gave their improved ground the lofty title of Le Stade de Paris. Later that season they completed a hat-trick of Cup wins.

St Ouen was one of four Paris stadiums used for the 1924 Olympic football tournament. Two years later when another Olympic venue, the Bergeyre Stadium, was demolished, Olympique de Paris moved to St Ouen to form Red Star Olympique. Since these deadly rivals had opposed each other in the Cup Final only five years earlier the merger was greeted with incredulity on both sides.

After the occupation in June 1940 the stadium was requisitioned for German military vehicles, but it was in use again for the wartime Cup Final in 1941, Bordeaux v. SC Fives.

In 1947 the stadium assumed the dimensions it has now; the track was removed and the existing main stand built. Otherwise Red Star's postwar experiences have been anything but peaceful. In 1946 they merged with another Paris sports club to form Red Star Olympique Audonien. In 1948 and for the next two seasons they merged with ailing club Stade Français, to form Stade-Red Star; in 1950, they dropped out of the League and spent two seasons at the Parc des Princes (Cercle Athlétique de Paris rented St Ouen), before returning to St Ouen as Red Star Olympique Audonien in 1952. They went non-League again in 1960, returned the following year, and in 1967 tried another short-lived merger, with Toulouse FC, now under the original name of Red Star FC.

S.A.M. / JEAN-CLAUDE BUGUIN

Executive box views for council tenants at Red Star's homely St Ouen ground.

Then, despite relegation in 1975, helped by their municipal landlords they built a new 7500 capacity stand fronting the Rue de Dr Bauer, with offices and a social club underneath. It was the brave act of a dying club.

A fatal combination of poor performances, political infighting and bad management saw Red Star decline rapidly, until finally, crippled by debts, they were forced into liquidation in 1978. Thus followed a humiliating drop to the amateur Division d'Honneur's Third Division – from great stadiums to neighbourhood pitches in one fell swoop – while ironically their place in the League was taken by a now-revived Toulouse. The 1978–9 season kicked off at St Ouen in front of just 366 spectators.

But as Red Star fans will tell you – theirs is not just a club, it is a symbol of St Ouen. In the next six years the club fought its way back to the Second Division and, on occasions, suggested that its traditional support could yet outstrip that of the capital's second club, Racing Club (recently known as Matra Racing).

Nowadays the Stade de Paris holds 21,000 and is covered on three sides. Both side stands are dark and basic, in the tradition of old British grounds. But one's eye does not turn to these nor to the newer end stand (which is all-standing and already weathered), but to a curiously triangular, flat-fronted housing block which overshadows the narrow, uncovered popular end. Each window provides a completely unencumbered view of the pitch, and all for a modest council rent. So if and when Red Star shine brightly again in the football firmament, the residents here will no doubt find themselves to be the most popular folk in St Ouen, as well as witnessing one of the great footballing comebacks of all time.

123

FRANCE

PARIS

PARC DES PRINCES

In a city which has long been subject to the architectural whims and conceits of its masters, the Parc des Princes is a prime example of the triumph of politics and sentiment over practical reality. With an all-seated capacity of 49,700, it is too big for club football, yet too small for a World Cup Final (which France wants in 1998). Nor could the stadium ever be suitable for the Olympics, because it has no track, and it is also in a heavily built-up area. Parc des Princes has therefore fallen between not two but three stools. It cannot even cater any longer for the cycling events for which it was once famous.

Otherwise it is, of course, a wonderful stadium.

Before the French Revolution life was much simpler for the Parc des Princes. It was, as its name suggests, a park reserved for the recreation of the royal offspring, part of a wide belt of green which circled the city's defences, *les fortifs*. Looking at a current map of Paris one can still see vestiges of this 'green belt', within which dozens of small stadiums and sports grounds are located.

The Parc des Princes lies in the southwest corner of the ring, between the Bois de Boulogne and Porte de St Cloud.

As a stadium it has had three, distinct lives.

From 1897–1932 it was essentially a velodrome which happened also to stage football. From 1932–67, after having been substantially rebuilt, it was both cycling venue and home to the capital's leading professional football outfit, **Racing Club de Paris**. Finally, since its second reconstruction between 1967–72, it has catered for rugby and football at both club and international level. Yet neither of its current resident football clubs, **Paris Saint-Germain** and **Racing de Paris**, have any links with the stadium's pre-1972 existence, nor indeed with any previous professional clubs.

To explain this unusual state of affairs, our first call is not to the stadium but to the labyrinthine archives of French football.

Racing Club de Paris were Parc des Princes's first and most famous resident club. Formed when professionalism was introduced to French football in 1932, they were a section of Racing Club de France (a long-established sports club, based at

Colombes). Their early years at the stadium were bright: they achieved the Double in 1936 and three further Cup wins between 1939–49. But thereafter Racing declined, were relegated in 1964, then, traumatically, two years later they went out of business. Other former footballing greats like Lille, Toulouse, Marseille and, as we have seen, Red Star (based in the north of Paris) suffered similar fates during this period, although unlike Racing all have since revived.

But Paris is different. In fact, until Paris Saint-Germain's formation in 1973, it had the worst record of any major European capital in the history of postwar club football. Only *one* Paris-based club had ever won a championship – Racing Club in 1936, and in the Cup, none of the capital's several struggling clubs achieved anything of note after 1950, despite Parisian teams having appeared in seventeen of the previous thirty-two finals.

Apart from Racing's early honours, the nearest Parc des Princes came to witnessing real success at club level before 1973 was when Stade de Reims (based 140 kilometres away) staged some of their European games in the stadium between 1955–63, including that historic first European Cup Final in which they lost 4–3 to Real Madrid in front of a sell-out 38,000 crowd. Paris was a most apposite venue for the final, since the competition owed its existence largely to the campaigning of a French sports newspaper, *L'Équipe*. Furthermore, *L'Équipe* was itself heir to an earlier publication, *L'Auto*, one of whose directors, Henri Desgrange, had first been responsible for creating a stadium at the Parc des Princes, in 1897.

From that year until Racing Club's formation in 1932, as has been stated, the stadium was known predominantly as a velodrome, for although it staged its first football international in 1906, v. Belgium, and alternated with Colombes for international duties during the 1930s, it was not until after its reconstruction in 1972 that it became the sole Parisian venue. Parc des Princes also played second fiddle to Colombes during the 1938 World Cup, staging only two games, Switzerland v. Germany and the subsequent replay.

Similarly, the first Cup Final at Parc des Princes was in 1919, but apart from five further finals staged there between 1938–44, Colombes held sway until 1967. This had little to do with the facilities on offer – after modernisation in 1935, Parc des Princes was probably superior in this respect. Nor was Colombes a very convenient

venue to reach by public transport. Colombes'
great advantage was that it was the larger of
the two stadiums, and, having no professional
resident club of its own, it was neutral.

Parc des Princes was, in contrast, closely ident-
ified with Racing Club after 1932, and it was
partly in response to their success, and the need
to provide a respectable finishing post for cycling's
Tour de France, that a major rebuilding programme was initiated in 1934–5.

The two stand entrances were the finest features
of the new Parc des Princes. Obviously influenced
by Jan Wils' Olympic Stadium in Amsterdam (see
page 133), Joseph Haour's exterior combined concrete horizontals with plain brick infilling, curved
bays and protruding concrete awnings. Three
flagpoles closely spaced above a circular 'PP'
emblem provided a focal point over the main
Tribune d'Honneur entrance, while on the stadium's opposite side the Tribune de l'Auto's
entranceway proclaimed in letters, graphic reliefs
and coloured glass that this was a velodrome, first
and foremost.

Indeed, the most remarked upon feature of the
new Parc des Princes was its distinctive pink cycle
track, 454 metres long around a lush green pitch –
these pink and green surfaces giving the stadium
a warm, winning glow.

Otherwise, it was a quite utilitarian, though
neatly balanced stadium, with open concrete terraces at each end, and wooden bench seats in two
long side stands. A tunnel in one corner of the
arena led cyclists onto the stadium track from the
Rue du Vélodrome outside, while behind one goal
a spiral tunnel gave cyclists and footballers an
entry point from an adjacent detached block of
changing rooms. There were 28,000 seats overall
(16,000 covered) in a total capacity of around
45,500, but this was later reduced to a more
comfortable 38,000.

As the years passed, and as cycling became
somewhat less of an attraction (while rugby and
football assumed a greater significance because
Colombes was falling into disrepair), Parc des
Princes found itself out of step with the times, yet
with no public funds in the offing for much-
needed refurbishment.

It was at this point of crisis, just as Racing Club
de Paris were in their final death throes, that fate
stepped in.

In 1965 plans were drawn up for a new Paris
ring road, Le Périphérique. Unfortunately its

The distinctive 1930s frontage of the Parc des Princes survived
barely thirty-five years.

intended route ran parallel to the Avenue du Parc
des Princes and required a two-lane tunnel to be
dug under one side and one corner of the stadium,
with a calculated loss of 17,000 places. So was this
the signal for Parc des Princes to be demolished
and, at last, the capital's long-held dream of an
out-of-town, multi-purpose national stadium to
be realised? Far from it.

The so-called Borotra Law stated that no sports
facility in Paris could be lost through development, even temporarily. If the Highways Department wanted to stick to their route therefore,
they were legally bound to pay a large indemnity
against the rebuilding of the 17,000 places, while
at the same time arranging that work on the tunnel
did not disrupt the use of the rest of the stadium.

But why bother? Instead of meddling piecemeal
with the old structure, here, out of the blue, was
a perfect opportunity to start afresh, to give Paris
the modern sports venue it so patently required.
Needing little persuasion, Paris City Council
grabbed its chance and thus a new Parc des Princes
was conceived. In the summer of 1967 the Tour
de France staged its last emotional finale on the
hallowed track, and then it was 'adieu la piste rose
et la verte pelouse, bienvenu M. Roger Taillibert'.

Roger Taillibert was, at the time, the Paris-
based Chief Architect of Civil Buildings and
National Palaces. He was also about to commence
work on what would be the acclaimed, futuristic
Olympic Stadium for Montreal. His creed was
simple. 'Concrete is the future,' he wrote. 'You
hold it in your hands and give it all the shapes
you want.' With advanced methods of prestress-

FRANCE

SIPA-PRESS

Roger Taillibert's Parc des Princes – a vast temple to the great god concrete in the midst of a dense residential area of Paris. To the left, the Stade Jean Bouin is used mainly for athletics. In the top right Le Périphérique motorway can be seen as it passes under one corner of the stadium. Had it not been for the construction of this road, the original 1930s' stadium design might well have survived. But should the site have been redeveloped at all?

ing, aided by computer-assisted calculations to the minutest degree, his designs promised to do for concrete what Munich's Olympic Stadium, being built at exactly the same time, would do for the concept of tent-roof construction; that is, provide a blueprint for the stadium of the future.

Taillibert's brief was plain enough – a 50,000 capacity, all-seated, all-covered stadium for rugby and football only. Yet it was this, quite short-sighted brief which now, barely twenty years later, puts Paris in the awkward position of having to finance another stadium if bids for the World Cup or Olympics are ever to be successful.

Demolition of the old Parc des Princes and work on the road tunnel took from July 1967 until the spring of 1970. (This caused little disruption to football, however, since the stadium had no resident club at the time.) Then fifty highly soph-isticated, prestressed concrete frames were formed around the original pitch, each one shaped almost like a wishbone and consisting of a curved column and cantilevered roof bracket. The uprights varied in height from 22–31 metres, while the brackets extended in length from 35–45 metres. Thus the roof rises and falls like a wave around its ellipsoid perimeter, but meets at a uniform height around the roof's inner ring, which forms a rectangular opening with rounded corners, corresponding exactly to the shape of the seating tiers below.

Aesthetically pleasing and technically advanced though the roof structure undoubtedly is, what makes Taillibert's design so perfect for spectators is that not only is every one of the 49,700 seats (on two tiers) well protected from the elements, but none is more than 45 metres away from the touchline. The Parc des Princes is, therefore, a quite intimate enclosure, despite its scale.

Furthermore, this was the first stadium in

126

Europe to have its floodlighting integrated into the roof structure, instead of being tacked onto pylons or gantries as an afterthought. Other technical innovations, borrowed from American stadiums and now *de rigueur* in all new European stadiums, included closed-circuit television cameras and computer-controlled lighting and sound systems.

The brave new Parc des Princes reopened its gates for the French Cup Final, Marseille v. Bastia, on 4 June 1972, in the presence of President Pompidou. It had cost the city 80 million francs, but compared with Munich or indeed any of the other West German super-stadiums then being built, this was a surprisingly reasonable sum.

As a national stadium, Parc des Princes has been well used since its reconstruction. At club level, Paris Saint-Germain moved in first, as we have noted, in 1973, although they were actually formed a couple of years earlier as Paris FC, with the intention of filling the gap left by Racing Club's demise. Before they even had any players signed up, Paris FC had 15,000 members, plus sponsorship from local well-wishers and from a municipality understandably anxious to install a successful club in its new showpiece stadium. By merging with an existing local club, Saint-Germain, Paris FC were then able to build a team and, just as importantly, avoid having to start from absolute rock-bottom in their quest for the First Division.

Undoubtedly the gamble worked. While consistently drawing crowds of around 20,000, in their first thirteen years PSG escaped the lower ranks, became the second Paris club to win the championship (in 1986) and also had two Cup triumphs (in 1982 and 1983). Their success no doubt also influenced the formation in 1982 of a second club to use the stadium – Racing de Paris, who from 1987–9 were lavishly, but hardly fruitfully, sponsored by a car company, Matra. (Racing, or Matra Racing as they were also known, had no links whatsoever with the defunct Racing Club de Paris.)

Apart from League matches, Cup Finals, internationals in both rugby and football, and the annual rugby championships, Parc des Princes has played host to European Cup Finals in 1975 and 1981, plus the European Cup Winners' Cup Final in 1978. It also staged three games in the European Championships, including the final, France v. Spain, on 27 June 1984 (even though it was actu-

Having to cater for rugby means the goals seem stranded, but viewing is otherwise superb.

ally the smallest of the seven French venues which were chosen).

One only has to look at the 1988 Olympic Stadium in Seoul to see how Taillibert's design continues to influence stadium architecture. Yet at the same time, as one walks around its now stained and graffiti-daubed concourses, and sees how hemmed in it is by surrounding houses and roads, Parc des Princes appears to be something of a period piece; a vast temple to the great god of concrete, a triumph of structural engineering, but cold to the human touch. It even makes one warm to the more colourful nuances of Post-Modernism, which in Paris never seem far away.

And what of the stadium's future? If, despite having failed to attract the 1996 Olympics, Paris manages to secure the 1998 World Cup, Parc des Princes will still be unable to stage either the tournament's opening ceremony or its final (for which FIFA require a minimum capacity of 80,000). Nor, because of its design and location, can the stadium be expanded.

But if a new stadium is built – probably somewhere in the northern outskirts of Paris – both football and rugby authorities will be under considerable pressure to use it, rather than the Parc des Princes, for their big games (since any new stadium can hardly be expected to survive on athletics alone). This would leave Parc des Princes with only the games of Paris Saint-Germain and Racing – all very well, but hardly befitting the stadium's original intended role.

Thus we say again, Parc des Princes is a wonderful stadium. It just happens to have been built to the wrong specifications, in the wrong place, and at the wrong time.

GROUNDWORK

Antibes, an unlikely World Cup venue, with the seashore and Alps beyond the north goal.

WORLD CUP 1938

OTHER VENUES

Apart from the six French World Cup venues already described, four more grounds were used in 1938.

Of all the grounds ever used in the history of the World Cup, none seems so obscure as Antibes, which staged Sweden's 8–0 rout of Cuba on 12 June 1938. Situated between Monaco and Cannes on the French Riviera, the **Stade du Fort Carré** is a quirky, barely developed ground, home of the minor club FC d'Antibes/Juan les Pins. Dominating the oval arena, opposite the low, basic main stand, is a strange terrace formed of high, stone-faced steps leading up to an imposing First World War memorial, from where the tall statue of a soldier looks down on the pitch like an impassive spectator. Behind him rise up the grassy ramparts of the star-shaped medieval Fort Carré, which guards the small harbour of Antibes below. Behind the north goal lies the Mediterranean shoreline, with the Alps a hazy, jagged edge on the distant horizon. Scenic maybe, but why stage a World Cup match here?

There are two reasons. Firstly, **FC Antibes** were one of the founders of French professional football

in 1932, and were members of the First Division until the Second World War. Secondly, their stadium held, in 1938, 24,000 people, which made it one of the largest in southeast France.

That said, it still seems an unlikely spot.

The home of the once-great club, **Stade de Reims**, staged Hungary's 6–0 win over the Dutch East Indies. Then called **Stade Vélodrome Municipal**, it has since been slightly modernised and renamed the **Stade Auguste Delaunne**. Its current capacity is 25,000.

Czechoslovakia played Holland in Le Havre, at the intriguingly titled **Stade de la Cavée Verte** ('stadium of the grassy sunken lane'!), which is now delapidated and used only by amateurs. **Le Havre AC**, meanwhile, play their matches at the new **Stade Jules Deschaseaux**, a modern, compact 22,000 capacity ground with four individual stands, three with vaulted, cantilevered roofs (like a smaller version of Nantes' old Marcel Saupin stadium).

Finally, Hungary played Switzerland in Lille, at the **Stade Victor Boucquey**. This was home to **Lille OSC**, one of France's top clubs in the decade after 1945, when the stadium was renamed after the club president, Henri Jooris. In 1978 the ground was demolished, and Lille now play in a completely new 25,400 capacity stadium, covered on three sides and called **Stade Grimomprez-Jooris** (Grimomprez being a former champion athlete).

GREECE

ATHENS

OLYMPIAKO STADIO

The new Olympic Stadium in Athens. Cream-coloured plastic has superseded marble.

When the first Olympiad was staged in 776 BC, there was just one sporting event – a sprint down a track measuring 600 feet, a distance known to the Ancient Greeks as a 'stadion'. The name stadion was then applied to the actual race, and finally to the arena in which the race was held.

This first stadium was, of course, in Olympia, which in its prime held 40,000 citizens on slopes overlooking the track, and in a useful life of eleven centuries staged the staggering total of 287 Olympiads, before the Games were finally abolished by decree in AD393.

And here we are in the twentieth century, yet to witness only our twenty-fifth Olympiad!

After Olympia, the next venue to stage the Games was, in 1896, the **Panathenaic Stadium** in Athens – surely the oldest stadium in the world still used for public events. Formed in a ravine, it dates not from 1896 but from 329BC. Around AD130 it was cloaked in shiny white marble, but fell slowly into ruin until it was beautifully restored for the revived Olympics, which began on 25 March 1896 with the running of a 100m sprint, watched by 69,000 ecstatic spectators.

After the Games, the Panathenaic Stadium was swiftly rendered obsolete. Being long and narrow (like Olympia) rather than oval, it could not accommodate a modern athletics track, nor indeed a pitch for the up-and-coming sport of football. But whether as concert venue, training area or tourist attraction, the old stadium retains every ounce of its dignity, as well as demonstrating

how much of modern stadium design has its roots in antiquity.

In 1996 – unless the IOC flout both sentiment and logic when the decision is made in 1990 – the Olympic torch will burn once again in Athens, but this time in the city's new 80 million dollar Olympic Stadium, built between 1980–2 on the cool, northeast plateau of Kalogreza. Greek Prime Minister Constantine Karamanlis had hoped the stadium would become a permanent home for the Games, as Olympia had been. But though disappointed in this respect, even the project's opponents were won over when it was revealed to be one of the finest, most technically advanced stadiums in Europe (and that was certainly never the case with Olympia, at least not once Delphi and the Romans got into the act).

The stadium's official title is OAKA 'Spiros Louis' (Olympic Athletic Centre of Athens – Louis, a Greek athlete, was the first marathon gold medallist, in 1896). It has two tiers, with pale cream plastic seats – not as dazzling as marble

129

GREEK OLYMPIC COMMITTEE

'Peace' reads the pitch, but sadly the new stadium has been plagued by hooliganism.

but kinder on the behind. The upper tier, partly cantilevered over the lower tier, breaks behind each goal to allow for two large video boards.

Leaning over the upper rim are four acutely angled, white floodlight masts, which seem to flout the laws of gravity, while down at ground level the pitch is a neat rectangle in a pool of terra cotta. If any of its sophisticated irrigation systems should fail, a spare pitch is nurtured nearby to provide replacement turf.

Unlike all but four of the previous Olympic stadiums, long before the 1996 Games proper the Athens stadium has been tried and tested upon numerous big occasions.

First came the European Athletics' Championships of 6–12 September 1982 (although the Marathon finale and the closing ceremony were held in the old Panathenaic Stadium). The first football match, Olympiakos v. Öesters Vaxjò in the European Cup, followed on 15 September, watched by a Greek record attendance of 80,000. A similar number attended the European Cup Final (Hamburg v. Juventus) the following year.

Since then the capacity has been slightly reduced to 74,160, while the stadium has become Greece's prime football venue, staging internationals, Cup Finals, the 1987 European Cup Winners' Cup

Final, and the League games of both **Olympiakos** and **Panathinaikos** – the country's two leading clubs (although when gates dropped recently, a subsequent loss of atmosphere persuaded Panathinaikos to revert to their own stadium for less attractive games; see page 132).

Despite its all-seated modernity, its moat and wide perimeter concourse, its own metro station and ample parking, Athens' new Olympic Stadium has not helped solve one of the city's worst social problems, hooliganism, which has plagued Greek football almost since the advent of professionalism in 1979. It became so bad that the authorities even shifted one Olympiakos derby with AEK to the distant island of Rhodes. The clubs have been repeatedly warned that damage inflicted upon the stadium, especially to the seating, will result in a withdrawal of facilities, but with regular gates of over 60,000, there is, in reality, nowhere else for a popular club like Olympiakos to go.

It is also true that few stadiums, least of all a lavishly equipped one such as this, can survive without the regular gate receipts which football provides. Olympia discovered the need for diversification also, which is why there was soon more to the Games than just one race of 600 feet.

PIRAEUS

STADIO KARAISKAKI

Before switching to the Olympic Stadium in 1982, Greece's most popular club, **Olympiakos**, and indeed the national team, played at the Karaiskakis Stadium, almost on the shoreline of Piraeus, the port adjacent to Athens. Named after Georgios Karaiskakis, a hero of the 1821 Greek War of Independence, the stadium was originally a velodrome.

Its present infrastructure – an open rectangle with slightly curved corners, clad in light-blue concrete and from the outside resembling a factory – dates primarily from 1958. But because, unusually, there is an athletics track set within the rectangle (instead of the usual, oval-shaped stands), and because there are long-jump areas and sprint straights on *both* sides of the track (instead of the usual one side), the effect is to make Karaiskakis appear disconcertingly wide, even if the pitch is in fact the standard size.

Perched above and behind the main, north side is a five-storey block housing press facilities and offices, in front of which is a section of white

marble seats for VIPs. A textile factory abuts onto the west end, while to the east are low-rise, modern apartment blocks. But the most arresting view is beyond the south side, where once the sea came within a couple of goalkicks of the stadium, but now has been pushed back to provide a site for the saddleback-shaped Peace and Friendship Stadium, a beautiful indoor venue holding 20,000.

Both this arena and the Karaiskakis Stadium are owned by the Greek Olympic Committee and will be used for the 1996 Games, but in the meantime Karaiskakis is mainly occupied as a community sports centre, and as home to Piraeus's second club, **Ethnikos**. This may seem something of a comedown for a stadium which once held 45,000 and has witnessed many great scenes in Greek football, as well as the European Cup Winners' Cup Final in 1971 – Chelsea v. Real Madrid.

But on 8 February 1981, tragedy struck. At the end of a game v. AEK, fans surged towards an exit in the southeast corner, and twenty-one fans died in the ensuing crush. As a plaque by the fateful gate records, these young *'philathlos'* – friends of sport – were all male and all aged between fourteen and thirty-four. Thereafter the stadium's capacity was cut to 34,300 – half what Olympiakos were subsequently able to attract when they moved, a year later, to the new national stadium.

GROUNDWORK

Once the pride of Piraeus, the Karaiskakis now plays a backstage role in Greek football.

GREECE

ATHENS

NEA FILADELPHIA

AEK's stadium has a special status in the Athenian community of Nea Filadelphia, for it was built and financed by Greek refugees who fled from Ataturk's newly proclaimed Turkish Republic in 1922. They formed AEK – Athletiki Enosis Konstantinopoulos – in 1924, choosing the double-headed eagle of Byzantium as their emblem, and although nowadays their support extends well beyond the locality, rivals still nickname them 'the harem girls'.

Actually the Sultan's concubines enjoyed rather more luxurious surroundings. Opened in 1936, AEK's 34,000 capacity stadium consists of a U-shaped bank of uncovered terraced seating, capped, at the south end, by a narrow, open-topped, double-decker stand, built in 1979. Immediately behind this is the local church – naturally in Byzantine style, while at the opposite end, pressed up against the terracing, is AEK's 3000 seater sports hall.

Apart from two sections of yellow seating on either side, and yellow fencing, the stadium remains a colourless, typically Mediterranean structure of poorly finished, bare, shuttered concrete, with a cinder track and rather too many rough edges.

But none of this shows when a full crowd

Steep terracing, low lights and high-rise surrounds at Panathinaikos.

squeezes in and the stadium comes alive, or even alight, as happened in 1982 when, with seconds remaining of a UEFA Cup tie v. Cologne, the floodlights failed. Anxious to assist, fans lit fires on the terracing, but UEFA saw only the dark side and fined the club. Cologne went on to win the replay 1–0, despite AEK cries of 'Turn off the lights, turn off the lights!'

● Enjoying a new lease of life is **Panathinaikos**'s 26,000 capacity **Stadio Apostolos Nikolaidis**, on Leofros Alexandras, a thoroughfare which runs across the northern edge of central Athens. Named after a club president, it was opened when English residents formed the club in 1908, and is now a typical inner-city venue. Hemmed in by tall blocks and houses, it has surprisingly low floodlight pylons, a small roof propped over the north side (which backs directly onto the main road, opposite the Supreme Court), and two steep, curving ends, both coated in a clay-coloured paint which contrasts warmly with the green railings and pitch.

Eight years after becoming the only Greek team to reach a European final (v. Ajax in the 1971 European Cup), Panathinaikos turned professional and in 1984 joined Olympiakos in the Olympic Stadium. But as gates fell for routine League games in the late 1980s, the old ground – used only for the occasional pop concert in the interim – was dusted down and on 8 January 1989, after a five-year gap, it welcomed an emotional full-house for a 2–0 victory over Levadiakos.

Bedrocks of the community – football and the church at Nea Filadelphia.

GROUNDWORK

HOLLAND

Amsterdam's Oude Stadion – opened 1914, demolished 1928.

AMSTERDAM

OLYMPISCH STADION

In footballing terms, much that is refreshing and innovative has emanated from the Netherlands over the past twenty years. As recent developments at Eindhoven, Utrecht and now Arnhem suggest, the same is true of stadium design.

But the Dutch contribution actually begins over seventy-five years ago. In what was then the southern outskirts of Amsterdam, Holland's first purpose-built stadium was opened on 5 April 1914, with an international v. Germany. Used also by local clubs such as Ajax and Blauw Wit, it was designed by Harry Elte and was essentially a pared down, though still substantial brick-built adaptation of the 1912 Stockholm Olympic Stadium, with a brick tower in each corner, one covered stand, and a capacity of nearly 30,000.

When Amsterdam won the nomination for the 1928 Olympic Games they hoped to use this fortress-like stadium, but it suffered three major drawbacks. It was too small, had no running

133

track, and, most crucially, it stood in the way of Amsterdam's planned suburban development. Thus, after staging its twenty-fifth and last major international on 22 April 1928, v. Denmark, the 'Oude Stadion' (Old Stadium) was relegated during the Games to the role of 'training stadium', and a few months later demolished to make way for apartment blocks (on streets all named after ancient Greeks). It had had just fourteen years of use – the shortest-lived major stadium ever to have been built.

The stadium which took its place was constructed only 300 metres eastwards, on a typically Dutch, boggy site, which needed the addition of 750,000 cubic metres of sand, over 4000 piles, then 10,000 cubic metres of concrete before the first stone could be laid, in May 1927.

The Amsterdam Olympic Stadium had to be different for two reasons. The 1928 Games were to be the first to invite female athletes, and the first to provide for all events to be held within one site – the so-called 'Cité Olympique' which had long been the dream of Baron de Coubertin, instigator of the modern Games in 1896.

In charge of Amsterdam's master plan was Jan Wils, a founder of the noted De Stijl school of Dutch architects. He was to design not only the Olympic structures but also every interior, every fixture and fitting, even the temporary marquees and the Olympic stationery.

Not all went smoothly. There were objections to Wils being chosen without the usual competition. His original cost estimates turned out to be grossly optimistic. There were also arguments over the tendering, followed by strikes among the construction workers (and the Italian World Cup organisers for 1990 thought their problems were so unusual ... !).

But the stadium was ready on time for the eighth Olympiad's opening on 28 July 1928, and the choice of Wils was, at least on aesthetic grounds, fully vindicated.

Two elements of the stadium's design highlight Wils' principal influences. What may be called its cubist composition – asymmetrical, rectangular blocks linked by thin concrete slabs – was consciously borrowed from the work of the American, Frank Lloyd Wright, one of the most inspirational architects of the modern era. But Wils' stadium was also dressed entirely in warm, natural bricks (2 million in all), a choice which ran counter to the growing fashion for bare concrete, steel and

glass, and which was undoubtedly influenced by Wils' mentor, Hendrik Berlage, an Amsterdam architect whose love of brick characterises much of the city's early twentieth-century architecture.

'I could have chosen a glass wall to reveal the structure,' Wils wrote in 1927, 'but it is a mistake to think that if we cover up the old, we can immediately clothe the new in glittering attire.'

In plan, the Olympic Stadium was an almost perfect ellipse (instead of having straight sides like Colombes or Wembley). There were both running and cycling tracks, and each side was covered with iron-framed, half-cantilevered flat roofs. For the Games it would hold 34,155, but by removing wooden benches afterwards this would rise to 41,433. At the back of the north curve was a scoreboard so big that its operation during the Games occupied twenty-five naval recruits.

On the west side, behind which flowed the Stadiongracht canal, the Grand Stand housed the Royal Box, while opposite was the Marathon Stand, facing onto a courtyard dominated by the tall brick, glass and concrete Marathon Tower. While neatly counterbalancing the horizontals of the stadium, the tower's principal purpose was to support the Olympic torch, plus the balconies from where trumpeters announced the arrival of the marathon runners, and the futuristic, angled sounding boards which amplified the loudspeakers.

Nowadays the tower looks like a prop from a 1950s' sci-fi 'B' movie, but in 1928 it was the harbinger of a new age, in which the Olympics, aided by the airwaves and airliners, would bring together the civilised world. It was also the precursor of more advanced towers at the Centenario Stadium, Montevideo (1930), the Comunale Stadium, Florence (1932) and the Olympic Stadium, Helsinki (1938).

Wils' Stadium continued to make history after the Olympics. We talk not of its great games, equestrian events, mass displays, or any of the multifarious events staged before the war. We talk, instead, of floodlighting.

For it was in the Olympic Stadium, Amsterdam that Europe's first permanent floodlights were erected in 1934, a full sixteen years before the rest of Europe started to catch on. In truth, stadium floodlighting was already commonplace in the United States and Latin America (where evening matches were preferred because of the daytime heat); but Amsterdam was not far behind.

Its first floodlit experiment took place on 23 October 1929, as part of an 'Edison Light Week' in the city. In front of a packed crowd, Dutch champions PSV Eindhoven (appropriately the team of the Philips electrical company), played an Amsterdam XI under a welter of lights strung randomly around the perimeter from tram wires. Although extremely bright, the lamps were vulnerable to being struck by the ball, which was itself plain brown leather and thus difficult to distinguish. (The Dutch had obviously not heard of an earlier floodlit match, at Blackburn in 1892, when balls dipped in whitewash were used!)

So successful was the first game that permanent lights were installed in 1934, on four double masts with arched frames at the top, each bearing sixty-four lamps. Looking at these same masts today it is hard to believe they are over fifty-five years old. But then the same could also be said of one of the players who took part in the inaugural game, a nineteen-year-old winger called Stanley Matthews (who helped Stoke beat an Amsterdam XI, 2–1).

The next major development followed a year later in 1935, in direct response to the imminent construction of a larger stadium at Feyenoord, Rotterdam. To meet the challenge, Jan Wils was called in to design extra tiers at both ends of the Olympic Stadium, thereby increasing its capacity to 60,000 (compared with 61,500 at Feyenoord). But Wils was unable to achieve this without diverging from his original style. Instead, he had to rely on unfaced reinforced concrete, glass curtain walling and a purely functional approach. This undoubtedly detracted from the stadium's external appearance, especially as it obscured much of the finely tuned details at each end – small towers, balconies, sunken entrances and projecting courtyards. The heightened tiers also necessitated the raising of each stand roof, in order to give occupants in the corners an unrestricted view of the pitch. (This explains why, when looking at each stand's façade, there is a gap between the brick retaining wall and the roof level.)

However, such was the rivalry between the two cities that Wils had little choice but to make these hasty alterations once Rotterdam made its plans known.

Since then, as the Olympic Stadium's current condition reveals only too starkly, events have firmly shifted in Feyenoord's favour.

One factor has been that apart from internationals and a few Ajax games each season, none

Amsterdam's Olympic Stadium – opened 1928, demolished ?? Note the end terrace extensions.

KLM AEROCARTO

of the stadium's former tenants ever achieved lasting success. Between them, Blauw Wit, De Volewijckers, and DWS (which stands for *Door Wilskracht Sterk* – Strong by Willpower!), only managed three championship wins. In 1972 they merged to form FC Amsterdam, but this proved neither popular nor successful, and in 1983 each club decided to operate separately, as amateurs, from their own grounds dotted around the city.

The Olympic Stadium did host the European Cup Final in 1962 and the European Cup Winners' Cup Final in 1977, and would have staged the 1987 Cup Winners' Cup Final had Ajax not been one of the finalists. Otherwise, there has been no athletics since 1953, no cycling since 1986 and, apart from the World Speedway Championships in 1987, the last major event was Holland's international v. Wales in September 1988, staged in Amsterdam only because Feyenoord was suspended due to crowd trouble.

But the principal reason for the stadium's decline – which has nothing to do with its inherent design – is that Amsterdam Council's fifty-year-old lease of the pitch ran out in 1987 and has not been extended, mainly because the stadium's proximity to Schiphol Airport and the sprouting up of smart residential developments in the vicinity has made it ripe for redevelopment. Poor road access has also been an increasing problem on major match days.

Meanwhile the city has plans to build a 54,500 all-seated stadium near Duivendrecht, in the southeast of Amsterdam. Although this was originally part of a bid for the 1992 Olympics,

HOLLAND

GROUNDWORK

Prewar lights, postwar memorial.

which failed, the intention to build the stadium remains, with Ajax almost certain to move in as permanent tenants.

And so the 1928 Olympic Stadium faces a lingering death. No money will be spent on bringing it back to scratch, while insufficient funds are currently available to build its replacement.

It is a depressing scenario. The paintwork has faded, while the gates are ruined by too much paintwork, in the form of graffiti. The later concrete additions, partially smothered in ivy, are corroded in parts, revealing rusting steel rods underneath; and inside the stadium, apart from yellow crush barriers, a large, flaking yellow scoreboard at one end and weathered maroon seats in the stands, the main splashes of colour are provided by numerous beer advertisements.

And yet, and yet, amid all this sad decay, there is a powerful dignity about the place. The strength and clarity of Wils' design shines through still, the 1934 floodlight masts continue to look modern, while at the back of the south curve stands a tall sculpture of a naked athlete – a memorial to the sportsmen who died in the Second World War. Almost as high up as the top of the Marathon Tower itself, the defiant figure seems to be warning potential developers, 'Hands off!'

But the end cannot be faraway now. There was no hesitating when it came to pulling down the Old Stadium in 1928–9, and there will be no reprieve this time either. Feyenoord Stadium will have prevailed, and the most Amsterdam's architectural buffs can hope for is that, at the very least, the Marathon Tower will be preserved, as a masterful structure in its own right, but also as a reminder of the great stadium it once overlooked.

AMSTERDAM

STADION DE MEER

Once there were four professional clubs in Amsterdam, now there is only one, **Ajax**. And though their modest, suburban stadium is hardly what one would expect of such an internationally renowned club, it is Ajax's record of shrewd management, combined with ownership of this ground, which has been their keystone of prosperity in a city otherwise relatively apathetic towards professional football in the postwar era.

We have all heard of Michels, Kovacs, Cruyff

and the 'total football' with which Ajax dominated Dutch and European football between 1966–74, yet it was an English trainer who helped establish the club in its early days. Jack Reynolds steered Ajax to their first championship in 1918 and was still in charge there when they won five League titles in the nine seasons before the Second World War.

It was this success during the 1930s which led to the construction of Ajax's 24,000 capacity stadium. Designed by a club member, architect Daan Rodenburgh, it consisted of brick-based, open terraces on three sides, and one main stand on the southeast side. Unusually, each side was cranked in three sections, to create better sightlines from the corners.

GROUNDWORK

From the cranked Reynoldstribune looking towards the scoreboard end at Ajax.

The stadium was opened in December 1934 and although officially titled 'Ajaxstadion' it became popularly known as De Meer, because of its location in the southeast district of Watergraafs Meer.

In 1956 a premier division was established for Holland's newly professional clubs, at which point Ajax, the first champions, took the unprecedented step of purchasing the ground from the municipality. Since then, the surprisingly small main stand – still with its propped, wooden-slatted roof – has been refurbished in stages, with the addition of red plastic seats in the centre, executive boxes suspended from the roof, and new offices and a sports medical centre built in a new block behind. The floodlight pylons, added in 1974, are also behind the stand, level with each 18-yard line.

Opposite the main stand is the Reynoldstribune, named after the former trainer, whose association with Ajax lasted fifty years. The word Ajax is picked out in white among the stand's blue and red seats, while the roof, also wooden slatted, was added in 1965.

Both end terraces were covered in 1984 and,

like the Reynoldstribune, are well fenestrated at the rear to allow light to seep into the tree-lined ground. With a dash of hi-tech about them, the terrace roofs have white plastic sheeting on a dark blue framework, glass screen ends and, to link them with both side stands, in each corner there are twee little translucent perspex vaults.

The northwest-end terrace has a rather vulnerable looking electronic scoreboard at the rear, which required the central roof section to be raised a few metres, while the opposite end houses Ajax's notorious F-side supporters. Despite the ground's spotless interior, the back of this terrace resembles a New York subway station. Some of the daubings make crude reference to the club's traditional Jewish support, which caused Ajax to suffer badly during the Nazi occupation but is nowadays an essentially meaningless tag, flaunted by the F-side and taunted by the opposition.

A more surprising feature of De Meer is that on three external corners, tucked into the angles between the stands, are small bungalows. Decked in ivy, with window boxes, and backyards formed by the rear walls of the stands, these curious dwellings house the groundsman, the concierge and one of the club's officials. Quite how their families cope during matches one can only imagine, though the properties are rent free and at least look out onto training pitches on two sides of the ground.

Permanent residents apart, De Meer's current capacity is 27,000, of which 11,000 are seated – plenty of room for normal usage, although small enough for the club still to need the Olympic Stadium for big occasions, and definitely too small for Ajax to earn any non-footballing income during the week. Thus it seems inevitable that in the event of Amsterdam ever building its promised new Olympic Stadium, the club's board will grab the chance of a move. From De Meer to de luxe, Ajax would then, undoubtedly, have *exactly* the kind of stadium one would expect of such an internationally renowned club. But then, in such new surroundings, would it still be the same club?

THE HAGUE

ZUIDERPARKSTADION

Of all the curious facts concerning **Den Haag**'s Zuiderpark – or South Park – Stadium, perhaps the least riveting is that the Rolling Stones once played a concert there.

Much more interesting are these bits of Zuiderpark trivia:

That in the lower central section of the north stand, between two wings of blue seats, is a portion of terracing called the 'Midden Nord' (Middle North). This terrace is unique in European football. Formerly the stand had two conventional tiers, with seats on top and terracing below, but on 1 March 1987, during a game v. Ajax, Den Haag's infamous hooligans started tearing up the terracing and attacking the police, who promptly tried to usher terrified fans out of the ground, only to find the exit gate locked. It was already Holland's worst ever football riot, but it could so easily have become another Heysel or Hillsborough.

That after this riot – in which forty were injured – the Dutch government ordered the north stand to be made all-seated, but Midden Nord regulars threatened the club so violently that the central section of terracing (which menacingly faces the directors' box in the opposite south stand), was, after all, preserved.

That to stand on the Midden Nord one must now have a special pass, and thus to possess such a pass is akin to having a hooligan's medal. Most membership schemes are designed to keep troublemakers out of football grounds; in The Hague it is felt better to have them under surveillance in one part of the stadium rather than keep them out on the streets. The city is, apparently, the most violent in Holland.

That, some two years before the 1987 riot, the Dutch government invested £200,000 on a computerised turnstile-cum-metal detector for the Zuiderpark, in order to test out a supporters' identity card scheme. Using technology developed for the Paris Metro, this turnstile was installed near a gate by the main, south stand. The night before its unveiling, youths broke into the ground, slipped sand into the card-slots, and thus rendered it permanently disabled. It has been hidden under a blue, corrugated hut ever since.

That the adjacent, cantilevered south stand, which has 3100 seats and was built in 1985, replaced a wooden stand dating back to 1927. One night in April 1982, at the end of one of Den Haag's occasional relegation seasons, a group of inebriated supporters set fire to the old stand. Three of them were subsequently caught and gaoled, but for three years Zuiderpark had no main stand, until a new, wealthy (and brave?) chairman came along and financed a replacement. One of the convicted arsonists then demonstrated such remorse that he was later appointed as a security officer for the supporters' club.

That in order to involve the club's more unruly elements, in 1988 an all-day cinema, the Ballenbios, was opened at the Zuiderpark, showing non-stop football matches to the public, free of charge. It was not a great success, since the sponsors failed to realise what sociologists had been saying for years – that few hardened hooligans are actually unemployed and have the time to watch films during the day.

That both end terraces have roofs because the municipality, which owns the stadium, decided in 1977 that building roofs would help save a few jobs in the city, and thus awarded the contract to a construction company which was otherwise in

Queer Street. One of the roofs, at the west end, is low and conventially rectangular, with netting to catch missiles from the crowd. The equally low, east terrace roof is actually curved in a slight arc, and is a classically simple, suspended cantilevered construction. Behind the terrace is a brick-lined slope, into which the roof's A-frame steel supports are embedded, with an additional vertical tie-beam at the back, anchoring the load to the foot of the slope. Not only was this choice of construction cheap – other small clubs please note – but it offers the layman a wonderfully clear lesson in the art of cantilevering.

That although most of the facings of the new stands are painted blue, Den Haag play in yellow and green.

That although it holds only 23,500 (including 11,000 seated), in 1987 the Zuiderpark Stadium staged the Dutch Cup Final. This was because no other stadium, not even the usual venue for the final, Feyenoord, wanted to stage a match which brought together the perpetrators of the March 1987 riot, namely Ajax's F-side and Den Haag's Midden Nord. So the Zuiderpark got the Cup

Den Haag, with the Midden Nord on the right.

Final by default, but with the crowd limited to only 6000.

That if one had no knowledge of these curious affairs, the casual visitor would think the Zuiderpark Stadium to be a quite charming, trim, and welcoming place, surrounded by beautiful parks and in a city known throughout Europe as the home of international justice.

That to judge the Zuiderpark only on the behaviour of a minority of its regulars would be most unjust.

UTRECHT

GALGENWAARD

We cannot be entirely sure of the origin of the name Galgenwaard. It could derive from the medieval term for where a river bends to form an oxbow – 'galghenwert', or, more intriguingly, it could mean 'the place of the gallows'.

We can, however, be absolutely certain that the present-day Galgenwaard, home of **FC Utrecht**, is one of the most innovative of all modern football grounds in Europe. Opened in August 1982, the new Galgenwaard holds 20,000, including 12,000 seats, and is a development of which every small-to-medium sized club should be aware. Already its safety features have attracted visits from European politicians and clubs like Real Madrid and Juventus, and have become standard requirements for all Dutch grounds. The stadium's associated commercial development also represents an inescapable trend for the future.

The first Galgenwaard was very much the shape

of the past. Built as part of a drive to provide employment, and opened in May 1936, it held 22,700 and was essentially a velodrome encircled by a narrow strip of terracing, with one covered stand, seating 1800, on the south side. Apart from two football teams (DOS and Hercules), it was used variously for motor-racing, gymnastics, American football, pageants and religious gatherings, but was always dominated by the wide band of the concrete cycle track, which divided spectators from the pitch. Apart from floodlights added in 1972, and temporary seating installed on the track, it altered little over the years.

One of the first moves which brought about change came in 1970, when three teams merged to form FC Utrecht. They were DOS, who won the 1958 championship, Velox, the Dutch amateur champions, and another local club called Elinkwijk (Hercules had already dropped out of the picture in 1967).

Now that the city had a new team, a new stadium became a priority. But it had to be self-financing, because the municipality had no money to spare, and, just as importantly, it had to be hooligan- and vandal-proof.

HOLLAND

The Galgenwaard before 1981, with cycle track and
original main stand.

Utrecht's hooligan problem was one of the worst in Holland, first erupting as early as 1948. The Hercules' club journal had once bitterly dubbed the ground 'Walgenwaard' – punch-up place, and from the late 1960s until the ground's complete reconstruction, there were regular pitch invasions, bottles thrown at referees and fights on the terracing. At the last match, v. PSV on 20 April 1981, fans pre-empted the work of demolition crews by mangling an entire metal framework of seating.

One of Holland's largest construction companies, Ballast-Nedam (actually a subsidiary of British Aerospace), was given the task of creating a new Galgenwaard and, by complete coincidence, it unveiled its plans for Utrecht in December 1977, only a month after Glasgow Rangers announced a similar revamp of Ibrox Stadium. Like Ibrox, Galgenwaard was to be transformed from an oval-shaped earth bank into a rectangular ground of four individual stands. Behind each stand there were to be retail outlets, offices and small workshops, while in one corner of the new stadium there would be the headquarters of a bank. By attracting substantial commercial investment – regardless of the football pitch in the middle – Ballast-Nedam thus ensured that the whole project would be self-financing.

After research into crowd behaviour, the problem of control and safety was addressed in a number of ways. Terracing was laid at each end, but was confined to the wings, with a funnel-shaped wedge of seating sandwiched in the middle, thus keeping potential hooligans away from the goal area. To keep fans off the pitch, the front rows of each stand were raised a couple of metres above pitch level, with steps along the front leading down to a sunken gangway surrounding the perimeter. This avoided the need for intrusive security fencing, facilitated quick and simple evacuation, and allowed the stands to be as close as possible to the touchlines (thus providing, as one publicity brochure put it, *'une ambiance toute britannique'*).

Work began on the site in May 1981 (on Galgenwaard's forty-fifth anniversary), while FC Utrecht decamped to a temporary 9000 capacity ground 3 kilometres north. Ironically the team then enjoyed its best season for years, reaching the final of the Dutch Cup. But the new stadium was ready for the following season, the temporary ground was dismantled, and FC Utrecht returned on 18 August 1982 amid ripples of interest from all over Europe.

Rather like a smaller version of Dortmund, the new Galgenwaard is architecturally quite unexciting, though eminently practical. The stands are conventional, single-tier cantilevers with blue facings, translucent plastic screen ends, and, it must be noted, plenty of leg room in front of each red and blue seat. Rather than being confined to a corner or behind fences, the disabled have access, via special lifts, to well located viewing platforms, while for women there is, at last, decent toilet provision. Even the terracing has been laid with slightly rounded-off edges to avoid chipping.

In the corners, whereas similar layouts at Dortmund and Ibrox have open spaces, the gaps between Galgenwaard's four separate stands are occupied by L-shaped, beige and brown, three-storey office blocks, whose rear windows look out both over the pitch and down onto small courtyards, filled with trees, bushes, shrubs, paving, the odd bicycle, and, we must not forget, the floodlight masts. A little incongruous, perhaps, but then a touch of the unexpected seldom goes amiss at a football ground.

Access is through fifteen gates set in the corner blocks and between the rows of shops and offices, which themselves occupy 30,000 sq. metres of space on three sides of the stadium. FC Utrecht's offices and club rooms take up the fourth, south side of the block.

The surrounding car parks and approaches are, as you would expect in Holland, tastefully landscaped. And if one passes by Galgenwaard on the street, the stands are so well masked by the

HOLLAND

KLM AEROCARTO

The new Galgenwaard – likely to become one of the most influential developments in Europe.

surrounding buildings that if it were not for the floodlights, the central purpose of the development might easily remain a mystery.

Altogether the Galgenwaard is a shrewd and stunningly simple design which, though a little lacking in colour, fully vindicates the efforts and research carried out by Ballast-Nedam. Indeed since its completion, at a cost of £17 million (of which only £4 million was for the actual stadium), the company has been commissioned by around twenty-five other Dutch clubs to rebuild stands (including Den Haag, Gronigen, MVV, Haarlem, and Sparta), while building entirely new stadiums in Saudi Arabia and the Far East. Further commissions in England and Spain are also envisaged. Thus the company promises to be in the forefront of European football ground design for at least the generation to come.

Wonderful for Ballast-Nedam's coffers, no doubt, but after years of hooligans setting the agenda in Holland, a welcome development for the game also.

ROTTERDAM

FEYENOORD STADION

It was 1931, and Feijenoord FC (now **Feyenoord**) – well-supported, successful on the pitch – were dreaming of a new stadium, as different from their small ground on Kromhoutstraat as a palace from a shed. Yet surely their dream was a fantasy. Formed in 1908 as a working-class club (unlike neighbours Sparta), many of Feijenoord's 600 members were unemployed, depression had plunged Holland into a crisis and the City of Rotterdam was itself in no position to help. The district of Feijenoord was no paradise either. Having grown around the south bank of the Nieuwe Maas River in the late nineteenth century, it was a drab and unpopular place to live.

HOLLAND

KLM AEROCARTO

De Kuip – Rotterdam's answer to Jan Wils. But the roof has never been extended and 'temporary' track-side seats are still in use, unlike the adjacent docks (top).

But Feijenoord's president, Leen van Zanvliet, was not to be deterred. If Amsterdam could have a famous stadium, so could Rotterdam. In fact he first approached Jan Wils, designer of the Olympic Stadium, but a combination of local chauvinism and criticism of Wils' work led to the hiring instead of two Rotterdam architects, Johannes Brinkman and Leendert van der Vlugt. This pair had just completed the much admired Van Nelle tobacco factory (next to Sparta's stadium), regarded as one of the most important modern industrial buildings of this century.

Armed with a petition from local businessmen, van Zanvliet procured his building permission, then, with a wealthy merchant, D.G. van Beuningen, tried to find others willing to guarantee a sale of shares in the new stadium. Bronze busts of these determined men now stand in the main foyer, but in 1932 they were not smiling. The share issue was so badly subscribed that the guarantors had to take up 85 per cent themselves. Even the

contractor, J.P. van Eesteren, and both architects, were asked to accept payment partly in the form of shares.

Against all the odds, the first pile of Feijenoord's dream stadium was sunk in July 1935, by the club's legendary player, Puck van Heel, in the midst of a vast expanse of flatland, next to the thriving (but now disused) Varkenoord shipyards.

As the stadium's steel framework arose from the earth, it was soon hailed as a dynamic example of the fashionable 'functionalist' style, which took its inspiration from the Eiffel Tower and dictated that all structural elements be allowed to stand unencumbered by superfluous decoration. Function was everything; technology had triumphed over art.

Of course a lack of funds made such an approach attractive – steel then was cheaper than concrete, which had been more widely used at the earlier 'functionalist' Stadio Comunale, Florence, designed by Nervi in 1930–2 (see page 36). But it was also likely that Feijenoord intended their stadium to look as different as possible from its Olympic rival in Amsterdam. (In fact the two stadiums neatly illustrate the rivalry of that period between Rotterdam's more progressive school of architects and the softer, more plastic work favoured in Amsterdam; Feijenoord's brutal steel v. Amsterdam's cubist brickwork. The difference was perhaps best summed up by the German architect Erich Mendelsohn, when in 1921 he described the City of Rotterdam as being 'analytical ...with deadly frost in its veins', whereas 'visionary Amsterdam' was 'devoured by the flames of its own dynamism'.)

Although a low-cost structure, the new Rotterdam stadium had one major innovative feature. After visiting Arsenal's Highbury Stadium in 1932, Feijenoord's directors opted for a double-decker arrangement of the tiers, but without interior support columns. This, unusually for 1937, was achieved all round the bowl.

Added to the fact that the west side was covered by a thin, cantilevered roof, we had here, in 1937, the model for several of the major stadiums built two decades later – Nou Camp in Barcelona being a prime example.

The 61,500 capacity Feijenoord Stadium opened with great ceremony on 27 March 1937. A team of runners carried a club pennant from the old ground to the new, where 38,000 people – Holland's largest recorded football crowd at the time – were waiting for the Queen's Chamberlain to cut the ribbon. Then Rotterdam's mayor kicked off (nearly knocking a Feijenoord player over in the process) and the home club went on to beat Beerschot of Antwerp, 5–2.

Since then the stadium has received many architectural accolades, but has barely been altered. Some would say this is preservation of a great building, others would call it neglect. The roof, for example, despite Holland's unfavourable climate, has never been extended, because of the expense.

Otherwise, floodlights were added in 1957, Feijenoord became Feyenoord in the early 1970s (to ease the spelling for foreigners), and the capacity has been slightly reduced to 58,000, after a limitation of the terracing behind each goal to just 4000 places.

Otherwise 'De Kuip' (The Tub), as the fans call it, is, almost eerily, little changed from the sparse simplicity of 1937. Even the 'temporary' seats, on what was intended as the running track, still

Built half a century before hi-tech, Feyenoord Stadium leaves its steel skeleton on view. But such raw functionalism found no takers among stadium architects.

remain, brown and discoloured. Fences behind each goal are tall and ugly (as indeed are some of the fans whose behaviour prompted their installation). Where decoration does intrude upon the technology, it is almost clinical – coloured glass and relief-work in the reception area, a gawky sculpture of a footballer by the restaurant. There is the look of a temporary exhibition which someone forgot to dismantle.

Art has had its triumphs though, from the 'total football' of Feyenoord, Ajax and Holland, to the visits of Bob Dylan and the Rolling Stones, all during the 1970s, and Michael Jackson, U2 and Madonna during the 1980s. Billy Graham has preached here, and in 1947 the stadium was the stage for a remarkable performance entitled 'Recapture of the Waterway', in which a wartime drama was enacted by 5000 players.

In one respect the functionalists were entirely successful. Feyenoord did supersede Amsterdam's Olympic Stadium as Dutch football's prime venue for internationals and Cup Finals. The stadium has also played host to six European finals: the European Cup in 1972 and 1982, and the Cup Winners' Cup in 1963, 1968, 1974 and 1985, a record bettered only by the Heysel Stadium.

De Kuip also paved the way, technically, for much of the stadium developments of the 1950s, even if, it has to be said, no-one ever copied the raw steel structural approach. The stadium remains, therefore, a period piece, a prototype, and as the architects intended, it functions. No more, no less.

SPARTA

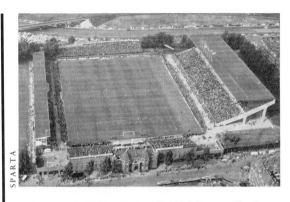

Sparta's Castle. The wide touchline (right) was to allow for rebuilding the main stand (left).

ROTTERDAM

HET KASSEL

Het Kassel – The Castle – is the delightful home of **Sparta Rotterdam**, Holland's oldest professional outfit. Formed in 1888 as a cricket and football club on an island in the Nieuwe Maas River, Sparta were the first Dutch team to use goal nets, in 1894, after a visit to England, and also, uniquely, they have used the same design for their match posters since 1906.

After four championship wins before the First World War, the club moved to the Spangen district, northwest of the river, in 1916. There they built a clubhouse in the form of a castle, to commemorate a fourteenth century moated castle, Slot van Spangen, which once stood nearby (rather

Mysterious monkeys above the door.

GROUNDWORK

as in 1905 the London club, Fulham, named their ground and built a pavilion in memory of an older building, the Craven Cottage).

Het Kassel, which holds 26,000 (15,000 seated), differs on all four sides. The 1916 clubhouse itself has been lovingly restored, although the upper level, formerly a grand balcony immediately behind the goal, was altered in 1988 to accommodate glass-fronted executive boxes. This ruined the fortress-like aspect which once faced the pitch – the street façade is mercifully unaltered – but at least the tall arched windows of the lower storey, overlooking a paved courtyard where the players enter the pitch, were preserved.

A touch more spartan is the original main stand, faced in red and grey. Yet even this humble wooden structure has a hint of self-importance, achieved by the simple extension of the roof in the centre and the provision of a podium for the directors, above a bay-windowed refreshment bar. Behind the stand is Sparta's training pitch.

Opposite is the disproportionately massive 10,000-seater Schietribune, named after the river which flows behind. A tall, two-tiered stand built in 1963, it offers a splendid view of the docks and a nearby space-age windmill, but its drab, concrete interior and rectangular structure is in stark contrast to the warm bricks and fanciful octagonal turrets of the Castle.

In one corner of the stadium, between the Schietribune and the Castle, is a childrens' playground, where no doubt young Spartans are toughened up.

Finally, opposite the Castle is the Boystribune, an open terrace lined at the rear by a blue and white striped fence (though Sparta's colours are red, white and black). Behind, across a main road and railway line, is the steely outline of the Van Nelle tobacco factory (built 1926–30), whose design so impressed Feyenoord's directors that they hired its two architects for their new stadium.

The floodlights date from August 1973 (inaugurated with a match v. Barcelona) but they were nearly extinguished only four years later when it was rumoured that Sparta would have to vacate Het Kassel to share with Rotterdam's third senior club, Excelsior (another uncanny parallel with Fulham). Indeed the ground's future hung in the balance until June 1987, when the City of Rotterdam, which owns the ground, finally opted not to redevelop the site for housing and instead gave Sparta a lease until 2010 (with the club paying 5 per cent of gate receipts as rent).

Before we leave this homely club, a quick glance back at Het Kassel reveals a mystery; two stone monkeys, footballs at the ready, flank either side of the Castle's main doorway. No-one knows why they are there or what their significance may be. This matters little, of course. They guard a century of tradition, and that is explanation enough.

EINDHOVEN

PHILIPS STADION

Of Eindhoven's 200,000 inhabitants, 35,000 work for the Philips electrical company and 17,000 hold season tickets for **PSV Eindhoven**. If ever there was a company town, it is Eindhoven. If ever there was a works team, it is PSV, the richest club in Holland, and in recent years by far the most successful – four of the club's eleven championships overall being won consecutively between 1986 and 1989. PSV (Philips Sport Vereniging, or Sport Club) have brought fame to a town which is otherwise quite anonymous, and glory to an electrical company which would otherwise be known only for . . .well, electricals.

But beware! PSV should never be referred to as plain 'Eindhoven', since the town has a second club, actually called plain 'Eindhoven', which plays at the leafy, barely developed Alsterweg ground, south of the centre.

PSV Eindhoven, on the other hand, could hardly have a more central location. Turn right out of the station, through an archetypical modern shopping precinct, past Emmasingel (the street in which Philips started making light bulbs in 1891), and a few hundred metres on, between the current Philips factory and the main railway line, you will find the Philips Stadium. The floodlights (supplied by Philips, naturally) are clearly visible in case you get lost.

Formed in August 1913 in the bosom of the electrical factory, PSV have played at the ground since their early days, but it was not until 1977 that the stadium really developed. PSV had just won two championships in succession, plus the Dutch Cup, and were about to gain their first major European honour, the UEFA Cup, in 1978. So where open terraces had stood before, three sides of the ground were quickly covered with identical low, grey cantilevered roofs. The railway side, to the north, remained as terracing, but both ends had green bench seats installed. In place of the small old main stand arose an unusual, reinforced concrete cantilevered stand. Holding 10,000 seats on two tiers, it appeared to sit inside a concrete cradle, like the side of a wide-bodied ship in dry dock. To accentuate its curving underbelly, especially when seen from the street, between each beam of the 'cradle', the surface was painted in long red and white stripes, which made it resemble a very wide deck chair.

Another unusual, even unique aspect of this stand was that a month before the builder's ten-year guarantee was due to expire, defects were found in the structure. Water and chemical corrosion was blamed, but since Philips' own building office had been responsible for its design in 1977, and it was insured, and – this is only a wicked rumour, of course – the club wanted a more modern stand anyway, after winning the European Cup in the summer of 1988 a new roof and upper tier were built in double-quick time, after a spectacular operation to dismantle the concrete 'cradle', piece by piece. At the same time the floodlights were upgraded to 1500 lux using an advanced Philips system called Arena Vision.

The new stand was opened v. AC Milan on 17 August 1988, and raised the capacity from 27,000 to 28,000 (of which 16,000 are seated). But more

PSV's shortlived 'deckchair' main stand, before demolition in 1988.

145

PHILIPS LIGHTING BV

A giant new stand and a new lighting system make for an electric atmosphere at the Philips Stadion.

importantly it added a whole new dimension to PSV's extra-footballing activities.

A modern white façade, interestingly composed of red, hi-tech steelwork and extensive two-tone glass curtain walling, fronts a six-storey complex which houses all the club offices, players' facilities and so on, but just as importantly in this day and age, there are spacious meeting rooms, restaurants and bars, all designed to attract income other than on match days.

From inside the stadium the new stand is over-powering and spectacular. There are two tiers, as before, each holding 5000 seats, but with two floors of glass-fronted executive accommodation in between. These seat 200 in individual boxes on the lower floor, and 850 above, in an open lounge with airline-type seating arranged in five rows, plus various catering facilities behind (very similar, in fact, to the lounges at Anderlecht).

But it is the new stand's roof which really dominates, hovering above the seats like the roof of an aircraft hangar, but fully enclosed at the sides by deep vertical glass screens linking up to the much lower roofs of both end stands. The enormous, slightly inclined roof surface itself is panelled also, looking like the cover of a record deck (Philips, of course), waiting to be flipped open.

The rest of the stadium has more modest accommodation, but PSV have certainly not forgotten their ordinary supporters.

All three remaining roofs are kitted out, seemingly, with as much gadgetry as the Aztec Stadium – loudspeakers, lighting and, on all three roof fronts, electronic information boards (supplied by you-know-who). And just in case one forgets 'who', there are advertisements for CDs, hi-fi's and videos for those in Eindhoven who have yet to get the message.

But there is one product positioned at regular intervals underneath the terrace roofing which is definitely not from the Philips range.

Unbelievably, these are gas heaters, which cast a warm glow over the faithful when the temperatures drop in winter. These heaters, and a lone sculpture in a garden area behind the west end stand – depicting a giant protecting his children – tell us that the team, its supporters and its stadium, are all in safe, secure hands ... (cue slushy music ...).

ARNHEM

EURODROME

If you thought Utrecht and Eindhoven were pretty smart, wait till you see what the small Dutch city of Arnhem has up its sleeve. Expected to open in mid-1991, the Arnhem Eurodrome is going to shatter all our preconceived ideas about what a stadium could and should be. The least part of it is that the 26,000 capacity, all-seated Eurodrome will play host to the matches of **Vitesse** football club.

But look at these other planned features:

● The Eurodrome will have two sliding roofs which will cover the entire playing area in a matter of minutes. This is no dream; the Eurodrome designers, Open Air Industriebau of Frie-drichshafen, West Germany, have already con-structed one such roof system for an ice stadium in Bavaria.

● Incorporated within the stands will be a retract-able stage, and sections of seating which can be moved around on hydraulic lifts, to suit the needs of more compact activities such as theatre, tennis or boxing. This is no dream; the technology already exists in the USA, for example, at the Houston Astrodome.

● To preserve the grass pitch during concerts and other events, the Eurodrome will have a false floor, half a metre above the turf. To support this, 120 hydraulically lifted columns are to be sunk into the subsoil at regular intervals, and topped by grass so that ordinary play will not be affected. These grass tops will be removable so that the supports can be raised and boards then placed across them to form a secondary floor. Using undersoil irrigation and ultra-violet lighting under the boards, the Open Air company reckon they can cover the pitch for two weeks, say, for an exhibition, without damaging the grass.

The Eurodrome is expected to cost in the region of £35–40 million, but much of its financing has already been raised. The architect, Joseph Wund, has invested heavily in the project, while subsidies

A model of the Eurodrome shows how a moveable stage can be incorporated into one stand. The two end roofs slide over each stand to meet in the middle.

from the Dutch government, the local province of Gelderland and the Arnhem municipality are also anticipated. With respect to Vitesse, it is the non-footballing potential which is most likely to inter-est investors. For example, an American pro-motions company, Leisure Management International, which already manages several sta-diums in the USA, are preparing a whole series of events at the Eurodrome. It could be Michael Jackson, it could be ballet, or even, heaven forbid, a Eurovision Song Contest.

Arnhem will not, however, be the only Super-drome in Europe. Antwerp are negotiating for one to replace the decrepit Bosuil Stadium. Others may follow at Nice, Cologne (a smaller version, not intended to replace the existing stadium), and possibly South London. Real Madrid are also said to be interested in Open Air's sliding roof for their revamped Bernabeu Stadium. Naturally each installation will be bristling with executive boxes, Business-Class seats and VIP facilities.

None of this is a dream. It is the future, and even if not all of it works – the false floor being perhaps the most unpredictable part of the package – the Eurodrome will catch on. From 'total football' to the 'total stadium'. And who knows, one day someone might even invent some half-decent half-time refreshments to serve to the ordinary fans. But no . . . that really is a dream.

HUNGARY

BUDAPEST

NÉPSTADION

Although the famous Hungarian national team of the 1950s took the football world by storm, playing thirty-four matches in succession without defeat, up to that time their national stadium was relatively archaic. Called the Millenáris Stadium, it was opened in 1886 as part of the celebrations for the country's millennium.

In common with several Central European countries, plans for a more substantial national stadium were drawn up in the 1930s (using a site

Socialist-Realism anticipates Post Modernism at the Népstadion's main entrance.

GROUNDWORK

in the Buda Hills) but shelved when war erupted in 1939. Under occupation by the Nazis, Budapest suffered appalling damage in the liberation battle of 1944–5 and thus the rebuilding of homes and factories should have taken precedence. However, public demand for a new national stadium gained strength with Hungary's unexpected success at the London Olympics of 1948.

The site finally chosen was just 500 metres from the original Millenáris Stadium (which is still used today), on the flat Pest side of the city, and work began in 1950. Architect Károly Dávid, who worked on other East European stadiums, drew up the plans, but the real credit belongs, as the stadium's name suggests, to the Nép, the people.

Fired with extra enthusiasm after Hungary won the gold medal for football at the Helsinki Olympics in 1952, some 10,000 workers were said to have given their labour 'voluntarily' during the three-year construction period. If not all were true volunteers, the prospect of toiling alongside Olympic medallists and the likes of Puskás, Kocsis and Hidegkúti must have inspired a great many. Certainly the historic link between the Népstadion's construction and the mingled sweat of both ordinary workers and legendary sporting figures remains potent to this day. Imagine, sitting on the very patch of concrete that Puskás laid!

The opening of the stadium on 20 August 1953 typified the community effort. Steeplechase runner Ladislav Yesensky built the obstacles one day, then raced over them the next. Immediately after the inaugural athletics meeting, the first football match to be played at the stadium was held, between Hungary and Moscow Torpedo.

With an all-seated capacity of 100,000 and a dramatic, sweeping upper deck of uncovered seats raised above the west side, the Népstadion was

WELCOMEPRESS

No shortage of toilet paper or Western adverts in post-*glasnost* Hungary.

certainly the most interesting and the most advanced of the 1950s Socialist super-bowls. Large display scoreboards, developed by Hungarian technicians, were installed in 1962, and floodlights were added in 1977, but the original plan to continue the upper level all around the stadium was never realised and the vast majority of spectators still remain without a roof over their heads. Safety considerations have also dictated a reduction of capacity to 72,000.

Nevertheless, the Népstadion has served the people well. All major '*foci*' internationals and Cup Finals are played here (*foci*, pronounced fozti, is the familiar term for football). The European Athletics Championships were staged here in 1966, and concerts by Louis Armstrong (in 1963) and Queen (1986) have filled the stadium to capacity. Basketball also drew large crowds in the early 1960s.

Nowadays, although the Népstadion has not kept pace with modern developments, its heroic scale is perfectly preserved. A monumental entrance block is pierced with an arched inset flanked by two white columns which support a white lintel bearing the Olympic motto. This block is, floodlights apart, the tallest structure on

the stadium's east side. Behind here in a formal garden are pine trees, one for each Hungarian Olympic medallist, leading out onto a wide, open 600-metre track lined on each side by sculptures depicting sportsmen and women, soldiers and workers, in the Socialist-Realist style which dates from the Stalin era and is so common in Eastern bloc countries. Current Budapest opinion is divided as to whether such sculptures should remain. Are they art or propaganda?

At the end of this heroic park stands a 16,000 capacity sports hall. We return, however, to the stadium's main entrance, pass through the marble hall and out into the arena. All around are concrete bench seats, while VIPs of course sit in the central main stand, where press and broadcasting booths are also located. Directly opposite the main stand, on the west side, is a small section for top Party functionaries, with its own underground access road allowing the curtained limousines to slip discreetly in and out of the stadium.

Breaking up the pure ellipse above the west side is a raised level of seating which curves around and finishes at an angle roughly level with the furthest corner flags. The floodlights are each mounted on four concrete legs and lean pre-

149

cariously over the seating, like cats on the prowl.

Due to Hungary's mixed economy, the Népstadion, unlike most in the Communist bloc, is considerably lightened by advertising hoardings. Surrounding buildings also add interest; to the north, for example, is the blue ceramic-tiled cupola of the Geological Institute, a typical example of Hungarian *Jugendstil* (Art Nouveau).

The Népstadion is representative too of its own era, a period when Hungary, having been pummelled by the Nazis, then overwhelmed by the Soviets, won a few victories of its own, on the football pitch and on the athletics track. The Népstadion was and remains thus, a potent symbol of national resurgence, paid for by the government, but built by the people."

BUDAPEST

ÜLLŐI ÚT

Should you be travelling from Budapest's Ferihegy airport towards the city centre, you cannot fail to see the stadium of Hungary's most popular club, **Ferencváros Torna Club**, or FTC. Indeed from the raised section of the highway, Üllői út, which runs within a whisker of the north side of the ground, one gains an excellent overview of this modern, though completely open stadium with its distinctive white, leaning floodlight masts. But don't slow down too much as you pass. There has already been one accident caused by an over-inquisitive driver.

His interest was understandable though. Since their formation in 1899 FTC have collected more honours than any other Hungarian club, and are the only ones to have won a major European title, the Fairs' Cup in 1965.

FTC first played at the ground in February 1911, at a time when, in honour of the ruling Austro-Hungarian Emperor, Franz Josef, the surrounding, mainly German-speaking area was called Franzenvorstadt, since translated into its Magyar form, Ferencváros. FTC are, in fact, most commonly known as Fradi, a diminutive of Franzenvorstadt, and are still tainted in some circles by their German connection.

Üllői út in its early days was a very atmospheric ground, with a cinder running track, a clubhouse in one corner and a main stand – Tribune A – which dated from 1911 and might have come straight from England.

In 1924 a rather grand, two-tiered wooden stand – Tribune B – went up on the opposite side, while to the west, at the so-called Town End, two angled covers, with a small gap in the centre, were

built over the terraces. The opposite, open end was looked down upon by a statue of a naked athlete, above a plinth commemorating the club's founder, Dr Ferenc Springer. This statue and plinth is all that remains of the old stadium.

Üllői út soon became a regular international football venue, and on 4 May 1947 was the scene of a match v. Austria to celebrate the first meeting of the two nations, fifty years earlier. Although only 37,200 tickets had been sold for the game and the ground held 38,600, poor crowd control and the issue of forged tickets – a familiar story – resulted in mayhem. With twelve minutes played and Hungary already 2–0 up, barriers in Tribune B collapsed under the weight of numbers. But in the second half worse was to follow. Elsewhere in the stadium, wooden terracing gave way, sending spectators tumbling several metres to the ground below.

'We all fell as one,' remembered one supporter. Bloodied and bewildered fans were hauled out from the twisted wreckage and ferried to local hospitals, and although the game went on – as had happened at even deadlier occurrences at Ibrox, Glasgow (1902) and Bolton (1946) – both sets of players were in a state of considerable shock. Some were crying, and one admitted afterwards, 'I was quite beside myself. I didn't know what I was doing on the pitch.'

Miraculously no-one died, but one young man was crippled for life and was subsequently employed and accommodated by Fradi for twenty-five years after the accident.

Üllői út was immediately closed by the authorities, and FTC, in the course of their own enquiry, traced the forged tickets back to an experienced criminal operating from a coffee house. But they also had to accept that the stands and wooden terracing had not been properly maintained and that stewards had not torn off

HUNGARY

WELCOMEPRESS

GROUNDWORK

The new Üllői út could hardly be more different from the old,
and yet as the prominent position of the Springer memorial (right) suggests, the past is never forgotten.
Note the electronic scoreboard behind the terrace (left).
Hungary has been exporting stadium information boards all over Europe since the 1950s.

ticket stubs, thus allowing tickets to be passed to others still queueing outside.

Apart from repairing their ground, like many Central European clubs with a strong prewar tradition, during the early postwar period Ferencváros had to bend to the will of their Communist masters. For one short spell they were made subordinate to the army club, Honvéd (see page 153). In 1950 they became ÉDOSZ, and from 1951 until the October 1956 Hungarian uprising they were known as Kinizsi. But when football resumed a few months later, FTC had regained their former identity, even if they failed to match their pre-1956 form until the 1980s.

In 1969 Üllői út was closed for rebuilding, FTC took refuge at the Népstadion, and only on 19 May 1974 were they able to return, for an inaugural match against their Budapest neighbours, Vasas (who spoiled the party by winning 1–0).

The new Üllői út was completely different from its predecessor; an orderly rectangle of concrete, uncovered stands, with a section cut away behind the east goal (rather like Sparta Rotterdam) to accommodate a modern clubhouse. This has a seated area on its roof and looks out over the Springer memorial, which the players pass by en route from the clubhouse changing rooms.

Although unquestionably sparse, almost to the point of being spartan, Üllői út is certainly a much safer ground which might easily be improved further if funds become available. From a capacity before 1969 of nearly 40,000, it can now accommodate 27,136, 10,000 of which are on bench seats. The minimal colour is provided by pale green facings, which make the white clubhouse and twin-mast floodlights, added in 1978, stand out in bright contrast.

There are a few links with the old stadium, apart from the presence of Dr Springer. On the side of one terrace is a plaque, commemorating a former trainer and player, István Tóth, who died 'a martyr' in 1945. Beyond the busy roadway can still be seen the ever-present ochre walls of the mint, which used to be a military barracks, while Fradi's training pitches still lie behind two other sides of the ground.

But for a real glimpse of the old Üllői út one must enter Fradi's unashamedly devotional museum inside the clubhouse. There, lovingly preserved, are photographs of the original stadium, a brick from Fradi's former clubhouse, and a clump of timber rescued from the old Tribune A. Call it sentimental, call it clinging to the past, but call it also typically Hungarian. Fradi may have a radically different ground, but underneath the new concrete, the spirit lives on.

151

HUNGARY

BUDAPEST

MTK STADION

Equidistant between the Népstadion and Üllői út, tucked between a railway line and the Hungária Boulevard, is the ground of Fradi's greatest rivals, **MTK-VM**: Magyar Testgyakorlók Köre (Hungarian Circle of Athletes), who merged with First Division neighbours VM (Vörös Meteor) Egyetértés in 1975.

Their 25,000 capacity stadium was inaugurated against Fradi in March 1912, although as a club MTK date from 1888 and the football section from 1902. From 1926–39 MTK were called Hungária and from 1949–56 had three other names – Textiles, Budapest Bástya, then Budapest Vörös Lobogó (Red Banner). Their more colloquial name, however, since seemingly everyone and everything has a nickname in Hungary, is '*Libások*' – literally 'the goose eaters' – a jocular reference to MTK's links with the Jewish community.

In this context the club, according to Fradi fans, is also supposed to be patronised by banking interests, but if this be true it is hardly reflected in the state of the stadium. Open on three sides, it has one simple post and beam stand, rebuilt after the Second World War, which, unusually, has barriers in front of each row of seats, as if to prevent the occupants from falling out. MTK were the last senior Budapest club to have floodlights. These, supported on four slender masts, and supplemented by an extra light gantry above the stand's yellow roof, were switched on in September 1987.

On the east curve the new lights flank two points of interest, both dating from 1978. One is a square blue sports hall (the club has twelve sport sections and nearly fifty Olympic gold medals to its name), and the other is a bust mounted on the terracing (like Pichichi's memorial at Bilbao). This commemorates György Orth, top goalscorer from 1917–28 during MTK's astonishing run of ten championship wins in succession (five times under

MTK

The MTK Stadion, but what is the building behind the open side stand on the left?

English manager Jimmy Hogan). Orth, considered one of Hungary's most talented players of all time, scored 138 goals in 167 games and won 30 caps before a serious injury hampered his form. He then went on to coach in eight different countries, and was en route back to Budapest in 1962 when a heart attack struck him down in Porto.

Yet an even more enduring image at the MTK Stadion, for visitors at least, lies just behind the open seated area opposite the main stand. At first glance it appears to be the back of an old four-storey warehouse with fading yellow walls. From the top of the terracing, however, one sees that it is in fact the massive grandstand of another stadium, only a few metres away across a narrow roadway. This is the haunting, echoing home of BKV Előre, a lower division club which attracts only a tenth of MTK's support but was for two seasons (1949–50 and 1981–2) in the same league division as its neighbours. Nowhere in Europe, not even in Dundee, Scotland, are two club stadiums so close together, and yet such worlds apart.

BUDAPEST

JÓZSEF BOZSIK STADION

For a club with such a lofty reputation, **Honvéd** possess a surprisingly modest ground. Situated in the southeast district of Kispest, between a slaughterhouse, railway line, factory and cemetery – all life is here! – it holds only 13,200, and comprises a small stand and a low bank of open terracing around a shale track. Were it not for bright red barriers, a red and black electric scoreboard, neat grey bench seats and leaning, latticework floodlight pylons, one might almost think Honvéd, Hungary's army club, to be quite without any privileges at all.

In fact they began life simply enough in 1909 as the Kispest village athletics club, with a ground opened three years later just south of the present stadium. Its stand burnt down during a match in

1934, and the sand pitch subsequently became a quagmire, so in 1939 a new stadium was built next door (while the old one became the cemetery). Then one morning in December 1949 Kispest became Honvéd and a few hours later took to the pitch under their new identity. But the ground remained fairly basic for the next thirty years because Honvéd, as the Communist regime's pet club, played most of their home games at the Népstadion. They returned to Kispest permanently in 1981, when the stand and terracing were modernised. A three-storey club centre overlooking the pitch, undersoil heating and new floodlights were added in 1986, after Honvéd's ninth championship win, and on 1 October of that year, as an illustration of how Hungarians never forget their heroes, the stadium was dedicated to József 'Cucu' Bozsik, a Kispest man who joined the club aged eleven, played 447 games for Honvéd, 100 times for Hungary, became an army officer, Honvéd president and a Member of Parliament. He died, aged fifty-three, in 1978.

● **Újpesti Dózsa**, in north Pest, are Hungary's oldest sports club (formed 1885) and have the city's second largest stadium, holding 30,000 in a completely open bowl, attached to a popular sports complex. Opened in September 1923, the **Dózsa Stadion** was a regular venue for internationals until the Népstadion was built, and was the first Hungarian ground to be floodlit, in 1972. Could this have been due to the proximity, nay the looming presence behind the ground, of the Tungsram lightbulb factory? György Dózsa, after whom both club and stadium are named, was not a footballer but a sixteenth-century noble who led a peasants revolt against the Turks and was burnt at the stake for his trouble.

Honvéd in mid-reconstruction, 1986.

HONVÉD

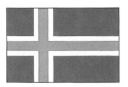

ICELAND

ICELAND FA

Europe's most northerly national stadium.

REYKJAVÍK

LAUGARDALSVÖLLUR

As Icelanders discovered when a Scotsman first introduced them to the game in 1895, football was a wonderful way to keep busy on those long summer nights when the sun never sets and the joys of playing chess and recounting sagas start to wear a bit thin.

But although a championship was established in 1912, the island had to wait until after independence from Denmark in 1944 to play its first international. This took place two years later, v. Denmark, on a gravel pitch at Melavöllur, in the west of Reykjavík. By then, eastwards along the city's northern shoreline, work had already begun on a proper ground at Laugardalsvöllur, a former bathing area of hot springs where Reykjavík women would gather to do their laundry.

But there was no hurry. In this, Europe's most northerly national capital, a few degrees south of the Arctic circle, life moves so slowly that it took fourteen years for the stadium to be inaugurated, on Iceland's National Day, 17 June 1957. The first

international match, v. Norway, followed shortly after on 8 July (the local FA's tenth anniversary).

Laugardalsvöllur currently holds 14,800 (3600 seated), although at least 18,000 attended a European Cup tie, Valur FC v. Benfica, in 1968. In a compact city of only 93,000, that represents an enormous percentage turnout for a football match.

Valur are one of four Reykjavík clubs, along with **Fram**, **KR**, and **Vikingur**, and for many years Laugardalsvöllur was used for most senior matches, there being few other grass pitches available. Nowadays, however, only Fram use the stadium on a regular basis. Attendances, once between 2–3000, now average around 950.

At present the stadium comprises no more than a pitch, athletics track, one stand and three sides of shallow banking. In order to meet FIFA's minimum international standards however, there are plans to add more seats and build a second cover, opposite the main stand.

But even these developments would barely rob Laugardalsvöllur of its invigorating air of innocence. Immediately to the south lies an indoor sports arena and floodlit artificial pitch (the main stadium needs no lighting since during the playing season the sun barely sets). To the east is a second grass pitch, used by teams from the lower divisions, while to the north is an open-air swimming pool. Like so much of Reykjavík, one imagines this all to be part of some trim Nordic holiday camp designed especially for world-weary refugees from the polluted metropolises of Europe. Indeed, even amid a packed, cheerful crowd at Laugardalsvöllur, knowing of the icy waters, rugged fjords, geysers and lava fields that lie so close at hand, it is hard to escape the sense of being in some stranded, but immaculately conceived outpost of humanity.

LUXEMBOURG

LUXEMBOURG

STADE MUNICIPAL

Not having won a match since their 2–1 European Championship victory in Rotterdam in October 1963, it is small wonder that the amateurs of Luxembourg are the worst supported national team in UEFA. But then there are only 370,000 inhabitants in the entire Grand Duchy, barely 80,000 of them in the city of Luxembourg itself.

With a current capacity of 12,000 (4700 seated), the Stade Municipal is the country's largest venue, but for League matches involving the resident club, **Spora Luxembourg**, it seldom welcomes more than a few hundred. Much of Luxembourg's real footballing interest in recent years has been focused instead 20 kilometres away on the most successful domestic outfit, Jeunesse d'Esch.

(It was to Jeunesse's tiny 7000 capacity Stade de la Frontière that the Luxembourg Football Federation, perhaps in the hope of ending their long run without victory, switched a European Championship match v. Scotland in December 1987. Luxembourg managed a draw, but there were still only 1999 to watch it.)

The Stade Municipal was opened in April 1940 with a friendly v. Belgium, only weeks before the German invasion, and since 1985 has undergone a steady renovation. There is now a new but small main cantilevered stand, which replaced the basic original 1000 seater in 1989. (During its construction Luxembourg were forced to play two of their home matches in the World Cup elsewhere. When they relocated the match v. Belgium to Lille, Switzerland, in the same qualifying group,

Night scene in Luxembourg, before the new stand was built in 1989.

complained that this virtually amounted to a home game for Belgium.)

The rest of the stadium consists of three open sides curved around an all-weather track. Opposite the main stand are 3500 uncovered white bench seats, behind which lies a floodlit training pitch flanked by tennis courts and a sports hall.

To the rear of the low west terrace, beyond a neat grass bank with clipped hedges, is a row of detached, suitably bourgeois residences, while beneath the east terrace, rebuilt in 1985, are the modern offices of Spora and the city's sports administration.

Trim and orderly though it is – like so much of this comfortable Euro-bland city – it is hard to imagine the Stade Municipal ever becoming a hotbed of soccer. But that was never the intention. As the Luxembourg motto so succinctly puts it, 'We want to remain what we are.'

155

MALTA

MALTA FA

TA'QALI STADIUM

Before Ta'Qali was officially inaugurated on 14 December 1980, Malta used to fill visiting teams with dread. The basic Empire Stadium in Gzira (facing Lazzaretto Creek and Fort Manoel, and now disused) held 30,000 and, it seemed, had that number of bumps and dips on its notoriously threadbare pitch. By comparison, Ta'Qali, also with a capacity of 30,000 – almost a tenth of the island's population, is positively luxurious; all seated, spacious, and as much geared to the needs of foreign clubs, who use the stadium's technical complex as an away-from-it-all training camp, as to the 700 or more Maltese players who use the facilities every week.

This can only be to the benefit of Malta's eight senior clubs, who play all their league and cup matches at Ta'Qali, usually staged as two double-headers each weekend; and since the stadium is judiciously located in the island's centre, on flat scrubland between Rabat and the more populated districts of Valletta, Sliema, Floriana and Gzira,

nowhere in Malta is more than a short bus ride away.

Great care had to be taken during Ta'Qali's construction. Because the site was formerly a Second World War airbase (abandoned only when the last British forces withdrew in 1979), it was feared the odd bomb or two might lie buried beneath the surface. That fear proved unfounded, and now only part of the runway and a hangar remain, while the old Royal Air Force Nissen huts, former living quarters of Spitfire and Gladiator pilots, now house a crafts village.

For a small island where gates average only 2000 – Hamrun Spartans being Malta's best supported club – Ta'Qali is a remarkable venture. An orderly oasis in the midst of a parched landscape, the stadium is bordered by three immaculate floodlit turf pitches, while shimmering on a rise barely a kilometre away are the domes and fortified walls of Mdina, the island's ancient capital.

The stadium itself, built by the Socialist administration of Prime Minister Dom Mintoff, is spotless. A hi-tech, inclined cantilevered roof is suspended from a web of steel tubing clamped onto the back of the single, main stand, which has orange seats on its airy, upper tier, and houses underneath sufficient fitness, training and recreational facilities to attract a number of Scandinavian, West German and Swiss clubs during their winter breaks.

The remaining three sides consist of raised open banks of concrete bench seats, curved around the track, with gateways topped by four flagpoles in the centre of each side. But the real pride of Ta'-Qali is the pitch – lush and smooth, despite the hard clay bed on which it is laid, and after Gzira like stepping from the wilderness onto the lawns of Eden. No-one dreads playing in Malta now.

NORTHERN IRELAND

BELFAST

WINDSOR PARK

Northern Ireland's international venue in West Belfast is the home of the province's richest, most successful club, **Linfield** – the 'Blues'. Yet for the people living less than a mile away, across the M1 motorway in the strictly Catholic area of Andersonstown, Windsor Park is nothing less than an alien stronghold of 'Orange' loyalists.

Ever since the city's foremost Catholic club, Belfast Celtic, disbanded in 1949 – partly in the wake of a riot at Windsor Park in December 1948 (in which a Celtic player's leg was broken by a sectarian mob) – football in Belfast has been a predominantly Protestant affair, with the Blues (formed in 1886 by workers at the Linfield mill) left to fight it out with their East Belfast rivals, Glentoran.

Windsor Park, known to hardliners as 'the shrine', was built on land previously called Bog Meadow, and opened on 2 September 1905 with a match v. Glentoran. Since then it has been developed in the best (or is it worst?) tradition of British football grounds – that is, in an entirely piecemeal fashion.

At the west end is the open Spion Kop, with two

Windsor Park, before the South Stand extension (right, with flat roof) was dismantled.

floodlight pylons of the leaning Scottish variety squatting near the front of the terracing. Newcastle United came for the inaugural floodlit game in October 1956. Behind the Kop is a pitch used by Linfield's reserves, the Swifts, with the Catholic Milltown Cemetery and the green hills of the Black Mountain rising in the distance.

At the east, or Railway End, is a low, gloomy stand which has a curved, latticework wooden cover of the type known, coincidentally, as a Belfast roof (also found commonly in England), with dog-tooth boarding along its fascia, like an old railway station. Part of this 660 seater stand was blown up by a terrorist bomb in April 1972 (during a four-year period when civil unrest forced Northern Ireland to stage all its home games outside the province). Next to it, in the southeast corner, is a block which forms part of Linfield's lucrative social club.

Windsor Park's most modern stand is on the north side: a £2 million, 6800 seater, cantilevered construction with red seats on its upper level, yellow below. This was opened by the London-based Minister of Sport (whose government donated half the costs) and FIFA President João Havelange, in October 1984. (Its construction by the Irish F.A. did not please everyone, however. Residents living directly behind found that

the draughts it created down their chimneys made it almost impossible to use their fireplaces.)

In complete contrast is the highly traditional main, or South Stand. Opened in 1930 with a match v. Rangers – Linfield's Protestant soul mates from Glasgow – it was built in collaboration with Britain's leading, though hardly very imaginative, ground designer of the period, Archibald Leitch. Clad in blue sheeting, it has a pitched roof, high balcony wall and an open paddock in front. But the stand only fills two-thirds of the south side, the remaining space having been formerly occupied by a much simpler stand extension which was dismantled after safety checks following the 1985 fire in Bradford.

The loss of this section and a tightening up of security all round has reduced Windsor Park from its original capacity of 60,000 to just 28,000, of which 9160 are seated – easily sufficient to handle average League attendances of around 3500. But the club's main gate money comes from internationals, for which Linfield receive 15 per cent of receipts in a contract which still has over ninety years to run; enough to guarantee the Blues stay in the black, and together with the club's other earnings maintain their poll position in Northern Irish football, if not in the hearts of all the province's population.

BELFAST

THE OVAL

Overlooked by the gantries of Harland and Wolff's shipyards in East Belfast is the Oval, home since 1899 of Linfield's fiercest rivals, **Glentoran**, popularly known as 'the Cock and Hens'. German air raids destroyed the ground in May 1941, a river then flooded it, and while swans swam in the bomb craters Glentoran had to share with Belfast neighbours Distillery, until the Oval was finally restored for use in August 1949.

It has changed little since then. The short main stand, decked in the club colours of green, red and black, has a pitched roof and 5500 seats. Opposite is a simple terrace cover, while the terracing at each end is open. On the taller Kop End, overlooking the shipyards, is a former Second World

War pillbox for which Glentoran were paid £1 per annum rental. The floodlights were switched on in December 1964, v. St Mirren, and two years later a record gate of 55,000 attended a European Cup tie v. Glasgow Rangers. Nowadays the Oval's limit is 20,000 and the crowds are smaller, but the Cock and Hens' mood remains as jaunty as ever. After all, someone's got to beat Linfield.

The Oval.

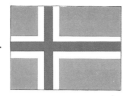

NORWAY

OSLO

ULLEVÅL STADION

Norway's national stadium was named after a farm which occupied the land until the turn of the century. And despite the busy roads and fast-food kiosks which now surround Ullevål, as one arrives at the stadium's tiny railway station in the north of the city, there still lingers the rustic air of a village halt.

The Ullevål has, however, begun its transformation into a late twentieth-century showpiece. To date only one section, the west curve, has been modernised (and duly renamed, after its sponsor, the Coca-Cola Stand). Built by private developers in 1986, from the street one would hardly guess that the building was part of a

Ullevål from the new Coca-Cola Stand.

NORWAY

stadium at all. It appears to be a regular four-storey office, shop and supermarket complex (suitably called Arena Mat) clad in black and red glass and steel. Only the old wooden Stadion Kro restaurant in the forecourt and the sight of floodlight pylons peeking above the roof hint at what really lies beyond the hi-tech façade.

From inside the stadium, the two-tiered Coca-Cola Stand has terracing on the lower level and 3400 orange and blue seats on the upper, with a line of windows behind the uppermost rows; a typical, modern cantilever not unlike those built, for example, at Manchester United's Old Trafford. The only difference is that the Ulleval windows belong not, as one would imagine, to private boxes but to the fourth floor offices of the development behind. What is more, the lease stipulates that they are not to be used for viewing during matches. (Well, would you hire out your office as an executive lounge?)

By 1992 it is hoped that the same cantilever design will be continued along the north side to replace the Ulleval's original grandstand (low, spartan, with a wooden façade, built in 1926 when the stadium was opened), and the east curve (a weathered, uncovered, concrete stand with faded red and green bench seats, built in 1939). All trace of the old dirt athletics track will be removed – no loss – and an underground car park may be built under the pitch (as at Monaco). Since at present frost and snow rule out football in Oslo from November to May, the new pitch will be heated.

Only the existing main stand, on the south side by the tree-lined railway line, will remain untouched. Filled with blue and red seats, the stand is a plain rectangular construction which houses the offices of both the Norwegian Football Federation (fotballforbund) and **Lyn Olso** football club (who have been very much out of the limelight since the early 1970s). The stand was opened in 1968, the same year the six floodlight pylons were first used, for a European Cup Winners' Cup tie between Lyn and Norrköping (Sweden).

The Ulleval's current capacity is 23,800, of which 5500 are standing places, although once redevelopment is complete the total capacity should rise to 32,000.

The Bislett Stadium's curious clubhouse, with its Nordic decoration, royal balcony and flagpoles at the ready.

● Also in Oslo is the 24,000 capacity **Bislett Stadium**, home of **Vålengerens IF**. Between 1913–51, Norway regularly staged soccer internationals at this surprising stadium, sunk in the midst of a residential area between the city centre and the Ulleval. Bislett came further to international prominence when it was chosen as the centre for the 1952 Winter Olympics, and since then it has become renowned as a major athletics venue; over sixty world records have been broken here.

At its heart stands a charming brick clubhouse, on the north side, which dates back to about 1913 and sports a clock tower, tiled roof, decorated railings and staircases, and a royal balcony whose curving roof is supported by a row of white poles, angled skywards like a missile battery. The surrounding terraces – there are no other seats – appear to undulate around the bowl towards a concrete cantilevered cover opposite the clubhouse. A curious gem indeed.

POLAND

CHORZÓW

STADION ŚLĄSKI

The real soul of Polish football lies not in the capital, Warsaw, but in the industrialised region of Śląsk, or Silesia – a dense agglomeration of mines and foundries, eleven towns and cities, 2.5 million people, and a football club around every corner.

And in the middle of all this, on the borders of Katowice and Chorzów, is the Wojewódzki Park of Culture and Recreation, once named after Stalin and now the setting for the Polish national stadium.

Designed, like several other Polish stadiums of the early 1950s, by the partnership of Bredy and Brzuchowski, the Śląski Stadium was built on land which, after years of mining, resembled a lunar landscape. It took three years to complete and was inaugurated on Poland's national holiday, 22 July 1956, with a game v. East Germany. Three years later Śląski's lights were the first in Poland – switched on for two matches on 2 May 1959, when another local club, Polonia Bytom, played Polonia Bydgoszcz, followed by Ruch v. Pogoń.

Since then, while the surrounding wasteland grew into a rambling park, the stadium has barely altered, though not through neglect.

In the mould of all great Socialist stadiums of the postwar period, the Stadion Śląski (pronounced Shlonski) is a vast, serious, open bowl, formed by earth banking and lined with bench seats divided into forty blocks. At both ends are tunnels, faced in severe, grey sandstone blocks, through which one might expect a train to emerge. Only one main feature distinguishes it from the

Śląski – Socialist superbowl and office block.

likes of Leningrad, Bucharest, Leipzig and Warsaw. Above a small VIP enclosure cut into the taller, west side banking, is a red and white striped tower block of offices and glass-fronted balconies. From the roof one gains a panoramic view of the nearest towns, the pitheads, chimneys and housing estates, plus the stadiums of three local clubs: GKS Katowice on the south east of the park, Ruch Chorzów to the west, and immediately behind the stadium's main entrance, the small ground of former giants, now amateurs, AKS Chorzów.

Unlike Poland's other large stadiums in Warsaw, Poznań and Wrocław, Chorzów's superbowl has been constantly occupied by internationals, Cup Finals, European ties and important League matches of neighbouring clubs, even the odd Second Division local derby. The players like its atmosphere, apparently, because with a sunken pitch and open banking, crowd noise reverberates around the bowl, just like the Hampden Roar in Glasgow.

Apart from football, the occasional Spartakiáda (mass sports display) and political rally, the Śląski Stadium has also staged athletics, two world gath-

161

ALAIN SCHROEDER

Polish subs warm up in the tunnel.

erings of Jehovah's Witnesses, and, since the track was adapted in 1973, several World Speedway Championships.

Full houses have been many, which until recent years meant 90,000 officially (but almost certainly over 100,000), and although the current limit is 75,000 all-seated, more are allowed in to stand at the back. This is just as well, for the intensity of footballing passion in the region makes the Śląski Stadium like a magnet, drawing in eager crowds from the surrounding towns and grounds, while in Warsaw, as we shall shortly learn, an almost identical stadium lies forgotten and unloved.

ŚLĄSK

OTHER VENUES

The doyens of Śląsk football, and until recently Poland's most titled club, are **Ruch Chorzów**, whose **Stadion Ruch** is better known by its address, on ulica Cicha – Silent Street – a gift for the headline writers.

Chorzów once straddled the German-Polish border (of which more in the following pages), but as soon as the Germans withdrew in 1918 Chorzów blossomed into a centre of Polish pride, which Ruch (meaning 'movement') did as much as anyone to bolster after their formation by foundry workers in 1920. In the course of their first four championships, won in succession between

Ulica Cicha and its swaying floodlights.

GROUNDWORK

1933–6, Ruch opened their present ground on 29 September 1935, with a match against another great prewar club, Warta Poznań. And although ul.Cicha has since been modernised in the 1960s – while Ruch lodged at the Śląski Stadium for two seasons – its basic format is unaltered: a shallow bank of terracing, without a single crush barrier, surrounds an oval of turf, with a small blue-clad main stand on the halfway line, seating 2000. The official capacity is put at 40,000, but in today's safety conscious climate that seems a trifle optimistic. Otherwise, apart from two squat cooling towers which dominate one end terrace, the ground's main feature is its pencil thin, blue steel floodlight masts, which sway quite alarmingly in the wind.

● Ruch are the only Silesian club not to be sponsored by the coalmining industry. **GKS Katowice** – GKS stands for Coalminers' Sports Club – were formed in 1964, a time when the Silesian capital, Katowice, boasted the most modern, automated mine in the world (which is perhaps why the workforce had more time off for football).

Situated on the edge of the Wojewódzki Park, but actually just outside the Katowice city boundary, **Stadion GKS** is better known as ulica Bukowa – Beech Street – even though those trees still within the actual ground, actually on the south end terrace, are oaks. Since a dynamic coalmine official became president in the mid-1980s and started to pump mining money into the club, the ground has become one of the most modern in Poland. It has a new cantilevered main stand on the east side, built in 1988, the track has been removed, new floodlights installed, and a multi-purpose sports hall started behind the north terrace. When finished the ground will hold around 18,000, but GKS's clubhouse will remain in a charming detached lodge behind the west stand, set amid trees on the edge of a large pond. Tradition has it that each new player is ducked into this pond, so it is fortunate for rookies that signings are only permitted in Poland during the summer months.

● By far the most successful miners' club are **Górnik Zabrze**, who, since overtaking Ruch's total in 1988, hold a record number of championships. But although the club formed in 1948, the **Stadion Górnik** has a longer history.

Under German rule before 1945, Zabrze was known as Hindenburg and, as in many German cities, a municipal stadium with swimming pool was built there to provide both recreation and employment. It was opened in September 1934 and given the same title as the distant stadium in Stuttgart, the Adolf Hitler Kampfbahn. Embarrassingly for the Führer, the master race rather slipped up in the opening game, which saw a German Silesian XI get whipped 7–2 by a Śląsk XI from over the Polish border, 3 kilometres eastwards. Had no-one warned the Germans of Ruch's rampant form at this time?

From thereon the stadium and its surrounding parade grounds were used mainly for Nazi rallies (which the Germans were at least good at), until after liberation in 1945 a team called Zjednoczenie Zabrze took up residence. Three years later (no doubt to the relief of future non-Polish commentators) they joined five other local clubs to form Górnik.

Despite becoming Poland's most successful and best supported club, with average gates of between 15–20,000, Górnik's ground remains quite basic. The original 1934 propped main stand has been revitalised with white paint and claret and blue seats, but the rest of the stadium is an open bowl with white bench seats on the lower tier, standing behind. The infrastructure does reflect Górnik's status however; an excellent pitch; floodlights, added in 1970 (after Górnik became the first Polish club to reach a European final – the Cup Winners' Cup v. Manchester City in Vienna); a synthetic running track, one of only four in Poland, laid in 1978; and a large electronic scoreboard, imported from Hungary in 1988. The current capacity is 23,000, of which 20,000 are seated, which means

that Górnik must still take their big games to Chorzów. The difference is that nowadays the people of Zabrze don't have to cross the German border to get there.

Oaks on the terracing at Beech Street, home of GKS Katowice.

Górnik Zabrze – simple stadium with mod cons.

Pure Śląsk – Szombierki Bytom's former ground.

GROUNDWORK

The bleakest Socialist superbowl of them all, built from the haunted ruins of Warsaw.

WARSAW

STADION DZIESIĘCIOLECIA

The 'Ten Years Stadium' was inaugurated on 22 July 1955, on the *eleventh* anniversary of the event it was meant to commemorate, the setting up of the first Polish Communist government in Lublin. Thirty-five years later and it is hard to say which looks more worn out and unloved – the Polish Communist Party or the stadium.

Built up by young 'volunteers' from the rubble of wartime Warsaw, the 100,000 capacity stadium is almost a carbon copy of the Śląski, but without a single diverting feature. For over two decades it was a showpiece – athletics, rugby, bicycle racing, a harvest festival, plus football internationals and Cup Finals all being held there. But its last international was in 1983, and its last big crowd – double the official capacity, plus 1.5 million in the surrounding park – was for the return visit of the Polish Pope, John-Paul II, also in 1983.

Since then there have been no thrills to witness in this no frills stadium. The press cabins have been removed, there are molehills around the pitch and a heightened state of gloom prevails. Built from the city's debris, and perhaps haunted by its dead, the Ten Years Stadium now threatens to become a ghostly ruin itself.

WARSAW

STADION LEGIA

Formed by Marshal Pilsudski's legionaries in 1916, **Legia Warszawa** inaugurated their present stadium in 1930 (with a match v. Barcelona), then in 1939 watched helplessly as the German army

Legia's war survivor.

turned it into a fortified artillery post. Trenches were dug into the pitch and the stand was occupied by SS men. Yet in the final days of the war, when every other building in the vicinity was destroyed, somehow Legia's stand survived. A wonderful period piece it is too, similar in appearance to the two classic 1930s' grandstands at Arsenal's stadium in London.

After the war Legia became the Central Army Sports Club (CWKS), won a few honours and enjoyed the odd European tussle in the Ten Years Stadium. But although they have their old name back, Legia have not won a championship since 1970, and with neighbours Gwardia (the police team) in decline, and the prewar railway team, Polonia, now in obscurity, football in Warsaw is looking a bit frayed at the edges. So too are many of Legia's blue and yellow bench seats, which fill three sides of their stadium's open, shallow banking.

The floodlights at Stadion Legia were switched on v. Aarhus in October 1960 – the first at a Polish club ground, and the present capacity of 21,940 is more than enough for Legia's current average gate of 8–10,000.

GROUNDWORK

WROCŁAW

STADION OLIMPIJSKI

Here's one for quizmasters. Which Olympic Stadium has staged the home internationals of two different countries? The answer is the Olimpijski Stadium, Wrocław, which, when opened in 1928, was within Germany's eastern borders, in a city then known as Breslau. Part of a typical German sports complex (called, inexplicably, the Sportpark Leerbeutel – which means 'empty sack'), it staged its first German international in November 1930, v. Norway, but was still unfinished when the Nazis renamed it, three years later, the Hermann Göring Sportfeld (which, considering both Göring's girth and his love of fine clothes, was the complete opposite of 'Leerbeutel').

As Berlin prepared for the 1936 Olympics, Breslau changed the stadium's name to Olympiastadion and made a brave bid for some of the events. Hitler would have none of it – he wanted Berlin to have all the limelight – though the Hitler Youth did use the stadium for rallies and Germany played another four internationals there (including v. Poland in 1935), before it was flattened during the Soviet advance in late 1944.

As Poland took over and renamed the city, public donations financed the stadium's complete reconstruction, and for many years it was one of the country's finest. Holding 48,000 (25,000 seated), there is a narrow, propped roof encircling the shallow bowl, interrupted on the east side by a square brick tower. On the front face of this tower is the Silesian white eagle, while under the stands are gloomy classrooms for the stadium's resident sports college. A large scoreboard, added in 1987, sits above the southern Marathon Gate,

Speedway at Wrocław's aptly-named 'empty sack'.

which itself leads into a circular, colonnaded main entrance, a unique feature of Richard Konwiarz's original 1926 design.

Nowadays, although the surrounding sports park survives unchanged, the predominantly brick-lined stadium is dour and neglected, with almost as much grass on the terracing as on the pitch. Poland rarely visit – their last appearance, in March 1987, was v. Norway (coincidentally Germany's first visitors), and it would seem that local army club **Śląsk Wrocław** prefer to build their own new stadium rather than use the Olimpijski regularly. (At present they play there only for European games, because it has floodlights, added in 1976, and because their present 14,000 capacity **Stadion Śląsk**, in the southwest suburb of Gajowice, could hardly be more basic.)

So, apart from regular speedway and the occasional pop concert, the future looks bleak for the Olimpijski. It may bear the status of 'a preserved monument', but what it really craves, like the Ten Years Stadium in Warsaw, is an active sporting role. Leave an 'empty sack', and its fabric will soon start to rot.

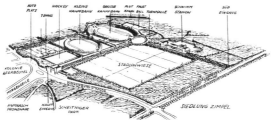

The original 1928 German Sportpark.

POLAND

Lech's unique floodlight masts are the difference between a dull, open arena and a visual treat. But that's little comfort for the fans on rainy days.

POZNAŃ

STADION LECH

As legend has it, the city of Poznań (meaning 'recognition') was born when the three original Slav brothers, Lech, Czech and Rus, met up by coincidence on an island in the Warta River.

KKS Lech Poznań were a somewhat later invention. Formed in 1922 by railway workers, it took them until 1970 to establish a First Division place, at which time they played at either of two stadiums belonging to Poznań's senior club, KS Warta (see below). Finally, in 1980 they moved to their own purpose-built Lech Stadium on the outskirts of the city.

Holding 23,734, the stadium is a U-shaped, single-tier of uncovered benches, sealed off at the open end, incredibly, by a railing such as one might find around a village pitch. Nothing else separates the stadium interior from the neighbouring pitches and approach road.

Still more surprising are the four floodlight masts, which each consist of two separate curved steel beams, splayed apart at the bottom, parallel at the top, with lamp holders clamped in between. What would otherwise be a dull arena is thus transformed into a visual treat.

Unfortunately, after only a decade *in situ*, these innovative masts already show signs of deterioration, but the same can hardly be said of Lech. Since moving here, the club has been champions twice and Cup holders three times.

● The club with whom Lech had earlier shared, **KS Warta**, made their name before the war at one of Europe's eeriest stadiums. On a windswept plain on the west bank of the River Warta (once the border between Germany and Poland), the enormous **Stadion Warta** opened in 1928 and held 72,000, until improvements made for the staging of the Polish Harvest Festival in 1974 reduced this to 50,000. Since then the place has slipped into decline, the floodlights have been removed from their pedestals, while the stadium's most haunting image is a solitary memorial behind the north curve. In Polish and Hebrew, this recalls thousands of labour slaves who were starved to death at the stadium between 1940–3, apparently because other German concentration camps nearby were overcrowded.

● Poznań's third venue is the 27,600 capacity **Stadion Olimpia**, home of **Olimpia Poznań**, a militia-run club who joined Lech in the First Division in 1986. Set amid dense woodland, with open bench seats around a speedway track, the ground is unremarkable, except that the adjacent athletics stadium has some unique, sculptural floodlight masts which not only rival Lech's unusual quartet but also, together with the synthetic running track, suggest that Olimpia are well looked after by their sponsors.

PORTUGAL

LISBON

ESTÁDIO NACIONAL

Considering this is a national stadium, it is remarkably well hidden. Ten kilometres west of central Lisbon and following signs to Caxias, one enters an area of dense, undulating pine forests, somewhere in the middle of which lies the stadium, like the hidden ruins of some lost world.

There is no stadium like it in Europe. Built into the side of a thickly wooded hill, it holds 60,000, all seated on stone benches, but, most unnervingly, has a gap where one would normally expect the east side of the bowl to be.

Cynics say that this gap, which leads down to a broad, ceremonial approach, flanked by flagpoles and turnstiles, exists only because the money ran out after work started on the site in 1939. Certainly, although the dictator Salazar kept Portugal nominally neutral during the war, the country did suffer economically. Five difficult years passed, therefore, before the stadium's inauguration, on 10 June 1944, with a match between Lisbon's two giants, Benfica v. Sporting.

Since then the stadium has staged most of Portugal's internationals and Cup Finals, and between 1945–54 many of Benfica and Sporting's big games too (before their own super-bowls were opened). Two other historic occasions have been Torino's match v. Benfica, a day before the Italians were tragically killed in an air crash, in May 1949, and the 1967 European Cup Final, Celtic v. Inter Milan.

The stadium would undoubtedly attract more top games if floodlights were added and the east

Gathering in the woods of Caxias, but, uniquely
not on the east side (centre left).

gap filled in. But to do the latter would be to rob the stadium of a unique characteristic.

And if it is disconcerting having only three sides, and the benches are somewhat unyielding, one can at least enjoy the classically unspoilt Elysian surroundings. Maybe that was the intended effect, because overlooking the west side is a dazzling white colonnade, with a marble rostrum in front, on which dozens of jubilant captains have hoisted trophies over the years.

The scene they have looked down upon has barely altered since 1944, apart from the addition of a now sun-bleached synthetic track. But the stadium's environs are quite different. Trees now mask the original view of the surrounding hills and nearby coast, and to the east, down in the winding valley of the River Jamor, lies a sprawling 200-hectare sports complex. Boasting all manner of facilities, this would undoubtedly make a most agreeable Olympic village. A three-sided Olympic Stadium, on the other hand, might not be such a great selling point.

167

PORTUGAL

LISBON

ESTÁDIO DA LUZ

Although strictly we should now call the largest stadium in Europe the 'Estádio do Sport Lisboa e Benfica', no advertising whizz kid, surely, could ever improve on its original name, Estádio da Luz – the Stadium of Light! Pure inspiration. A name of such ethereal quality, even if the reality is a touch more down to earth.

To explain, the name Estádio da Luz arose, not because this was the first ground in Portugal to have floodlights, nor even because its interior is especially bright, but because, rather boringly, the stadium just happens to be situated close to the Estrada da Luz, Luz being the name of the district.

There is certainly nothing illuminating about its location. Heading west along the highway from Lisbon airport, no sooner have you slipped into top gear than you see it, looming out of the dust. Or at least, first you see a stadium to your right, look frantically for a turn off, then, a kilometre or so further on, see another stadium, on your left. Despite the heat, you are not seeing double. The first super-stadium belongs to Sporting, our next stop, the second belongs to Benfica. Like Partisan and Red Star in Yugoslavia, or Liverpool and Everton in England, Lisbon's greatest rivals do not have to look far to see what the opposition are doing.

To put this rivalry in its context, since the Portuguese League began in 1934, apart from 1946 (when Belenenses nipped in), only three clubs have ever won the title – Benfica, Sporting and Porto (Benfica having won it more than the other two combined). Each club has an enormous all-seated stadium which forms part of a much larger sports complex, and each has more than 70,000 *socios*, or members. Portugal may be, as one travel writer put it, 'a peanut of a country', but in footballing terms it is the stomping ground of giants – three giants.

Benfica's official title, like that of the stadium, is **Sport Lisboa e Benfica**, a name which derives from a merger in 1908 between Grupo Sport Lisboa (formed by sons of the wealthy in 1904), and Sport Clube de Benfica (formed in 1906, mainly as a cycling and athletics club). GSL had several good players, a club motto – *'E Pluribus*

Unum' (All For One), the emblem of an eagle, but crucially, they had no ground. SCB, meanwhile, had a ground, but not much else.

Their Campo da Feiteira – little more than a pitch in the shadow of Benfica's Parish Church – was to be the first of six grounds in the club's history, while Benfica itself was, at this time, barely more than a village separated from Lisbon by farmland.

By late 1912 Benfica had left Feiteira and were playing at venues all around Lisbon, until their new Sete Rios ground, in Palhavã (both names of current metro stations), was opened in October 1913. But as crowds grew and the club's activities branched out to include several other sports, in November 1917 the Eagles returned to Benfica, to the Avenida Gomes Pereira. This became a 'stadium of light' in its own right when, in September 1919, it staged the first two experimental floodlit matches in Portugal.

Artificial light did not catch on, and nor did the new ground. After eight years Benfica moved again, to Amoreiras, a hilltop area just west of central Lisbon. The Estádio das Amoreiras, with two low covers behind each goal, and both sides open, was inaugurated on 13 December 1925, Benfica's match v. Casa Pia (another Lisbon club) being watched by a full house of 15,000.

At Amoreiras Benfica won their first national honours: the Portuguese Cup in 1930 and 1931, and a hat-trick of League championships between 1936–8. And although an intended palatial façade was never built, the main stand was enlarged, a library opened for the club's 5000 *socios*, and in 1936 detailed plans were drawn up for a multi-purpose stadium on the site, which if built would have made it one of the most modern in Europe. Instead, in July 1940 Amoreiras faced a rather more comprehensive redesign, when it was expropriated to make way for the Avenida Duarte Pacheco viaduct. (The heights of Amoreiras are now most conspicuous for Tomás Taveira's startling pink and green Post-Modern shopping centre.) By way of compensation the Ministry of Public Works assigned Benfica a plot on a large expanse of open land called Campo Grande, which had formerly been home to their great rivals, Sporting Club between 1917–37. (In fact it was practically next door to where Sporting still played – the site now occupied by their present-day José Alvalade Stadium.)

And so, as the Germans advanced on Moscow

and Japan prepared to bomb Pearl Harbour, in Salazar's 'neutral' Portugal construction of a national stadium was underway near Caxias, while Benfica prepared ground number five, Campo Grande, their largest yet, with raised open terracing on three sides and what amounted to a long covered balcony along the rear of the main seated area. In a symbolic opening ceremony on 5 October 1941, samples of soil from each of Benfica's previous grounds were mixed with the new pitch, as if to put a seal upon the club's hitherto wandering existence.

But Benfica were victims of their own popularity. This was a period (from 1940–55) when between them, Benfica and Sporting won just about every honour in Portuguese football, but were forced to play many of their games in the new national stadium, because their own stadiums were too small. Thus, in 1951 plans were drawn up by architect J. Simões, a former Benfica athlete, for a 60,000 capacity stadium, to be built on fields between Benfica and Campo Grande. The first ground was broken in June 1953, by club president Joaquim Ferreira Bogalho, and this time he ensured there were to be no half measures. Posters, lotteries, exhibitions and publicity drives all drew attention to Benfica's ambitious plans for a sports village, and brought a flood of donations from excited members, many of whom visited the site for tours of inspection.

The Estádio da Luz was finally revealed to the world on 1 December 1954. The Eagles had landed!

Their new nest was, by the standards of the day, quite plain – an open bowl, with two tiers of predominantly concrete, terraced seats, no athletics track, and a pitch sunk so deeply that the upper tier was raised only marginally above ground level. The surrounds were also completely open, which promised not so much plenteous car-parking space – remember, this was one of Europe's poorest countries at the time – as acres of room for the future provision of other sporting installations.

Porto were guests for the first game, and in winning 3–1 the northerners exacted revenge for Benfica's 8–2 victory at the opening of their own stadium, two years earlier. Porto won again at Luz on 19 January 1958, for Portugal's first flood-lit match in modern times.

Floodlights were only the beginning, however. Eight months later construction began on the erec-

'E Pluribus Unum' – gateway to the Eagle's nest.

tion of a third tier, on stilts behind the east side, which, when opened by the Portuguese President on 5 October 1960, boosted Benfica's capacity to 75,000 (while membership had already topped 50,000). Two months later Eusébio arrived from Mozambique, and the rest, as they say, is history.

In the eighteen seasons between 1960 and 1977 Benfica won fourteen League titles (Sporting managed the other four), celebrated two European Cup wins, in 1961 and 1962, and in the same competition made three further final appearances, in 1963, 1965 and 1968. But there was also a flair, a fallibility even, about Benfica, and above all at Luz, an intensity of emotion, which lent Benfica romance at a time when otherwise Portugal was in the grip of political and social decline, followed by the turmoil of revolution in 1974 and then democratic renaissance.

Only when the dust settled and Benfica had recovered from a few barren seasons in the late 1970s, did work start afresh on completing the Stadium of Light. Two Doubles and an appearance in the 1983 UEFA Cup Final provided the impetus for the third tier to be completed and for the stadium thus to lay claim, proudly, to the title of largest venue in Europe (since the Bernabeu's capacity had been reduced for the 1982 World Cup). The last section on the west side, which included a new entrance block, was inaugurated on 21 September 1985 v. Dynamo Bucharest, in the presence of President Eanes, Prime Minister Soares, and of course the former 'King', Eusébio. The Stadium of Light now held an astonishing 120,000 people, all seated, mostly without cover, but all dazzled by the sheer enormity of what Benfica had achieved.

PORTUGAL

Stadium of Light – and white, if no great comfort.

And so with this history in mind, we pull off the highway and with a growing sense of awe, approach the main, west entrance, where a giant black, metallic eagle is perched above the central door. *'E Pluribus Unum'* reads the motto underneath. This could almost be an airport or government building.

Inside the echoing, cool foyer one is confronted by yet another eagle, this one sculpted in granite in 1955 by the same man who designed the east side upper tier, Soares Branco. It originally stood outside the stadium on a plinth. In adjoining chambers there is a club museum containing 15,000 trophies, and a hall containing portraits of every club president.

Entering the stadium, one is then torn between two reactions. On one hand, is this all? Three tiers of concrete benches, a few sun-bleached red seats, no roof, and four stained, brown, concrete floodlight towers peeking over the rim? It is big alright, but then there are plenty of other stadiums which look even bigger.

On the other hand, as the eye starts to absorb

detail one begins to see patches of white – walls, barriers, seats. One notices that the oval pitch area is, unusually, entirely grassed, with not even a sliver of a perimeter track. It is like looking down into the crater of a volcano, half-filled by a deep, still, green pool. Gradually one begins to see why the stadium is so aptly named. There is hardly a shadow in the entire arena.

In fact the only real contrast is provided where the rear of the middle tier of seats, occupied by 230 very simple, private pens (each seating five), is cast into shadow by the overhang of the upper tier. One section of the middle ring, on the west side, is glassed-in, presumably to save dignitaries from too much contact with José Public, while directly below them is a long press gallery, covered in perspex, apparently to save radio commentators from similarly irksome encounters.

The third, or upper tier, covered in white bench seats, is the deepest of the three, and on the east side it rises up in the centre like a saddleback. At each end is an electronic scoreboard on a concrete plinth, while the lights, as already noted, are on concrete towers, like those one sees used for fire-fighting practice. At the top of each tower is a red, neon eagle, while at the base, now outside the stadium, is a chequerboard of white tiles. Each tile bears the name of a supporter who contributed money to the stadium's construction, which could explain why, in a city which has been disfigured more than most by the spray can, there is hardly a drop of graffiti in the entire Benfica complex.

Of course Benfica, like Sporting and Porto, is much more than a football club. Walking round to the south of the stadium one sees an athletics track, donated by a supporter in 1972 (for which he ascended to the honorary rank of Golden Eagle, along with the likes of Eusébio). Then, in addition, there are various training pitches, an indoor sports hall, two indoor swimming pools and twelve tennis courts.

This brings us to the rear of the east stand, which, with its red paintwork and white concrete walls, is beginning to show its age a little. But it

Lights of the stadium, with the neon eagle on top ...

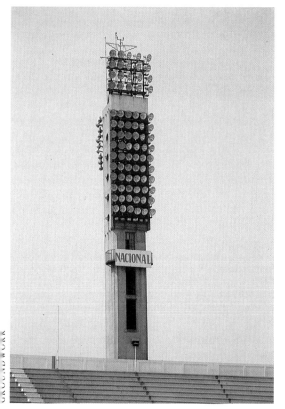

... and the names of honoured Eagle supporters on tiles below.

is also the busiest part of the stadium, for it includes a restaurant, club shop, young players' hostel and, most surprisingly of all, right under the stand, a web of basketball courts, sprint tracks, and even a 3000-seater sports arena. On a rise behind this stand are blocks of modern apartments, built by the club as a lucrative investment and occasionally rented by the players.

In all, the complex caters for twenty-two different sports, apart from football, for a membership which in 1989 had reached *socio* number 90,000. Furthermore, Benfica have now been settled at the stadium for over thirty-five years, and for a club which had five grounds in its first forty-five years, this must surely give one sufficient justification to ink it in as Benfica's permanent address. But not under the name of Estádio do Sport Lisboa e Benfica. Whatever the club may say, it is still the Estádio da Luz, and should always remain so. Take away the 'Light', and you may take away the glow of inspiration.

171

LISBON

ESTÁDIO JOSÉ ALVALADE

Contrary to popular assumption, Portugal's largest and arguably most popular club is to be found not at Luz but a couple of kilometres back along the highway at the José Alvalade Stadium, another massive, concrete presence by the roadside, just before Lisbon Airport. This is the base of **Sporting Club de Portugal**, which boasts over 100,000 members in twenty sports, and 140 affiliated clubs, some of them very senior indeed – such as Farense and Portimonense, who currently play alongside Sporting in the First Division.

The use of the English word 'club' in their title, instead of the Portuguese 'clube', is indicative of Sporting's origins among the wealthy scions of Lisbon, in 1904. Having formed Campo Grande FC – named after the rural area northeast of Lisbon, in which most of the members resided – a split occurred between those who preferred social gatherings, and those, led by José Alvalade, determined to concentrate on sport. Thus Sporting were formed on 1 July 1906, and courtesy of José's landowning grandfather, Viscount Alvalade, a site was purchased on Campo Grande itself – a large tract of open fields and gardens which would in time play host to several other Lisbon clubs, Benfica included.

Aided by the Alvalade family fortune, Sporting's facilities rapidly developed to embrace tennis, fencing, athletics, show-jumping and gymnastics – all favoured pursuits of the nobility. José himself proved to be a demanding, ambitious leader. When the first pitch was found to be 15 centimetres too long he insisted it be relaid. And when another club, Lisboa FC, vacated their adjacent plot, number 412, on Campo Grande, Sporting snapped it up and built a new ground for themselves on the site. This was opened on 1 April 1917 v. Benfica.

Meanwhile, close by on Campo Grande, Alvalade was involved with a company building an athletics ground, the Estádio de Lisboa. This was subsequently rented by FC Barreirense and called Lumiar (after the nearby district).

By 1926 Sporting's boundaries had moved a little closer to Lumiar, after the father of one of the directors made a gift of 40,000 sq. metres of land adjoining the club's existing plot, 412. Then, ten years later, Sporting purchased another neighbouring plot, a pitch away from Lumiar.

By now claiming around 5000 'Lions' (as members are called), Sporting's empire reached its furthest extent in 1937, when Barreirense were told, with some justification, that since they were supposed to represent Barreiro, a town south of Lisbon, they would have to play in that town or else change their name. Conveniently for Sporting, therefore, Barreirense vacated Lumiar, thus leaving the Lions a quite sizeable stadium to develop.

Then, out of the blue, Benfica turned up on their doorstep.

As we have already noted, in 1940 Benfica's Estádio das Amoreiras was commandeered for a road scheme, and they had been assigned plot 412 on Campo Grande – exactly the one on which Sporting had played between 1917–37.

Between 1941–5, therefore, Sporting and Benfica were virtually next door neighbours, but both were also busily hatching schemes for their own new super-stadiums. Benfica coveted land in Luz, a couple of kilometres west of Campo Grande, while Sporting decided in 1945 to develop the site they already owned. Campo Grande had, after all, been the club's birthplace.

This meant, ironically, that while Benfica were able to play on at Campo Grande during their new stadium's construction at Luz, Sporting had to move out in order to develop theirs, because Benfica were occupying the only other usable part of the site.

From 1945–56 Sporting flitted between three smaller venues, belonging to Futebol Benfica (now a Third Division club), Atlético Club (in Alcantara, near the 25 April suspension bridge), and Casa Pia's Estádio Pina Manique (2 kilometres southwest of Benfica).

Even more ironically, Sporting's eleven years of exile turned out to be the most successful in their history. Inspired by a forward line nicknamed 'the five violins', Sporting won the championship seven times and the Cup four times. Had European competition started earlier, argue fans of the Lions, theirs would have been the team to dominate the Continent, far moreso than Benfica's European conquerors of the early 1960s.

Buoyed by this unprecedented success, plus, as at Benfica, a massive campaign of fund raising, the José Alvalade Stadium was finally ready for

PORTUGAL

GROUNDWORK

Stadium of green and white, with the more recent east side seating (right) clearly distinguishable from the original end terracing.

inauguration on Sporting's fiftieth anniversary, 1 July 1956.

The new 49,089 capacity stadium differed from Benfica's in several respects. Firstly it had a roof (concrete, slightly vaulted and cantilevered over the west side). Secondly, there was only one, deep tier of concrete bench seating, which, like the Estádio Nacional, did not fully extend around the east side. Instead, a lower tier of terracing filled the gap.

Sporting also laid an athletics track in their new home, and it is this which nowadays lends the stadium a rather sickly hue for, unlike most tracks, Sporting's is pale green. Added to bands of green and white plastic seating under the roof, one is left with little doubt as to the club colours.

Since 1956 there has been only one major alter-ation – in the mid-1980s the east gap was filled in, which raised the capacity to 75,230, all-seated. In this respect, and also in terms of sporting facilities both in and around the stadium, Sporting do lag slightly behind Benfica. Part of the reason is that since winning the European Cup Winners' Cup in 1964, Sporting have been Portuguese champions and Cup winners only ten times in total (compared with twenty-five for Benfica). In Portugal, where only three clubs dominate, that is almost tan-tamount to failure.

It might also be said that the Lions have gained more headlines for their in-fighting and indebt-edness, which partly explains why the stadium began to look a little rough by the late 1980s. Refurbishment eventually began in 1989, but it will be a while before the club's plans are finally realised. Exactly like Porto (see page 175), Sport-ing are to dig up their athletics track, lower the pitch and extend the tiers of seating downwards, to create a capacity of 120,000. There are also plans for a hotel and various other installations in the immediate vicinity, because in Portugal it is not simply a matter of what is achieved on the football pitch, but how the club as a whole is managed. Thus, while Sporting fight hard to keep up with Benfica and Porto in the honours stakes, around the José Alvalade Stadium, bulldozers rumble, the earth moves, and the pale green track grows ever paler in the hot, dusty sun.

● Unseen by tourists, a few blocks behind the marble Jerónimos Monastery and the famous Belém Tower in southwest Lisbon, is the **Estádio do Restelo**, intriguing home of **Os Belenenses**, Lisbon's third club. Formed in 1919 after a split at Benfica, Belenenses' major feat was to win the 1946 championship, thus becoming the only club ever to break the Big Three's monopoly.

Situated in the residential district of Restelo,

173

PORTUGAL

The Estádio do Restelo's terrace-top view over the Tagus.

the stadium holds 40,000 all-seated, and has very English, square floodlight pylons. But the location is unique. Cut into a hillside, there is a high, walled embankment behind the north curve, and cantilevered roofs over blue seats on either side of the lower tier and running track.

But it is towards the south end that one's gaze is drawn, to a marvellous view, over the monastery roof, of the River Tagus, with the slender threads of the 25 April suspension bridge linking Lisbon with the distant bank. With a view like this, it's no wonder the stadium restaurant is so popular.

● Across the suspension bridge the motorway heads south to Setúbal, Portugal's third city. **Vitória Setúbal** play at the 30,000 capacity **Estádio do Bonfim** (literally Stadium of Good End), whose architecture need not detain us – modern, concrete, like a smaller version of Sporting. But the entrance has an interesting plaque, commemorating Bonfim's opening in September 1962, by the despised State President, Admiral Amerigo Thomás. His name has since been violently erased, because on 25 April 1974 he was deposed in a coup and sent packing to Brazil.

Until 1962, Vitória played nearby at the tiny Campo dos Arcos, a sandy ground bordered by

an ancient viaduct. History is still at hand at Setúbal's current home – the fourteenth-century Chapel of Saint Bonfim actually abuts onto the stadium concourse. Although Bonfim is the patron saint of local fishermen, every year on Vitória's anniversary the players and officials pack the chapel to pray for the club. Judging by their honours list – two cups in seventy years – it looks like the fishermen get the better net response.

**God on their side?
Behind the terracing at Setúbal.**

OPORTO

ESTÁDIO DAS ANTAS

After the Eagles and Lions of Lisbon, we go north to the Dragons of Oporto. Like the region's wine, **FC Porto** travel well (1987 World Club Champions in Tokyo, for example), and have improved with age (by becoming Benfica's main challengers in recent years, in place of Sporting).

Porto formed when a certain José Monteiro da Costa returned from a trip to England full of enthusiasm for the game and, as president of a local horticultural society, managed to convert a nursery into a sports ground. Called Campo da Reinha (the Queen's Ground), and situated on what is now Rua Antero de Quental, the first game was in December 1906, v. Boavista (formed three years earlier and still Porto's local rivals). On 26 January 1913 they opened a new ground, close by on Rua da Constituição, with a tour-

nament involving Benfica, Oporto CC and Real Vigo. The Campo da Constituição still exists, on one of Oporto's busiest streets, and is worth a visit if only to form an impression of a typical, early twentieth-century Latin ground. Hidden behind a whitewashed wall, only the name 'Football Club de Porto' above a gateway, numbered 900, announces its presence. Leaving the city bustle behind, inside one finds a dusty haven, like an old courtyard, with trees and segments of the old terracing surrounding a sandy pitch, now the haunt of energetic schoolchildren – future '*Portistas*', no doubt.

It was in this backyard at Campo da Constituição that Porto became first national champions in 1922, and, thereafter, the main challenger to the two dominant Lisbon clubs.

In common with both Sporting and Benfica, Porto moved to their present stadium in the 1950s. Built in the Antas district of northeast Oporto, on a rise which in the late nineteenth century was found to contain prehistoric graves, the stadium's main feature was a wafer-thin cantilevered roof

Das Antas in 1988. The former pitch level was where the new, lighter terracing meets the old.

GROUNDWORK

175

over the west side, echoed at the rear by a smaller cantilevered canopy over the main forecourt. Otherwise the Estádio das Antas was a more modern, though marginally smaller version of the Estádio Nacional; it too had an athletics track, was shaped like a 'C', with a gap on the east side, and had terraced seating for 50,000 on its three sides. Benfica provided the opposition for the inaugural game, on 28 May 1952, but then ruined the party with an 8–2 victory (although, as we have previously noted, Porto did gain revenge two years later by winning the opening game at the Estádio da Luz).

Unlike the national stadium, das Antas had floodlights installed and lost its gap, both in the 1960s, followed in 1976 by the addition, above the new east side, of an extra, open deck on top (the Spanish 'anfiteatro'). This upper deck forms, in effect, a separate stand whose rear balconies rise four storeys high, but whose base is rooted in terracing used for the training pitch behind (as seen at Dynamo Zagreb also).

The completion of this stand – with brackets at the back ready to support a future roof – increased the capacity to 70,000, but this was only part of the expanding Porto empire. Already the complex had a 7000 capacity sports hall, an indoor swimming pool and a large bingo hall.

Getting a 'full house' was not Porto's problem, however. Creating a larger one was, principally because surrounding access roads made building up the existing stands an impossibility. Porto therefore had to take the opposite route – downwards. So while the team sought refuge at Boavista (see below), the turf was, literally, rolled up in coils, and then 110,000 cubic metres of soil excavated, thus lowering the pitch by 6 metres and allowing the creation of 20,000 extra places in space formerly occupied by the running track.

When the Estádio das Antas is empty the new, lighter-coloured lower tier is clearly distinguishable from the original upper tier. They meet at what used to be ground level. Yet when das Antas has its full complement of 90,000 all-seated spectators, so neatly has the extra space been achieved that one might easily believe the stadium had always been this cavernous. Turf now covers the entire oval-shaped ground, which adds a pleasing unity to the new layout.

Das Antas reopened on 17 December 1986 with another game v. Benfica, but since then, elsewhere in the complex, building work has continued apace, with the laying out of new training pitches, a cultural centre, new club offices and an Olympic-sized indoor swimming pool. For a club with 70,000 members and 20 different · disciplines, money seems to be no object.

But lest anyone forgets the transient nature of modern success, in complete contrast to Porto's bourgeoning facilities, on a high ridge behind the stadium's north curve and visible to all, is an archetypical ramshackle, chaotic car scrapyard. How long before the Dragons swallow up this land too? And how long before das Antas, along with Lisbon's three other major super-bowls, forms the basis of a Portuguese bid for the European Championships? UEFA could do a lot worse.
● Two kilometres west of Porto, in the district of **Boavista**, is the **Estádio do Bessa**. After the cultured curves of SCP, SLB and FCP, here is a ground straight out of the English Fourth Division (apart from its Continental-style floodlight masts). Decked in black and white, to echo Boavista's black and white chequered shirts, the ground is basic, has narrow terracing, and is overlooked by modern office blocks. It is to das Antas what St Ouen is to the Parc des Princes, or St Pauli to the Volksparkstadion. Need one say more?

Straight out of the English Fourth Division – Boavista's compact and unassuming Estádio do Bessa, a really traditional football ground in a country well blessed with concrete superbowls.

REPUBLIC OF IRELAND

DUBLIN

LANSDOWNE ROAD

In terms of wealth and respectability, soccer in the Republic of Ireland (or Eire) has for many years trailed behind rugby and both traditional Irish sports, Gaelic football and hurling. For this reason, compared with the Irish Rugby Football Union's plush headquarters at Lansdowne Road, or the Gaelic Athletic Association's 75,000 capacity Croke Park, also in Dublin, the national soccer stadium, Dalymount Park (see page 178), has remained very much the humble abode of Irish sport.

Since 1971 however, and especially since Eire's successes in both the 1988 European

Lansdowne Road – irregular terracing, a railway under the West Stand and heaps of Irish charm.

PETER BARROW

177

REPUBLIC OF IRELAND

COLORSPORT

The West Stand and pavilion.

Championships and the 1990 World Cup qualifiers, soccer's status within the Republic has risen dramatically, and short of hiring Croke Park for the more important internationals – about as likely as there being stock-car racing at Lord's – the FA of Ireland has had little choice but to go, old-school tie and cap in hand, to the rugby chaps.

In fact, hiring Lansdowne Road is nothing new, for not only is it the oldest surviving international rugby venue in the world (the first match, v. England, having been in 1878), but it is also, whisper this, the world's second oldest football international venue still in current, regular use after Cardiff Arms Park, Wales. England's visit to Lansdowne Road in March 1900 predates the international debuts of the Racecourse Ground (Wales) in 1905, and both Hampden Park (Scotland) and the Parc des Princes (France) in 1906 (although it is true that football did not find a regular spot at Lansdowne Road until after 1971).

In common with many rugby venues, there is a comfortable innocence about the ground. Along Lansdowne Road itself, the ornate boundary walls are decked in ivy, while facing the pitch on either side of the main, West Stand are detached, mock-

Tudor pavilions, belonging to the two resident rugby clubs, Wanderers FC and Lansdowne Club. The West Stand itself has a tall upper tier covered by a pitched roof, dating from 1955, and a lower tier remodelled in 1977. Occupants of this stand are well used to feeling the earth move, because directly underneath the upper tier's concrete framework runs the Dublin to Dun Laoghaire railway line, which emerges from under the stand into a small station just across Lansdowne Road itself. To enter the rear of the West Stand there are tunnels underneath the railway line.

Both end terraces are uncovered and irregularly shaped to fit in with the boundary roads, but this only adds to the charm of the stadium.

The fourth side of Lansdowne Road is the most dramatic. Designed by Ove Arup, the new East Stand was opened in February 1984 and has 13,000 dark green seats on two decks, covered by a deep, white panelled, cantilevered roof, which rather disconcertingly does not extend the full length of the pitch, because residents in the houses behind objected to the loss of their natural light.

Apart from having to pay the IRFU 15 per cent of gate receipts, Lansdowne Road has two drawbacks for the FAI. Firstly, there are no floodlights, which means all games must be played in the afternoon. Secondly, because it is first and foremost a rugby pitch, the turf is bumpier and has coarser grass than is usual for soccer.

But can the FAI really complain? Even though the profits of Eire's international success are to be ploughed into modernising Dalymount Park, its capacity will never match that of Lansdowne Road, which for football is licensed to hold 49,000 (25,000 seated). Of course if the national team reverted to its former losing ways the choice need never arise. But until that is the case, one can only stare philosophically into one's Guinness and declare that there are indeed worse fates in this world than having to play on a bumpy pitch in the middle of the afternoon.

DUBLIN

DALYMOUNT PARK

After the tweeds and college scarves of Lansdowne Road, a few kilometres north of the River Liffey

the narrow back alleys of Phisborough lead us to another side of Dublin's 'fair city' – Dalymount Park. No calm suburban streets here. No pavilions, no clubhouses. Just terraced houses, busy streets, Mountjoy Prison and a typical working-class community with a crumbling football ground at the end of its back garden.

But Dalymount Park, so long a victim of soccer's struggle to survive in Eire, now looks like being the major beneficiary of its revival, having been purchased by the FAI from its owners, **Bohemian FC**, in 1989, for just £600,000. It could have been sold to a commercial developer for more, but Bohemians were persuaded by the FAI's pledge to refurbish the ground and give the club a 99-year lease.

Of course Dalymount represents an excellent long-term investment for the FAI, but considering that its new found profits from international success could have gone towards building a modern, out-of-town stadium, the rescue act could be interpreted as a purely sentimental gesture. Maybe, but in 1987 the famous old Milltown ground of Shamrock Rovers, in south Dublin, was lost to developers – a crushing blow to Irish football – and more grounds would have followed. In saving Dalymount therefore, the FAI has become one of the few football associations in the world to have won the gratitude and admiration of the ordinary fans.

Bohemians are Eire's oldest surviving senior club. Formed in 1890, they opened Dalyer, as it is known locally, on 7 September 1901, and hosted their first international, Ireland v. Scotland, in March 1904. But not until after the Southern Irish split from the Belfast-based Irish FA in June 1921 did Dublin really come to the international fore. The newly independent FAI's first guests at Dalymount were the USA, in June 1924, and from 1929 until 1971 Dalymount was *the* home of Eire soccer and Cup Finals, renowned for its tightly packed terracing, which brought the crowd within a metre or so of the touchlines.

The post-Bradford and Hillsborough era finds Dalymount not quite so quaint or appealing. For example, the main entrance, such as it is, is reached via the sort of narrow back alleyway where one would normally seek out a cheap car mechanic, not a national stadium.

The main stand – a traditional, foot-stomping iron and wooden construction, built in 1928 with a corrugated pitched roof and a red balcony wall – is about as primitive a stand as one can find at any senior European venue. Perhaps it's just as well that watching over it is the spire of the local church, St Peter's. The State keeps an eye on Dalymount too, for in one corner of the open

Dalymount Park –
a base for the future with its roots in the past.
Its purchase made the FAI the toast of Dublin football.

east, or Tramway End, terrace, is a tall block of government offices.

Opposite the main stand is the open, grass-topped north terrace, which backs onto a row of houses and gardens, while the only standing cover at the ground is provided by an old barrel roof over one half of the west, St Peter's Road terrace. Poking through this roof is one of the floodlight pylons. The roof has been there since 1945; the lights were first used on 7 March 1962, for a match between an Irish XI and Arsenal.

Since then the place has barely changed, which is why the capacity has been steadily reduced to only 22,000 (2000 seated), compared with Dalyer's record gate of 47,600, on 19 May 1957. (When the visitors that day, England, scored a late equaliser, it was said the silence could be heard a mile away in O'Connell Street!)

When modernisation plans are eventually implemented, the projected all-seated capacity of around 28,000 will still require that Lansdowne Road be used as a back-up. But never mind. Dalymount will be a base for the future, with its roots in the past. And so what if Bohemians rarely attract gates of more than 2000, or that **Shamrock Rovers** (who currently share Dalyer) are only marginally more popular. Having played third and fourth fiddle to other sports in the Emerald Isle for so long, the FAI wants to build on what strengths and traditions it now has in its grasp, before the international bubble bursts and the opportunity to consolidate may be lost forever.

ROMANIA

BUCHAREST

STADIONUL 23 AUGUST

In common with their Soviet bloc partners, the people of Romania did not get down to the serious business of building a national stadium until the early 1950s. But once started, their stadium was completed in great haste – by volunteers of course – in readiness for the 1953 Socialist youth and student festival. The name 23 August refers to the date of the first uprising against the occupying Germans in 1944, now commemorated as a national holiday.

The 65,000 capacity, all-seated stadium is a typical Eastern European venue; at first glance it could almost be Leipzig, Chorzów or Warsaw. Built into a natural hollow in the centre of the expansive Parcul de Cultură Și Sport, east of

Pre-match entertainment in Romania. Nicolae Ceaucescu holds a Party in his own honour.

central Bucharest, it is essentially a vast open bowl with a single tier of green and yellow bench seats, circled by a tree- and bush-lined concourse around the upper rim.

The main focal point, cut into the west side, is a somewhat incongruous neoclassical loggia, ornamented in yellow brick, with columns, pilasters and an upper balustrade. This provides the stadium's only covered viewing – for a handful of dignitaries, naturally – but also rather thoughtlessly blocks the view from seats immediately on either side (these are not, as a consequence, counted in the overall capacity). Behind the viewing balcony lie marble halls through which honoured guests enter from the neighbouring park. (In the park stand two tall gantries; one for television cameras, the other, chequered red and white, not for radar as it would appear but for training parachutists.)

Leaving the Party bosses in their marble isolation, we continue around the concourse, which is ringed by small green flagpoles marking the aisles, and also by ornate drinking fountains. Water may be plentiful in Romania – not much else is – but alcohol is strictly banned from all stadiums. Yet if there is no drink, why does the ground behind the loggia seem to sink eerily beneath your feet? That, apparently, is the result of an earthquake in 1977, when the walkway dropped by 30 centimetres or so.

Further along the concourse we pass under the stadium's extraordinary floodlights (the only ones in Romania until Steaua recently lit up). Erected in 1970, the leaning pylons, with their upturned heads and two supporting legs, resemble giant cats, alert and watchful over the proceedings.

At each end of the stadium are scoreboards, the more advanced one dating from 1981, when the 23 August Stadium hosted the international student games. For that event a synthetic track was laid and, immediately opposite the loggia, two sets of five simple white concrete arches were erected

GROUNDWORK

It's August 23rd so it must be Bucharest.

along the concourse, on either side of a giant torch holder. At the foot of the earth banking behind these arches is another neoclassical entrance hall from where the players enter the stadium. Beyond lie the modern flats of the Socului district, their upper floors overlooking the arena.

The stadium hosts most of Romania's international matches, occasional major European club games, plus all domestic Cup Finals, but it is also the country's prime athletics venue. Here, for example, the Romanian Cusmir broke the women's long jump world record in 1985.

Although Romanians have had precious little else to celebrate in recent years, unless one also counts Steaua's achievements on the football field, the illusion of economic success and political unity is stoically maintained at the national stadium by such predictable slogans as 'Long live our dear country, free and independent', and 'Long live the Romanian Communist Party led by the Secretary General, Comrade Nicolae Ceaucescu'. Most ironically of all in this benighted country, prominently displayed on the loggia's flat roof is Romania's national emblem, depicting wheat, fir trees, oil and sunshine – a veritable land of plenty one would think. The punters on the flaking bench seats know differently.

BUCHAREST

STADIONUL STEAUA

In Romania, as in Bulgaria, football is dominated by two clubs from the capital backed respectively

by the army and the police. **Steaua Bucharest,** Romania's army club, can just pull rank in terms of domestic honours – they are also the only Eastern European team to have won the European Cup (in 1986) – but in terms of stadium facilities Steaua easily outgun their main rivals, Dinamo.

Yet strangely, Steaua – or Star – were homeless until 1974. Formed in 1947 as ASA, they adopted

ROMANIA

Steaua pave their way to success.

their present name in 1960 and played at various venues, including Rapid Bucharest's Giuleşti Stadium, the 23 August Stadium and the Republic Stadium (built 1921). The Steaua Stadium, in the dusty western outskirts of Bucharest, was then a mere juniors' pitch, where in 1956 a small boy was spotted playing football by the club's tennis coach and persuaded to change disciplines. His name – Ilie Nastase.

The football stadium was opened on 9 April 1974, with a friendly v. OFK Belgrade, and until recently held 30,842 (although see below). A very basic rectangular stadium with four open banks of bench seating, the only cover is provided for broadcasters in cabins along one side.

Opposite, where Steaua's more vocal supporters congregate above the tunnel, a sign reads, 'Steaua, don't forget we want victory!' (which rhymes in Romanian), and in the adjacent corner, the 'tribuna copiilor' is reserved for under-14s, all of whom are admitted gratis. A paved walkway, lined by green drinking fountains (as at the national stadium), surrounds the pitch, which is said to be the best in the country.

Otherwise, one would hardly imagine the stadium to be home to such an illustrious club. Recognising this and awash with income from success in Europe, in July 1988 Steaua initiated a major reconstruction programme, involving the installation of floodlights and an extra tier of seating all round, to expand the capacity to 55,000, although there will still be no cover.

But football is only one activity in this extensive, though by Western European standards, spartan, complex, which is neatly landscaped with conifers and trim pathways in best military tradition. In fact the Steaua club is brimming with champions. Members have won seventeen Olympic gold medals, and in 1987, of the twenty-three sports represented by the club, eighteen became national champions. Furthermore, unlike the rest of Bucharest, Steaua's facilities are improving all the time. There are plans for a 15,000 capacity rugby stadium, an Olympic-sized swimming pool, a 3000 seater tennis arena, a speedway track, a 10,000 capacity athletics stadium and a ten-storey hotel. When completed it will amount to one of Eastern Europe's finest sports centres, and one of the neatest, since it is maintained by soldiers from the neighbouring barracks. In short, despite Romania's limited resources, Steaua thrive on their army service, while every other club, it would seem, must fall into line.

● Bucharest has four other senior venues, the most important being the plain 18,000 capacity **Dinamo Stadium**, belonging to Steaua's rivals, **Dinamo Bucharest**, and, with the same capacity, the **Giuleşti Stadium**, home of the capital's traditional favourites, **CS Rapid Bucharest**, the team of the railway workers. Built in the late 1930s, the Giuleşti is situated in the district of that name, has a narrow running track and is nicknamed 'the horseshoe' because of its U-shaped stands.

AGERPRES

The Giuleşti Stadium, home of Rapid, the railway workers' favourite.

SCOTLAND

The English may have invented the modern game of football, but it was the Scots who refined it. The same is partly true of football ground design. While the majority of early English grounds were relatively small or humble affairs, by 1908 Scotland, or rather Glasgow, was able to boast the three largest grounds in the world: **Ibrox Park**, home of the staunch Protestant club **Rangers**; **Hampden Park**, property of the amateurs **Queen's Park**; and **Celtic Park**, home of Rangers' Catholic rivals, **Celtic**. These three grounds – essentially vast open, oval-shaped bowls with one main stand – were laid out by a Glaswegian engineer, Archibald Leitch, the man who was to dictate the shape and form of almost every major British ground built or redeveloped between 1900–1939.

Hampden Park, the national stadium, was in fact the largest in the world until Brazil's Maracana Stadium opened its doors in 1950. The all-time record attendance for any European football match belongs to Hampden, for Scotland's match v. England on 17 April 1937, when 149,415 paid

admission and a further 10,000 were said to have entered illegally. Just seven days later Hampden chalked up the European club record, this time for Celtic's Cup Final v. Aberdeen, watched by 147,365 (although 20,000 more were reportedly locked outside the ground).

Hampden's third major record is for an attendance at a European competition match. Despite it being played on a midweek evening, 136,505 attended the European Cup semi-final, Celtic v. Leeds, on 15 April 1970.

Nowadays the mere fact that Hampden still exists is something of a miracle. By the late 1960s it was a crumbling wreck, and it took years of political manoeuvring and public appeals before a £3 million refurbishment programme could begin in 1981. Yet so advanced was the stadium's state of decline that even after this expenditure it remained an extremely basic, albeit much safer venue, with only 10,000 seats in a total capacity of 74,370.

Hampden could have remained in that state

Hampden Park, reborn with half its former capacity but facing an uncertain future.

Celtic Park has all-round cover but too few seats for internationals.

SCOTLAND

ACTION IMAGES

Leitch's superb South Stand (left) is all that remains
of the old Ibrox Park. Its red brick frontage, fortunately,
is classed as a listed building, although the interior has been
altered to accommodate executive boxes.

ACTION IMAGES

Ibrox Park's three new stands are built on the goalpost principle,
with the roof suspended under the 'crossbar'.
Note the South Stand's criss-cross balcony wall –
that was the trademark of Archibald Leitch.

indefinitely had it not been for FIFA's 1989 pronouncement that after 1992 no standing will be permitted at World Cup matches.

There are many who believe that a second phase of improvements to Hampden would be a waste of resources and that the stadium is an anachronism, because of its layout, location and ownership (still in the hands of Queen's Park, who, eerily, attract League gates of only a few hundred to the stadium). On the other hand, if Hampden is not converted into an all-seated stadium – and it would require roofs to be built over the two open sides of the ground – what are the alternatives for the national team?

Pittodrie, the home of **Aberdeen**, was the first all-seated ground in Britain, but though admirable it holds only 22,568. Celtic Park holds 61,800 and is completely covered, but with only 9000 seats it is hardly more suitable than Hampden.

This leaves Ibrox Park, a ground with an eventful history. In 1902 it was the scene of the world's first football disaster, when part of a tall wooden terrace collapsed, sending twenty-six people to their deaths during an international v. England. After its subsequent redevelopment Ibrox then grew to hold 118,000, which made it the world's second largest ground after Hampden. But more tragedy was to come. On 2 January 1971, after an 'Old Firm' derby v. Celtic, sixty-six fans died on one of Ibrox's notoriously steep exit routes known as Stairway 13. It was this second Ibrox disaster which prompted the introduction of the Safety of

Sports Grounds Act in 1975, legislation which was to have a profound effect on British grounds over the next decade.

Burdened with the stigma of their dangerous ground, in 1977 Rangers unveiled a plan to transform Ibrox completely on three sides, leaving (fortunately) Leitch's distinctive 1928 South Stand intact. In a similar fashion to Utrecht, but on a much larger scale, Ibrox's elliptical bank of terracing was cleared and replaced by three identical rectangular stands. Because Rangers are the richest club in Britain they were able to complete this £10 million programme in just three years, but it was an enormous risk. From a huge, antiquated bowl holding 100,000 in 1977, Ibrox had become by 1981 a 44,500 capacity modern marvel, in which the vast majority of spectators – 36,500 – were seated.

The gamble worked. A set of supporters formerly notorious for invading the pitch now sat happily in comfort with not a perimeter fence in sight, which, combined with their subsequent policy of lavish spending on top players, enabled Rangers to regularly fill the stadium with trouble-free (if not entirely bigot-free) crowds.

That it took the 1971 tragedy to bring about this state of affairs is to be regretted, but that Ibrox is now one of Europe's finest and safest football grounds, and one which will inevitably stage Scotland's future World Cup games if Hampden is not upgraded, is vindication enough of Rangers' bold and imaginative initiative.

SOVIET UNION

MOSCOW

CENTRALNY STADION LENINA

'The Civil War fronts are still ablaze, starvation and ruin hold the young Soviet Republic in a vice, yet we are today starting our campaign for mass physical culture.'

So spoke Nikolai Podvoisky in 1920 as the foundation stones were laid for the International Red Stadium. And although that particular structure never quite lived up to its grandiose billing, the stadium which took its place in 1956 has indeed become a mecca for the masses. Named after Podvoisky's boss, Vladimir Ilyich Lenin, father of the Russian Revolution, the Central Lenin Stadium is probably the biggest and most popular sports complex in the world (in Russian the term '*stadion*' refers to the whole complex, not just the actual stadium). Official statistics claim that on average over 10,000 people use its 140 separate sports installations every day. These include a 13,000 capacity Palace of Sports, a 10,500 capacity open-air swimming arena, the 4000 seater Druzhba multi-purpose hall (sometimes used for circuses), 22 smaller sports halls, 11 football pitches, 4 athletics tracks, 3 skating rinks, 55 tennis courts, and last, but not least, one statue of Lenin himself, overcoat unbuttoned, chin up, looking out from his plinth by the main stadium entrance as if expecting Trotsky to turn up with the match tickets.

The 100,000 capacity, all-seated stadium is also kept busy, with football internationals, Cup Finals, the home games of **Spartak Moscow** (the capital's most popular club) and a host of other events, both cultural and sporting – the most famous having been the 1980 Olympic Games. It also has, underneath the seating tiers, a cinema, a theatre, a hotel, a restaurant, and an internationally respected sports medical centre.

Under the spotlight yet again – Lenin at the Lenin Stadium.

GROUNDWORK

185

SOVIET UNION

COLORSPORT

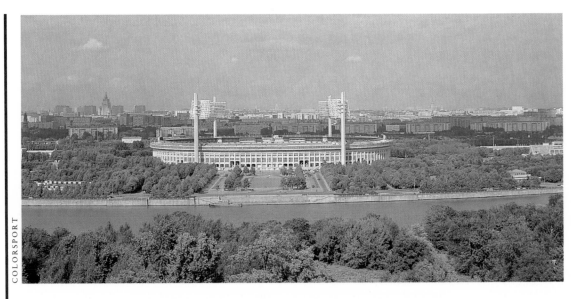

View from the Lenin Hills. Spot Stalin's wedding cake skyscrapers on the horizon.

The best view of this veritable 'city of sport and culture', which is also called Luzhniki Park, is from the Lenin Hills, on the opposite bank of the Moskva River. There, from a platform in front of Moscow State University (one of the city's seven wedding cake skyscrapers built during the Stalin era), one can see that the Lenin Stadium occupies what is almost an island, formed by the Moskva doubling back on itself as it skirts the south-western edge of central Moscow.

Before 1917 the heights of the university were known as the Sparrow Hills, the stadium site was occupied by the Moscow River Yacht Club, and those who were playing in the thriving Moscow football league were either foreigners or members of the Russian bourgeoisie. Then came the Revolution and suddenly sport belonged to the state.

According to James Riordan's *Sport in Soviet Society* (see bibliography), one of the first events at the International Red Stadium was in the summer of 1920 when, as part of a mass display of sport and gymnastics, an International XI of foreign delegates to the Third International Congress (including John Reed, author of *Ten Days That Shook the World*) lost heavily to a Moscow Select team, whose players received a jar of fruit and a bag of flour for their efforts.

Spartak Moscow were formed at the Red Stadium two years later as the Moscow Sports Club, then in 1935 adopted their present name

after becoming affiliated to the trade union for producers' co-operatives (which is why they are sometimes nicknamed 'lavochniki' – the shop-keepers). In the same year the first fully national league got under way, with Moscow clubs forming almost half the number of participants. Spartak, Dynamo Moscow and CSKA (see page 188) led the honours list until 1961 when Kiev finally managed to break the Muscovite monopoly. (Spartak might, however, claim to have the Soviet Union's worst behaved fans, a malaise which looks set to spread as *glasnost*, regrettably, unleashes bigotry and malevolence in equal proportion to free-thinking and democracy.)

The Lenin Stadium as we know it today was the work of an architect called Polikarpov, and although it avoids the overladen decoration which afflicted so much Soviet architecture of the immediate postwar period (some of it dubbed Stalinist Gothic), by contemporary Western European standards it was still a rather dour, monotonous design; a building impressive in scale if not in style.

It opened on 5 August 1956 for the staging of the first All-Union Spartakiad, an event which brought together 34,000 athletes from all over the USSR in a superbly drilled display of human tableaux, gymnastic demonstrations, parades and, not least, sporting competition. This was an era when great socialist superbowls were opened all around the Soviet Bloc – in Prague, Warsaw, Chorzów, Leipzig, Bucharest and Sofia, all serving up the same diet of propagandist events.

There were similarly lavish presentations to mark the staging of the 1980 Olympics, an event for which the Lenin Stadium was substantially improved. The most noticeable change was the installation of four massive steel floodlight masts, measuring approximately 8 x 5 metres at their base and each carrying over 190 lamps. From inside the stadium these floodlights seem to be poised over the rim of the bowl like giant fly-swatters.

In the centre of the east side, a tall Olympic torch holder was set proudly aloft, framed by a curving band of bronze to give it emphasis.

The Lenin Stadium sparkled during the 1980 Olympics, the Russians proving that they could put on a show as good as anything the capitalists had ever managed (although they never quite matched the tastelessness displayed at Los Angeles four years later).

But on a bitterly cold night in 1982, the Lenin Stadium saw the darker side of mass physical culture. Spartak were 1–0 up against Haarlem of Holland in the UEFA Cup when sections of the 15,000 crowd started to leave down an icy ramp. Spartak then scored a late goal, and as those leaving, having heard the cheers, tried to turn back, a fatal crush ensued; perhaps caused by slippage on the ice, perhaps by poor policing. Probably we will never know.

What we do know, however, is that the incident went unreported in the Soviet Union for the next seven years, despite leaked reports in the West which spoke of around twenty deaths. Then came *glasnost* and with it more openness in the reporting of Soviet accidents. In 1989 *Sovietsky Sport*, the official government sports newspaper, telling the story for the first time in the Soviet press, put the death toll at sixty-nine. Some foreign newspapers, meanwhile, put the figure as high as 340, but this seems unlikely.

Certainly ice is a regular visitor to the Luzhniki Park, where each winter the stadium concourse is deliberately turned into a huge public ice rink. And as we skate by the stadium's cinema entrance we see a large, rather ornate thermometer which offers its own chilling comment on Moscow's climate, for it registers only from 3 degrees down to minus 5 degrees centigrade. Any warmer and it's a bonus. Any colder and it's on with the fur hat or risk losing your ears.

● Climactic extremes provide Soviet football's greatest problems, and in order to squeeze in a full fixture list from March to November, clubs in Moscow and Leningrad have taken to playing their early and late season games on full-size artificial pitches in indoor stadiums. The Russians call it *'comnatny futbol'* – 'drawing-room' football – because of the lack of atmosphere. But one cannot help but be impressed by the two indoor Moscow venues – the Olimpiski, capacity 35,000, and the CSKA Palace of Sports, capacity 7000. Nothing remotely like these enormous covered stadiums exists elsewhere in Europe – at least not with full-sized football pitches.

Not that playing on an artificial surface is anything new in Moscow. On May Day 1936 a huge green fibre carpet was rolled across part of Red Square and a game staged between two teams from Spartak Moscow. In 1942 and 1943 the exercise was repeated and commentaries relayed to troops a short distance away on the front, to help boost morale.

For the war fronts were still ablaze, starvation and ruin held the Soviet Republic in a vice, yet in Red Square . . . they played football.

MOSCOW

STADION DYNAMO

Most cities would be delighted with the range of facilities on offer at the Lenin Stadium complex. But in Moscow, a city of 8 million inhabitants, there is much more on offer. Along the tree-lined, busy Leningradsky Prospekt, for example, there are four major sport installations within a short distance of each other; the Stadium of Young Pioneers, the CSKA Palace of Sports, the Dynamo Small Sports Arena (including Europe's biggest gymnasium), and most visible of all, thanks to its prominent leaning floodlights, the 51,000 capacity all-seated Dynamo Stadium.

Until the Lenin Stadium opened in 1956, the Dynamo Stadium was the largest in Moscow. It

187

GROUNDWORK

Dynamo Stadium, Moscow – the Secret Policeman's Ballpark?
Note the top-heavy floodlight pylons, for improved surveillance.

Lokomotiv Moscow keep on the right track with their
neon diesel loco logo.

was built in 1928 and opened with an attempt at a Communist Workers' Olympiad (Frankfurt having staged the Socialist Workers' Games in 1925). It was then revamped in the 1950s and again for the 1980 Olympics. But the Dynamo Stadium is still no more than a completely open bowl with blue and white bench seats, and four portico entrances in what may be described as the 'proletarian classical' style popular between about 1930–53 (sparse, orderly and rather institutional).

There is, however, an interesting frieze over one portico, depicting footballers in playing gear manning artillery. A plaque nearby records the formation at the stadium of a sportsmen's brigade, on 27 June 1941, just five days after the German invasion began. Few of them would return.

Two clubs currently play at the Dynamo Stadium: **CSKA** (the Central Army Sports Club), formed in 1923 and known as the '*Konyushniki*' (stable boys), and **Dynamo Moscow**, who also formed in 1923, after absorbing Orekhovo Sportivny Klub (a pre-Revolutionary club which itself had started as Morozovtsi, a team established by British mill owners). It was perhaps ironic that OSK, having successfully eluded the Tsarist secret police, despite its operation as a front for revolutionary activities, should have become Dynamo, because their sponsors were the new regime's own security forces (which nowadays includes the KGB). Although this relationship was barely admitted until recently, Dynamo have, nevertheless, long been nicknamed '*gorodoviki*' – a Tsarist name for policemen.

● Moscow has two other clubs who regularly appear in the Premier League. **Torpedo Moscow** were formed in 1924 as the team of the motor workers, and named after the first Soviet-built production car, the Torpedo. They play in the so-called Proletarian district of southeast Moscow, in the barely developed **Torpedo Stadium** (capacity 21,000), on the banks of the Moskva.

Much more interesting is the 30,000 capacity **Lokomotiv Stadium** of the railway workers' team, **Lokomotiv Moscow**, out in the distant northeastern suburb of Preobrazhensky. The stadium has two white cantilevered stands, multi-coloured bench seats and an unusual running track composed of black rubber tiles. Best of all, above its street frontage is a wonderful neon sign depicting the club logo, a locomotive, powering down the line. Lokomotiv, Torpedo, Dynamo! Full speed ahead. How could they fail?

GROUNDWORK

TBILISI

STADION DYNAMO

As Naples is to Milan, so the Georgian capital of Tbilisi is to distant Moscow – a southern, slightly exotic hotbed of football fervour. The language is different, the climate is subtropical, but at least the name of the local team has a familiar ring.

Formed in 1925 as one of Dynamo Moscow's many offshoots, **Dynamo Tbilisi** moved into their stadium in 1935, the same year as the All-Union League championship began. First called the Stalin Dynamo Stadium (Stalin was a Georgian, as his original name, Djugashvili, indicates), the decorated columns from that original single-tiered, open stadium can still be seen today, though they have been comprehensively enveloped by a modern concrete shell which was added in the mid-1970s. This was designed by the father and son team of Archil and Georgi Kordiani and consists of a second upper tier, covered all around by a plain, concrete, cantilevered roof. Unusually, the floodlights are grouped in four long, low clusters mounted on the roof and barely visible from inside the stadium.

Inaugurated in 1976 for a European Cup Winners' Cup tie v. Cardiff (a competition Tbilisi eventually won in 1981), the remodelled Lenin Dynamo Stadium, as it is now officially titled, holds 74,324 all-seated and is best described as spacious, functional, but just a touch colourless (a word which certainly doesn't apply to the almost Italianate surrounding district of Didubeh, or indeed the rest of Tbilisi). The bench seating is grey, as are many of the concrete facings, and behind each goal, in order to accommodate the synthetic track, the original lower tier has been cut away to form a high, granite-clad retaining wall.

To Western eyes it seems incredible that such a large stadium has no perimeter fencing or moat, despite the passionate nature of the fans. This is because the front rows are always occupied by a ring of soldiers – a practice adopted at all major Soviet venues since a crowd riot in Leningrad in 1937. Nevertheless, to one grown accustomed to seeing pitches lined by mini-versions of the Berlin Wall, the lack of barriers at Tbilisi lends the stadium a rather intimate, even innocent air. This is reinforced by the fact that like most

Tbilisi – no need for barriers.

Soviet grounds the stadium remains open during weekdays and thus passers-by wander in and out of the stadium, to stroll, jog around the track, or use the sports facilities under the stands. To inspire them, displayed on the stadium's outer columns are lists of all Georgian entrants to past Olympic Games, plus notices detailing the various requirements for the GTO fitness programme (GTO stands for 'Ready for Labour and Defence' and is a national fitness programme open to 7- to 60-year-olds).

There is also a sign proclaiming: 'Keep the stadium clean, beautiful and orderly.'

Beautiful it may not be, but neither is the scene a sterile one. A glance up at the stadium's ornate Georgian-style railings, at the distant mountains, across to the adjacent children's playground, or at the animated mustachioed men watching a schoolboy game on the cinder pitch behind the main stand, and it is quite clear that this is a long way from the moody seriousness of Moscow. The club may be Dynamo in name, but it is most definitely Tbilisi in spirit.

Outside the Dynamo Stadium, colourful boards show the First and Second Division placings.

GROUNDWORK

GROUNDWORK

SOVIET UNION

KIEV

RESPUBLIKANSKY STADION

In Kiev, august city on the banks of the broad River Dniepr, there are no half measures. Greatness and tragedy lace its history. Windswept heights, towering monuments and heavy stone buildings cast light and shadow upon its brooding mass. And in its midst is a stadium which fully reflects this *gravitas*, the Republican or, as it is officially titled, the Ukrainian Republican Central Stadium, home of the mighty **Dynamo Kiev**.

In fact the stadium could hardly be more central. Situated on Ulitsa Pervomaiskaya (May Day Street), which is itself a continuation of Kiev's stately main shopping street, Kreshchatik, the stadium is to Kiev almost what the Bernabeu Stadium is to Madrid – just one institution among

many in a prime location. And with its elaborate, gold-embossed iron railings, its large front courtyard and its entrance portico with Corinthian columns, were it not for the prominent floodlights one might even mistake the stadium for a museum. Even the ticket booths look as if they had once been gatehouses for a Tsar's palace.

Built on what had been the grounds of possibly the last ever Tsarist Russian exhibition (held in 1913), the original stadium on the site, called the Krasny – or Red – Stadium, was built by youth brigades after the Revolution, and opened on 12 August 1923 with a game of 'live chess', in which humans acted the part of chess pieces on an enormous board (with real horses for the knights).

After the formation of Dynamo Kiev in 1927, rebuilding of this simple venue began prior to the first All-Union League championship in 1936. Designed by architect Grechina in the so-called Stalinist Gothic style of the period, it had red granite terraces, a large, classical-style pavilion, and held 50,000 in one open, elliptical bowl. But it took five years to complete, and although 50,000

The Ukrainian Republican Central Stadium – like a public square.

GROUNDWORK

invitations were sent out for the inaugural match between Dynamo Kiev and CSKA, scheduled for 22 June 1941, on the morning of the great day, at 3.00am, the Germans invaded.

In the course of a brutal two-year Nazi occupation the new stadium was destroyed, the Germans having used it as a vehicle depot and then smashed it up on their retreat in November 1943. However, nine months later it was back in action, for an athletics meeting, and in September 1945 its long-awaited official inauguration, now under the name Central Stadium, took place. All the original invitees were asked back, and although no record exists of how many of them actually attended, it is unlikely more than half survived, since 200,000 people had died in the city between 1941–3. (In 1988, just 26 of the original 50,000 were known still to be alive.)

Since the war, of course, Dynamo Kiev have achieved probably the highest international profile of any Soviet club. They were the first non-Muscovite club to win the championship, in 1961. Then in 1975 they were the first Soviet club to win a European honour, the Cup Winners' Cup, a competition they won again in 1986. The players also spent a few gruelling years serving as the basis of the Soviet national squad.

The stadium, meanwhile, had been renamed in 1962 after Nikita Khrushchev (despite his statement several years earlier that nothing should ever be named after a living person). After Khrushchev's downfall – sorry, retirement – in 1964, it reverted to being the Central Stadium, the name by which it is still known popularly, despite the more recent addition of the weightier title of 'Ukrainian Republican'.

Dynamo's success had made it the Soviet Union's best attended venue, so between 1966–70 a second tier of seating was added, cantilevered over the first, which more than doubled the capacity to 104,000 all-seated (now slightly reduced to 100,164). A broadcasting centre was also built on tall, concrete stilts above the main entrance pavilion (since most Premier League matches go out live on local television), and floodlights and an electronic scoreboard installed. The last series of improvements were carried out in 1978–80, when the pitch, track, scoreboard and floodlights were all upgraded for the 1980 Olympic soccer tournament, which Kiev shared with Moscow, Minsk and Leningrad.

Like many Soviet venues, the Republican

Ticket booths, Kiev style.

Central Stadium seldom rests. Dynamo's average gates are around 69,000 (attendances doubled after pre-match lotteries were introduced in 1987), and over 5000 members of the public use the facilities every week for fitness classes. But the stadium also plays an important social role. The elderly stroll in from the street and sit gossiping in the stands, mothers push prams around the perimeter track, while school kids can be seen giggling in the VIP section while puffing on illicit cigarettes. Thus the stadium functions rather like a public square – open to all, on just one condition. No-one may go on the pitch, for, East or West, hell hath no fury like a groundsman scorned.

● Kiev has two other stadiums. The picturesque but confusingly titled **Dynamo Stadium**, set in a hillside park between the river and Komsomol Square (more central than the Central Stadium itself), holds 30,000 and is a busy sports centre.

A few kilometres northeast, on Ulitsa Marshala Rybalko, is the small **Start Stadium**, where a poignant sculpture commemorates the infamous 'match smerti' (match of death) which took place there in August 1942. Despite much of Kiev's population having been enslaved and starved during the Nazi occupation, the Germans 'invited' the locals to a game, which the Ukrainians had the temerity to win, 5–3. Within a few days their entire team was rounded up. Two were spared for work duties, one escaped, the rest were executed. Not content with wreaking death and destruction upon an entire continent, the Nazis could not even bear to lose a game of football.

191

This flamboyant curiosity is the Dynamo Stadium in Minsk. Opened in 1934 and with an extra tier added in 1979 (in preparation for hosting Olympic football in 1980), not surprisingly it is home to Dynamo Minsk, and currently holds 50,682 – gladiators no doubt enter for free.

LENINGRAD

STADION KIROVA

Of all the great Socialist superbowls, none is quite so bracing as the home of **Zenit Leningrad**, the Soviet Union's most northerly senior club. Built on the extreme western tip of Krestovsky Island in the River Neva delta, with the Gulf of Finland on three sides and Victory Park forming a long, straight approach from the east, the Kirov Stadium feels as if it were poised on the very fingertips of Mother Russia.

In design it is unremarkable – little more than an oval of open banking, with the standard electronic scoreboard behind one end, a VIP viewing section on the west side, and rather too much distance between the terracing and the pitch.

And yet otherwise it is quite distinctive. The floodlights in particular, added for the 1980

Olympics, are like silvery space rockets, thrusting upwards into the clear northern sky. The players' tunnel, 60 metres long with coffered walls, even in summer is chilling and dark like a railway tunnel, while up on top of the banking one can gaze out over the watery horizons and watch hydrofoils slip by en route to the naval base at Kronstadt.

More than most Soviet clubs, the players of Zenit have to be extremely adaptable. When the season opens in March, the Kirov is usually under snow, so the club plays its first few matches either in southern resort towns or goes through the sterile motions of '*comnatny futbol*' (drawing-room football) at the Lenin Sports and Concert Complex, an impressive indoor arena which accommodates 19,500 spectators and a full-sized West German Polygrass artificial pitch.

Back in Leningrad – locked in ice for a third of the year – once the Kirov pitch has thawed, then dried out, that usually leaves from mid-June to October to enjoy normal conditions. Then, as the surrounding sea level rises, the groundsman must pray for no early frosts during the final weeks of the season. Otherwise it's back to the drawing-room.

Amid all this, the Zenit player must routinely travel distances of, for example, 2500 kilometres to the Armenian Republic, to play Ararat Erevan, near the Turkish border, or 4000 kilometres to arid Kazakhstan, in order to play Kairat Alma-Ata, near the Chinese border.

To compound Zenit's difficulties, Leningrad – the outdoor museum, as it is called – is no hothouse of football. Which makes it all the more surprising that when formed in 1931, Zenit were initially called Stalin Leningrad, the first known example of a football club falling victim to a personality cult. The folly of this association was eventually realised when the team started losing, thus reflecting badly on Uncle Joe's reputation, and so in 1940 they took on the name of their sponsors, the Zenit camera company. (Imagine, however, had the Soviet leader's projected 200,000 capacity stadium ever been built in Moscow there

might have been a Stalin Leningrad v. Stalingrad Cup Final at the Stalin Stadium.)

Sergei Kirov, after whom the Leningrad stadium is named, was himself no shrinking violet. He was the tough but charismatic boss of the large, influential Leningrad Communist Party when the stadium project was first hatched in 1932. Krestovsky Island was then a swamp which would be reclaimed only after tons of sand had been dredged from the bay and then topped by more than 1 million cubic metres of earth.

Kirov, meanwhile, was involved in a cover-up job of a different nature. On 1 December 1934, while working at his desk, he was killed by a Communist gunman. Stalin, said to have been his best friend, took charge of the murder enquiry, bore Kirov's coffin at the funeral, and promptly unleashed the Great Terror which cost thousands of innocent lives and sent many more into exile, famous footballers among them. And yet recent evidence suggests that Stalin himself was the instigator of Kirov's assassination. And people say that football is a funny game ...

The Kirov Stadium – most bracing of all the great Socialist superbowls.

SOVIET UNION

GROUNDWORK

Lights aplenty at Leningrad. The use of advanced Western metal halide lamps would no doubt cut the numbers required, but reduce the visual impact considerably.

Sergei Kirov in ticket-collecting pose outside the stadium's grand stairway and colonnade.

GROUNDWORK

194

Only in 1938 did construction of the actual Kirov Stadium begin, and by the time war broke out the work was only half complete. But it was bread, not circuses, that the people craved. During the Germans' 900-days siege of the city over 500,000 people died, mostly of starvation – more than the combined total of war dead suffered by Great Britain and America. What did it matter that a stadium lay half-built out on a reclaimed swamp?

In fact the stadium came through the war unscathed, being far from any centre of population or industry. Its banking was used as an anti-aircraft gun platform and that long, dark players' tunnel became an ammunition store. Zenit even managed to win the Soviet Cup in 1944, only months after the siege was lifted.

The stadium was finally inaugurated on 30 July 1950, an emotional day for the many 'volunteers' who had participated in its completion and for the survivors of Leningrad's war-time nightmare. Also unveiled at this time was a statue of Kirov, at the eastern entrance to the stadium. His Lenin-like attire and bearing was surely no accident, in this, the final years of the Stalin era.

Apart from the floodlights and a few cosmetic additions, the stadium has remained virtually unchanged since 1950. In 1980 the capacity, once 100,000, was reduced to a more comfortable 75,000, all-seated (although Zenit average barely a third of that figure). There are plans to erect a roof and, most welcome of all, to extend the Leningrad metro up to the stadium entrance, thus saving a long, though pleasant trek through Victory Park.

The park, incidentally, also contains the small Dynamo Stadium. Before the war, Dynamo Leningrad were the city's top team, although they now play in the lower divisions at the rebuilt 25,000 capacity Lenin Stadium, on Petrovosky Island. That this should be so, that Leningrad should only be able to sustain one senior team, and not a wildly successful one at that (only one championship to its name and a dismal record in Europe), is an indication of how the size of a city bears no relation to the success of its football representatives. There are, after all, 5 million inhabitants of Leningrad, which makes it the largest, least successful football city in Europe, and as Sergei Kirov himself discovered only too painfully, it is not the size of one's constituency which matters, but the quality of one's friends.

SPAIN

BARCELONA

CAMP NOU

There are stadiums great by reputation and association which, when first encountered, disappoint. The Nou Camp (pronounced No Camp and sometimes referred to as Camp Nou) is not among them. This cauldron of Catalan fervour is big in heart as well as scale and, though it lacks the international status of Real's Bernabeu Stadium, when full it is indubitably one of the world's most breathtaking sporting arenas.

It has a capacity of 115,000, of which 85,000 are seated, and in Europe only Benfica's Stadium of Light is larger. Not that **FC Barcelona** (known locally as Barça) are content with that; plans are afoot to remodel the already substantial west stand, so that those occupying its uppermost tiers will feel closer to the stars of the firmament than to the stars on the pitch.

But we begin our tour halfway up the west stand, in the club's quite outstanding museum. Here we learn that, like so many Spanish clubs, Barça owed its creation to a foreigner, the Swiss-born Joan Gamper, in November 1899. Seven grounds were used in the first decade, including a velodrome and racecourse, until on 14 March 1909 the club's own ground on the Carrer de la Indústria was opened with a match v. Catalá. The museum model of this simple enclosure, with its sand pitch and one tiny, wooden, double-decker stand, could well depict that of any football club in its early days. Some grounds, thankfully, have remained that way for years.

For Barcelona the turning point came over Christmas 1921 when two games were staged against Sparta Prague, not in their home ground but at the Estadio Fuxarda (now used for rugby). So popular were these holiday games that Barça purchased a bigger site, on the Travessera de Les Corts, a kilometre or so east of Nou Camp.

The Camp de Les Corts opened on 20 May 1922 with a match between a Catalan XI and the Scottish club St Mirren (who spent eleven days travelling to Spain overland). The following day the Scots took on Barcelona, then four days later the English club Notts County. Les Corts also staged the first ever international to be held in Barcelona, when Spain played Austria in December 1924. The club then had about 5000 *socios* (members), whose loyalty was severely tested the following June when Les Corts was closed for six months by order of the Spanish dictator, General Primo de Rivera, after fans had whistled irreverently during a royal march played at half-time. Joan Gamper, after whom a street is named near the site of the old stadium (near Les Corts metro station), was forced to resign the club presidency, and it was left to the members to keep both club and ground in order. More seriously, during the Civil War, eleven years later, membership dropped to 2500 and Les Corts proved to be the club's only tangible asset.

Yet Franco's authoritarian policies – for example, banning the Catalan language, thus forcing the adoption of the Castilian title 'Club de Fútbol' instead of 'Futbol Club' – only served to stoke the fires of nationalist passion, so that during Spanish football's boom years in the 1940s, Barça's membership shot up to 22,000. But though previously successful in local championships and the Spanish Cup (moreso than Real Madrid), only by the late 1940s did the club begin to make a

195

genuine impact on the Spanish League.

It was during this period that Les Corts evolved into an all-concrete 40,000 capacity ground. In 1944 a remarkably advanced, deep, cantilevered roof was slung low over the main seated area. Its curvaceous underside was ribbed in a style which presaged the modern vogue for metal cladding. The remaining three sides were open. Floodlighting arrived in 1954 (early for Spain), and as the city expanded so Les Corts became increasingly strangled by surrounding developments.

Barça's only escape from suffocation was to move westwards, further out of town, where a large expanse of small gardens and allotments was bought. The first stone of this 'camp nou' (new ground) was laid in March 1954, the 66 million pesetas project being financed entirely by club socios, who bought bonds and season tickets in advance for periods of up to five years.

The 1950s were buoyant years for Barça; a flood of goals from the Hungarian Kubala, two championships and four Cup triumphs. Even before the new 90,000 capacity stadium was inaugurated with a match v. Warsaw, on 24 September 1957 (Barcelona's patron saint day), the Catalan architects, J.Soteras Mauri and F.Mitjans Miró, had made provision for a second-stage expansion to 150,000.

A plaque (in Castilian, of course) commemorating the opening can be seen in the main foyer of the stadium. There is also a bust of Joan Gamper, while outside the museum you can sit on the trainers' original green bench taken from Les Corts. (Barcelona retained the old ground until it was bought for redevelopment in 1966.)

Also by the museum entrance are displayed ceramic tiles donated by some of Barça's 391 peñas (supporters' clubs) from seven countries (including, surprisingly, the USSR).

Before entering the stadium proper, a stroll around the 15 hectare Nou Camp site reveals the extent of Barça's empire. Across the car park from the main entrance, past guard dog kennels under the main access ramp, is the Palau Blaugrana (blue-red), an indoor sports hall with a capacity of 6400 which was built in 1971. This is used by the club's basketball, roller hockey, handball and volleyball teams and will host the 1992 Olympic judo competition. Ice hockey is played next door in the Ice Palace, and Barça also have sections for rugby, athletics and baseball.

Beyond these two buildings, across a wide road but connected by an overhead walkway, is, astonishingly, another football stadium. Used by Barcelona Atlétic (the second team) and Barcelona Amateur, the Mini-Estadi would be the pride of many a medium-sized town anywhere in the world. Holding 16,500 in two tiers – red seats on top, blue below – like its big brother across the road it has three open sides with a cantilevered roof sheltering the west. The Mini-Estadi was opened on 23 September 1982, a day before the Nou Camp's twenty-fifth anniversary.

Not content with two excellent stadiums, the Barça estate unfolds further onto six more training fields (the first team has its own facilities elsewhere), a substantial club office block and a second indoor sports hall.

Our stroll, now something of a trek, continues back towards the stadium, past a moonscape car park, which buzzes with taxis during the week, past the cemetery of Les Corts (for we are not far from the old ground) and, still past the northern curve of the Nou Camp, to a somewhat incongruous detached building set amid landscaped gardens on a slight rise. Built in 1702, this old Catalan farmhouse, 'La Masia', with its scrubbed brickwork and rustic tiled roofs, was formerly the club offices but since 1980 has become a residence for Barça's football school.

The object of these students' dreams lies a couple of goal kicks away, across a busy road and yet another training pitch. Towering above the street, it is the Nou Camp's massive video scoreboards which first catch the eye. Smooth, white, slightly curved slabs, balanced along the top of the tall terracing, their sheer scale makes one gasp in anticipation. If the scoreboards appear so enormous from the exterior, how voluminous must be the interior?

Entry to the Nou Camp is no disappointment, full or empty. Like Benfica's Stadium of Light, its three tiers just seem to go up and up, higher on the uncovered east side than at the ends (although the pitch is actually 8 metres below street level), until only distant mountains and the upper floors of nearby skyscrapers are visible beyond. Remembering the dust, the traffic and the urban clutter from which we have just retreated, the Nou Camp's concentric rings of blue and red seats, the neat paving stones which, unusually, surround the pitch (and thus give it emphasis), even the regular shadows cast by the overhanging tiers and the dramatic roof, combine breathtakingly to give the

EDICIONES CAMPAÑA

The Barça empire – Nou Camp and its little brother, the Mini-Estadi, sandwich the Palau Blaugrana (left) and Ice Palace. Having floodlights mounted along the rim of the bowl, as at Nou Camp, is a common feature of Spanish football grounds.

impression of a deep, refreshing lake of precision.

Full to the brim, however, the Nou Camp presents us with a wall of humanity. When a drum sounds from one of the small terraced areas behind each goal, the plunging bowl itself becomes a drum, reverberating with sound.

And still it is destined to expand.

The first major remodelling between 1980–2 cost 1,288 million pesetas and in effect saw the completion of the original plans from 1957. Three of the architects from that period were involved in the work, the main element of which was the addition of a third tier on the three uncovered sides. This raised the capacity not to 150,000, as originally intended, but to 120,000, because of the current requirement for seating rather than standing room. (This total has since been reduced by 5000 with the installation of even more seats.) The two video boards, an electronic information board on the first tier balcony, and new floodlights were also installed for 1982.

A second plaque in the foyer (in Catalan this time) commemorates the inauguration of the remodelled Nou Camp for the World Cup's opening ceremony, on 13 June 1982, when 85,000 saw Belgium beat the holders, Argentina, 1–0. This turned out to be the highest attendance for any of Barcelona's five World Cup matches, not that Barça's president Josep Lluís Núñez and his directorate were disappointed. With a bigger stadium they were able to push membership levels higher, so that when the Pope paid a visit only a few months after the World Cup on 7 November, he was ceremonially enrolled as member number 108,000 (since when membership has topped 110,000, making Barça the largest football club in the world). No less reverential but rather more boisterous crowds have since welcomed such stadium luminaries as Michael Jackson, the Rolling Stones and Bruce Springsteen. On the footballing front the Nou Camp has staged two European Cup Winners' Cup Finals (1972 and 1982), the 1988 European Cup Final and numerous internationals.

197

SPAIN

As mentioned earlier, Barça's most recent plan to improve the stadium, unveiled in 1985, is to revamp completely the main or west stand, which was structurally unaffected by the 1982 remodelling. If ever carried out, the plan is to add, vertiginously, two additional tiers holding 10,000 seats above the existing roof line, to be sheltered by an even higher, suspended cantilevered roof. There will also be two underground parking areas, plus numerous restaurants, lounges, private boxes and, of course, lifts to the uppermost seats (which otherwise could only be occupied by the super-fit). Less dramatically, but no less controversially, Barça are also considering installing seats in the popular standing areas behind each goal.

This second remodelling may be completed in time for 1992, when the Nou Camp will host the main games of the Olympic soccer tournament, but it will not greatly increase the overall capacity. Instead it aims to enhance spectator comfort and,

And still Barça want to build higher.

perhaps just as crucially, keep Barça ahead of even Real Madrid's intended stadium improvements. Nou Camp may not be so new any more, but it certainly looks like improving with age.

Like a deep lake of precision amid the dust and urban clamour of Barcelona, Nou Camp's interior is, in the modern American fashion, refreshingly free of the usual stadium clutter.

GROUNDWORK

Sarriá – a typical Spanish inner-city venue which Español don't want to leave.

BARCELONA

ESTADIO DE SARRIÁ

Two kilometres east of Nou Camp, **Real Club Deportivo Español** can be found nestling in the densely built-up district of Sarriá.

Formed by students in 1900 (only months after FC Barcelona), Español used several grounds in their early years, including the site of the Monumental bullring. Finally in 1923 the La Riva family, wealthy textile industrialists, bought Español some land not far from Barcelona's new Les Corts Stadium. Because the site was said to resemble a Caribbean jungle it was known as Manigua – the local name for Cuba – and Español members were thus dubbed *Los Periquitos* (the parakeets). The ground was also called Can Rabia – White House – after an old villa which stood directly behind the south goal. It had a balcony overlooking the pitch and became home to Español's younger players.

Opened on 1 February 1923 with a local match v. Sants, the ground's first stand was built three years later, and in 1928 Español became founder members of the national league (along with Barcelona and another local club, Europa).

Apart from two Cup wins (1929 and 1940), Español rarely outgunned Barça, and after the Civil War, when Franco decreed that all club presidents be nominated from Madrid, the La Riva family demanded the return of their land. So, while other clubs enjoyed a postwar boom, Español were hampered by a prolonged dispute, resolved only in 1951 when the club finally gained ownership of the ground.

Development followed almost immediately with the demolition of the Can Rabia in 1952, to make way for the south terrace. Since then the jungle of Manigua has become a concrete one, culminating in 413 million pesetas worth of reconstruction for the 1982 World Cup, when three matches were staged, involving Argentina, Brazil and Italy. Sarriá's capacity was then 44,000, but is now 41,000, of which 19,000 are seated.

Sarriá is a typical inner-city venue, with steeply

raked stands on two sides (hence the ground's nickname, *La Bombonera*, or Chocolate Box) and open terraces at each end. Modern apartment blocks enjoy an almost unrestricted view from the north (though some residents brazenly display rival loyalties on match days).

The blue and white seated east stand gained its upper tier and roof in 1974. Behind lie Español's training pitches. The west stand with its *anfiteatro* (amphitheatre) – an upper, uncovered tier of seats and/or standing common at Spanish grounds – was erected in 1956 under the supervision of J. Soteras Mauri (co-architect of the Nou Camp). Colourful murals decorate the otherwise jaded main entrance, depicting aspects of local history – Columbus, the work of innovative architect Gaudí, and scenes from Catalan folklore. Across the Carrer de Ricardo Villa (no relation to the former Argentinian international) is a garage where Español once had an indoor sports hall.

The floodlights, English style on four corner pylons, date from 1959.

They might not light up this tightly packed ground much longer, for there is now pressure on *Los Periquitos* to fly their urban nest. Local politicians want Español to use the Montjuïc Stadium (see below), expensively rebuilt for the 1992 Olympics, to save it from becoming a white elephant. But although government money might be added as a sweetener, the club would still need new training grounds. Meanwhile Español's 18,000 *socios*, accustomed to their Chocolate Box, dread becoming lost in the larger setting of a 70,000 capacity multi-purpose stadium. They may have an important ally, however. A former roller-hockey player for Español in 1942 and a present member of the club is none other than Juan Samaranch, President of the IOC. A few squawks in the right direction and *Los Periquitos* might yet remain ensconced in their much-loved concrete jungle.

BARCELONA

ESTADIO OLIMPICO MONTJUÏC

Montjuïc was to be the Wembley of Spain. Instead it became a decaying memorial to the vainglory of dictator Primo de Rivera. Not even Franco could stop the rot. The public simply never liked Montjuïc, and it would have crumbled into obliv-

ion had the city of Barcelona not decided it was worth substantial reconstruction for the 1992 Olympics. (Nou Camp is unsuitable since it has no room for an athletics track.)

Certainly few stadiums have a finer location. Set on the summit of Montjuïc (Hill of the Jews) above the National Palace, overlooking the Mediterranean and surrounded by parkland, the 55,000 capacity stadium was designed by Pere Domènech for the 1929 Exposició Internacional and formed the centrepiece of Barcelona's unsuccessful 1936 Olympic bid. But despite staging several Cup Finals and internationals between 1930–50, thereafter Montjuïc fell gradually into disrepair.

Its recent transformation, under the direction of Milanese architect Vittorio Gregotti (who has also designed new stadiums in Nîmes and Genoa), has been remarkable and costly – around 6,000 million pesetas. Preserving only the shell – with its palatial façade, central cupola, bell-tower and massive Marathon Gate – the interior has been completely gutted, the pitch lowered 11 metres and two new tiers holding 70,000 seats constructed. A cantilevered roof over the west stand is barely visible from the exterior, hence, mercifully, leaving the lines of the monumental frontage unaffected.

But will Montjuïc decline a second time, after 1992? It could happen, especially if Español cannot be persuaded to move from Sarriá. Otherwise the

Montjuïc before restoration. It was reopened in September 1989 for the athletics World Cup.

stadium can hardly expect to attract many major football games, especially being so close to Nou Camp. Indeed Montjuïc will see none of the 1992 Olympic football action. The five venues are to be, instead, Nou Camp, Sarriá, Zaragoza, Valencia and Sabadell.

VALENCIA

ESTADIO LUIS CASANOVA

Famous for genuine paella and the scent of oranges, Spain's third largest city boasts a typically cavernous, inner-city stadium with a surprise or two behind its concrete exterior. Best of all, bathed in the city's wonderful natural light, is one mighty roof, which juts out into the sky and throws shadows across the bright white seats and barriers below.

Valencia Club de Fútbol was formed by students and foreign residents in 1902, then reformed with essentially local players in 1919 at a modest ground in the Parque de Algirós.

The present stadium, opened on 20 May 1923 v. Levante, was originally called Campo de Mestalla, after a small nearby river. It staged its first international, v. Italy, in June 1925 and, as a convenient venue for opposing clubs from Barcelona and Madrid, hosted Cup Finals in 1926, 1929 and 1936. Los Chés ('*ché*' is a familiar term of address in Valencia), meanwhile, reached the First Division in 1931.

Spain's Civil War hit the club badly; adjacent military barracks and the importance of Valencia's docks put the ground right in the firing line, with inevitable consequences. Under president Luis Casanova, however, who held office until

Another cavernous Spanish ground in a concrete jungle.
Valencia's roof resembles a prewar British design with its supports knocked away, while the pitch was formerly a few metres higher.

GROUNDWORK

201

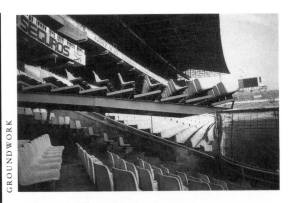

GROUNDWORK

Open Sesame! Not an inch is wasted.

1958, the club emerged powerfully from the ruins and in the next decade won the League title three times, the Cup twice and made three appearances as losing finalists.

The stadium, first rebuilt in 1940, grew to accommodate this success, particularly in the 1950s. Then in 1978 the pitch was excavated in order to extend the lower tier. Valencia's reward for this mammoth operation came during the 1982 World Cup, when it staged all three of Spain's first-round matches, against Northern Ireland, Honduras and Yugoslavia. Each game was a 50,000 sell-out. The current capacity is 49,398, of which 33,053 are seated.

The stadium's layout is on the familiar Spanish model – a rectangle with curved corners, two open terraces to the north and south (the standing areas being above the seats), a high, open slab-like upper *anfiteatro* on the east side (again with standing at

the summit), and a covered double-decker stand on the west.

But what a stand it is! Built in 1954 (after another Cup triumph) and covered with thin corrugated sheeting, the cantilevered roof seems daringly high and deep for its age. It is as if a traditional stand from prewar Britain has been hoisted up into the sky and its supports knocked away. In contrast to its shadowy steelwork, flanking the roof are modern white, three-storey, glass-fronted radio cabins (echoes of Bordeaux?), sitting high on the stadium's upper tier of terracing. In such a setting the four original corner floodlight pylons, first used in March 1959 (v. Stade de Reims), seem almost inconsequential.

So much has been packed into the available space – the touchlines are particularly tight for such a large stadium – that there is barely room for the players' tunnel, and photographers have to crouch in low dugouts. Even the tunnel entrance for pitch maintenance equipment, in the southwest corner, has been concealed by seating, mounted on a platform which can be hydraulically raised. Not an inch is wasted.

With no room to expand, and apartment blocks and a tall, Post-Modern town hall annexe breathing down the stadium's neck (right behind the club offices), Valencia have considered building a new stadium 9 kilometres away at Paterna. But since this might antagonise the fans, not to mention the stadium's resident colony of cats, Luis Casanova's legacy looks secure for the time being, and in 1992 Valencia will be one of the soccer venues for the Barcelona Olympics.

ELCHE

ESTADIO MANUEL MARTÍNEZ VALERO

Flat scrubland stretches out under a wide sky, crisscrossed with telegraph wires like the American midwest. Palm trees sway and rustle on the horizon. Behind us lies Alicante and the Costa Blanca. Ahead, the small city where they make shoes, Elche. But here in no-man's land, stands a massive cylindrical hulk, all alone, beyond the factory roofs at the end of a long straight road. Is

it an ancient temple, a monument to some lost civilisation? A vast launching pad for an alien spacecraft?

Before finding the answer, we move on, a kilometre or so into Elche, and on rough ground behind some newly built flats we stumble across another enigma. Towering above the palms are two lampless floodlight pylons; skeletons against the sky, their rusting enamel advertisements flapping in the breeze.

There are diggers close by and so it seems that the pylons, so incongruous amid the building rubble, must soon topple, watched perhaps by a few old timers who recall what the lights once illuminated; a patch of green, a bank of terracing, a lifetime of memories.

For this is the tale of **Elche Club de Fútbol**, who chose the path of progress and ended up in the wilderness.

Having started life in 1910 at a ground called El Clot, the club was formally constituted in 1923. Three years later they moved to the Altabix district, where they would remain until the diggers arrived half a century later. Altabix was a neighbourhood ground; rectangular, uncovered, holding 18,000 at a pinch, and perfect for a lower division club. But Elche didn't remain in the lower divisions. They reached the First Division in 1959, purchased a 49 per cent share in Altabix, added terracing to cope with the crowds and erected those hardy floodlights in 1961. But it was always a struggle, in what was then the First Division's smallest, most uncomfortable venue, yet also – to maintain Elche's status – the most expensive.

Manuel Martínez Valero became president in 1962, and realising that one day Altabix would have to be sold to finance a new stadium, launched a drive to buy up those shares of the land still in outside hands. Once this lengthy process was completed, Elche were ready to move on, despite their relegation in 1970.

But before selling Altabix, Elche needed cash to buy another site, so Martínez offered car park spaces at the projected stadium for 100,000 pesetas each, and as there were going to be 1700 spaces, he suggested the new ground be called 'Estadio de los 1700'. The actual site, beyond the outskirts, out in no-man's land at the end of a long straight road, cost 29 million pesetas and in 1974 Elche made ambitious plans for a sports city. As one Spanish FA official remarked when work began a year later, 'A lot of stadium for such a little city!'

There were a lot of problems too. The municipality would only allow half the Altabix site to be redeveloped (hence the survival of the two pylons), the mayor proved unsympathetic, a loan from the government sports department failed to materialise, and, just as ominously, few of Elche's members bothered buying up the vital parking spaces. A less dogged man might have abandoned the scheme there and then, yet even when Elche were threatened with a 1 million peseta fine for starting construction without a building permit, Martínez refused to yield. He knew the city was rapidly expanding – its population would double to 300,000 in a decade – and boldly forecast that Elche would one day host a World Cup, a claim which only a few years earlier would have seemed

Skeleton against the sky – all that remains of Altabix, Elche's home for half a century.

laughable, but which was to prove correct.

Amid all these obstacles came the thorny question of a name for the new stadium. 'Nou Altabix' was much favoured, as was 'El Palmeral', after the locality's famous palms. There were too many former club presidents for just one to be honoured, and local names were thought to be too confusing for outsiders. For example, Ilicitanos, residents of Elche, call their city Elx.

Finally, after a secret vote and newspaper poll the dull compromise title of 'Nuevo Estadio' was chosen, and Martínez was offered the consolation of having a street, a bust or a plaque in his name. (The stadium was only named after him posthumously, in 1988, as was a shoe factory. Few Ilicitanos do not have connections with the trade.)

Elche's Nuevo Estadio was opened on 8 September 1976, the president's wife kicking off a club friendly v. Mexico. The stadium then consisted of one tier, holding 28,000, and although the first attendance was only 25,000, so clogged did the single approach road become that it took two hours to cover the kilometre or so back into town. Nevertheless the local bishop called the stadium

GROUNDWORK

SPAIN

PAISAJES ESPAÑOLES

The Estadio Manuel Martínez Valero – 'a lot of stadium for such a little city'.

a miracle, and the club responded by asking for his prayers, since they now had to face their creditors.

Completing the Nuevo Estadio turned out to be as great an act of faith as was starting it. Some argued that a capacity of 28,000 was sufficient. Martínez argued, only half jokingly, that since the club had not yet paid for the first phase, why not double the debt?

Meanwhile the government loan was still not forthcoming, Altabix had yet to be fully sold, building prices had rocketed, and, after only two seasons in their new home, Elche were relegated to the Second Division again.

They were still there when 1982 approached. Only then did the government's money arrive, and the stadium was completed to create a capacity of 53,000 (since reduced to 38,750, all seated), in time for Elche to host the World Cup. Redevelopment of half the Altabix site also finally began, although the remaining half was still undeveloped as recently as early 1989.

We tell this story in detail not only because Martínez himself left us with such a detailed and entertaining account of the saga (in his book, *Nuestro Estadio*) but also because, to be brutal, Elche's experience might serve as a warning to any small, but ambitious club.

The stadium itself, although weathering in the wind, daubed in graffiti, spartan inside and still

with inadequate approach roads, is perfectly serviceable. The architect, former club vice-president Juan Boix Matarredona (who sounds like a cross between a bullfighter and footballer), cannot be faulted. With its green and white seats, two open tiers and ample parking space the stadium would be the envy of many a larger club. Surprisingly, it has a grass sloping moat instead of the usual concrete.

But no sports city was ever built, and despite all the '*palmeras*' around their new stadium, Elche have not chalked up any '*palmares*' (honours). Apart from one appearance in a Cup Final, in 1969, they have spent much of the last two decades flitting between the First and Second Divisions, with average gates of 18–20,000 only in the top flight. Furthermore, despite all the build-up, Elche's three World Cup games in 1982, involving Hungary, El Salvador and Belgium, attracted less than 40,000 fans altogether.

There is no doubt that at the time, Altabix was no longer viable, or that the World Cup put Elche on the map, albeit fleetingly. But the Nuevo Estadio in the wilderness was a hugely expensive gamble, completed against all the odds, and it could just be that a less ambitious, smaller project would have served both the club, and the city, far better. Instead, one could say, the club of the shoemakers got too big for their boots.

ALICANTE

ESTADIO JOSÉ RICO PERÉZ

COLORSPORT

Alicante – scene of Herculean deeds.

As gateway to the Costa Blanca, Alicante was an ideal World Cup venue in 1982, even if local club **Hércules** could hardly claim membership of the footballing jetset. Their stadium, named after a club president, was inaugurated on 3 August 1974 v. Barcelona, during a four season burst which saw Hércules rise from the Third to the First Division and outgrow their small, inner-city ground at La Viña.

It proved to be a successful move. For the next eight seasons Hércules outshone neighbours Elche in the League and in March 1977 hosted their first international, v. Hungary. In 1982 three World Cup games were staged, the holders Argentina playing Hungary and El Salvador, plus the third place play-off, Poland v. France.

With a capacity of 38,700 uncovered seats, the stadium, close to the ancient hippodrome, consists of one lower tier with raised, slab-like upper tiers on either side. There are the ubiquitous tower blocks beyond the north end, and a modern municipal sports hall behind the south. Four white box pillars carry the floodlights.

Nice stadium, nice weather, but by 1986 Hércules found themselves, ruinously, back in the Third Division, and facing, like their namesake in antiquity (the son of Zeus), the Herculean task of emerging once more from the lower world.

MÁLAGA

LA ROSALEDA

Málaga staged three World Cup games in 1982, involving Scotland, New Zealand and the USSR, but, like Alicante, was selected more for its seaside location than the status of the local club, **CD Málaga**. Formed in April 1933, Málaga first played at an exotically named ground, Los Baños del Carmen, before purchasing a field of rose bushes (hence La Rosaleda) on the banks of the River Guadalmedina. The stadium was opened on 14 September 1941 with a game v. Sevilla, whom Málaga joined in the First Division nine seasons later. La Rosaleda's first international, against Greece, was in February 1973.

For the World Cup, however, a major overhaul of the tight but completely open, rectangular stadium was required. New upper tiers were built, a moat dug, a typically Spanish row of lights erected on high gantries above each side, and wide bands of blue and white seating installed on two sides. The pitch, normally thirsting for life in July, was relaid with tougher seeds to withstand use during the hottest, driest part of the year.

La Rosaleda has since been expanded by having its corners filled in, thus creating a 42,000 capacity (22,000 seated), two-tiered, all-enclosed stadium. The outside world still gets a look in, though. To the north lies the sierra, to the south the sea, and all around dense clumps of apartment blocks remind us that in today's Costa del Sol, concrete thrives just as much as roses.

The river is dry (bottom right) but Málaga's pitch thrives.

PAISAJES ESPAÑOLES

SEVILLE

ESTADIO BENITO VILLAMARÍN

Of Seville's two major clubs, **Real Betis Balompié** ('*balompié*' is a traditional term for football) have usually played the underdog. But in typical Andalucian style they have never let this sully their *joie de vivre* or dampen their colourful past. Indeed, it would be hard to assess the bricks and mortar of their green and white stadium (the colours of the Andalucian flag) without being seduced by their heartiness, humour and hospitality.

'Er Beti', as local dialect calls them, were the product of a merger between two clubs in 1914: Sevilla Balompié, formed in 1907, and Betis, who came into being in 1909 after a split among members of Sevilla FC (shades of Liverpool and Everton). Betis was the Roman name for Seville's River Guadalquivir.

King Alfonso XIII became the new club's Honorary President, hence the title Real, though this pedigree was hardly evident when the first derby match against Sevilla in 1915 ended in an unseemly brawl involving both fans and players.

Under the direction of an Englishman, Mr 'Papa' Jones (no-one knew his first name and he later disappeared mysteriously), Betis's first ground, in the Prado de San Sebastián, was called 'Las Tablas Verdes', because it was enclosed by green boards. In 1918 Betis transferred the

boards to a ground in the Patronato district, and it was here their unpredictable League career began in 1928.

A year later Seville staged the major Ibero-Americana Exhibition which, apart from providing the city with some fine, individual buildings – the ornate Guatemalan pavilion can be seen en route to Betis from the centre, saw the construction of a new stadium, named after the district, El Estadio de Heliópolis. This 18,000 capacity venue, whitewashed and perfectly proportioned, was inaugurated with an international v. Portugal on 17 March 1929.

Meanwhile, still at Patronato, Betis reached the First Division, played in the 1931 Cup Final, and in 1935 won their first and only championship. Flushed with success they decided to move on, and in 1936 signed a lease for Heliópolis. Their timing could not have been worse. Less than forty-eight hours after arriving on 16 July, the Civil War began and, with it, fighting in the streets of Seville. The club offices were bombed, most of the team fled the country and over the next three years membership fell to less than one hundred.

Peace in 1939 found Er Beti back at Heliópolis, but in disarray. By 1947 they had slipped into the Third Division, where they remained for seven years, finally returning to the top flight in 1958. (In the process they became the only Spanish club to win the championships of all three divisions.) Behind their resurrection was a Galician (from northern Spain), Benito Villamarín, president from 1957–65, who masterminded the club's purchase of Heliópolis in August 1961.

The stadium which subsequently took his name currently holds 47,500 (22,500 seated), and was almost completely rebuilt for the 1982 World Cup. It retains, however, much of the original ambience, especially with its whitewashed, almost Moorish latticework on the retaining walls behind each goal.

Refurbishment began shortly after Betis won their first ever Cup, in 1977, and for a while the team was forced to share Sevilla's stadium. A new pitch was laid, and the old floodlight pylons which dipped curiously over the terracing came down. Twenty-seven kilos of dynamite were used to demolish the old main stand – several agonising seconds passed before it toppled, apparently – and in its place arose a tall and imposing, free-standing, triple decker, cantilevered stand decked splendidly in wide bands of green and white seats. The

Resplendent in whitewash – Heliópolis before redevelopment. Note the dipping floodlights.

GROUNDWORK

Vibrant with identity – the Benito Villamarín Stadium. No question of what colours Betis play in. Only the end terraces survive from old Heliópolis.

opposite bank was raised, fully seated and also given a new roof.

Altogether the work cost 510 million pesetas, but it was money well spent. The two World Cup matches staged here, Brazil v. Scotland and v. New Zealand, were well attended, and the stadium is now a truly modern football ground in the best traditional sense – seats on both sides, standing at the ends – as one would expect from a club with strong working-class support.

Above all, the Benito Villamarín Stadium is vibrant with colour and identity. For example, to protect the tunnel entrance is a retractable green and white canopy, like a shop front. The stadium's main entrance bears the club name and crest in decorative tiles – typical of the region – while across the car park stands a row of characteristic Sevillian white villas, their walled gardens lush with orange trees.

Opposite the main stand is a large bank of green and white seats, topped by an angled, half-cantilevered roof, with green steelwork and green

facings. Both open end terraces are liberally dotted with green crush barriers and lined at the rear by crisp white walls. The floodlights, needless to say, are on shiny green stalks in each corner.

Behind the north goal are palm trees and the now familiar – in Spain at least – tall apartment blocks close by. Beyond the south goal and a line of eucalyptus trees lies the club's training ground, where the groundsman's ramshackle hut doubles as a lively bar and meeting place for Betis staff.

Betis have one other distinction. Inexplicably, theirs is the only Spanish stadium ever to have appeared on a Mozambique postage stamp. Though dated 1982, the stamp unfortunately depicts the old stadium and a player wearing blue! Imagine, Betis, in blue!

More laughter echoes around Heliópolis before a darker moment in the club's history is soberly recalled. In February 1948 the area was completely submerged by a flood. So loyal were the fans, it is said, that they rowed to the stadium in boats. But only to see if the match was on, of course.

Red steel at sunset – amazing grace at Sevilla's Sánchez Pizjuán Stadium.

SEVILLE

ESTADIO SÁNCHEZ PIZJUÁN

With their larger stadium and marginally better track record, **Sevilla FC** have usually had the slight edge over Betis in this football crazy city. The Sánchez Pizjuán Stadium holds 70,000 (28,552 seated) and is Seville's first choice for internationals, although to maintain some equality, like Betis, it hosted only two games in the 1982 World Cup – Brazil v. USSR and the memorable West Germany v. France semi-final – watched by a total of 110,000 spectators. Since then the stadium has also staged the 1986 European Cup Final, Steaua Bucharest v. Barcelona.

Formed in October 1905, Sevilla originally played on the Prado de San Sebastián. Their first enclosed ground, El Campo del Mercantil, next to the grounds of the famous April Fair, was opened in January 1910, an event attended, according to contemporary reports, by many beautiful women who were presented with bouquets of violets and roses.

Eight years later urban development prompted a move to the Paseo de la Palmera, where Sevilla used the Victoria tavern as a changing room. The Campo de la Victoria, as the ground became known, was inaugurated with two matches against Unión Sporting Club de Madrid in October 1918, and staged Seville's first international, v. Portugal, in December 1923. It also staged the 1925 Cup Final, Barcelona v. Arenas.

Three years later, construction work for the Ibero-Americana Exhibition of 1929 (see page 206) forced Sevilla to move yet again, but this time the club invested 200,000 pesetas on a huge tract of land in the Nervión district, where they have remained ever since (and profited greatly from selling off surplus land). The Nervión Stadium was opened on 7 October 1928, during the Spanish League's inaugural season, but Sevilla's rivals Betis stole the show with a 2–1 win. Furthermore, despite Sevilla winning the Second Division, the rules prevented promotion that season, and Sevilla had to wait until 1934 to follow Betis into the First Division. The following year the honours were all square – Betis took the Championship, Sevilla the Cup.

It was around then that Ramón Sánchez Pizjuán, president since 1932, started planning a new stadium. Even in the midst of Civil War, realising that real estate would be the club's most valuable future asset, Sánchez Pizjuán purchased an extra 42,000 sq. metres of land around the stadium. A few years later he sent delegates to quiz Real Madrid about the construction of their new Chamartín Stadium, by which time Sevilla had accumulated 50 million pesetas for their own project. Helenio Herrera, Sevilla's coach in the mid-1950s, described Sánchez Pizjuán as 'the most intelligent man I have ever met'.

But not even the president foresaw the problems facing engineers at the new stadium's site, directly adjacent to Sevilla's existing ground. Poor subsoil meant that 800 concrete piles had to be sunk before building could commence, and it soon became apparent that 50 million pesetas would cover only a third of the costs. Sánchez Pizjuán meanwhile died unexpectedly in October 1956.

But construction continued. Designed by one of Real Madrid's architects, Manuel Muñoz Monasterio, and built by Catalan contractors, the stadium was finally opened, albeit in an unfinished state, in September 1958. Betis were again the visitors, and again they had the nerve to win.

Since then the stadium's surroundings have changed greatly, as Sevilla have sold off parcels of land for development. But the actual body of the stadium was not completed until 1975, when 78 million pesetas was needed to complete the upper tier and fill in the corners. Finishing touches were then applied for 1982, the most noticeable being the erection over the main stand's upper tier of a quite stunning red, steel-framed roof. Like a dinosaur's neck in profile, it arches upwards towards the pitch, leaving its tail suspended over the rear of the retaining wall, delicately poised on its axis on a series of stilts, high above the seats. It may not keep out the wind, but it creates a graceful counterpoise to the three remaining sides of the bowl. These are open – the concrete bleached in the hot Andalucian sun – with floodlights on leaning red gantries around the summit.

Another striking feature of the stadium is a

Santiago del Campo's distinctive mosaic dominates the stadium's street frontage.

mosaic above the main entrance. Three bays wide and almost as tall as the stadium itself, this mammoth work was created for 1982 by local artist and Sevilla supporter, Santiago del Campo. Costing 6 million pesetas and using only local materials, the mosaic depicts the club crest in the centre, surrounded by the crests of sixty major clubs from Spain and around the world who have visited Sevilla. Set in shields along the base are important dates from the club's history.

This eye-catching, mainly scarlet and white mosaic looks down on a tarmac car park where the original Nervión Stadium stood. The remaining surrounding land is open, dusty, uneven, and of course ripe for development. Apartment blocks on two sides of the stadium already occupy part of the club's former estate, and no doubt much of the remainder will eventually be gobbled up. Sevilla will then find themselves hemmed in yet again, although this time the profit will be theirs. As Herrera had earlier suggested, Sánchez Pizjuán was no fool.

MADRID

ESTADIO SANTIAGO BERNABEU

Imagine if the Parc des Princes were situated on the Champs Elysées or if Wembley were on Park Lane. For this is the measure of the Bernabeu Stadium's location, on Madrid's most prestigious thoroughfare, the wide, straight Castellana, home of museums, ministries, mansions and banks. No other football club in the world can boast such an esteemed address, but then few other clubs can lay claim, as can **Real Madrid**, to being such an integral part of the national fabric. Barcelona may boast a bigger, better stadium and almost twice as many members as their age-old rivals, but the Bernabeu occupies a niche in the very corridor of power, while Real are, in effect, a Spanish institution.

Real formed officially in March 1902 under the title Sociedad Madrid Foot Ball Club (although some chauvinistic Madrileños claim that earlier Madrid teams predate those of Bilbao and Barcelona). They played first on fields at Moncloa, then quickly moved to the more central area straddling the famous Calle de Alcala, between the Prado and the Monumental bullring. There, on the corner of Calle Velázquez and Calle José Ortega y Gasset, they called their pitch Campo de la Estrada, after a marble cutter whose workshop was close by. According to Real's official club history (see bibliography), to which I am much indebted, Señor Estrada thought these young men kicking a leather ball around were quite 'loco', until, that is, he heard they had named a rectangle of grass after him.

Madrid's next pitch was a few blocks southeast on the Avenida Felipe II, between the present-day Goya metro station and the Palacio Deportes. Although partly owned by Queen María Cristina, it was actually a rubbish dump, and the players had to dig trenches to prevent carts from further dumping. Hardly surprisingly, they soon moved, this time a short distance to a field closer to the Plaza de Toros.

Madrid played in the shadow of the bullring until 1912, although popular games against Basque and Catalan teams, and several of the early Spanish Cup Finals, were also staged at a larger ground on Madrid's racecourse.

But the club's first enclosed ground was back near the old rubbish dump, on the corner of Calles O'Donnell and Narváez. Known as the Campo de O'Donnell, it had a wooden stand for 200 and was inaugurated in October 1912, v. Sporting de Irún. The club then had 450 members, and spent 13,000 pesetas on the ground, which, notes Real's history proudly, had ventilated toilets. More significantly, among the volunteers who helped level the pitch and erect perimeter fencing were two teenage brothers, Marcelo and Santiago Bernabeu. It was at O'Donnell that Santiago would make his name as a dashing young inside-forward.

In 1920 the club was granted permission to use the prefix Real (Royal), and growing support forced another move. But the ground they chose, a newly constructed velodrome in the distant northeast district of Cuidad Lineal, proved to be a mistake. It held only 8000 and, although there were good bus and tram links, it was too far from the hub of Real's support. Therefore less than a year after its inauguration, on 29 April 1923, v. Real Unión de Irún, in the presence of King Alfonso XIII and the Infante Don Juan (the present king's father), Real were on the move again.

This time they employed an architect, José María Castell, who planned a proper 15,000 capacity stadium with a 4000-seater stand. Named after the district, Chamartín Stadium occupied the area immediately behind the current stadium's east side. In design it echoed the traditional British football ground of the period, with three open sides, parallel to the pitch, and one main stand with a central, pointed gable on its pitched roof – very much, in fact, after the fashion of Britain's leading stadium architect, Archibald Leitch. Appropriately, in this respect, the stadium opened on 17 May 1924 with a visit from Newcastle United, the English Cup holders.

Unlike the Bernabeu, Chamartín never became Spain's first-choice Cup Final or international venue. The Civil War, moreover, left the ground a ruin. The pitch was destroyed, the wooden stand broken up for fuel, and it cost Real 300,000 pesetas to restore the ground before football could resume in October 1939.

Four years later in 1943, Bernabeu's reign as club president began. Since injury had forced his retirement as a player, he had become a lawyer, and also served the club as secretary. Within a

The original Chamartín Stadium c.1930. Central Madrid had yet to overwhelm the area.

year of assuming the presidency he had initiated the purchase of 5 hectares of prime real estate bordering the stadium and the Castellana (then called the Avenida del Generalísimo Franco), for the huge sum of 3 million pesetas. Construction of a new stadium on this land was to cost a further 38 million pesetas, an astonishing amount for that period and indicative of Real's standing in Franco's postwar Madrid. But although Bernabeu was himself a Franco sympathiser, as were the majority of Real's members, and Franco and his ministers were often to be seen at home games, allegations that the government gave Real actual financial aid have never been proved, while Barcelona have always been the wealthier of the two clubs. (It is also true that both before and after Franco's years in power, Real were still seen as the pet team of the Spanish Establishment.)

Work on the new Chamartín Stadium began, literally, around the old one, in October 1944. In fact the old stadium's corner actually abutted on the new terraces and pitch, which were laid several metres below the old boundary wall.

Bernabeu himself broke the first ground, after the usual blessing of the site by a priest, then, in order to finish the southeast corner, the old ground was closed in May 1945. Real had in the meantime signed an agreement to share Atlético de Madrid's Metropolitano Stadium, on condition that Atlético members be admitted free to Real's matches!

The concession lasted for one and a half seasons, until Real's new stadium was inaugurated on 14 December 1947, with a friendly v. Belenenses of Lisbon. Designed by Luis Alemany Soler and Manuel Muñoz Monasterio (who was later commissioned by Sevilla), the stadium originally had three sides of open, two-tiered stands, with a lower bank of uncovered terracing on the east side (where the old stadium had got in the way) atop which, in the centre, was a neoclassical tower (rather like La Coruña).

But the architects originally planned to have four much larger towers, one in each corner, as at, for example, the Old Stadium in Amsterdam (built in 1914), or the University Stadium, Illinois, (1927). Only two of these towers were ever built, both in 1954 when the east side was remodelled. This pair of now familiar rectangular white towers flanked a new third tier – the splendid open *anfiteatro* (amphitheatre), as it is called – which extended above the line of the other stands and increased Chamartín's capacity to a prodigious 120,000. But it was the understated, refined lines of the new east side, rather than its scale, which gave Chamartín an undeniable pedigree. This, and the stadium's location, made it a landmark edifice more than any other football stadium in any other European capital.

Real, meanwhile, underwent a very lean spell at the time of their move in 1947, finishing fourth from bottom in their first season at Chamartín. In fact, up until 1953 their city rivals, Atlético, had won more League titles. Since then of course, as no-one needs reminding, Real have dominated their domestic league to a degree no other major Western European club can rival, winning the championship in all but a dozen seasons since 1954. They also swept the Continent by winning the European Cup in each of its first five seasons, between 1956–60, adding a sixth trophy in 1966.

In addition, after 1948 Chamartín became Spain's main Cup Final venue (with only six exceptions in the next forty years), including a historic Final in 1980 when Real won 6–1 against their own reserve team, Second Division Castilla (who also play at the Bernabeu). Yet in playing terms Real have hardly gained from having finals on their own patch – as is often alleged. Of their nine Cup Final appearances at the Bernabeu from 1958–80, Real won on only four occasions (once on penalties).

The stadium has also staged more internationals than any other Spanish venue – the first v. Portugal in March 1948 – plus the European Cup Finals in 1957, 1969 and 1980. In the early 1950s it also hosted boxing, cycling, baseball, handball and American football.

From 1954 until the 1982 World Cup there were only minor changes. In January 1955 the name Estadio Santiago Bernabeu was officially adopted. The floodlights, on gantries along each side, were first used on 18 May 1957, for a game v. Recife of Brazil, although officially they were inaugurated twelve days later for Real's European Cup Final v. Fiorentina (watched by 124,000 spectators). These lights were replaced in 1969 by mercury halide projectors which boosted the light from 400 lux to 1420 lux, a mark of how much lighting technology had advanced in only a decade or so. To add to the drama of floodlit games, both towers were fitted with illuminated club crests.

Real, however, were still looking to improve their lot. They had already opened, in Franco's presence in 1963, a huge multi-sport training complex north of the city, and in 1973 Bernabeu announced plans to convert the existing stadium into a green space and build in the north of Madrid a new 120,000 capacity stadium, with a floating roof and space for 8000 cars. This time, however, the old president did not get his way. Despite some support from Real's members, the Town Hall dismissed the project out of hand.

So the Bernabeu Stadium survived, and as a result of its greatest moment of international celebrity, the 1982 World Cup, it thrived too. Completely refurbished for the occasion, Bernabeu staged four World Cup matches: the second round games involving West Germany, Spain, and England, and the final, West Germany v. Italy. A massive aggregate of 345,000 people (out of a possible 360,000) watched those games, a total far outstripping that at any other venue. (Another 120,000 turned up at the stadium on 3 November 1983 to see the Pope, and if any supporters among them did sneak in the odd prayer or two it certainly had the right effect, for on the very same day Real won a Cup Winners' Cup tie in Budapest.)

The huge World Cup attendances were something of a relief for Real, since more money had been spent on the Bernabeu than any other Spanish venue – over 700 million pesetas, of which half was for a new roof. Real's share of the outlay, 530 million, was also greater than that incurred by any other stadium proprietor.

The main work for 1982 included: the installation of more seats, thereby reducing the capacity to 90,200 (60,000 standing); the building of a 150 metre long footbridge (since removed) from the west side to a press centre across the car park and main road, and the refacing and strengthening of three sides of the façade, partly in order to support the new cantilevered roof.

This three-sided roof has become one of football's most familiar images. Like a clean white plastic lid snapped tightly onto a bowl, it caps off the stadium with pleasing precision. Underneath its apparently smooth surface, however, lies a sophisticated structure.

Prefabricated roof beams, so large they had to

REAL MADRID

One of the finest sites in modern football, with the *anfiteatro* bathed in light and framed by those famous towers, each topped by the club crest in neon. Real's unique roof caps it all.

be delivered at night to avoid disrupting traffic in central Madrid, were erected in stages to allow Real to fulfil their playing commitments. These beams support a concave ribbed upper layer formed by a particularly lightweight fibre cement called Cemfil, which has the added bonus of blending in well with the surrounding urban landscape. (Remember, this is no ordinary part of town and there are tall buildings which must look down on the roof.)

From underneath the roof it is apparent that the lower layer is actually a see-through false ceiling made up of thin white panels; and that instead of a solid, black infill, which one would expect from seeing the roof fascia – which is like a liquorice sweet with thin white layers and a solid black centre, there is a void between the upper and lower sections. Floodlights are sandwiched between them on the west side.

On the east side, where the roof comes to an abrupt halt as it reaches the towers on either side of the amphitheatre (itself too high to cover), the shape of the roof section is clearly visible. It is as if the liquorice sweet had been neatly sliced at each end, then squashed in the middle. This elasticity is accentuated behind each goal, where the two white layers diverge to accommodate video screens (the first at any club stadium in the world, inaugurated with a club friendly v. the USSR in February 1982).

The roof – streamlined, bright and modern – is, it has to be said, the most impressive feature of the Bernabeu. Heretical though such a statement may seem, much of the remainder is disappointing.

The main entrance on the east side, for example, is fronted by a crumbling open-air swimming pool – unused for years – and a small circular patio and garden under an obtrusive elevated ramp. In this shadowy garden stands a bronze bust of Santiago Bernabeu, dedicated just before the 1982 World Cup. (The great leader himself died in June 1978, and as a measure of his status the Spanish team then playing in the World Cup in Argentina wore black arm bands.) The bust is mounted on a globe, which is itself supported by replicas of Real's famous six European Cups. Next to the garden is the club chapel, where players used to attend Mass before each home game.

Inside the cool, almost bare main foyer – understated as is all genuine wealth – is a plaque commemorating the World Cup, donated by the IOC President, Juan Samaranch, who although a Catalan and *socio* of RCD Español is also a Real member, number 572. The club's most illustrious supporters are, however, King Juan Carlos and his wife Sofia, although for balance their son is supposed to have pledged his allegiance to Atlético – another indication of the role football plays in Spanish society. (Imagine catching a member of the current British royal family at Tottenham or Arsenal on a Saturday afternoon!)

Further into the lobby one passes a sculpture of two players, Sotero Aranguren and Alberto Machimbarrena, both heroes of the O'Donnell period. The sculpture formerly stood in the garden of the old Chamartín Stadium.

But the goal of every visitor to the Bernabeu is Real Madrid's treasure chest, the famed trophy room, which turns out to be a long, thin chamber where cabinets bulge with an overwhelming array of silverware.

The first major trophy dates from Real's initial Cup triumph in 1905, while the most valuable (worth 13 million pesetas apiece) are the six Ramón de Carranza trophies, awarded for one of Spain's many prestigious pre-season competitions. Then there are the trophies which mark Real's astonishing achievement of having won a hat-trick of League championships *four* times.

But pride of place at the end of the room goes to Real's record number of six European Cups. Add to this the fifteen Spanish Cups (less than Barcelona's tally however), two UEFA Cups, seven European basketball cups and you have, surely, the most illustrious collection of silverware in European club sport. Altogether there are 5500 items on display, seen annually by quarter of a million awestruck visitors.

The interior of the stadium itself is equally awe inspiring, yet also rather old-fashioned. White balcony walls, white barriers and, of course, the familiar towers lend some dignity. Otherwise, the overall impression is of cold, grey concrete. The pitch is surrounded by a rough, sandy track, while the infamous Ultra Sur terrace is fronted by tall poles which support high anti-missile netting during sensitive matches.

If the Ultra regulars are so volatile, how come there is no moat? Herein lies perhaps the Bernabeu's most hidden secret. It would be impossible to dig a moat because right under the sacred pitch, running diagonally from the southwest corner to the east side, is a metro tunnel. In some areas the roof of this tunnel is said to lie less than a metre under the grass, and indeed if one stands near the southwest corner flag as trains pass beneath, the vibrations are quite palpable.

But then the Bernabeu has always made the senses tingle – especially in one's nether regions if one buys a seat ticket but does not hire a cushion. For the Bernabeu is also a rather uncomfortable venue. It has too few seats, and most of them are no more than concrete benches with iron armrests. The public concourses are dingy, there is no museum, custom-built souvenir shop or public reception area, and, as we have noted, the approach to the main entrance is quite run-down. In short, despite its new roof, the whole place is badly in need of a face-lift if it is to maintain its standing in the world game.

But as one would hope and expect, Real intend to put all this right.

Firstly, the eastern approach is to be completely revamped, with a new sports club replacing the swimming pool. Secondly, although barely seven years old, incredibly, the roof is to be removed, piece by piece for safekeeping, to allow Real to add a third tier to the Bernabeu. The effect of this would be to raise the overall height to that of the existing amphitheatre, and thus increase the capacity to approximately 105,000, including 65,000 seats. Thirdly, the existing concrete benches will be, thankfully, replaced by modern plastic seats and executive boxes installed between the two lower tiers.

This mammoth operation will cost the club around 2,500 million pesetas, so inevitably Real have had to curb their spending on players. As president Ramón Mendoza announced in 1989, after Barcelona broke the bank to pay for Ronald Koeman of PSV Eindhoven, 'We are not going to give up our plans for the stadium to sign any player, no matter how good he is.'

Will this policy of putting spectator comfort before big-name players jeopardise Real's dominance of the Spanish game? One might as well ask, would King Juan Carlos ever dare to admit a dislike for football?

Real will improve their stadium, and they will maintain their standards. If you live on the Castellana, noble sirs, nothing less will do.

MADRID

ESTADIO VICENTE CALDERÓN

Forever, it would seem, destined to live in the shadow of their powerful neighbours, it comes as no surprise to find **Atlético de Madrid** on a street called Melancólicos. But if their trophy cupboard is not quite so replete as Real's, as far as their stadium is concerned they have no cause for unhappiness. The 62,000 capacity, all-seated Vicente Calderón Stadium has a quite unique location and a charm all of its own.

Atlético have had three different names and used several grounds since their formation as a branch of Athletic Bilbao in 1903. As Athletic de Madrid (note the English spelling) they played first at the Ronda de Vallecas, in the vicinity of Rayo Vallecano's stadium (see page 216), then in 1913 moved to the O'Donnell area, to where their rivals, Sociedad Madrid (later renamed Real), had moved the year before. Ten years later both clubs opened new stadiums: Real at Cuidad Lineal and Athletic, two weeks later – on 13 May 1923 v. Real Sociedad, at the new Metropolitano Stadium, near the Avenida Reina Victoria in northwest Madrid. Watched by his mother, Queen María Cristina, the Infante Don Juan (the present king's father) kicked off that first match.

After such a regal start, Athletic struggled. In the eight seasons before Civil War broke out in 1936 they were relegated twice and vacated the Metropolitano twice – for reasons not entirely clear – using the Estadio de Vallecas and various other grounds between 1930–4.

After the war they fell under the wing of the air force, were renamed Atlético de Aviacón, and took off immediately. They won the 1939–40 championship while based at Real's Estadio Chamartín, then repeated the feat the following season, back at Vallecas, which had only just been reconverted from its wartime role as a concentration camp for POWs. By 1943 the Metropolitano had also been rebuilt, so Atlético moved back, playing the first game v. Real Madrid on 21 February.

The club's current title, Atlético de Madrid, was adopted in 1946, but they continued to fly

On the banks of the Manzanares, Atlético's cut-away stadium makes way for the ring road.

high, winning another pair of championships in 1950 and 1951. Meanwhile the Metropolitano, still a very basic stadium, was becoming hemmed in by development, and so in 1959 Atlético purchased a much larger plot in the southwestern outskirts of Madrid, by a gas works on the banks of the River Manzanares. Work proceeded slowly, and a few years later, short of funds, Atlético spent one humbling season at the Bernabeu while their new stadium lay unfinished. They then returned to the Metropolitano where they played one last glorious season, winning the championship in 1965–6. Finally, on 2 October 1966, seven years after building began, the Manzanares Stadium was ready – though still incomplete – and was unofficially opened with a match v. Valencia. In the same week bulldozers arrived at the Metropolitano, sending it crashing into oblivion.

Atlético's president during this crucial period was Vicente Calderón, whose name the new stadium took in September 1971 when it was, at last, nearing completion. The official inauguration followed on 23 May 1972 with an international friendly v. Uruguay, in the presence of both Franco and his named successor, King Juan Carlos. After Franco's death the King and his wife paid a return visit, in January 1976, their first public appearance at a sporting

215

event as reigning monarchs. This has been interpreted as tacit recognition that, unlike Real, Atlético were unaided by Franco's patronage.

That is almost certainly too simplistic a judgement, just as it would be misleading to portray Atlético as either a working-class or *nouveau riche* club compared with the aristocrats of Real. Membership of Atlético is actually more expensive, and less popular (roughly 30,000 *socios* compared with 60,000 at Real). Nevertheless, the Vicente Calderón does lie in the heart of an industrial and working-class district, a complete contrast to the surroundings of the Bernabeu.

Viewed from the air, Atlético's stadium is in a most extraordinary situation. Three sides are typically Spanish; two-tiered, uncovered, curved around the pitch and with floodlight gantries along the lip of the bowl. But on the west side, as if sliced by a giant guillotine, the tiers end abruptly as they come up against a swathe of tarmac, the six-lane M30 Madrid ring road, which runs alongside the ground, parallel to the touchline.

It seems odd enough that Atlético should have chosen such a site, knowing of this rather formidable obstacle. But they have overcome it with panache, simply by building their huge main stand on stilts, above the road. To test the engineers' ingenuity further, the back of this stand is anchored on the very bank of the Manzanares as it flows past the stadium.

Although Lansdowne Road in Dublin sits over a railway line and Vigo's main stand, in northern Spain, straddles a river, there is truly no other grandstand to match Atlético's. Underneath, lorries and cars speed through a dark, low-roofed concrete alley, past the stadium's main door (which looks as if it might be the entrance to some secret, basement dive). Above, the upper tier vibrates with the rush of traffic.

Because of its riverside location, and because the suspended cantilevered roof has no screen ends, the Vicente Calderón Stadium can be a cold and windy venue. This is mitigated partially by two enormous Mitsubishi video boards which cut off the corners on each side of the main stand. These giant displays were installed in 1982, when Atlético hosted three World Cup matches, involving France, Austria and Northern Ireland.

But even without the video boards the stadium is far from dull. Decked liberally inside and out in red and white stripes – hence its nickname, *El Campo Colchónero*, the ground of the mattress makers – it stands out in what is otherwise a rather grim locality. Most admirably, to soften its bare concrete facings, the external upper balconies, certain stairways and internal walls have been draped in hanging plants and evergreens. Someone, obviously, cares a great deal about appearances, but then when you are number two, you must always try harder.

● Madrid's third football venue is in the area of one of Atlético's former haunts. The 19,500 capacity **Estadio de Vallecas**, home to **Rayo Vallecano**, is next to Portazgo metro station in southeast Madrid. Rebuilt in 1976, the stadium appears to have been shoehorned into a neighbourhood block, with two double-decker stands on either side, and a terrace behind the south goal so narrow that in one corner there is barely room for a single line of spectators.

VALLADOLID

ESTADIO JOSÉ ZORILLA

They call the home of **Real Valladolid Deportivo** '*El Estadio de la Pulmonía*' – the stadium of pneumonia – and with good reason. Standing on an exposed plain, 713 metres above sea level and a couple of kilometres out of town, the new José Zorilla Stadium is like an ice box in a wind tunnel. It really is enough to turn Valladolid's members, '*Los Violetas*', quite blue, especially those who fondly recall the old José Zorilla Stadium.

Opened in 1942, Valladolid's former ground held 18,000 and was on the south bank of the River Pisuerga, next to the Hipica showjumping grounds in the city centre. But it had the usual drawbacks: too few seats, no parking, poor access, and since it belonged to the town council and was coveted by developers there was no escaping its fate. A branch of Spain's most popular department store, El Córte Inglés, now occupies the site.

Work on the new ground began in November 1980 and although it eventually cost nearly double the original 350 million peseta budget, it was at

Private boxes (some unglazed) were installed to enclose Valladolid's windy north end.

least completed a mere thirteen months later. Certainly Valladolid received much welcome publicity as a result. The stadium was officially inaugurated on 20 February 1982, with a League match v. Bilbao. A few months later it staged the 1982 Spanish Cup Final, Real Madrid v. Sporting Gijón. Then in June Valladolid hosted three World Cup matches involving Kuwait, the USSR and France.

Since it was the only venue purpose-built for the tournament, the designers had to follow strict specifications laid down by the Organising Committee (including the provision of cells), although its capacity of 29,990 actually fell 10 short of the specified minimum! Since 1982 the accommodation has expanded to 37,500 (26,500 seated).

The stadium started essentially as one open tier curved around the pitch (standing at both ends, seats on the sides), with two matching covered stands on each side. But such are the prevailing winds that the open north terrace proved a pretty inhospitable place to stand, so, to act as a weathershield, in 1984 the two side cantilevered roofs

were continued round to form a horseshoe. Rather than expose seated spectators to the wind under the new cover, the club then made provision for private boxes, 120 in total, on three levels. The effect of this curved wall of boxes (not all of them, surprisingly, glassed in) is not as awkward as one would imagine, and their presence certainly encloses the arena. Even so, the wind was still not beaten. On 25 July 1986 an 80 kph gust lifted the new roof high off its frame. Had there been anything behind, serious damage would have undoubtedly resulted. But there is only open land – seemingly miles of it – and no-one, fortunately, was hurt. The replacement roof is now said to be strong enough to withstand winds of up to 150 kph, but watch this space ...

Despite the wind, the cold and its inhospitable location (which should soon change with the construction of new housing in the vicinity), the stadium itself is well designed. There is a sloping concrete moat around the pitch, which makes viewing easier and allows for good pitch drainage; the stands have clean, uniform lines, accentuated

GROUNDWORK

by bright yellow steelwork and green roof cladding, and the main stand seating is in bands of violet and white. The open south terrace, with yellow steel barriers, has two low floodlight pylons (the other lights being mounted along the roof fascia) and is lined by a high white wall. In the centre is a 45 million peseta German electronic information board, which like Solna in Sweden, rotates on its axis in order to relay advertising to the passing world during the week.

This leaves us with one last question: who was José Zorilla? Amazingly he was not a former club president but one of Valladolid's most famous sons – a romantic poet and dramatist of the nineteenth century, best known for his still-performed play *Don Juan Tenorio*. Back in town there is his statue in the Plaza de Zorilla and a museum in his former abode. As a romantic, however, the new stadium would have surely left him cold, in his extremities if not in his heart.

VIGO

ESTADIO BALAÍDOS

Spain's most westerly club is **Celta de Vigo**, whose very name celebrates the fact that here, on the Gallego (or Galician) Atlantic coast, lies yet another piece of Spain's jumbled cultural jigsaw. Closer to Porto than to any other senior club, Celta's fans may sound more Portuguese than Spanish, but when it came to choosing a name for the newly formed club in August 1923 (after a merger of two other clubs), it was Gallego's ancient and cherished Celtic links which the founders sought to stress, at a time when antipathy to Madrid was running particularly high.

Celta began life at a ground called Campo de Coya, venue for the 1922 Cup Final, but played their first match at Balaídos, a 7–1 trouncing of Unión de Irún, on 30 December 1928. After that the 'light-blues' drifted between the First and Second Divisions, without honours, while their stadium changed little until 1970.

Then, to celebrate Celta's return to the First Division, three sides of the stadium were rebuilt, in a style similar to Bordeaux's Parc de Lescure, except that the reinforced concrete, cantilevered roofs had pointed, rather than rounded vaults. They were also divided into two sections of differing heights.

The taller roof ran along the north side and around the curved east end, in the shape of a 'J', with seats on the upper deck, standing below. This was linked to a lower roof at the west end, which covered a single tier of terracing. All that remained of the original stadium was a simple, cantilevered main stand on the south side, behind

which flowed the Rio Lagares. Though quite narrow, the river was a continual source of flooding in the region, so when Vigo was chosen as one of the venues for the 1982 World Cup, the water authorities and the stadium's municipal owners decided that they could kill two birds with one stone.

Thus the Lagares was rerouted through a channel laid underneath the foundations of a completely new main stand. The result was an odd-shaped stand, totally out of scale and harmony with the three sides of lower concrete roofing, but one which nevertheless solved the Lagares problem and gave Balaídos room for extra facilities for the public. The stadium now held 33,000 (including 30,000 seated), and became, in appearance, a stadium of two halves.

The concrete vaulted roofs, terraces and bench seats on the three older sides are unremittingly grey, and thus blend in comfortably with the anonymous apartment blocks which line the streets north and east of the stadium.

The new stand, conversely, is a lively hi-tech construction with a web of red steelwork supporting its deep overhanging roof. At the rear, red cladding covers the space which was created by having the concrete framework splayed over the covered river channel, and in this space are facilities for squash, badminton and volleyball.

From the uppermost levels of the new stand (opened in 1982 in time for Vigo's three World Cup games), one can look down onto the older concrete roofs, and see how protective fabric has been draped across the top (presumably because so much rainwater collects in each vault). One also sees, immediately behind the east end, a small, but modern athletics ground. Alongside this, the Lagares comes up for air again and demonstrates quite pungently why covering it up was no great loss.

POSTALES FAMA

Balaídos, with the murky Lagares flowing under the bright new hi-tech main stand.

Across a road behind the new stand is the sprawling factory of Celta's main sponsors, Citroen Cars, and in the east corner of the stand, tucked into the shadows, is a branch of the local police station.

Balaídos has two memorials honouring men who helped form the club in 1923. On the cinder track by the players' tunnel is a bust of José 'Pepe' Bar, a patron of 'Los Deportistas de Vigo', while outside the north stand, on the street which bears his name, is a much grander monument to Manuel de Castro. This was donated by members of the 1924 Uruguayan Olympic football team, several of whom were Gallego exiles living in Montevideo. Under his pen name of 'Handicap', Castro had been a champion of Galician sport, until his untimely but accidental death under a train in the early 1930s.

Gallego separatist graffiti has since rather despoiled the monument, but Castro would no doubt have been sympathetic towards the perpetrators. What he would have felt about underground polluted rivers and French car manufacturers we can only guess.

LA CORUÑA

ESTADIO DE RIAZOR

On Galicia's northwestern Atlantic coast lies one of Spain's most individualistic stadiums. The sole 1982 World Cup venue to double as an athletics stadium, Riazor, the home of **Deportivo**, has spectator accommodation on three sides only, and although this normally results in a loss of atmosphere for football matches, the stadium's design more than compensates with its colourful, quirky detail.

Above all, literally, stands its tall Marathon

SPAIN

GROUNDWORK

Nautical imagery embraces La Coruña's splendid Marathon Tower.

Tower, in the centre of the semicircular east terrace. This simple, neoclassical tower, like an obelisk on a pedestal, has balconies on both lower floors, the upper one carrying the flags of Spain and Galicia. In an arched niche above the lower balcony, facing the pitch, is another tower, this one a 3 metre tall bronze model of the Torre de Hércules (the oldest working lighthouse in the world and La Coruña's most famous landmark).

Before development of the west end of the stadium, the Marathon Tower had an unimpeded view across to the sea, a couple of hundred metres away. But Deportivo (officially Real Club Deportivo de La Coruña – try chanting that after a few glasses of Rioja) were once based even closer to the water. After forming in 1904 and becoming founder members of the Second Division in 1928, they settled right on the Atlantic coast at the Campo Riazor, named after an adjoining beach.

The old ground, now part of a school playground, was used until October 1944, when the present municipal Estadio de Riazor opened across the road. Official inauguration took place on 6 May 1945 – as the rest of Europe anxiously awaited peace – with an international v. Portugal. Two years later Real Madrid and Español were the visitors for the 1947 Cup Final.

Over the years Riazor grew to accommodate 40,000 spectators, essentially in one horseshoe-shaped bank surrounded by a solid, rough-cut stone wall. There was a single cantilevered roof over the north side, while at the seaboard end, instead of terracing, there were open arches leading to a training area.

The stadium today is almost entirely different. Preparations for the World Cup revealed, in 1979, structural defects which necessitated almost total reconstruction. Two double-decker stands went up on either side, each designed to reflect the city's maritime heritage, with white, dipping roofs being suspended from a series of tall, red pointed masts, as if hauled up like giant sails. The red cable braces are anchored, like mooring ropes, on concrete blocks behind each stand. On the underside of the roof, red steel framework looks down on bands of blue and white seating.

Two similarly playful stands are curved around the east terrace, with the Marathon Tower sandwiched between. For sure their proximity robs the tower of much of its former presence, though it could also be said that the tower's stark simplicity is enhanced by its new hi-tech neighbours. Whatever, the municipality is to be congratulated for preserving the tower. Stadiums would be dull indeed if all vestiges of the past were swept away and designs reduced to a formula.

Riazor staged three games in the 1982 World Cup, involving Peru, Cameroon and Poland. But the 500 million pesetas spent on the 28,956 capacity stadium (14,456 seated) was not squandered on prestige alone. As we have noted, there is a running track (synthetic and well used) around the pitch. At the west end, apart from a small raised terrace for children in one corner, the grassed space behind the goal is taken up by a large athletics scoreboard, behind which stands a dome-covered Sports Palace (opened in 1970 and holding 4900), an indoor swimming pool (opened 1977) and a fronton court.

Deportivo, who rent from the municipality at a peppercorn rate, could hardly have built such a complex on their own, especially as they have celebrated so few honours on the pitch. But they cherish other fond memories. Behind the main stand are three monuments – one to Juan Acuña, a former reserve international goalkeeper, one to Luis Otero, a member of Spain's Olympic XI before the Civil War, and one to recall FIFA president Dr João Havelange's visit for the World Cup in 1982. Not much to boast about if you're from Madrid or Barcelona but, as this municipal enterprise with its nautical references demonstrates so delightfully, they have other sources of pride in La Coruña.

GIJÓN

EL MOLINÓN

El Molinón – the Big Windmill – sounds idyllic, but the reality is quite different. Although on the edge of a spacious park, on the outskirts of this industrial Atlantic port, the home of **Sporting Gijón** is a sparsely-finished, functional stadium whose gaunt, concrete exterior, painted green and liberally daubed with graffiti, puts one less in mind of windmills and more of the dark satanic variety.

Inside El Molinón one is further unsettled. Quite simply, none of the stands seem to fit together. It is as if someone has taken a perfectly good stadium, shaken it all up, then reassembled the parts wrongly.

Before delving further, we find much of Sporting's early history to be similarly fragmented because their records were destroyed during the Civil War. It is known, however, that the club formed in 1905 and played at various grounds called Beronda, Campu Ronda, La Flor de Valencia and, intriguingly, La Matóna (literally 'the female bully'). All were in the same area as El Molinón, where Sporting first played on 5 August 1917. In 1920 the new ground hosted the Cup Final, Barcelona v. Athletic Bilbao, and eight years later – shortly before Sporting became founder members of the Second Division – El Molinón staged its first international, v. Italy, on 22 April 1928.

Development proceeded, piece by piece, but if there ever was a masterplan, it was never followed. In the late 1950s a low, concrete half-cantilevered roof was erected over the north terrace. Later painted red on its underside, the roof is currently in a sorry, crumbling state, yet it was the only part of El Molinón to survive redevelopment during the 1970s. Gijón's trade fair grounds lie behind the terrace, linked to the stadium by an overhead walkway.

The remaining three sides were rebuilt between 1971–7, increasing El Molinón's capacity from 35,000 to 45,000 (18,000 seated), although the stadium has never been filled, not even for Gijón's three World Cup matches. (They were memorable games however, in West Germany's controversial group with Austria, Chile, and Algeria.)

On the west side, twice as high as the north end, is an all-seated main stand – parallel to the pitch with a flat roof – which backs onto the Parque Isabel la Católica and houses a police station in one section. The more modern south stand, with red steelwork and green cladding, curves around the pitch with a tier of seats above a terrace. This links up on the east side with the Tribuna Nueva, which, as the name suggests, was the last section to be built. It is also the tallest, its

GROUNDWORK

El Molinón's awkward roofs fail to cover some poor design.

upturned cantilevered roof dominating the rest of the stadium.

Taken separately, each section of El Molinón, though different in style, functions perfectly well. It is the attempt to link the four sides which fails, quite dismally.

For example, between the tall Tribuna Nueva and the low north terrace (the spot, incidentally, where the original windmill was said to have stood) covering the upper corner seats is what can best be described as a freestanding hood on stilts, perched embarrassingly in the air, halfway between the two different roof levels.

If the intention is eventually to demolish the north end, then this odd little canopy will presumably be linked up with another rather curious corner roof, at the north end of the main stand. Thus El Molinón will be fully enclosed and covered, even if each corner roof does resemble a torn-up cardboard box adapted hastily to cover an unforeseen gap.

But afterthought or not, and aesthetics aside, this still does not explain why the seats and open balconies in both corners of the main stand are arranged at right angles to the rest of the seating (that is, parallel to the goal lines) and set back against the corners of the stand. This not only creates awkward areas to cover, but also forces the occupants to turn to one side to see the pitch; literally a pain in the neck.

Not to put too fine a point on it, these are such basic design errors that for fear of being accused of sexism one hesitates to point out that overseeing El Molinón's redevelopment was a female architect, María del Mar Benito, and that El Molinón is the only major stadium in Europe to have had 'a woman's touch'. Certainly Sporting Gijón are said to be 'not amused' by the results – memories of La Matóna perhaps – especially because, though tenants of the municipality, they must still bear all the stadium's maintenance costs. Since 1988 they have at least had one consolation. Thanks to a sympathetic mayor, who also happens to be a director of the club, Sporting's rent has been reduced to just one peseta per year. Despite El Molinón's design faults therefore, Sporting will not be pleading for a rent rebate quite yet.

OVIEDO

ESTADIO CARLOS TARTIERE

A short distance south from Gijón and in complete contrast is the small but immaculate municipal stadium used by **Real Oviedo**, a prime example of how simple design can overcome the twin obstacles of limited space and resources, yet still retain the best characteristics of an intimate enclosure.

The Carlos Tartiere Stadium had just celebrated its fiftieth anniversary when the World Cup came to town in 1982. In fact the three games staged (involving Chile, Austria and Algeria) were the first international action seen at Oviedo since the stadium's official inauguration, with a match v. Yugoslavia, on 24 April 1932, when Carlos Tartiere was both mayor and club president. Oviedo had, however, played at the ground – then holding only 10,000 and known as the Buenavista Stadium – since forming in 1926.

Until 1982 the stadium had remained basic, even by the standards of the Second Division in which Oviedo have spent much of their time. Surrounded by open land, it had one reinforced concrete cantilevered main stand dating from 1932 – one of the first such stands in Europe, designed by Juan Junquéra and named after a prominent Spanish structural engineer, Sánchez del Río – and three fenced-in earthen banks of terracing, one of which was covered by a simple metal roof.

On the open side of the stadium was a small central tower and behind the open goal stood two small houses. It was an archetypical unspoilt, provincial ground, with just a hint of the future in its advanced main stand.

Whizz forward a few years and the surroundings, if not the Carlos Tartiere, had changed entirely.

Urban development pressed up against three sides, so that as 1982 approached, the architect responsible for rebuilding the stadium, Florencio Muñiz Uribe, had to balance carefully the interests of football with those of the local residents.

He did a splendid job.

Though based, for the sake of continuity, on

No awards for style,
but Oviedo's rebuilt ground proves yet again
that simple ideas
usually work best for football.

the character of the Tribuna Sánchez del Río (which like many a prototype had not withstood the test of time), the Carlos Tartiere is now covered on all four sides by metallic cantilevered roofs (slightly lower at the ends because of adjacent apartment blocks), and has a capacity of 22,284 (5004 seated).

There are no frills. The stadium's exterior is in plain brickwork, to blend with surrounding high-rise municipal housing. The single-tier interior is compact and tidy, with blue and white seats on either side and terracing with white barriers at the ends. The rear walls of these terraces carry a nice touch – the crests and names of Oviedo's twenty-three Asturian '*peñas*', or supporters' club branches.

In one corner of the main stand is a brick-built block, from which Oviedo's newest brainchild is controlled.

This is a system of portable, electronic ticket-readers which, since 1988, the club officials have used to check against ticket forgeries in each of their sixty turnstiles. The system, adapted from supermarket checkouts, cost Oviedo about 260,000 pesetas (£1300) per turnstile, and has aroused great interest among other Spanish clubs, not to mention English clubs facing government legislation on computerised identity cards. In fact many English clubs would actually feel most at home at the Carlos Tartiere; it is a model medium-sized stadium, dedicated to football, in the heart of the community it serves.

ATHLETIC BILBAO

Artist Arrúe's view of San Mamés in 1913, with the Casa de Misericordia beyond.

BILBAO

SAN MAMÉS

San Mamés – La Catedral – is more than just a stadium, and **Athletic Club de Bilbao** more than just a football club. Both are potent symbols of Basque pride (Real Sociedad and Osasuna notwithstanding) among a people whose language, culture and political aspirations often cause ire and frustration in Madrid but inspire intense loyalty on the football pitch. Athletic do not, on principle, field non-Basque players, which is both their strength and their weakness.

Bilbao was the birthplace, or rather first entry-point, for football in Spain. British miners and foundry workers arriving during the trading boom of the 1890s astonished the locals with their footballing antics and baggy shorts, and were soon joined by the sons of Bilbao merchants who had

picked up the game in English schools. The first organised match is thought to have taken place in May 1894, and Bilbao FC, essentially a British team, formed four years later; then in 1901 they merged with another club, Athletic (whose one English member, though a resident for twenty-five years, was said never to have learnt Spanish).

Playing first at Lamiaco, then at a ground called Jolaseta, Athletic Club de Bilbao made an immediate impact on the infant Spanish scene, and after the club had won a fourth Cup victory in the competition's first decade, the members voted to build a proper ground on fields at the end of the city's main thoroughfare, the Gran Vía.

Then, as now, the grandest edifice in that area was a refuge for orphans and homeless people, the Casa de Misericordia, a solid nineteenth-century institution with domes and turrets, built on the site of a hermitage where the saint and child martyr, Mamés de Cesarea, had been venerated. (Because of the saint's association with lions, Athletic were later nicknamed Los Leónes.)

In a solemn ceremony attended by players, members and priests, the first stone of the San Mamés stadium was laid on 20 January 1913, and only seven months later the first match took place, v. Cup-holders Racing de Irún, on 21 August. Legend has it that an Athletic player called Pichichi scored the first goal. More of him anon. A few days later Shepherds Bush, an amateur team from London, visited for two challenge matches, the second of which was honoured by the presence of King Alfonso XIII and his wife. (Unfortunately the royal couple arrived late and the match had to be stopped while they made an entrance.)

San Mamés then consisted of an ornate red and white wooden stand, perched on a grass bank above a narrow strip of terracing (with flower beds at each end), and opposite, a crescent-shaped wedge of open terracing. The local pressmen waxed lyrical, one preposterously claiming that only Chelsea's ground in London could compare with San Mamés, and certainly not Crystal Palace (which held around 100,000!). San Mamés did have one thing in common with its London counterparts however. The pitch was planted with English grass.

Altogether San Mamés cost Athletic's members 89,000 pesetas, a huge sum for the period. But the sports-mad folk of Bilbao did not let them down. The 10,000 capacity ground soon developed, and on 7 October 1921 it staged the first ever international on Spanish soil, Spain beating Belgium 2–0. In the same year San Mamés also hosted the Cup Final (the only one to be played at the stadium), between the home club and Athletic de Madrid.

(When Franco clamped down on anglicisation after 1939, both clubs had to adopt the Castilian 'Atlético', but only Bilbao reverted to their former name after his death in 1975.)

By the early 1950s the fields and meadows surrounding San Mamés had been swallowed up by urban development, which made impossible complete redevelopment along the lines of, say, Real Madrid or Sevilla. Instead, Bilbao concentrated on rebuilding their main stand, and boldly opted for a form of roof construction unseen at a football stadium – a giant arch. The original plan was to build on each corner of the stand a square screening block lined with open balconies, these blocks to support a gargantuan coffered arch. No doubt it would have looked monumental, but its rear wall would have to have been prohibitively

tall and would thus have provided the centre seats with no real shelter from the elements.

After a rethink, therefore, the two five-storey, stone-faced screening blocks were built but with a huge steel arch bridging the gap, beneath which a flat roof was suspended. Under the direction of engineer Carlos Fernández Casado and three architects, work on the ambitious San Mamés arch and 12,000 seater double-decker stand began in February 1952 and was finished in March 1953. Had it not been for a shortage of materials (owing to an industrial crisis at the time), the stand might have been extended and hence given Bilbao the world's largest reinforced concrete roof (larger than aircraft hangars in Maine and South Dakota, USA).

Nevertheless the San Mamés arch quickly became a revered and popular image in Spanish football, while on match days the corner units were like blocks of flats with the occupants out in force to enjoy the view. At that time the opposite east terrace was open and backed by a high wall and just one of the end terraces was covered.

By 1962 La Catedral was complete. There were now double-decker stands on the remaining three sides, their flat roofs supported by pillars. Each stand was shaped irregularly because of the surrounding roads, and the narrow corner between the south and west stands was filled by an L-shaped block of balconies. With so little room remaining, the new lights, switched on v. Flamengo of Brazil on 28 April 1962, were mounted on stumpy gantries on three roof corners and along the roof of the new east stand. San Mamés was now a tightly enclosed den, sealed off from the surrounding trees, hills and buildings; an intimidating bastion of Basque fervour.

It remained thus until the run-up to the 1982 World Cup, when further remodelling began, not to increase capacity so much as spectator comfort. But what a delicate operation it proved to be.

The aim was to link up the main stand with two new double-decker stands at either end, which entailed demolishing the space-consuming five-storey corner blocks. But since these bore the load of the famous arch, which Athletic insisted on preserving, they could not come down until an alternative method of support had been constructed. It proved to be an immense challenge.

First, prefabricated cantilevered brackets were inserted into the stand, underneath each end of the arch. Then, while cranes took the weight of

SPAIN

ATHLETIC BILBAO

The famous San Mamés arch – the corner blocks are gone but the theme has been revived at Genoa.

the arch, the corner blocks were demolished – an operation which required seven blasts of dynamite – and finally the new brackets were moved into position to accept the weight of the arch. If this sounds simple, the reality was very different. The massive structure of the arch – and therefore the roof below – was in constant danger of buckling throughout the process, and so precise were the movements that electric censors and heating elements were needed to keep the new concrete at exactly the right temperature. When the arch finally settled onto its new supports it was found to have shifted only 5 millimetres, an astonishing feat of engineering.

Throughout the operation, work also proceeded on the two new end stands. These were essentially more streamlined, cantilevered versions of the earlier structures, but with extra seating and moulded white-clad roofs, illuminated from the rear by a line of windows. The east stand was untouched apart from the installation of seats in the lower tier. The original lights were also replaced by new lamps along each roof.

The reborn Cathedral of San Mamés held 46,223 but had more seats (36,000) and much improved facilities all round. Even so, the massive investment of 1,100 million pesetas precluded any possible profit from the World Cup, in which San Mamés, surprisingly, staged only three games, all involving England (v. France, Czechoslovakia and Kuwait).

Was it all worth it?

Arch or no arch there is no denying that San Mamés was, before 1982, a rather dour concrete fortress. New red seats, two Mitsubishi video boards (as at Atlético), and the generous use of white cladding externally have brightened up the stadium considerably, imposing a much needed

uniformity on what is really a collection of irregularly shaped-stands. Every odd angle, every corner of the stadium has been filled with seating. There is even a narrow balcony of seats alongside one video board, perched above the main body of the south stand.

Above all, however, towers the inescapable white San Mamés arch, crisply defined against the sky. One may question its structural validity – such a roof span could nowadays be easily supported by other means of cantilevering – but its physical presence is undeniable. San Mamés would not be the same without it.

But then Bilbao is a city rich with traditional emblems. Among the uppermost seats of the main stand is a small bronze bust whose significance carries far beyond San Mamés. This is the memorial to Rafael Moreno, one of Athletic's best-loved goalscorers from their earliest days. Nicknamed 'Pichichi' (nipper), his trademark was a distinctive white skull cap. The bust, dedicated in December 1928 shortly after his early death, used to stand, facing the pitch like a face in the crowd, on a pedestal at the rear of the old north terrace, and it was customary for teams paying their first visit to San Mamés to place flowers at the base. In addition, every season since 1928, Spain's top scorer has been granted the Pichichi Award. (The best goalkeepers receive the Zamora Award, named after Spain's prewar international keeper.) The street behind the main stand, where new hi-tech exhibition halls face the main entrance, is also named after Pichichi (Pitxitxi in Basque).

There are two other sights for the inquiring visitor. One block behind the south stand is a small, delapidated football ground called the Campo de Garellano. Floodlit with a sand pitch and sagging crossbars it has no connection with Athletic but is a poignant reminder of how some of our great football stadiums once looked.

In complete contrast is Ibaigane, a quite stunning building in which Athletic's offices are to be found, near the River Bilbao on the Alameda de Mazarredo. Built in 1900, it is a detached seignorial mansion in neo-Basque style – deep overhanging roof, brick and timber reliefwork and iron balconies – which belonged originally to a prominent Basque merchant shipper, Ramón de la Sota, who was knighted by Queen Victoria but dispossessed during the Civil War. After Franco's death the mansion was returned to the family but stood empty for years, until 1988 when Athletic

ATHLETIC BILBAO

San Mamés today. The Casa de Misericordia still stands, but all else is different.

offered to restore it and use it as their club offices.

There is not space to describe Ibaigane's full splendour – its polished oak panelling, the stained glass ceiling depicting scenes of Basque peasantry, the central gallery and grand staircase, and the numerous paintings of San Mamés and Athletic players during the early years. And yet reminders of Athletic's rich past appear all over Bilbao. One only has to enter a bar, especially in the old quarter, to see archive photographs of San Mamés and its heroes, lovingly exhibited with pennants and mementos collected by the club's besotted supporters. San Mamés is truly their cathedral; Athletic, the defenders of their faith.

SAN SEBASTIÁN

ATOCHA

By the time you read this, **Real Sociedad** of San Sebastián (Donostia in Basque) may have moved on, in which case this will serve as a memorial to their hopelessly inadequate but lovable ground a few steps from the railway station, huddled in between the main line, a fruit market and San Sebastián's only (dreadful) modern office block.

After the craggy hillsides and baroque splendours of this delightful coastal resort, Atocha exudes a distinctly plebeian air. Inaugurated in 1913, its first and only taste of international action was v. France, in January 1923. A year later it

Real Sociedad fans joke that the office block is really Atocha's changing rooms.

staged the Cup Final, Unión de Irún v. Real Madrid. After the 1950s however Atocha lagged far behind stadium trends in Spain, hence its pre-

cious individuality and absence from the World Cup scene in 1982.

Holding 27,400, the ground is an intimidating hothouse for visitors, covered on all four sides (each with a different style of roof) and with barely a metre between its touchlines and perimeter fence. The white north stand roof, apparently concrete, is actually lath and plaster, and the general facilities are basic, to say the least.

None of this mattered while Real were dubbed '*el equipo ascensor*' – because of their ups and downs – but recent European appearances, two League titles (1981 and 1982) and a Cup win in 1987 have proved to be Atocha's undoing. In 1988 plans for a modern, though hardly larger, municipal stadium in the southern outskirts of the town at Anoeta were unveiled, while Atocha is expected to become a public park. Better that, one supposes, than another ugly office block.

ZARAGOZA

LA ROMAREDA

In the spirit of nostalgic reverie with which readers should now be quite familiar, we begin not at the current home of **Real Zaragoza** but at the forlorn remains of its old, abandoned hunting ground, El Campo de Torrero.

Like Elche's former Altabix Stadium, Torrero has obviously suffered a long and painful decline since Zaragoza departed in 1957. By early 1989

The ruins of Campo de Torrero's terracing, over thirty years after the last big match.

all that remained were two retaining walls, the skeleton of one terrace, and the barest hint of a pitch amid weeds and building rubble.

Built on the same fields that were used for Napoleon's artillery barrage of the city in 1808, Torrero belonged to a club called Iberia and was opened on 7 October 1923, with a match v. Osasuna. In 1926 it staged Spain's first ever women's football match, a year later Unión de Irún played their Cup Final here v. Arenas, and in April 1929 France were the visitors for Zaragoza's first international. Iberia, meanwhile, became founder members of the Second Division, then in 1932 merged with neighbours Zaragoza to form the present club.

Torrero was typical of its era – rectangular, surrounded by narrow streets and houses, but with one unusual feature; a line of balconies above one terrace, overlooking the pitch. As a First Division venue however it had no future, and the last match took place on 28 April 1957. For several years Torrero resisted the grasps of property developers, but Zaragoza eventually had to sell in order to rescue their flagging finances. Apartment blocks now occupy part of the site.

La Romareda, named, it is thought, after the area, opened on 8 September 1957, and Osasuna, again, were the visitors. A municipal venture designed by Francisco Riestra, it was spurred on by a sympathetic mayor and cost 21.5 million

GROUNDWORK

La Romareda – 'twixt hospital and convent with a long way to the back of the net.

pesetas. In plan it was straight at the sides and semicircular at each end, but only the main stand had a roof until 1976–7, when both end terraces were built up and also covered. This left just the east side to be roofed over, as part of a 120 million peseta refit in 1982, which included new floodlights and the construction behind the main stand of a press centre. Zaragoza had hoped to convert this centre into club offices after the World Cup, but the municipality pulled rank and installed its own offices instead.

La Romareda now held 46,920 and staged three World Cup games. To commemorate this there are concrete flagpoles on either side of the main entrance, bearing the names of the participants – Honduras, Yugoslavia and Northern Ireland.

Since then the stadium has been further improved and brightened up by the installation of blue and white seating, thus reducing the capacity slightly to 43,349, of which 16,600 are standing and 1487 are in small open pens or 'palcos', which form a band around the stadium, between the upper and lower tiers.

La Romareda is overall a tidy, functional stadium with few distinguishing features. Set in an open piazza on a main road, the exterior is a continuous wall of concrete verticals and brick infill. Blue floodlight box pillars stand slightly away from the main body. Inside, the unbroken cantilevered roof on red steel framework covers the top tier only, with electronic scoreboards supported above the roof line at each end. Should the need arise, both Zaragoza's body and soul should be in safe hands; behind the east stand hovers the massive silhouette of the Miguel Servet Hospital, while behind the south terrace lies the Convent of Jerusalem.

La Romareda has two other distinctions. Firstly, since 1971 it has been the only venue, apart from Valladolid (once), to break Madrid's monopoly of the Spanish Cup Final, in 1983 and 1987. Secondly, Zaragoza must surely have the deepest goalnets in European football! The nets go back nearly 4 metres, so strikers beware – if you want to hit the back of the net at La Romareda, give it some welly.

SWEDEN

OLLE AGNELL

Goal! Olle Agnell's portrayal of Örjans vall, Halmstad, captures the charm of small-town Swedish football. In 1958 delightful grounds like this played host to the world's best.

WORLD CUP 1958

SMALLER VENUES

There will never again be a World Cup like 1958, at least not in Europe. Sweden chose to use twice as many venues as had the Swiss in 1954 – twelve in all – in a deliberate attempt to take international football to small towns and grounds which nowadays would be regarded as totally inadequate for major games.

The **Olympia** ground, built on a plateau above the medieval castle of **Helsingborg**, was typical of Sweden's eight smaller World Cup stadiums. In 1958, when West Germany, Czechoslovakia and Argentina were the visitors for two games, it was oval-shaped with one small, wooden stand flanked by bleachers (wooden planks on scaffold), and billed as having the best pitch in Sweden, with a capacity of 30,000. (The highest gate was, in fact, 20,257, for an international v. Switzerland a month before the World Cup.) Today, only the wooden stand survives; Olympia was rebuilt in 1985 on three sides with open concrete terracing parallel to the pitch.

The resident club there is **Helsingborgs IF**, once a regular First Division outfit but currently in the lower divisions.

Örjans vall, Halmstad, was another homely venue, more like a country club. Built on the banks of the River Nissan, on the site of a medieval leprosy hospital, the ground currently holds 19,125 and is used by **Halmstads BK** and a lesser club, Halmia (most Swedish grounds are shared). The old wooden stand from 1958 was replaced during the late 1970s by a neatly functional cantilevered stand. A smaller cantilevered stand, named after the Swedish football pools company, Tips, was built opposite in 1986, thus blocking the view of houses whose prim gardens adjoin the ground. One marvels that the likes of Argentina, Czechoslovakia and Northern Ireland once sought international honours in such a leafy, unassuming riverside spot.

In a similarly refined suburban setting, in the town of **Örebro**, is **Eyravallen** (named after an ancient Nordic god), home of **Örebro SK** (and BK Forward), where Scotland played France in 1958. Here, to adapt a cliché, is a stadium of two halves: on one side, a cramped, low, ornate wooden stand dating from 1923, in pale green with yellow benches; on the other, a streamlined, propped, cantilevered stand with angled, glass screen ends and roof beams which jut out over the pitch like gargoyles.

But the most surprising feature of Eyravallen is a tall, Disney-like statue who peers into the ground over the main turnstiles. Sporting a cowboy hat, number nine shirt, Adidas shorts and clumpy brown boots, this is the cartoon character Kronblomm, Örebro's mascot and a curiosity for the whole town.

The iron and steel town of **Eskilstuna** also staged one World Cup match, Yugoslavia v. Paraguay, at **Tunavallen**. The ground's record gate of 22,491 came, however, in 1963, for **IFK Eskilstuna**'s match v. GAIS. Virtually unchanged since 1958, there is just one wooden stand, holding 874 seats, and three low, open sides curving around a new all-weather track. Hidden mysteriously among trees and granite boulders behind Tunavallen is a large speedway stadium.

Yugoslavia also played two World Cup matches (v. Scotland and v. France) at **Arosvallen, Västerås**. This remains a typical community sports ground, holding 11,200, with one 1200 capacity stand – a low construction with vaulted concrete roofing – wooden bleachers and a pristine running track. The record gate is 14,208, for **Västerås SK** v. Sandvikens IF in 1956.

Sandviken's own 21,000 capacity stadium, used in 1958 for two matches involving Wales, Hungary and Mexico, is the most northerly venue ever used during a World Cup final, being just 550 kilometres south of the Arctic Circle. In a town known primarily as headquarters of the mighty Sandvik Steelworks, Sandviken's football ground, **Jernvallen** (the Iron Ground), reflects little of the surrounding area's corporate sterility and remains the most basic of the twelve Swedish venues from 1958. It has a brown, bare main stand backing onto an ice-hockey pitch and training complex, a dishevelled dirt track, grass banks for standing and precious little iron or steel in evidence.

Borås, a textile town in the Lancashire mould, staged two matches (Austria's games v. England and v. USSR) at **Ryavallen**, which currently holds 18,526 but has a record gate of 22,654, for **IF Elfsborg** v. IFK Norrköping in 1961, the golden era of Swedish club football. Ryavallen has two plain white stands with low open banking curved around a modern running track. Behind the east terrace is Knalleland, the mail order capital of Sweden.

A classically simple half-cantilevered stand dwarfs the tiny main stand (just visible, bottom left) at Eyravallen, Örebro.

Finally, **Rimnersvallen** in **Uddevalla** (population 36,000) was built especially for the World Cup. The sole match staged there, Austria v. Brazil (yet to field Pelé at the time), drew 17,778 people, still a ground record and commemorated by a plaque on the main stand, which is unchanged since 1958. Nestling between a tree-covered granite ridge (decked in advertising) and winding suburban lanes, Rimnersvallen is used by **IK Oddevold** and typifies the quintessentially Swedish, classless, orderly calm which pervaded much of the 1958 tournament. Never again would a World Cup setting seem so innocent or so close to the heart of its host community.

Barely altered since 1958, the wooden main stand at Tunavallen, Eskilstuna, shows how expectations for the World Cup have changed. But at what cost?

SCANDIA PHOTOPRESS/RICHARD CONRICUS

Malmö's giant half shell from 1958 (right) faces its 1988 partner.

MALMÖ

MALMÖ STADION

Before 1958 sporting endeavour in Malmö had largely been confined to the compact Malmö Sports Ground. When opened in 1896 this was the first of its kind in Scandinavia and was regularly packed for events such as equestrian parties, wrestling (for which Malmö became famous) and soirées at the adjacent 'Boston', a much-loved *palais de danse*. Of course there was also football, which by the 1920s was dominated by the rivalry between the Sports Ground's resident club, **Malmö FF**, Sweden's most successful domestic outfit, and nearby Helsingborgs IF.

Nowadays the quaint old Sports Ground with its original wooden stand occupies a corner of Pildamm Park, a haven of woods and water bordering the city centre. Yet only a few hundred metres distant, through the trees and across a wide thoroughfare, we find the 1958 World Cup stadium in a completely contrasting situation, on the edge of a vast postwar development in which every road is straight and no tree is out of line.

Development of the Malmö Stadium took place at the same time as Gothenburg's new World Cup Stadium, and, as the designs clearly indicate, both were the work of the same architects, Fritz Jaenecke and Sten Samuelson. The two stadiums even opened within twenty-four hours of each other, Malmö being inaugurated first on 28 May 1958 with an athletics meeting. The first football match, one of four at Malmö during the World Cup, was Argentina v. West Germany, on 8 June 1958 – the opening day of the tournament, the attendance establishing the ground record of 30,953. (The highest for a Malmö FF match is 29,328, v. Helsingborgs IF, during Malmö's seventh championship season, in 1967.)

Fluid design characterises this graceful stadium. Like a giant half shell, the main stand's roof appears to embrace one side of the arena, high in its centre, tapering behind each goal. So pronounced is this taper that at each extremity the upper tier of the stand is reduced to just one row of blue seating, beyond which the white exterior wall veers away from the bowl to form a screen between the interior of the stadium and the surrounding landscape.

The large openings of this purely cosmetic screen are echoed inside the stand by the extensive use of glass between both tiers, so that light floods in. Two ramps flank the central entrance, as at Gothenburg, leading to a concourse which is framed by a pair of abstract murals by local artist C.O.Hultén. The four freestanding floodlight pillars were added in 1960.

In 1988, in anticipation of Sweden staging the 1992 European Championships, the harmony of Jaenecke and Samuelson's original design was slightly unbalanced by the addition of a second, much plainer 3000 seater stand, opposite the main stand (thus marginally reducing the overall capacity to 30,000, of which 15,500 are seated). This was part of a SKr38 million refit of the stadium complex, which also includes training pitches, a bowling hall, ice stadium and an indoor arena called the Baltic Hall (also designed by Jaenecke and Samuelson), which houses Sweden's only sports museum.

Malmö Stadium thus forms the focus of one of Europe's largest sports complexes, a complex which, situated as it is on the edge of a flat, drawing-board estate of uniform housing blocks and landscaped greenery, evokes only too clearly the postwar planners' vision of an orderly and scientific world. Yet confronting this brave new world as one emerges from the meandering woods of Pildamm Park, one sees instantly that it is the stadium, and perhaps the stadium alone, which lends this modern vision a human face.

NORRKÖPING

IDROTTSPARK

One of four venues due to host the 1992 European Championships, the Idrottspark (Sports Park) was the smallest of Sweden's four main World Cup venues in 1958. It staged three games: Paraguay v. France and v. Scotland, and France's quarter-final v. Northern Ireland.

Norrköping itself is an elegant, baroque town sometimes dubbed the 'Paris of the North', but the football ground, opened in 1903, is very Scandinavian and will need considerable improvement to meet UEFA's standards for 1992. The Idrottspark's current capacity is 21,200 (including 7,200 seats), but the record attendance is 32,234, when home club **IFK Norrköping** met Malmö FF on 7 June 1956 in a match which led to IFK winning their sixth championship.

The most basic section is the north or Klockan – Clock End – terrace, which consists only of a tall bank of bleachers – terracing comprised of wooden planks on scaffolding, and these will undoubtedly have to be replaced for 1992.

The 4000 seater main stand is small but quite adequate. A large propped construction whose façade is bedecked in ivy, it was built in 1958 and is still called the VM Läktaren (World Cup Stand).

Opposite is the Tips Stand, dating from 1987 and financed, as at Halmstad, by the Swedish pools company.

But one's attention is most drawn to the southern end, to the Berget, or mountain. Its lower terracing is carved out of granite blocks, while its upper half is a neatly trimmed grass mound dotted with white barriers and topped ceremonially with a single white flagpole, as if it had once been captured in a battle.

One hopes that development of the Idrottspark will not destroy this proud hump, but with 1992 looming and FIFA urging the installation of individual seats at all major venues, the mountain may yet be conquered.

View from the Norrköping 'mountain' – white barriers on a grass slope, bleachers at the opposite end. Will 1992 destroy its air of innocence?

GOTHENBURG

NYA ULLEVI

In a cityscape dominated by cranes and ships' masts, the Nya – or New – Ullevi stadium with its twin pillars and steel cables makes an apposite architectural statement, one which might almost have inspired Munich's Olympic Stadium fourteen years later. Broadly translated as 'temple of Ull' (the god of sport), Ullevi was designed by Jaenecke and Samuelson, architects of Malmö's stadium, which was built at the same time and opened one day earlier. In Gothenburg they employed a similar shell-like roof design – high in the centre, low at the ends – after aerial views of

Helsinki's Olympic Stadium revealed that spectators naturally gravitate towards the halfway line on both sides. But whereas the roof at Malmö is self-supporting and covers only half the stadium, at Gothenburg the all-round roof is suspended at its highest point by thirty-eight steel cables – each capable of bearing 80 tons – hung from two 52-metre tall concrete masts. These towering white verticals, with floodlights at their peak, frame the approach and main entrance to the stadium, lending poise and drama to the undulating roof of the bowl.

Construction on this, Sweden's largest stadium, began in May 1957 on the clay bed of Levgrens Meadow, which needed 52,000 metres of stabilising piles (varying from 6 to 67 metres long) before construction could begin. (Until then, Gothenburg's main venue had been a few hundred

FRITID GÖTEBORG

Malmö's sister stadium – the New Ullevi in Gothenburg. Old Ullevi can just be seen, centre right.

metres away at the Gamla – or Old – Ullevi, opened in 1916 but now destined to make way for a cultural centre.)

Nya Ullevi was opened on schedule, though massively over budget, with a speech by actor Tore Lindwall and a match between Sweden and a Gothenburg Xl, on 29 May 1958, a week before the World Cup. During the Finals it staged six matches, including Pelé's first ever World Cup appearance (v. USSR), one quarter-final, a semi-final and the play-off for third place. But the highest football match attendance, of 52,194 (a Swedish club record), came a year later, for IFK Göteborg's vital promotion match v. rivals Örgryte on 3 June 1959. There has been one, even larger crowd for a sporting event at Ullevi, in September 1958, when 53,614 saw Ingemar Johansson knock out Eddie Machen of the USA, in a bout which lasted 2 minutes 16 seconds.

But the stadium's all-time record is 126,856 spread over two nights of Bruce Springsteen concerts in June 1985. Ullevi (and residents for miles around) did not entirely welcome the Springsteen experience. As his amplified music filled the stadium the roof shook visibly – an alarming experience, according to witnesses – and the stadium's municipal owners subsequently had to install concrete panels in order to stabilise the roof, and then insert 7000 limestone rods under the pitch to absorb future vibrations.

Other Ullevi happenings have included rock concerts by David Bowie, the Rolling Stones and Bob Dylan, plus ice hockey matches, athletics, speed skating (on the world's first artificial ice-track), speedway (the Kaparna team are in current occupation), and a freedom rally in 1983 which drew 100,000 demonstrators chanting 'Give Peace a Chance'.

Football remains Ullevi's bread and butter, however.

It plays host to three of Sweden's most successful clubs: **Örgryte IS**, the country's second oldest club, which dominated Swedish club football until 1930; **GAIS** (Göteborg Atlet & Idrotts-sällskap); and, the best-known and best-supported, **IFK Göteborg**, nicknamed the Angels or Blåvitt (blue-white). Thus the Ullevi can stage up to twelve local derbies a season, with the unwritten rule that the 'home' club fans are always allowed to occupy the much-favoured N-section above the halfway line.

Surprisingly, Ullevi has staged only one Euro-

Glowing totems and a mystic silver sphere at Gothenburg's 'Temple of Ull' – still one of the most finely poised and dramatic of Europe's modern stadiums.

pean final – Aberdeen's Cup Winners' Cup victory over Real Madrid in May 1982. Additionally it also enjoys a fond place in the history of women's football, having staged Sweden's first international in 1975, v. England, a match which helped convince the conservative male hierarchy that women's football was, after all, both worthwhile and entertaining.

Until recently the capacity remained at its original level of 52,000 (21,139 seats), although interestingly, in winter, when spectators dress in thicker clothing, only 50,000 could squeeze in. Modernisation work under the east side has, since 1989, reduced the capacity to 45,000, though thankfully the sweeping line of the roof has not been affected. One always has to return to that startling roof and its supporting masts, for they are the stadium's trademark, the features which will always ensure Ullevi's ranking among the most attractive stadiums in the world.

● Two other Gothenburg venues deserve a mention. Just south of Ullevi, the grandly titled **Valhalla** (house of the gods), was Sweden's first proper grass pitch and now sports an artificial surface. It hosted many important matches, including Sweden's second ever international match, in 1908. The **Slottskogsvallen**, though better known as an athletics stadium, also staged soccer internationals during the 1920s. Opened in May 1923 with room for 20,000 on its solid granite terracing, it features, uniquely, four viewing towers, like bandstands, one situated on each corner of the pitch.

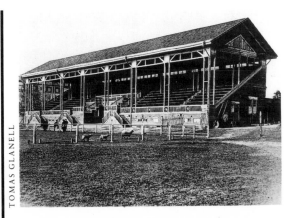

The original main stand at Råsunda. Sheep were often grazed on football pitches before the First World War – it saved on mowing and yielded an income from local farmers.

SWEDEN

TOMAS GLANELL

SOLNA

RÅSUNDA STADION

Sweden's national stadium, home of the Swedish FA and leading club **AIK** (Allmänna Idrotts-klubben – General Sports Club), is sometimes referred to as Solna (a municipality north of central Stockholm, rather as Colombes is to Paris), sometimes as the Fotbollstadion (to distinguish it from the Stockholm Stadium, see page 238), but officially its title is Råsunda Stadium (named after the district within Solna).

Since football began on this former lake bed, on a sand pitch in 1898, three major changes have occurred. The first was in September 1910 when a 2000 seater wooden stand was opened by Crown Prince Gustav Adolf, thus beginning a close relationship between the royal family and Råsunda. Nine months later, a grass pitch was laid for Råsunda's first international, v. Germany, on 18 June 1911 (attendance 3000). The stadium also staged several games during the 1912 Stockholm Olympics.

The impecunious Swedish FA took an enormous gamble in developing and subsequently buying the Råsunda site for SKr37,000, and by 1921 it had to be baled out by the successful Solna club, AIK, who began renting Råsunda for SKr4000 per annum (until then the resident club had been Vikings).

AIK (which stands for General Sports Club) were again at the fore when Råsunda was completely remodelled in 1937 – apparently on Arsenal's Highbury Stadium, though the resemblance is slight – and opened by King Gustaf V, who caused considerable mirth by declaring, 'I hereby pronounce this tennis stadium open ...' That was on 17 May 1937, before an international v. England, although the first game had been on 18 April, AIK v. Malmö FF.

Thoroughly rectangular, concrete and modern, the revamped Råsunda held 52,000, with uncovered terraces on two tiers at both ends, an open, double-decker stand for seats on the west side and a two-tiered main stand with glass screen ends on the east side. Best of all, the stands were close to the touchlines (this, at least, was like Arsenal).

From 1937 Råsunda became Sweden's prime football venue and, because they owned it, was the Swedish FA's natural choice for the 1958 World Cup Final. Yet Brazil's epic 5–2 victory over Sweden in the final did not attract Råsunda's record gate. That came on 26 September 1965 when 52,943 – an all-time football record for the country – saw Sweden fail in their World Cup qualifier v. West Germany. The record for a club match at Råsunda is 48,894 for Djurgårdens IF v. IFK Göteborg in October 1959, during the World Cup-inspired peak in Swedish attendances. Earlier, in August, the floodlights were switched on for the first time, for a derby game, AIK v. Djurgårdens. (Cup Final attendances at Råsunda have never been high, the largest being 34,966 for the 1944 final between IFK Norrköping and Malmö FF.)

Other events at the stadium have included a Floyd Patterson v. Eddie Machen boxing bout in 1964 (Machen lasted twelve rounds this time), and in 1982, singing 'The Boxer', Simon and Garfunkel in concert. Rod Stewart, AC/DC and the Rolling Stones have also played here.

Nowadays Råsunda holds 41,700 (21,700 seats), a reduction caused by the third major redevelopment in 1983–5. This saw the 10,000 capacity west side double-decker make way for an unusual stand with 4200 seats on a lower tier, above which a line of private boxes overhangs from the back of a tall, blank wall. Behind this wall is an office complex with five projecting bays, linked, in the southwest corner, to a sixteen-storey, reflective glass-fronted office block, nicknamed 'Dal-

236

lashuset' (although by Dallas standards it would be regarded as titchy). Six hundred people work in these offices, which were financed jointly by two insurance companies, Skandia and Folksam, each of whom bought a 48 per cent share in the stadium company. The Swedish FA owns the remaining 4 per cent.

As an office development the new west stand has an attractive scale which knits well with the cantilevered roof. But from inside the ground the effect is less pleasing, mainly because there was insufficient money to complete the row of boxes along the upper level. The stand therefore looks bare at the wings.

One cunning feature however, mirrored in the main stand, is the random use of blue, orange and red seats, so that when gates are low – as they frequently are – the stands do not look so empty.

In true Råsunda tradition the new west stand was opened, in April 1985, by a member of the royal family, Princess Lilian (actually a former English commoner), wife of Prince Bertil. A year later the much-criticised pitch was replaced by a state-of-the-art surface with seven layers, one metre deep. Visitors can see a cross-section of the pitch in the stadium foyer.

Other innovations are more obvious. For example, Råsunda has, unusually, television camera platforms on both sides. At the rear of the south terrace is a 55 sq. metre video screen which acts as a scoreboard during matches and revolves round 180 degrees to keep the people of Solna informed for the rest of the week. Uniquely, Råsunda's ticket office is linked by computer for sales in post offices all over Sweden, and the west stand roof, though wood-panelled, is lined by gas heaters (as at PSV Eindhoven).

The technical wizardry might not stop there, since plans have been drawn up to cover the stadium with a giant, retractable roof (as is being built at Arnhem, Holland).

But with domestic attendances low, any funds that are available will go towards completing the west stand in time for 1992, when Råsunda will stage the European Championships. No need for multi-coloured seating to disguise the empty spaces then, surely.

Råsunda today, with the *Dallashuset* a silvery presence behind the new west stand.

GROUNDWORK

SWEDEN

STOCKHOLM

STOCKHOLMS STADION

When architect Torben Grut accepted the commission to design Stockholm's Olympic Stadium for 1912 he turned for his inspiration not only to Athens (the first modern Olympic Stadium, built in 1896), but to the entire gamut of Swedish revivalist architecture. The result, still gloriously intact, was a stadium part castle, part mansion, part cloister, part pageant, but altogether magnificent and built entirely out of Swedish materials. If Hans Christian Andersen had combined with Walt Disney to design an antidote to the concrete super-bowls of Pier Luigi Nervi in Italy or Manuel Muñoz Monasterio in Spain, the Stockholm Stadium, surely, would have been the result.

Clad in grey-violet Helsingborg bricks, decked in ivy, topped by a tiled roof and circled by flag-poles, it is certainly the best-preserved pre-1920

stadium in existence and one of the last important stadiums in Europe to have adopted the vernacular style before reinforced concrete transformed the horizons of architects and brought about the new generation of super-stadiums in the 1920s.

For international football, the 'Stadion', as it is known simply in Stockholm, was Sweden's main venue between 1912 and 1937, before Råsunda (the second Olympic football venue) was revamped. Since 1936 it has been the home of **Djurgårdens IF** (formerly based at the third Olympic football venue, the Traneberg Athletic Grounds), whose offices are in the Klocktornet (Clocktower), one of two castellated towers which cap the northern end of the U-shaped stand (the club boardroom is actually the old Olympic fencing hall). The gentle chimes of the clock lend a timelessness to the most modern of matches. Even the copper-covered awning, which in 1912 protected the King and his entourage, is still perched on poles in the middle of the stand. Directly behind the stand at this point is the King's

PRESSENS BILD/LASSE HEDBERG

Part castle, part pageant – Grut's masterpiece. Note the King's awning, still in place (right).

entrance, which is marked by gold crowns on black railings.

Every granite sculpture and carving, every wooden column, brick motif and painted Nordic symbol has been lovingly preserved, yet the stadium remains in regular use and has a modern running track (which replaced the original track, laid in 1912 under the supervision of a Mr Charles Perry, of the Stamford Bridge grounds, London, home of Chelsea FC).

Djurgårdens' record gate is 22,108, for a derby v. AIK in 1946, and despite modern safety requirements the stadium still holds 22,000 (17,000 seated), barely less than the total in 1912. There are, however, a few concessions to modernity. Firstly, just before the 1912 Olympics it was discovered that the pitch was too small to comply with FIFA regulations, so all participating teams had to sign an agreement not to protest against the dimensions. The pitch has since been altered. Secondly, two sets of floodlights peek incongruously from the top of the towers, and, thirdly, at the north end, where formerly there was an open terrace built into a rising rock face and backed by a wall of arches, there is now a cranked, two-tiered stand with cantilevered roof which, thankfully, detracts little from Grut's original concept.

It is true that Springsteen has played here, and the Eurythmics, but the Stadium's real lyricism harks back to a bygone era of Kings and Corinthians, when stadiums aspired to majesty and participants played for fun. Certainly the official report of the 1912 football tournament makes interesting reading for those who had World Cup matches in Mexico kicking-off under the midday sun. Midsummer games, said the report, should not start before 18.00 hours 'at the very least'. 'A football player cannot do his best when working in the midst of a blazing sunshine.'

Torben Grut himself was the stadium's finest eulogist. 'Silent and calm lie the brooding horizontals of the stadium,' he wrote of the leafy arcade around the medieval South Gate. 'No unnecessary "architecture" disturbs the feeling as of moaning pine forests ... Inside the building, in the arena, live noble rivalry, song, the stage, jousting, warlike strife. Little space is there for contemplation ... the arena itself is the central figure; flags and horn-signals its array. Within the Stadium, our growing generations shall be fostered to feats of strength and manly courage.'

The South Gate. Every column is decorated.

Grut's masterpiece lives on. So does the pageant of sport. But if the pine forests do still moan it is for a world which has long since passed away, leaving the Stadium as a relic of the past, not, sadly, a model for the future.

● Also in Stockholm is the small but perfectly formed **Söderstadion** – or South Stadium, home of **Hammarby IF**. Built in 1966 with a capacity of 12,000, the Söderstadion is characterised by green and white stripes on each of its four plainly covered stands. Hammarby's record gate here is 14,221, v. IFK Göteborg in 1982 (although the club also uses Råsunda for big games). However, the most remarkable feature of the Söderstadion is its neighbour, the newly constructed indoor ice stadium, whose massive white spherical roof dominates the skyline like an overgrown golf ball.

A crown marks the King's personal gateway.

SWITZERLAND

BERNE

STADION WANKDORF

Switzerland – home of both FIFA and UEFA, and host to the 1954 World Cup and six major European finals since 1961 – faces a dilemma, a dilemma which has a bearing not only on the future of the national stadium in Berne but on all the country's major venues. The Swiss football authorities want another bash at staging the World Cup, in 1998, but do not have a single stadium which meets FIFA's minimum standards for the competition.

The central government, or Bund, has already stated it cannot guarantee any potential deficit should the Swiss bid succeed, but even if the Swiss Football Federation could find private funding to rebuild eight or ten stadiums, it would still face enormous obstacles. First, it would have to reconcile the needs of World Cup football with those

of Switzerland's own, impecunious, domestic game, and second, it must persuade a conservative public that the effort is worthwhile. In a small nation in which football is hardly woven deep into the social fabric, that could prove an insurmountable hurdle, especially as all major undertakings involving public expenditure in Switzerland have to be voted on by referendum.

There were no such uncertainties on 4 July 1954, when 55,000 packed the Wankdorf Stadium to witness a riveting World Cup Final in which West Germany snatched a late 3–2 win against Hungary, a team unbeaten for the previous four years. But that was only the last act in a whole series of dramas at the rain-soaked stadium. Six days earlier a violent quarter-final encounter between Hungary and Brazil – the so-called Battle of Berne – culminated in players from each team fighting each other in the dressing rooms.

Nowadays, of course, it is the fans who must be kept apart. Thus when the Wankdorf staged the European Cup Winners' Cup Final between Barcelona and Sampdoria, on 10 May 1989, over 1000 policemen were on duty to keep the peace among the restricted capacity crowd of 45,000.

That Berne was the match venue at all was a contentious issue. A stadium with only 9300 seats, little cover, few adequate barriers and barely sufficient means of segregating rival fans, seemed an unlikely choice, especially following sharp criticism of the use of Heysel Stadium for the riot-torn 1985 European Cup Final. Equally surprising was the fact that UEFA, who are based in Berne (read into that what you will), only switched the game to the Wankdorf after it was decided that the venue chosen originally, Lausanne, was too small to cope with the combined followings of Barcelona and Sampdoria. One wonders which

The Wankdorf Stadium in 1954, still the biggest and best Switzerland can offer.

two clubs UEFA had expected to reach the Final – maybe Glenavon and Flamurtari?

As it transpired there was crowd trouble at the game, mainly in the form of missiles being hurled from one set of fans to the other, over the heads of policemen stationed in the central dividing zone of the main terrace, the Nordrampe. But UEFA were lucky. It could have been a lot worse; for example, on both corners of the Nordrampe, where there is no actual terracing, spectators were allowed to stand precariously on sloping ground.

The stadium had, in fact, barely altered at all since it was reconstructed for the 1954 World Cup (having been opened originally in 1925).

Located in the northeastern district of Wankdorf, its slightly cranked, two-tiered main stand seats only 4600, under a propped, vaulted concrete roof. Behind the stand are two training pitches. Opposite is the Nordrampe, a tree-lined bank of paved, uncovered terracing which dates back to 1937 and backs onto an athletics track, while the ground's most distinctive features are two rectangular towers on the north corner of both end terraces. These towers display clocks and advertisements, and house offices for rent.

The east end, or Ostrampe, has a lower tier of terracing, behind which is an upper level of exposed bench seating. The Westrampe is single-tiered with a narrow corrugated roof at the rear (added in 1960, along with the unusual floodlights on four twin-mast, concrete towers). Underneath both end terraces are workshops, garages and warehouses – all for rent, naturally.

The Wankdorf remains the national stadium (and Cup Final venue) because it is still the biggest and best, and because the city of Berne, though Zurich, Basle and Geneva are all larger, is the country's political capital. But it is no hotbed of football, and the resident club, **BSC Young Boys**, who formed in 1898, seldom attract gates of over 10,000, even though their record crowd is 62,000, for a European Cup semi-final v. Stade de Reims in 1959. Two years after that, Wankdorf also staged the European Cup Final, Benfica v. Barcelona, but only 33,000 attended on that occasion.

Will a European Final ever come Berne's way again? Very likely yes, if a £52 million redevelopment plan unveiled in June 1989 is ever carried out. Following Utrecht's example, the intention is to have large-scale office and commercial space integrated within the stands, in order to finance the stadium's reconstruction (since no public

The Wankdorf, with its concrete floodlight masts and wide Nordrampe stepping (right).

funding is likely), plus an underground car park.

But will this new development be suitable for the 1998 World Cup, or should it even try to be?

In recognition of the difficulties facing small to medium-sized countries like Switzerland, FIFA have promised to consider reducing the minimum required capacity for venues staging the World Cup opening ceremony and Final from 80,000 to 50,000.

But even this concession might not help Switzerland's bid – which will join those of France and probably Morocco when the serious lobbying begins in the spring of 1991 – if only because the French already seem determined to meet FIFA's existing standards without any compromises. The chances of a small country like Switzerland staging the World Cup are, indeed, slimmer than ever before. With respect to the city of the Young Boys, the Big Boys may well be the only ones left who can shoulder the burden.

Old-time half-time scoreboard and overgrown terraces on Berne's Nordrampe in 1988.

BASLE

STADION ST. JAKOB

Nudging up against the French and West German borders, on the banks of the Rhine, the city of Basle faces even more acute problems with its stadium than does Berne.

This is unfortunate, because the St. Jakob Stadium – or Joggeli, as it is affectionately called in local dialect – has a wonderful air of innocence. Apart from a classic 1950s'-style cantilevered main stand, built for the 1954 World Cup and holding 8200 on two tiers of bench seats, the rest of the stadium consists of three open banks of terracing, so traditional that there is even a railway line running along the top of one side, as used to be the case at Bolton Wanderers, in England. But as an indication of how standards differ between England and Switzerland, the St. Jakob terracing, though officially listed as holding 51,816, has not one single crush barrier. And yet this is a ground which staged six games in that World Cup (games which yielded an incredible haul of forty-four goals), and since then, largely because of its location, has played host to more European Cup Winners' Cup Finals than any other venue apart from Rotterdam (in 1969, 1975, 1979 and 1984).

Actually the main north terrace does have some

steelwork. Right in the centre is an electricity pylon. Another quirk is that although **FC Basel** (formed in 1893) are tenants of Joggeli, another club called Concordia owns the licence for the bar and café in the main stand. Concordia were, apparently, the original users of the pitch before the stadium was built around it for the World Cup. (Before 1954 Basel played on the north bank of the Rhine at the Landhof Sportplatz, which they still use for training.)

Also rather oddly, in Joggeli's southeast corner is a house, whose balcony not only provides its occupier, the groundsman Herr Meier, with a perfect view on match days but is also a prime spot for watching the stadium's regular rock concerts. Though horribly damaging to Herr Meier's pitch, so lucrative have these concerts become that extra electricity supplies have been connected to the ground to cope with the surge in current (not via the pylon, however).

FC Basel, regrettably, of late languishing in the Second Division, don't generate quite the same level of interest as Michael Jackson, the Rolling Stones or Tina Turner, although in the 1970s they were Switzerland's best supported club, with average gates of 18,000.

But nowadays the income from football barely pays the electricity bills, and so, as at Berne, there are plans to redevelop St. Jakob into a 35,000 capacity, all-seated venue, at a cost of £76 million – an astronomical sum, even for such an

BAL/RIBA – PETER HEMAN

St. Jakob sports the pure 'modern' look of the 'fifties.

adventurous project (but, this being Switzerland, a sum which will have to be raised privately).

New stands incorporating exhibition, trade and leisure facilities are to be built on three sides, and the existing main stand completely refurbished. A railway station will be built behind the ground, and, intriguingly, in the event of Switzerland's bid for the 1998 World Cup being successful, provision is to be made for mobile stands to hold an additional 15,000 spectators.

Fear not for Herr Meier – he will be accommodated in the new plan, no doubt, although with the stadium's even greater potential for staging rock concerts he might wish to find a quieter spot. But at least the concerts will place less of a strain on the national electricity grid. This is because the new stand roofs are going to be covered with solar panels, the first known installation at a football ground anywhere in Europe.

Basle in 1954. Although it has hardly changed since, the presence of the railway line behind the north side terrace (bottom left) will prove to be a valuable asset when the new Joggeli takes shape in the 1990s.

NEUCHÂTEL

STADE DE LA MALADIÈRE

Having seen the problems faced by two Swiss cities with large, ageing stadiums, we take a brief detour from the 1954 World Cup circuit to the lakeside town of Neuchâtel, home of the small but perfectly successful **Neuchâtel Xamax FC**, the club which rose from obscurity to win the Swiss championship in both 1987 and 1988.

Their compact Stade de la Maladière, named after the district, was originally used by a club called Cantonal, who formed in 1906, merged first with Neuchâtel Sports in 1969 and then a year later with Xamax. For their part, Xamax formed in 1912 and owe their palindromic name to a founding member and Swiss international, Max 'Xam' Abegglen.

The ground's main stand, the Tribune Nord, was built by Cantonal in 1952, but has since been completely modernised. Flanking the stand are two unusual floodlight masts with lamps fixed to a circular, horizontal mounting (described more fully on page 249), while behind it rises the tree-covered hill of Chaumont.

The small, double-decker Tribune Sud, opposite, with its red roof, red seats and wooden

floor, started off as a small structure behind the east goal before being moved to its present position in 1982. This prompted the jovial regulars in the Tribune Nord to ask for a price reduction, since their scenic view across Lake Neuchâtel was blocked as a consequence. But the new stand did at least stop Xamax losing balls in the lake behind. (More recently the shoreline has been reclaimed and a covered ice hockey arena built behind the Tribune Sud.)

Both end terraces are open. The west terrace,

Neuchâtel's Stade de la Maladière, looking towards the refurbished main stand and the verdant hill of Chaumont. Note the unusual circular floodlight mountings, a common feature at Swiss sports venues.

behind which lies a narrow street lined with houses, has a video board, a mod-con usually only seen at much larger venues, while the east terrace is only four steps deep with a circular indoor sports hall and all-weather training area behind.

Despite all these improvements, Xamax remain a charmingly informal, hospitable club, largely owing to the character of their unconventional president, Gilbert Facchinetti. A former Cantonal and Servette player, Facchinetti inspires the kind of devotion for which most major club presidents would willingly spend millions to attain. But never expect to see him in the directors' box at Maladi-

ère, for he and his wife refuse to give up their seats in a corner of the main stand, even though a pillar blocks their view.

Maladière's current capacity is 22,139 (nearly two-thirds of the local population), including 5600 seats, but it has been known to expand to 25,500, for example when Real Madrid visited in the UEFA Cup in March 1986. This extension is achieved by erecting temporary stands behind both end terraces. Not everyone is happy about this, however, especially those residents in the houses behind the west end. No need to ask why – the stands block their view of the pitch.

LAUSANNE

STADE OLYMPIQUE

Returning to the World Cup trail, we move down to the northern shores of Lake Geneva, where on 16 June 1954 the Stade Olympique de la Pontaise

(to give it its full name) staged the opening ceremony before France's match v. Yugoslavia, the first of five World Cup games in the city.

There had been a stadium on the Pontaise site since 1926, but the present structure was completed in 1953 and named the Stade Olympique when Lausanne made a bid, unsuccessfully, for the 1960 Olympics. (The presence of the IOC headquarters in the city obviously carried no

Technicolour dream stadium – Lausanne, Lake Geneva and the snow-capped Alps.

EDITIONS G.JAEGER

weight. Their offices, incidentally, were designed by the architect of the Aztec Stadium in Mexico City, Pedro Vasquez.)

Architecturally, the Stade Olympique is the most complete of all the Swiss venues, similar in detail to Turin's stadium built for the 1934 World Cup. Designed by Charles Thévenaz, it is elliptical in plan, with identical concrete cantilevered roofs cranked around each side and open terraces at each end, dipping to a low point behind the goals. When opened it held 40,000, but with the addition of extra seats it now holds 28,000 (10,000 seated).

At the main entrance behind the north, main stand, there is a formal courtyard with the Olympic emblem and a small abstract tower. Under the south stand is an indoor tennis court. Floodlights arrived in 1959 and were supplemented by two extra masts to illuminate the sprint track, which, unusually, lies not in front of the main stand but on the opposite side (so that there has to be a press box in each stand, one for football, one for athletics).

Lausanne-Sports (formed in 1896) are the resident club, although the stadium is occasionally used by Second Division **FC Malley**, whose charming 6000 capacity ground, **Bois Gentil** – just a few hundred metres northeast of the Stade Olympique, has a quaint wooden stand but no floodlights.

GENEVA

STADE DES CHARMILLES

Across Lake Geneva from Lausanne we find a very British-looking ground. Home to **Servette FC**, the Stade des Charmilles holds 30,000, but has only 3700 seats. It is privately owned (unusually for Switzerland), has four covered stands bunched tightly around the pitch (ditto), and is hemmed in by roads, a railway line, a cemetery and (very British, this) the site of a demolished factory.

Servette are the top club in French-speaking Switzerland and second only to Grasshoppers of Zurich in terms of honours. Formed in 1890 as a rugby club in the Servette district, which lies next to Charmilles, the club's first ground was across the railway line from the present stadium and was called simply the Parc des Sports.

Servette had just won their sixth championship when on 28 June 1930 the Stade des Charmilles was opened for the start of an ambitious nine-day international tournament involving the champions of ten different countries. (Újpesti Dózsa of Budapest were the winners.)

With all eyes on the star players of the day, one feature of the new stadium went virtually unrecognised. This was the main Tribune Nord, which featured an early form of cantilevered roof. True it was, and still is, a rather shallow roof, composed of wooden slats on concrete supports, and it falls both technically and stylistically short of the reinforced concrete stands Messrs Nervi and Bonatz would design two years later at Florence and Stuttgart respectively. Nevertheless it may yet be the earliest example of its type still extant.

For the World Cup in 1954, when Charmilles staged four games, a similar cantilevered roof went up over the opposite, south side. Its original clean lines are impossible to discern, however, since a propped roof extension was erected along its front in 1982 to provide cover for the lower section of terracing. At the same time propped roofs were also built over both end terraces. Clad externally in the club colour of claret (hence Servette's nickname, 'Les Grenats'), these quite basic roofs give the ground a warm, colourful sense of enclosure. Very British indeed.

The floodlights, conversely, are typically Swiss. Like those at Neuchâtel and Grasshoppers (see pages 243 and 249), the lights are mounted on horizontal platforms atop slender, tubular steel masts. But instead of the mountings being circular, as elsewhere in Switzerland, at Servette they are square.

A once familiar feature of the ground, which sadly no longer exists, was the Charmilles factory, which had loomed large behind the south side since the ground's earliest days. Specialising in precision engineering, the company decided to close this section of their works in the mid-1980s with the loss of 800 jobs, a crushing blow to local morale and tradition.

The days of the existing Stade des Charmilles also appear to be numbered. As at Basle and Berne, Servette have drawn up a £58 million scheme to rebuild the stadium completely, World Cup or

SWITZERLAND

GROUNDWORK

Servette's Stade des Charmilles. The modest, concrete cantilevered main stand (right) may possibly be the earliest example of its type. Note that the floodlights have square horizontal mountings, instead of the circular system seen elsewhere in Switzerland.

not, into a 30,000 capacity, all-seated venue, with a hotel, underground car park, offices and commercial space (subject, as always, to the approval of local residents).

In football, as in all business, you can only reap what you sow, and with Servette's attendances currently averaging between 5–7000, and seldom rising above 12,000, the club has little choice but to exploit every inch of its property if it is to sustain its challenge as a leading force in Swiss football.

On the other hand, for Servette 'The End of the World' is always nigh, for that is the area of southeast Geneva in which their Second Division neighbours, **Etoile Carouge**, play at a delightful 10,000 capacity ground called **La Fontenette**, where the grass-banked terracing backs onto the rushing waters of the River L'Arve.

● Used for one match only in the 1954 World Cup (Italy v. Belgium) was the **Stadio di Cornaredo** in Lugano, which as its name suggests is in the Italian-speaking region of Ticino.

Opened in November 1951, the stadium holds 25,200 - not bad for a town of only 29,000 inhabitants – but the proximity and lure of Milan and Turin across the border mean that **FC Lugano** attract gates which can often be accommodated within the stadium's single 2200 seater stand. But it's a fine stand all the same, with a Florence-like, reinforced concrete, cantilevered roof arched over its central section. The remaining three sides, curved around a synthetic track, are shallow open terraces, last filled to capacity by another incursion from Italy, this time by the Pope in 1984.

ZÜRICH

STADION LETZIGRUND

The Letzigrund is a prime example of how people-power operates in Switzerland and of how striking architectural concepts often result in unsuitable stadiums.

First constructed in 1925 by the mainly working-class members of **FC Zürich**, the Letzigrund was adopted by the city council ten years later, and would have played a part in the 1954 World Cup had the ratepayers not rejected a refurbishment plan by 53,000 votes to 26,000. Redevelopment was finally sanctioned in 1956 (by 36,000 to 21,000 votes), but even so, when unveiled in August 1958 the new design must still have given traditionalists quite a start.

The east stand was as it had been since 1930. But the new west, or Hauptribüne, was most unusual, rising up in the centre to a point (not in a curve, as at Malmö, for example) and tapering at the wings like a triangle.

This was all very well and innovative, but at the two end Kopftribünes (head stands), the architect, Prof. Dunkel, showed that he cannot have understood the football fan's mentality at all. In plan the idea looks sensible enough – both 'V'-shaped end terraces join with the triangular west stand to form six sides of an octagon. But in elevation, while the west stand peaks in the centre, the Kopftribünes slope down from the corners to a low point behind each goal.

Awkward though this was at first to Kopf regulars, the opening of the new Letzigrund heralded FC Zürich's best ever run, including seven championships and five Cup wins between 1963–81. Also during this period the stadium, which is shared by the Zürich Athletics Club, became one of the most popular venues on the international athletics scene, especially for its fast 100-metre straight in front of the Hauptribüne.

It had been hoped eventually to complete Prof. Dunkel's octagonal plan by replacing the old east

GROUNDWORK

A new angle on stadium design – but Prof. Dunkel's Letzigrund has never been copied.

SWITZERLAND

stand with a copy of the west stand, but since this would have meant building over the adjacent road the plans were stopped by public protest in 1969. Instead, the two end terraces were covered (which resulted in awkward pillars in the wrong places), and in 1984 a new, rectangular east stand was built. This consists of a steeply raked, single tier of orange and green seats, and a cantilevered roof with glass screen ends and green steelwork – a colourful accompaniment to the rich terra cotta of the synthetic track. Underneath the stand are the offices of the Zürich Municipal Sports Authority and a covered 120-metre training track.

For all its quirks, the Letzigrund currently holds 26,880, of which the total number of seats, 11,880,

is greater than any other Swiss venue. And for one man and his family the Letzigrund really is home sweet home. Herr Glauser, the groundsman, does not so much live 'over the shop' as under it, or at least under the south Kopftribüne, where his front door and floral window boxes are on public display on one of the stairways leading up to the terracing. It says a great deal about the FC Zürich fans who frequent that end of the ground that in eighteen years' residence the Glausers have never once had their property damaged. The family are fans themselves, however, if only because with a noisy terrace above their ceiling, what choice do they have but to emerge on match days and see what's happening in their back garden.

ZÜRICH

STADION HARDTURM

A kilometre or so north of the Letzigrund, but on the other side of the main Zürich to Basle railway line, the Hardturm Stadium is home to the **Grass-hopper Club**, Switzerland's most successful, but hardly most popular outfit.

Although they are currently trying hard to change their image, Grasshoppers have always been regarded as the club of the Zürich elite. But privilege alone has not brought them peace of mind, and so we end our tour of Switzerland as we began it, in Berne, with a stadium caught at a crucial moment of transition.

Grasshoppers were formed in 1886 by English students, and moved to the Hard area of north-west Zürich in 1909. The Hardturm Stadium (named after a nearby medieval turm, or tower) was inaugurated on 28 April 1929, with a match v. Alessandria of Italy, and held 25,000 standing on three earth banks, with a wooden stand for 2400 on the north side.

The stand did not last long, and in retrospect it was not surprising, for there had been a whole spate of suspicious fires at Swiss football grounds, including Olten in 1928, Aarau and the Letzigrund in 1929, and the Hardturm in May 1934 (after a match between Switzerland and West Ham). Ten years later Cantonal's stand at Neuchâtel also went up in flames. But if there ever was an arsonist

with a grudge against football, he or she was never apprehended.

While a new stand was built at the Hardturm, Grasshoppers decamped briefly to the Letzigrund, and by the time of the 1954 World Cup, Hardturm was also able to offer seating in the Treml Stand (named after a former club trainer), perched on stilts behind the west end terrace.

Five World Cup games were held at the ground, which now held 35,000 (5600 seats), including the third and fourth place play-off, Austria v. Uruguay, then in April 1956 the floodlights were inaugurated for Switzerland's first floodlit international, v. Brazil. It was a bright year for Grasshoppers too. They won their sixth Double in thirty years, but then proceeded to win nothing for the next fifteen. To add to their frustration, fire struck the main stand again, in June 1968, and forced a return to the Letzigrund, where FC Zürich were just celebrating their third championship of the decade.

By the early 1980s Grasshoppers had recovered their winning ways, and then set about planning for a radical reconstruction of the Hardturm. But it was no simple matter, and not only because of the usual political and social obstacles which face major building projects in Switzerland.

The Hardturm land is owned by the Schoeller textile company. It was largely due to the generosity of Walter Schoeller – 'Mister GC' – a founder member of the club, that Grasshoppers had been able to build the stadium there in the first place. But times change, the later generation of Schoellers are reportedly less committed to football and, more importantly, land values in the area have rocketed since the construction of a motorway and adjoining industrial and commercial premises.

Grasshoppers' lease is due to run out in 1995, so before the club considered any ground improvements it had to ask, would the Schoeller company dare to evict such a national institution – a club which counts among its supporters some of the most influential figures in Zurich?

Taking no chances, and in spite of the constrained economic climate of the period, Grasshoppers decided in 1983 to redevelop Hardturm as quickly and cheaply as possible, not only to enhance their own earning power (by installing private boxes, for example), but also to create a stadium substantial enough to make their eviction less likely.

So far they have been able to complete half the project, and the situation remains uncertain to say the least, if only because the late 1980s found Grasshoppers deeply in debt and with gates down to an average of 6900 in season 1987–8, despite winning the Cup that year.

The Hardturm today is most definitely a stadium of two halves. At the west end the Treml Stand survives, with its covered bench seating on the upper level and an odd little roof extending from its front balcony to provide shelter for those at the rear of the terrace below. The main, north stand, completed in 1969, is a plain, single-tiered construction with green, orange and blue seats under a flat, propped roof. Behind is a multi-storey car park.

The two new stands, on the south and east sides, were designed by Alfred Dora and are linked to form an 'L' shape. Each is patently a low-cost construction, with a raised tier of seating covered by a propped, metallic roof, wooden floorboards on a steel frame, and uncovered terracing in front without a single crush barrier.

The south stand houses offices and meeting rooms, and has a line of glass-fronted boxes between the upper and lower tiers. The occupant of box 21 obviously has a sense of humour. Embedded in the glass is a football, as if it had been planted there by a burly defender's thunderous clearance.

Along the rear of the south stand's lower terrace is a real sign of the times at Hardturm – a wall where supporters and companies have paid for the privilege of doing what most graffiti artists

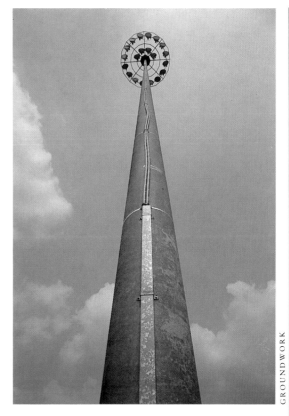

GROUNDWORK

Jean Rubeli's floodlight masts at the Hardturm Stadium are distinctive and easy to maintain.

gladly do for free – that is, scrawl their name or message on the wall (and in indelible paint), at 100 Swiss francs per brick.

The east stand, finished in late 1986, has no boxes and is cranked around the goal-line to provide better sight lines. Surprisingly, there is a large electronic scoreboard taking up valuable room in the centre of the upper tier – exactly where many supporters would no doubt love to sit. Why this scoreboard could not have been placed in the far corner of the ground, next to the Treml Stand, is a mystery.

The Hardturm's new floodlights are worthy of comment. Like those already seen at Neuchâtel and Geneva (but present at numerous Swiss venues), with horizontal mountings on a steel mast, they were designed by Jean Rubeli of Geneva and are said to have several advantages. Among these is the fact that the wheel-like mountings can be lowered down the masts by electric

249

GROUNDWORK

Half-finished Hardturm, with the old Treml Stand at the far, west end and the new L-shaped stands to the left. In the hills beyond, FIFA's headquarters are to be found.

motor, thus saving money and time on maintenance (not to mention attacks of vertigo). Also, because the mountings are horizontal they create very little wind resistance, thus allowing the masts to be tall, slender and less costly to erect. They are aesthetically pleasing too.

In its half-finished state the Hardturm has a capacity of 37,000, including 8500 seats, but if ever finished the total will rise to 38,000, including 10,000 seats.

But would the Hardturm then be a stadium fit for the challenges of the 1990s or even the 1998 World Cup? Can it be adapted to earn money during the week? Can the terraces be made all-seated?

These are crucial issues for a stadium whose master plan appears to have been based on the thinking of the 1970s, which was built in the 1980s, and which in the 1990s already looks like becoming obsolete. But then June 1989 brought good news for the club. Schoellers' new boss, Uli Albers, announced a change of heart and stated that once their lease expired Grasshoppers would be allowed to stay at the Hardturm after all. Of course a lot can happen between now and 1995, but as Switzerland continues to prepare its bid for the 1998 World Cup, at least the name of Hardturm can now be inked in among the list of potential venues.

The French, leading contenders for 1998, will not, one suspects, be greatly perturbed by the news.

TURKEY

ISTANBUL

İNÖNÜ STADI

It is all as one imagines: the shimmering Bosphorus, the domes and minarets, the dusty roads and cypress trees on rocky slopes. As Paul Bonatz, architect of the Neckar Stadium, Stuttgart, put it, 'In situation and architecture, Istanbul is surely the most fairytale-like place in the world.'

And sure enough, there, dreamily nestling amid parkland which tumbles down from the heights of the Taksim business district to the Dolmabahçe Palace, on the shores of the Bosphorus, is the İnönü Stadium, its lush pitch a splash of bright green on the hazy landscape.

Designed by a Milan architect, Dr Paolo Violi, the stadium is home to one of Istanbul's three top clubs, **Beşiktaş**, who were formed in 1903 and sponsored by one of the ruling Sultan's most trusted generals, Osman Pasha. Sultan Abdul Hamid II was, at this time, notoriously suspicious of just about anything he believed might threaten his Ottoman rule, including football clubs, and thus even Osman Pasha had to transport his footballers around in veiled carriages. Since then, Beşiktaş's rivals have always dubbed them '*Arabacılar*' – those who travel in horsecarts.

Happily, Beşiktaş outlived the Sultan, and when their new stadium opened on 23 October

Asia ahoy! The İnönü Stadium and Dolmabahçe Palace on the European bank of the Bosphorus.

1947 with a match v. AEK of Athens (appropriately, since Beşiktaş a bustling district east of the stadium, originated as a Greek colony), it was given the name of another former Turkish statesman, Mithat Pasha. The current title dates from 1973, and honours Ismet İnönü, second president of the Turkish Republic.

After gradual expansion over the years, the İnönü Stadi currently holds 40,000 (12,000 seated). It has two identical stands, each with an upturned concrete roof, and three tiers of open terracing at the north end, curved around a running track. Yellow, green and blue barriers add a dash of colour, even though Beşiktaş play in black and white strip. At the stadium's south end, flanked by two solid rectangular stone towers, is a single tier of open terracing, in the centre of which is a gateway, where a plaque quotes from a speech given by Ismet İnönü in 1936, exhorting Turks to build new stadiums.

Unusually, corner pylons were erected, but no lights ever installed, and these pylons were then removed during renovations in 1987 when, most importantly, a new pitch was laid. (Beşiktaş patently missed their old threadbare surface, because in their first match back at the İnönü they were mowed down, 5–0, by Dynamo Kiev in the European Cup.)

Because of its stunning location, one cannot ignore the İnönü's surroundings. Behind the north terrace, parkland rises up towards the tall, modern Hilton Hotel, in Taksim, and the older buildings of the Technical University. More landscaped greenery lies behind the main stand, while between the stadium and the district of Beşiktaş, to the east, is the Küçük Çiftlik Park.

But the most enduring images lie immediately behind the south terrace, where amid trees and ornamental gardens, the Dolmabahçe Mosque and Palace stand proudly on the water's edge, facing towards Asia on the distant shore. The nineteenth-century palace housed the Sultan's last harem before the fall of the Empire, and was also where Atatürk, founder of the Republic, died in 1938. There are few more restful spots in this bustling city, except, of course, on match days.

ISTANBUL

ALI SAMI YEN STADI

In complete contrast to the serenity of the İnönü, **Galatasaray** are based in a typical inner-city stadium, hemmed in by flats, offices and a six-lane motorway. Turkey's top football club of late, Galatasaray are also the country's largest and wealthiest sports club, with 8000 members in ten different sporting branches.

Their name derives from Istanbul's most prestigious college, the Lycée Galatasaray, which, under French influence at the turn of the century, was a hotbed of liberal thought, and thus the focus of much suspicion from the ruling Abdul Hamid (the neurotic Sultan we encountered at Beşiktaş). As the Ottoman Empire crumbled around his palace, he forbade Turks from even forming football clubs, fearing these might act as fronts for political subversives. So when pupils of the college were first introduced to the game by the English Robinson brothers, around 1897, in order to fool the Sultan's secret agents, several Turks shaved off their moustaches, dyed their hair, adopted English names and played under the guise of the 'Black Stocking FC'.

Ali Sami Yen was one of the Galatasaray students who set up a defiantly Turkish club in 1905 (three years before the Sultan lost power), but the stadium which bears his name, in the northeast district of Mecidiyeköy, was not developed until the period 1940–5, and even then only with an earthen pitch and basic terracing. Not until Gala-

'Sixties symmetry at Galatasaray.

tasaray came to the footballing fore in the early 1960s (by winning two championships and four Cup Finals in succession), was grass laid and the present stadium built.

Essentially a concrete bowl constructed on stilts around a running track, it has two cantilevered roofs protecting the upper tier on either side. Opening day, on 20 December 1964, brought great excitement to the city, as around 45,000 fans packed the new stadium for an international v. Bulgaria. Unfortunately it was too many. When a small fire broke out in a refreshment hut on the upper tier, there was a panic, a barrier broke, and, as one newspaper reported, there followed 'a human avalanche' as spectators spilled over a balcony wall down onto the terracing below.

Incredibly, no-one died, although seventy were injured, and since that day a limit of 35,000 has been enforced.

Otherwise the stadium has changed little; there are still no floodlights, for example. Outside the stadium, however, the surroundings are very different; tall, grey, utilitarian office and apartment blocks have arisen, and the urban motorway, noisy and dusty, comes within a whisker of one end terrace. Not at all what one would expect of the heirs to the Lycée Galatasaray tradition, but then what worth has an old school tie and a beautiful stadium when compared with a full and shining trophy cabinet?

ISTANBUL

FENERBAHÇE STADI

Only in Istanbul must clubs travel to a different continent in order to play a local derby. For while Beşiktaş and Galatasaray dominate the European heart of old Constantinople, across the Bosphorus, via Europe's longest suspension bridge, **Fenerbahçe** are ensconced in Kadıköy, a densely populated district on the Asiatic side of this sprawling conurbation.

Football was introduced to Kadıköy in 1895, by an Englishman, James Lafontaine. But because, as we have already noted, the paranoiac Sultan subsequently banned football among Turks, the college students who formed Fenerbahçe had to keep their heads down for two years, before finally going public in 1908, after the Sultan had been mercifully confined to his palace.

Their ground was known as the 'Priest's Marsh', on the banks of what locals called '*Kur-*

It took twenty-one years to rebuild the Fenerbahçe Stadium, but marsh-like conditions still plague the pitch.

bağlidere' – the Frog River. This flowed into the Sea of Marmara, and thus when Istanbul was under Allied occupation between 1918–20 (following the collapse of the Ottoman Empire), the football ground made a perfect spot for smuggling weapons out to the republican forces of Kemal Atatürk. Atatürk himself was said to be a Fenerbahçe supporter – he had signed the visitor's book in May 1918 – and the club was closed several times for its role in arms smuggling. Fittingly, in this respect, shortly after a republic was declared, the ground witnessed one of the most symbolic victories in Turkish football, when Fenerbahçe beat a British Army XI 2–1, in June 1923.

Heroes though they were, Fenerbahçe still had to wait until 1929 before they could take full possession of the ground, when their president – who just happened to be Atatürk's Minister of Justice – arranged for his club to buy the site for the symbolic price of one Turkish lira.

Thereafter, few changes occurred until 1960 when Fenerbahçe went off to share with Beşiktaş to enable a completely new stadium to be built on the site. But redevelopment was painfully slow, and it was not until 1981 that the ground could

be used again. Not that exile did Fenerbahçe any harm. They won eight championships during this period (in a record total of eleven), then returned and won the Double in 1983.

For a venue which holds 32,500 (all-seated), the new stadium is deceptively large, perhaps because it is a rare patch of open space amid a crowded quarter of high-rise apartments, narrow, busy streets, and, close to the stadium perimeter, a high school and mosque. Rising above this urban clutter like a clay fortress on rough ground, the stadium is a colourless concrete bowl, sweeping up at the sides and with vomitories for access dotted around the terracing. There is one grey, corrugated roof, sitting on tall pillars high above one side (to allow stiff breezes from the Bosphorus to pass through).

One of Fenerbahçe Stadium's main problems is that although the Frog River has long since dried up, the condition which gave rise to the name, Priest's Marsh, still persists. Hundreds of logs have been driven into the ground to stabilise the pitch, but the groundsman wages a constant struggle. On the other hand, for one Turkish lira, can Fenerbahçe really complain?

IZMIR

ATATÜRK STADI

Turkey's biggest stadium is not, as one would expect, in Istanbul nor even the capital, Ankara, but in the Aegean port of Izmir, the country's third largest city (known by the Greeks as Smyrna).

Situated alongside a motorway in the flat, open northwest of the city, the 70,000 capacity, all-seated Kemal Atatürk Stadium was built specifically for the 1971 Mediterranean Games, and

Izmir – the Turk's delight.

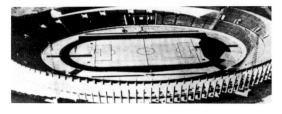

named after the founder of the Republic – along with at least seven other Turkish stadiums. It is a cavernous, rather featureless arena, characterised by its deep, single tier of scrubbed white concrete seating all around – almost blinding on a bright day when the crowd is small. On one side there is a narrow roof over the upper tier.

This was the first stadium in Turkey to have an artificial running track and an electronic scoreboard, and is the country's only floodlit football venue. There are sports halls underneath the stands, a training stadium immediately behind the main stand, and numerous other training pitches in the surrounding complex.

Although now used by the less successful of Izmir's two First Division clubs, **Karşiyaka**, as far as most Turks are concerned, the Atatürk is an *'uğurlu stadyum'* – a lucky stadium for the national team. This may be due to Izmir's better weather conditions, or it may have something to do with the stadium's quality pitch, but whatever the reason, since the Turkish side needs all the help it can get, Izmir is the popular choice.

WALES

The world's oldest surviving international soccer venue in current use is not a football ground at all. It is a rugby ground – **Cardiff Arms Park**, home of the Welsh Rugby Union. Wales made their first appearance at the Arms Park on 16 March 1896, suffering a 9–1 defeat at the hands of the English. Five more games were staged there until **Cardiff City** opened their new ground called **Ninian Park** in September 1910. From then until 1989 Wales shared its international fixtures between three club venues; over half have been at Ninian Park (capacity 40,000), another third at the **Racecourse Ground** (22,000), home of **Wrexham**, and the remainder at the **Vetch Field** (23,000), home of **Swansea City**.

For eighty years Wrexham, home until recently of the Welsh FA, in the north has argued with Cardiff in the south – rugby country – that football internationals should be at the Racecourse Ground, where northerners claim the real heart of Welsh football lies. But in 1989 FIFA complicated matters by decreeing that after 1992 no standing will be permitted at any World Cup games. Since between them Cardiff, Wrexham and Swansea can muster only 14,000 seats, in the short term at least the Welsh FA seems to have little choice. With 37,818 seats (in a total capacity of 58,196), the Arms Park not only offers the FA a much larger potential income from games, but it is also, since its complete reconstruction in the 1970s, a quite magnificent stadium to boot. One of the finest in Europe, in fact.

Wales's first match back at the Arms Park since 1910 was v. West Germany in May 1989, and although the pitch was a touch coarse for soccer, 31,000 safe and comfortable spectators (and Franz Beckenbauer apparently) were all terribly impressed. The north-south debate could well be over.

FIFA's decree on all-seater stadiums was a blow to Ninian Park's international prospects.

Cardiff Arms Park – the mecca of Welsh rugby, now in demand for football. On the banks of the River Taff, the ground of Cardiff Rugby Club is neatly integrated into the rear of the main stand. The open end of the main stadium cannot be covered because it would cut light from the adjacent buildings.

WEST GERMANY

MUNICH

OLYMPIASTADION

The Olympic Stadium, Munich, needs little introduction. Like a twenty-first century bedouin tent draped across a fertile oasis, it is Europe's most instantly recognisable stadium and one of West Germany's most popular tourist attractions. There has never been another stadium like it, and in all probability there never will be. The total bill for the stadium, not including the surrounding Olympiapark, came to DM137 million, a staggering 55 million of which was spent on the roof alone, more than it has cost to build entire stadiums elsewhere in West Germany.

But the Olympiastadion is mesmerisingly

beautiful, of that there can be no doubt, and it has certainly done no harm to mighty **Bayern München**, who moved to the stadium in 1972, just at the point when their team – Maier, Müller, Beckenbauer, Breitner et al. – was blossoming into one of Germany's finest ever. Yet not long before then, Bayern (which means Bavarian), were no more than a quite average German club, barely on par with their neighbours, **TSV 1860 München** (remember them?), who, unlike Bayern, were founder members of the Bundesliga in 1963. Since 1972, however, inspired no doubt by their unique surroundings, Bayern have dominated both Munich and the Bundesliga, as well as becoming West Germany's wealthiest club. This is just as well, since apart from the DM1 paid by every tourist entering the Olympiapark, Bayern's rent (10 per cent of gate receipts) has been a major factor in offsetting the stadium's enormous maintenance costs.

Before the Olympiastadion opened, club football in Munich was concentrated on the 35,000 capacity **Stadion an der Grünwalder Strasse**, which still exists in the southern district of Geising, and which by the standards of many other cities would be an admirable, medium-sized venue. With one simple cantilevered main stand, an older stand opposite, two open terraces at either end and floodlights on four steel columns, Grünwalder Strasse staged both 1860 and Bayern's first Bundesliga games. In 1965, 1860 reached the European Cup Winners' Cup Final, and a year later won the Bundesliga. But though they moved to the Olympiastadion with Bayern in 1972, 1860 have long since returned to Geising. In 1982 they lost their professional licence and then slipped down into the regional Oberliga. (Apart from 1860's games, Grünwalder Strasse also currently

Grünwalder Strasse in 1988 – still playing host to TSV 1860.

WEREK

Munich's Olympiapark from the TV Tower – space-age Bedouin tents across a fertile oasis.

stages Bayern's second team fixtures, and there has been recent talk of even playing some of Bayern's first team games there, when low attendances are forecast.)

Returning to the northwest of the city, planning for the Olympiastadion and its surrounding parkland – said to be the largest sports and recreation centre in Europe – began with a design competition in 1965. Among approximately one hundred architects and engineers who entered were Jaenecke and Samuelson of Sweden (architects of both Malmö and Gothenburg stadiums), and, surprisingly, Werner March, whose design for the 1936 Olympic Stadium in Berlin was hijacked by a certain A.Hitler.

The first entry of winning architect Prof. Günter Behnisch, from Stuttgart, was actually quite conventional; only when he collaborated with designer Prof. Frei Otto of Warmbronn did the eventual tent-roof concept emerge.

Otto, a former Second World War fighter pilot who was strongly influenced by lightweight aircraft technology, had long been experimenting with tent structures. In 1964, for the Lausanne Exhibition, he switched from using canvas to more sturdy membranes, then for West Germany's pavilion at Expo '67 in Montreal he created what may be considered the prototype for Munich. The basis of his asymmetrical, undulating roof was a network formed by steel cables, supported on steel masts and covered with 4mm acrylic glass panels. But the Munich roofs had to cover fifteen times the area of the Montreal pavilion, and be permanent.

Behnisch had certainly never worked on anything so freely formed or technically adventurous. Much of his early work was in designing school buildings. But his collaboration with Frei Otto and project director Volker Jansen of Munich, plus a host of other technical aides, combined with the imagination and largesse of his Munich clients, resulted in the largest and boldest use of the tent-roof ever seen.

The site chosen for this structural exhibitionism *par excellence* was enormous – 385 hectares – yet still within Munich's city boundaries. Originally called Oberwiesenfeld, it was the location of the airfield where in September 1938 the British Prime Minister, Neville Chamberlain, made his infamous flight to seal the Munich Agreement with Hitler, Mussolini and Daladier, whereby the Sudetenland was ceded to Germany.

But the Olympiapark was to be more than merely a stadium. For the first time in Olympic history, participants in the 20th games – 10,000 in all – were to perform and be accommodated on the same site, in apartment blocks built up on the edge of the sports complex. This Olympic Village was, of course, where 'Black September' Arab terrorists murdered two Israeli athletes on the morning of 5 September 1972, ten days after the Olympics opened, followed by a shoot-out at a military airfield near Munich, where all nine Israeli hostages died in a bungled rescue attempt. As one emerges from the stadium's main underground station, there is a memorial to the murdered Israelis in the forecourt of the former village complex, but even without this sombre reminder, the apartment blocks display the dreary, threadbare aspect which has blighted so many low-cost, high-rise developments all over Europe.

On a brighter note, the stadium was actually inaugurated three months before those fated Olympics, on 26 May 1972, when Bayern's ace striker, Gerhard Müller, made himself instantly at home by scoring all four goals in West Germany's 4–1 win over the USSR. Since then the Olympiastadion has staged, most famously, the World Cup Final in 1974 and the European Championship Final in 1988. It has also become West Germany's favourite international venue, marginally ahead of Hamburg and Düsseldorf (although to its credit, West Germany has always spread its international games around; fourteen venues have been used since 1972 alone). Munich also staged the 1981 European Cup Final, Nottingham Forest v. Malmö.

Predictably, the Rolling Stones have performed there, in 1982, as have Michael Jackson, Pink Floyd and also, inevitably, the Pope (Bavaria being a staunch Catholic province).

But many people visit simply to stroll around and stare in wonderment. The Olympiapark is an extensive, rambling area of lawns, lakes, trees and, overlooking the stadium, an artificial hill created from the Münchner Schuttberg, a mountain of rubble left over from the war. Towering above everything is the 275-metre tall Olympia-Turm, an observation platform which provides the best possible view of the whole complex, and, as many fans have noted, a bird's-eye view of the Olympiastadion's pitch. Some 300,000 people ascend this tower every year, and with good cause. Such are the complex shapes and patterns woven by the tent-roofs that at first sight, from ground level, it is almost impossible to gain a clear understanding of the Olympiapark's layout, as if one had been caught in a giant spider's web without knowing its source or extent. How do the roofs link up, what do they cover and is there any method behind these free-flowing forms?

When one first gazes down from the Olympia-Turm, the shapes seem to make no sense, but gradually, as the eye becomes accustomed to the 75,000 sq. metres of acrylic roof panels and the shimmering surface of the lake, one does discern a pattern – albeit an irregular one – forming on the ground below.

Nearest to the tower is the Olympic swimming pool, its draped roof supported by one wire, tensioned like a pulley from the top of a tall, cigar-shaped mast. Tension wires on all sides tie down the ragged hems of this plastic, sensuous roof to the surrounding concourse. The roof then spreads, almost drifts, towards the stadium, like a trail of sand dunes, to the larger Olympic hall, while the lake juts into the concourse before slinking away around the edge of the stadium.

The stadium itself is an almost perfect circle, with its playing surface sunk deep down below ground level, and its own tent-roof forming a crescent over the far, west side. There are eight masts supporting this roof, which rises and falls like waves above the main seated area. Two short floodlight gantries are angled above the roof's edge, with two pylons leaning over the nearer, open side.

Beyond the stadium is the Olympic velodrome, with a much simpler vaulted roof and now with covered tennis courts in the centre. To the right is the main approach road, crossed at one point by a long, taut wire suspended from one of the roof masts. Wires and roads form the only straight lines in view.

Descending from the tower we approach the stadium and, as we walk, discover that many of the tent-roofs actually cover the concourse areas and that to reach the stadium we must pass under their weird shapes, skip around the steel masts and duck under the lowest tapering points of the translucent roof panels. We can see and touch

ALLSPORT/DAVID CANNON

Inside the tent – fantasy or folly?

these lowermost panels, and discover how they are bolted and tied onto the netting by yet more tension cables, like telegraph wires, and cushioned with rubber grommets. We can see how age has distorted the acrylic panels, made them bumpy like the battered, riveted panels of an old aircraft. Scores of visitors have scratched their names onto them, which as an act of desecration actually seems rather reassuring, like finding a lump of chewing gum stuck onto the side of the Space Shuttle.

But only when we actually reach the edge of the stadium bowl does the true picture emerge, for we now see that the Olympiastadion is less haphazard than we had at first imagined, and more breathtaking than we could ever have dreamt. The roof – light, sweeping, skeletal against the sky – at last makes sense. The floodlights, conversely, appear skew-whiff, their uppermost gantries being curved and densely clustered, each with 144 lamps. More light clusters hang from under the roof, so that at night the transparent roof is pierced by light, while the rear of the west stand is lit up by the

booths which hold 1700 members of the press.

The actual bowl, striped with vertical aisles, rises up like a saddleback, 29 metres above the halfway line on the covered west side, then drops, as the roof tapers away, to a height of 14 metres at each end. Behind the open east side, towards the Olympia-Turm, one sees just the tips of the concourse and swimming pool tent-roofs, undulating and shiny, like polished graphite. In the distance is a silvery tower block, like a giant piston – not part of the Olympiapark at all but the centre of BMW's neighbouring factory and museum. For a moment one wonders, are we still in the twentieth century?

But back inside the stadium, now that we have the place sussed out, it is not long before cool appraisal supersedes our earlier awe. We notice that the seats are pale olive green – yes, this is the twentieth century – and that the stadium's barriers and steelwork are grey, thin and pale. Wind rushes in under the roof.

When it rains, water cascades along channels in the roof and splashes down into open grilles along the concourse. This is a structure with its guts on display, with nothing to hide. Even Post-Modernism, which at least plays with colour, is not this frank.

But it is also a roof which leaves much uncovered. At both ends of the stadium the concourses are better protected from the elements than are the actual terraces. In winter the open seats can induce soggy, freezing misery.

And as bad as it is in poor weather, so the stadium seems grossly flamboyant when poorly attended. With a capacity of 77,895, the Olympiastadion was the largest in West Germany when opened in 1972, and remains so, although the addition of 3000 extra seats for the European Championships in 1988 has since reduced the total to 74,000, of which 47,519 are seated (but only 24,700 of those covered). Bayern may average about 30,000 – the second highest in West Germany – but when gates falls below 25,000, Grünwalder Strasse seems not such a bad old stadium after all.

The Olympiastadion is really in its prime only for the big, fair-weather event. One can relax and enjoy the grounds before the match, rather as fans did eighty years ago at London's Crystal Palace. Viewing is unobstructed all round, and if the game is dull the surroundings never fail to lift one's spirits. Everywhere one looks there are angles, textures and shapes to tease the eye.

But what really makes the Olympiastadion so extraordinary is that it is both beautiful and yet also somehow stark – cold and unforgiving – as if science had at last usurped nature, and when reaching down to touch a leaf we had found it to be made of steel.

Only the lush pitch, with its bright terra cotta running track around the touchlines, conforms with one's expectations of a stadium.

In every other way, the Olympiastadion shatters these expectations, leaving one unnerved and excited at the very same time. Nothing is as it should be, and yet everything is in its place.

NUREMBERG

NÜRNBERGER STADION

The Nürnberger Stadion is home to **1.FC Nürnberg** and dates from a period when, shortly after the First World War, 'Club', as they are known, dominated German football. In common with many of its German contemporaries the stadium is part of a much larger sports complex but, uniquely, it is eight-sided, like an elongated

octagon. The architect, Otto Ernst Schweizer, actually won an Olympic Gold Medal for the project in 1928, and then went on to design the Prater Stadium in Vienna.

The Nürnberger's inauguration took place in July 1929 with a workers' sports festival, and the following September it staged the first of several internationals, v. Denmark. More recently Nuremberg also hosted the 1967 European Cup Winners' Cup Final, Bayern Munich v. Rangers.

But for most people the stadium is inextricably linked with the Nazi period, when the adjoining Turnwiese (Gymnastics' Meadow) became the 'Reichsparteitaggelände', a parade ground where huge, stage-managed gatherings were held to rally the Party faithful. The area is fenced off now, but one can still see Hitler's rostrum and the faint shadow of swastikas which once adorned the surrounding stone columns.

Of the original 60,000 capacity stadium, only the main, west stand survives. Supported by grants from the Bavarian State government – although Nuremberg still clings to its separate Franconian identity – some DM30–40 million has been spent since 1988 on transforming the stadium into a modern, two-tiered, covered venue, still eight-sided, and with a capacity of 55,670, of which 29,898 are seated.

Club's new roofs go up, then down.

STUTTGART

NECKARSTADION

Now the Federal Republic's third largest venue, the 67,693 capacity Neckar Stadium (with 35,113 seats) forms the heart of a major sports complex on the banks of the River Neckar, between the spa of Bad Cannstatt and the oldest car factory in the world, home of Daimler Benz.

Apart from hosting matches of **VfB Stuttgart** (and, in 1988–9, **Stuttgarter Kickers**, whose 15,000 capacity Degerloch ground did not conform with Bundesliga First Division standards – much like the team, as it transpired), the Neckar Stadium is best known for staging World Cup matches in 1974, the European Athletics' Championships in 1986, and in May and June of 1988, the European Cup Final followed by the European Championships semi-final.

But Stuttgart was not always in the vanguard of international sport. Indeed by the late 1920s, unlike most large German cities, it had no senior stadium at all. This was hurriedly remedied in 1933 when, three months after the Nazi takeover, the 40,000 capacity Adolf Hitler Kampfbahn (or should that have been Mein Kampfbahn?) was opened on Cannstatter Wasen, a drill-ground and aerodrome where the Stuttgart beer festival had been held since 1818.

The designer was Prof. Paul Bonatz, celebrated architect of the city's monumental railway station (and adviser for the German autobahn programme from 1935–40), whose modernistic, reinforced concrete, cantilevered main stand with concrete roof was a sign of how the pseudo-classical indulgences found in earlier German stadiums, such as Berlin and Frankfurt, were now a thing of the past. (Although Nervi had already broken the mould at the Comunale Stadium in Florence a year earlier, Bonatz was undoubtedly more influenced by such renowned modernists as Peter Behrens, Mies Van Der Rohe and Le Corbusier, who each contributed to Stuttgart's model housing colony built in 1927.)

The inaugural match, an inter-city meeting between Nürnberg/Fürth and Stuttgart, was on 25 June 1933, followed in July by the Deutsches Turnfest (gymnastics festival). After this Stuttgart rapidly became part of the German sports circuit,

Paul Bonatz's striking cantilevered stand at Stuttgart in 1933.

staging international football, rugby, hockey and athletics, plus, inevitably in this period, political rallies. Wooden terraces were built in 1935 to boost the stadium's capacity to 74,000, but dismantled three years later for safety reasons; then, just before the war, 65,000 saw a heavyweight boxing match between Max Schmeling and Adolf Heuser which lasted just 71 seconds.

Football and athletics continued once the real fighting began, despite the occasional bomb, and only days after VE Day a game billed rather optimistically as France v. Russia was held between a Tunisian Army XI and recently liberated Russian conscript workers. American troops also played baseball and gridiron here during the occupation.

But the most significant postwar match at the now-renamed Neckarstadion took place on 22 November 1950, when the Federal Republic played its first official international, against Switzerland, watched by an emotional crowd estimated at 103,000.

Since then the Neckar Stadium has steadily improved. The hastily built foundations of 1933 were strengthened in 1951, both end terraces were enlarged in 1955–6, floodlights were installed in 1962, and in 1969 the first Tartan all-weather track in West Germany (and only the second in Europe) was laid.

But the stadium as we know it today dates mainly from the period 1970–3 when, in preparation for the 1974 World Cup, DM21 million was spent on a new main stand, a cover for the opposite side and new hollow-mast floodlights.

From the main entrance on tree-lined Mercedesstrasse (which leads of course to Benzstrasse), the new main stand is characterised by a line of white, freestanding, concrete masts, angled like tent pegs, into which the cantilevered roof beams are clamped at the top, above a line of twenty first-floor windows which resemble giant

WEST GERMANY

SPORTAMT STUTTGART

The Neckar Stadium in 1974 – West Germany's third largest venue.

exhaust outlets – perhaps a deliberate allusion to the nearby car factory. Around these windows, artist Lothar Schall has painted red and blue abstract forms, like flickering flames; a worthy attempt at enlivening the bare concrete façade, but the overall effect is unsatisfactory. The murals appear unfinished and even detract from the more interesting porthole windows.

Flaming exhaust outlets on Stuttgart's Mercedesstrasse frontage.

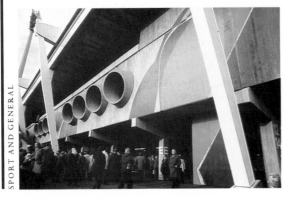

SPORT AND GENERAL

From inside the stadium this unusual stand's cantilevered roof, open at both ends, rises then dips over the seating rather like the crooked wing of a gull. Opposite the main stand is a simple cover with internal columns, which, though echoing the lines of the opposite roof, was intended only to be a temporary structure to meet FIFA's requirements for the World Cup.

Both curved ends of the stadium are open and thus provide views of the stadium's surroundings. To the west, behind the home fans' Cannstatter Kurve, is the 10,000 seater Hanns-Martin Schleyer sports hall and a large industrial estate. The River Neckar, though not visible, flows alongside training pitches behind the main stand, while behind the east or Untertürkheimer Kurve, where there is an electronic scoreboard dating from the 1986 European Athletics' Championships, beyond a series of yet more training grounds lies the towering mass of the huge Daimler Benz works.

The factory has been there since the days of the Adolf Hitler Kampfbahn in 1933, and so has one other part of the Neckar Stadium – the pitch, over fifty-five years old and still growing strong.

FRANKFURT

WALDSTADION

Hidden amongst the trees of West Germany's largest municipal woodland, the Wald – or Forest – Stadium is the lair of **Eintracht Frankfurt**, and was used during both the 1974 World Cup and 1988 European Championships.

The original Waldstadion, when plans were unveiled just before the First World War, was to be the heart of a sports complex on the city outskirts, linked to the centre by public transport. Although common in Germany by the mid-1920s, at the time this was a quite novel concept.

The site eventually selected was a former army shooting range, closed in 1919 under the disarmament clauses of the Treaty of Versailles. It was an ideal choice, since the protective earth banks behind the gun targets were readily adapted to form the new stadium's terracing.

With Germany still reeling from the economic effects of the peace treaty, construction of the Waldstadion was delayed until 1921 and even then bedevilled by stoppages. Donations from local sports clubs failed to keep the work in progress, and by the time the authorities finally gave the project priority status, inflation had soared so devastatingly – from an exchange rate of £1:760 marks in 1922 to £1:16 million marks by November 1923 – that the city's original subsidy of 20 million marks was only just enough to buy one discus and a measuring tape!

Nevertheless the stadium was completed after four years' work, not least because there was never any shortage of labour. Fittingly, in this respect, the Waldstadion's first major event was the inaugural Workers' Olympiad, held in July 1925, although the first football match had taken place earlier on 24 May – a local Main XI v. Boca Juniors of Argentina, watched by 35,000.

Of those, only 1500 were seated, but what a stand they occupied! Possibly modelled on the Idraetspark, Copenhagen, it was an indulgent concoction of pediments and columns, balconies and pitched roofs. Approached from a long driveway which emerged from the woods, its façade resembled a palace more than a grandstand – which was of course the intention. This was a palace for the people, in a golden age of German

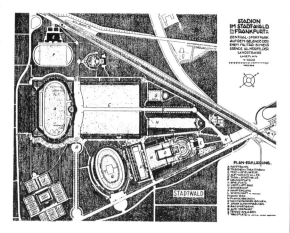

Impecunious but ambitious, Frankfurt's municipality created a model sports park in the woods. The Festival Grounds (C) led to the stadium (A). Nearby was a velodrome (Q), swimming complex (O) and tennis courts (bottom left). The layout is the same today.

liberalism. Too bad that it was hopelessly inappropriate for a major sports venue; in 1925 it was a symbol of revival, destined to become a monumental landmark of German sport for nearly half a century.

The Waldstadion provided a tremendous boost to sporting life in Frankfurt, and in 1937 the capacity was expanded to 55,000. Two years later the World 400m record was broken by Rudolf Harbig on the stadium's 500m track. When reconstruction began in 1953, this track was converted to 400m, the pitch excavated to a depth of 3 metres, and the excess soil used to raise the terracing, thereby enlarging the capacity to 87,000.

Eintracht responded to these developments by winning their first championship in 1959 (and reaching the classic 1960 European Cup Final v. Real Madrid). But for all its scale and charm, with such an inadequate main stand the Waldstadion still had little chance of staging major European matches. That was, until the 1974 World Cup.

For two years before the competition, the stadium was completely refurbished, during which time yet more soil was shifted and 7000 cubic metres of concrete laid. Sadly, but inevitably, the old grandstand had to be sacrificed, and thus we have only photographic reminders of its splendour. Still, it was unfortunate that no part of the structure could have been integrated into the new stand – as achieved so excellently at Lens (see page 120), for example.

263

WEST GERMANY

Frankfurt's original main stand, a palace for the people.

Sentiment apart, the new stadium is clearly a vast improvement, holding 61,992, with almost half of those seated. The 7000 seater main stand, or Haupttribüne, is half-cantilevered with uncovered seats on the lower tier. It backs onto two training pitches and was further improved for the 1988 European Championships.

The opposite stand, or Gegentribüne, holds 13,000 covered seats and also has a front tier of open seating. Its roof is deeper and sweeps further round the pitch but, unlike its opposite, is rooted into the apex of the original earth banking.

Both end terraces are open and lined with tall trees, so that however vast the stadium appears, it still feels nicely enclosed by the woods. Yet this is no arboreal retreat. Frankfurt airport, Europe's third busiest, is a noisy hop away beyond the scoreboard end, while a short distance behind the opposite terrace is a main railway line.

Elsewhere in the woods are other, barely modernised remnants of Frankfurt's pioneering municipal sportpark; particularly the adjacent 1925 velodrome with its charming grandstand and two ice rinks in the centre, and an open-air swimming pool, set in landscaped gardens leading up to the stadium hotel. Meanwhile, lurking in the trees behind the Gegentribüne is another set of buildings, this time modern ones. They house the offices of several sports bodies, among them the DFB, West Germany's football federation. No hiding in the woods for Eintracht, then. The gamekeeper is always close at hand.

SVEN SIMON

The Waldstadion in 1987 – no arboreal retreat.

Cologne's Müngersdorfer Stadium – another 'twenties municipal marvel in modern garb.

ALLSPORT/DAVID CANNON

COLOGNE

MÜNGERSDORFER STADION

Although its modernisation was completed too late for the 1974 World Cup, the Müngersdorfer Stadium was justly chosen as a venue for the 1988 European Championships. Situated in Cologne's western district of Müngersdorf and host to Bundesliga club **1.FC Köln** (formed in 1948 after a merger between Kölner BC 01 and Sülz 07), it was West Germany's first all-enclosed stadium and is of such a uniform design – a two-tiered ellipse – that it might almost be considered characterless; a sort of Wembley Stadium without the bits and bumps. But there is nothing dull about the stadium's surrounding facilities, which leave Wembley and a score of other major international stadiums far behind.

Following Frankfurt's example, the city of

Cologne first adopted the concept of an all-embracing sports park shortly after the First World War. When opened in 1923, the 55 hectare Müngersdorf complex was the largest in Germany, mainly due to the drive of Cologne's mayor at the time, Konrad Adenauer (who later became the Federal Republic's first Chancellor, from 1949–63).

The core of this development was the 63,000 capacity main stadium, or Hauptkampfbahn, which had shallow open banks of terracing all round and one small covered stand on its west side. Its most interesting feature was a modern brick gateway (still extant on the Aachen road), which led between four training pitches to a ceremonial arched gate at the stadium's north end, which was itself flanked by two L-shaped administration and changing-room blocks with square-columned modern porticoes. It was 1920s' civic modernism on a grand scale, and a complete contrast to the more ornate style employed at Frankfurt's Waldstadion during the same period.

Between 1923 and 1973 there were few changes

265

to the Cologne stadium, apart from floodlights in 1958 and the addition of more seats in 1962. But around the stadium sprouted a complex which developed into a real hothouse of German sport, akin to a similar postwar centre in Leipzig, East Germany. Bordering the stadium were built three smaller stadiums, eleven training pitches, several tennis courts, a swimming complex, an open-air pool, a velodrome, a national hockey and judo training centre, a horse-riding centre, a trainers' hostel and academy, and last but not least the German Sports College, in which many of the country's top performers have since been groomed for stardom. (Did we mention parking for 12,000 vehicles?) From 55 hectares in 1923, the Müngersdorf sports park had expanded to an astonishing 200 hectares by 1975.

Moreover, unlike some sports complexes, Müngersdorf is no stark expanse of turf, tracks and fencing. Each section is richly enveloped by trees, and there is also an artificial lake behind the stadium, leading onto parkland.

Plans to rebuild the stadium were first drafted in 1961, and had the project not been dropped in 1971 for lack of funds, Cologne might yet have staged games in the 1974 World Cup. As it was, the go-ahead was delayed until October 1973, and the stadium did not officially reopen until 12 November 1975. (During rebuilding work 1.FC Köln played in the neighbouring velodrome, now demolished.) In order to keep costs down (to DM44.5 million), the original banking was retained, though modernised, while an upper, all-seated tier was built above, to form what looks from the inside like a double-decker stand.

The surprisingly plain interior is shrouded by deep shadows cast by the unbroken, quite low elliptical cantilevered roof, extending just over the track to give spectators complete shelter. There are electronic scoreboards under the roof at each end, while perched on top of the roof in each corner are large, twin-pylon, leaning floodlight gantries (each carrying ninety small lamps), which from inside the Müngersdorf appear to be as tall as the stands themselves.

Such a smooth, wide sweep do these stands make around the stadium that it is hard to believe the capacity is only (only?) 60,584, of which 28,108 are seated. And yet with average gates of around 21,000, and there being an expanse of nearly 30 metres of terra cotta running track plus its pale green outer edges between the touchlines and the front row of terracing, Müngersdorf can at times seem like an oversized, echoing vault; yet one more example of how West German super-stadiums are geared to the main event, not the mundane.

DÜSSELDORF

RHEINSTADION

As Lancashire is to England, or Silesia to Poland, so the heavily industrialised area of North Rhine Westphalia is to West Germany. Apart from being its wealthiest and most populous 'Land' (or province), Nordrhein Westfalen has the greatest concentration of Bundesliga clubs, and in its provincial capital it boasts one of Europe's most dramatic venues, the Rheinstadion.

Fortuna Düsseldorf are the resident team. Formed in 1895, they have played at the stadium since its opening on 28 April 1926 for an international v. Holland. But although it staged a further six internationals and three Cup Finals, until 1972 the Rheinstadion was never more than a basic, traditional venue, holding 50,000, with three open sides around a running track and one 2500 seater stand – similar in fact to the original Müngersdorfer Stadium in Cologne. However, four years of reconstruction between 1968–72 and an expenditure of some DM52 million transformed the Rheinstadion beyond recognition. Sepp Maier, the former Bayern Munich goalkeeper, called it the most beautiful venue in the country, after he had played for West Germany in the new stadium's inaugural match, v. Switzerland, on 15 November 1972.

Much of the stadium's attraction lies in its location. Situated on the edge of one of Düsseldorf's most exclusive suburbs, Kaiserswerth, and set amid chestnut trees on the banks of the Rhine, from a distance the Rheinstadion seems to float above the surrounding greenery like a piece of modern sculpture.

But the stadium is also a focal point of considerable activity, being at the heart of a 50 hectare sports complex (which includes forty-seven tennis

SPORT AND GENERAL

The Rheinstadion and pool – welcome relief from the predictable superbowl.

courts, two running tracks, an indoor and outdoor swimming pool and various sports halls). Düsseldorfers have long utilised the area as a picnic and recreational spot, and anyone can use the complex facilities for a small fee – municipal sport at its very best.

Only 600 metres away is Düsseldorf's thriving Nowea exhibition centre, which contributes towards the stadium's admirable total of 25,000 car-parking spaces, while the sky above is frequently filled with the roar of jets approaching the nearby airport. Yet for all the surrounding bustle, the immediate vicinity of the stadium is calm, leafy and welcoming, almost idyllic when approached from the river.

The Rheinstadion itself is a breathtaking example of prestressed concrete and cable-braced construction, similar in principle to the design of Düsseldorf's three striking bridges across the Rhine. In fact the bridges and stadium were designed by the same man, a local architect, Prof. Dr Freidrich Tamms.

Around three sides of the Rheinstadion, in the shape of a horseshoe, are sixty-two angular concrete masts, rising like pointing fingers to a height of 37 metres. Two cables are slung from each masthead and support the broad sweep of the roof, while four of the masts thrust 8 metres higher and hold the solid mountings of the floodlights, which lean over the roof and dominate the

267

ALLSPORT

Düsseldorf's horseshoe with a light touch.

riverside landscape. (There are additional lamps mounted along a catwalk under the roof.)

What makes the Rheinstadion so striking is that far from hiding its roof construction, it makes of it a positive virtue, so that from both outside and inside the stadium one is always confronted by interesting angles. Had the stadium been completely enclosed, instead of being left open at the south end, the effect would have been far less appealing.

The roof actually covers only half of the 68,360 capacity, mainly those in the upper tier. This has 27,900 orange seats, with one section nearest the uncovered south end being kept for standing (and thus Fortuna's more vocal fans). The lower tier, which has uncovered seats at the sides and standing at each end, corresponds to the lines of the original stadium banking.

A large electronic scoreboard looks down on the open south terrace, which is overshadowed by tall trees which provide a welcome contrast to the surrounding horseshoe of steel and concrete. Directly behind these trees is a large open-air swimming pool. Stadiums and pools were often directly linked in prewar Germany, as we see at Hamburg and Berlin.

When unveiled in 1972, Prof. Tamms' design and Dr Erwin Beyer's engineering won an award from the Association of German Architects, for technical achievement as much as for aesthetic quality. Since then, apart from five matches in the 1974 World Cup, the Rheinstadion has staged the first athletics World Cup, in 1977, several of nearby Borussia Mönchengladbach's major European games (until their own stadium was rebuilt in 1978), a number of West German internationals and the opening match of the 1988 European Championships. During those championships the Rheinstadion also played host to the first historic athletics meeting between the Federal Republic and its East German neighbours. A previous East German visit had been from Carl Zeiss Jena, who played Dynamo Tbilisi in the 1981 European Cup Winners' Cup Final.

Modern engineering in the 1970s, for all its ability to overcome structural problems, seldom produced stadiums of visual merit. At the Rheinstadion, however, the marriage of technology with design created an exciting alternative to the more common fare of soulless concrete bowls. Indeed, like the city of Düsseldorf itself, the Rheinstadion remains today stylish without being fussy, efficient without seeming dour; a horseshoe with a light touch.

MÖNCHENGLADBACH

BÖKELBERGSTADION

Between Düsseldorf and the Dutch border, the textile town of Mönchengladbach shot to prominence in the 1970s, thanks to the herculean efforts of its hitherto little-known team, **Borussia Mönchengladbach**. Formed in 1900, Gladbach

Plenty of terracing but no running track up on the Bökelberg.

KRAPOHL

reached the Bundesliga in 1965 and in one whirl-wind decade between 1970–80 won the cham-pionship five times, the Cup once, and reached no less than five European Cup Finals, winning the UEFA Cup twice.

During this sensational run, Gladbach often switched games to Düsseldorf, as their own, quite unassuming, centrally located ground on Bökel hill could not cope. Gladbach remedied this in 1978 by building an 8722 seater, west, or main stand, with a dipping cantilevered roof, and

improving the remaining three sides of open ter-racing to create the current capacity of 36,800. The ground is now owned by the municipality, and is unusual in West Germany for having no running track, three sides of terracing, and for being located so close to the gardens of some of the homes which characterise this otherwise quite opulent district.

Improved greatly though Bökelberg is, it does seem to have one drawback. Since 1979, Gladbach have not won a single major honour.

GELSENKIRCHEN

PARKSTADION

In a country well blessed with super-stadiums, the Parkstadion stands out as one which, for all the logic behind its choice of location and design, simply fails to capture the heart. Fortress-like and in splendid isolation on the edges of this former coal- and steel-rich conurbation, the Parkstadion appears to have been cast out from the community and left to survive in no-man's-land, buffeted by the wind and by the traffic speeding along the nearby motorway. For sure, it is convenient to reach by car – plenty of space to park, too, for 15,660 cars – but it is also so, so difficult to get excited about.

There had been talk for some years of a 100,000 capacity stadium to serve the whole Ruhr area, West Germany's densely populated industrial centre (which takes in neighbouring centres like Bochum and Essen). But there was always too much rivalry for a neutral site to be found, and when West Germany received the nomination for the 1974 World Cup, Gelsenkirchen, with a popu-lation of over 300,000, decided to go it alone. Few people outside the Federal Republic had heard of the place, but most people in football knew of its team, the miners' team of **Schalke 04**, which had dominated German football during the 1930s, a period when the Ruhr stoked the boilers of indus-trial revival. Schalke played in the traditional 35,000 capacity Glückauf Kampfbahn, still to be seen en route to the Parkstadion from the centre of Gelsenkirchen. Opened in 1928, the ground fell below the standards of other Bundesliga giants in

terms of facilities, access and parking, but was at least in the Schalke district.

The site chosen for the city's new multi-purpose super-stadium was a few kilometres north, an airfield next to the immaculate grounds of the Schloss – or Castle – Berge, a popular recreational park for visitors from all over the Ruhr (hence the stadium's name). Waste from local coal mines was ferried onto the site, in order to build up the banking, and it cost around DM54 million and took three years for the stadium to be completed, a year before the World Cup. The inaugural match, Schalke 04 v. Feyenoord, took place on 4 August 1973.

With a total capacity of 70,298, three sides of the Parkstadion are open, with 13,786 uncovered seats on the higher, east side, and one massive, towering stand on the west side, holding 22,248 seated on two tiers. Sunk into the side of a huge bank – which is split at ground level for road access to the main entrance – this main stand rises six storeys above the adjacent training pitches. Fear not for the health of visiting dignitaries however; there is a lift to whisk them up to the top floor. Furthermore, because the pitch is sunk some way below ground level, uniquely there is an escalator to convey the players from their dressing rooms down to the pitch and back again. Perfect for those tired limbs after ninety minutes.

The stand roof, 120 metres long and 40 metres deep, is dramatically cantilevered 32 metres above pitch level and is cranked around the bowl with screens at either end. How necessary these screens are one can determine by standing on top of the exposed banks which form the terracing, and which also provide panoramic views of the sur-rounding flat landscape of parkland, car parks and, behind the north terrace, the motorway

SPORT AND GENERAL

The Parkstadion put Gelsenkirchen on the map but left Schalke fans in the cold.

between Cologne and Hannover. Only four coal mines remain in the area, whose main industry nowadays derives from oil processing, mechanical engineering and chemicals.

On a good day, when Schalke are winning, the stadium is full and the surrounding parkland looks lush, the Parkstadion is a fine place to be. But life, and football, is not always like this, and when the wind blows and times get hard (such as they have been since Schalke recently dropped into the

Second Division) there are surely not a few blue-and-white fans who must survey this wide open bowl with its athletics track and featureless surrounds, and long to be back amid the cramped quarters of the Glückauf Kampfbahn.

The Parkstadion is undoubtedly an admirable civic achievement and is perfect for the big event. But as a regular football venue it is oversized and impersonal. The Schalke miners of old were, after all, used to having to huddle together.

BOCHUM

RUHRSTADION

Vfl Bochum are one of Germany's oldest sports clubs. They formed in this once heavily indus-trialised city in 1848, but it was another ninety

years before a football section emerged, and another forty-one years after that before they had a stadium of note.

But it was worth the wait. The photograph says it all. The Ruhrstadion could hardly be more different from the Parkstadion in neighbouring Gelsenkirchen.

Bochum's decision to rebuild the Ruhrstadion completely cost the city DM26 million – a relatively small amount for a deceptively large, all-covered stadium holding 49,417 (including 11,327 seats), and with parking space for 12,500 cars. But the money was well spent, for when the stadium reopened in July 1979 it was to universal acclaim. Identical cantilevered roofs cover each side, with plenty of glass at the rear and sides, and just the smallest of cut-away sections in each corner allowing the floodlight masts to peep through.

As at most West German stadiums, there is a running track at the Ruhrstadion, but as far as football fans are concerned it is where it belongs, outside the stadium.

SPORTAMT BOCHUM

Bochum's best.

DORTMUND

WESTFALENSTADION

If one were to ask the average supporter to design a perfect football ground, the chances are that he would come up with something strikingly similar either to Bochum's Ruhrstadion, or to Dortmund's Westfalenstadion: four rectangular stands, all close to the pitch, plenty of standing room, all-round cover, good transport links and plenteous car-parking. Who needs great architecture when you have all this? As one journalist said of the Westfalenstadion, 'The sort of football arena that fans all over the world dream about.'

The players like it too. According to one survey of Bundesliga players in the 1970s, Dortmund was their favourite football venue.

And yet what makes it so popular is that Germans consider its atmosphere to be *'typisch englisch'*. In an age, regrettably, when the English may be considered the worst role models for any sensible supporter, perhaps a better phrase would be 'traditional football' atmosphere, for the fans of **BV 09 Borussia Dortmund** need no lessons from the English when it comes to passion. The 'Dortmund Roar', no doubt well-lubricated by the city's famous local brew, has cheered Borussia on to victory in the European Cup Winners' Cup (in 1966), and three championships (1956, 1957 and 1963).

Borussia played in those days at a 'typically German' ground, the Rote Erde Kampfbahn (literally, the Red Earth Ground), which still exists

directly behind the new stadium's west stand. This old venue, now used for athletics and training, held 30,000 and was part of a larger sports complex laid out in 1925. Like similar developments during the Weimar Republic, such as Cologne, Dresden and Frankfurt, the Dortmund Volkspark was the product of progressive municipal government. There was an open-air swimming pool directly behind the Rote Erde, a sports hall, tennis courts, training pitches and, of course, direct links with public transport.

Nowadays the 70 hectare complex, renamed the Westfalenpark – Dortmund is Westphalia's largest city, has spread to include Europe's largest indoor arena, the Westfalenhalle (which holds 23,000), an ice stadium, a television tower, numerous modern sports halls, hotels, and, 'typically English' indeed, a rose garden boasting 3000 varieties. Immediately behind the Rote Erde is another remarkable sports installation, the 5000 capacity ultra-modern Helmut Körnig Halle, an indoor athletics venue which, when finished in 1979, had the largest clear roof span of any European sports hall. (Still smaller, however, than two such indoor arenas in Moscow.)

In comparison, the adjacent Rote Erde looks like some medieval refuge, with its rusticated stone perimeter wall and pilasters, one covered stand and three sides of terracing around a track. Formerly, stone arcades with tiled pitched roofs used to break up the open sides to give the tree-lined arena a more stately appearance, but that any of the Rote Erde has survived at all is something of a miracle. During excavations for the new stadium next door in 1970, no less than thirty-four unexploded bombs were dug up.

271

MARGRET REIMANN/STADT DORTMUND

Rote Erde with its successor – different solutions for different generations.

Since then, Rote Erde has been rather dwarfed by its steel and concrete neighbour, which opened, exactly on schedule, on 2 April 1974, with a Ruhr derby, Dortmund v. Schalke 04. Two weeks later the Westfalenstadion staged the first of several internationals, West Germany's World Cup warm-up v. Hungary; Rote Erde by comparison had staged only two internationals, v. Ireland in 1935, and v. Albania in 1967. In July 1974, Dortmund then welcomed the World Cup, the only one of nine venues used not to have an athletics track. Three of its four games, each involving Holland, attracted a full house, which, for the Westfalenstadion, meant 53,970, including 16,430 seats. Nowadays Borussia attract average crowds of around 31,000, the highest in West Germany.

Both technically and architecturally, Dortmund's pride is by no means innovative or stylish. It is, instead, eminently practical.

To reduce costs the four stands were built from identical prefabricated, reinforced concrete units – twenty-six in total – each stand being a separate entity. Their propped steel-framed roofs – not cantilevered unfortunately, again to save money – extend over the perimeter fence, with inclined blue fascia boards to deflect rain and wind from spectators. Glass screen ends provide further protection. Each corner is open, which allows good pitch ventilation, and dominated by a distinctive red hexagonal floodlight mast, topped by elongated gantries like lacrosse racquets.

In two respects the Westfalenstadion is not 'typisch englisch' at all. Firstly, there are 9100 parking spaces in the Westfalenpark complex – a third more than even Wembley's total. Secondly, between the anti-hooligan perimeter fence and the first row of seats or terracing on all four sides are wide gangways with shallow steps, which facilitate quick and safe access either through ground level vomitories in the stands or via the open corner passageways. The stands therefore fill from the front upwards, rather than from the rear downwards – a simple enough design feature, but one seldom found at older English grounds.

Not only does the Westfalenstadion look different from most other West German stadiums, it cost much less; only DM33 million, compared with, for example, DM54 million for the Parkstadion, Gelsenkirchen. One factor was, however, 'typically German', and that was the stadium's funding, which came from the Federal Government, the regional authority – in Dortmund's case North-Rhine Westphalia, a national lottery and the City of Dortmund itself, which contributed DM6 million to the project plus the architects and engineers needed to oversee the construction.

Such a public initiative has never happened in England, which is a great pity, for venues like the Westfalenstadion would be a credit to any city or football club. If only it were a 'typical' football ground.

Dortmund – eminently practical.

HANNOVER

NIEDERSACHSENSTADION

For sheer convenience and congenial surroundings, Hannover's Niedersachsenstadion – or Lower Saxony Stadium – is a rare pleasure. A ten minute stroll through the city centre, into a formal park bordering the imposing Town Hall, and there it stands, between the shores of the Maschsee lake and two branches of the Leine River. To the south is a sports park with an indoor swimming pool and sports hall. To the north lie the old drill grounds, the Schützenplatz, now used for parking and funfairs. Trees, water, green open spaces and cobbled walkways – who said all inner-city stadiums were bad?

And while spectators inside the stadium can admire the green baroque dome of the Town Hall and sailing boats on the Maschsee, promenaders around the lake can look up at the stadium's ultra-minimalistic floodlight masts. These date from 1967 and resemble giant leaning ballpoint pens. Otherwise, considering its scale, the stadium barely intrudes upon Hannover's townscape, which was all but flattened by bombing during the Second World War. Indeed without the bombs the stadium might never have been built, since 2 million cubic metres of debris were used to form the massive bowl, thus saving the enormous cost of transporting the rubble further away. (Hamburg, Munich and Leipzig all did the same.)

Work started in 1951, when the west bank of terracing was raised 24 metres above ground level, with the narrower eastern bank kept lower, to allow a view of the Maschsee. Only one small stand was built, on the east side, since the city could ill afford to spend more than DM4 million on the whole project. But if the stadium was acutely short of cover, it compensated in other ways. When finally opened on 26 September 1954, the Niedersachsenstadion not only had a longer name than most other stadiums, it also had a capacity of 86,500 (including 11,500 on temporary stands), which made it the Federal Republic's second largest after Berlin. Not surprisingly, it soon became one of the country's busiest sporting venues.

The first of many internationals took place on 16 October 1954, v. France, and the stadium later staged eight Cup Finals, from 1962 until 1985 (when finals were moved to Berlin). Other events have included a handball international v. Norway in 1955, which drew 50,000 spectators, athletics meetings, music festivals and religious gatherings.

Yet curiously the stadium had no major resident club of its own until 1962, when **Hannover 96** transferred from their 25,000 capacity Eilenfeldstadion, which was opened in 1925 and originally called the Hindenburg Stadion, after the German president who took office that year. Still in use by the club's amateurs, Eilenfeld is situated directly next to the Stadthalle, near the zoo.

To remedy the Niedersachsenstadion's lack of cover, in 1974 a vast, sickle-shaped, cantilevered roof, reminiscent of Gothenburg and Malmö, was

WEST GERMANY

The Niedersachsenstadion – a big name with a low profile in Hannover.
In the distance lies the Town Hall dome (centre), while the Regieturm, the pen-like floodlights and the adjacent indoor pool (right)
maintain a discreet presence on the shores of the Maschsee.

rooted into the apex of the west bank, as part of a DM26 million refit for the World Cup. To improve the exterior view of the stadium, thousands of trees were planted, so that from the river bank below the west bank now resembled a hilltop fortress in a forest. Inside the stadium, 16,300 seats were constructed to replace 38,000 standing places on the west side's upper tier, while to compensate, two open seated sections on either side of the east stand were converted to terracing. For safety purposes, both these terraces were divided into four pens, each holding 2000. This left covered standing for only 3810, under each tapering wing of the new roof.

Thus the Niedersachsenstadion juggled its accommodation and reduced its overall capacity from 75,000 to a still respectable 60,355, of which 41,000 are seated (albeit still only 19,000 of those covered).

The original 6026 seater east, or main stand,

with its eleven vaulted, cantilevered roof sections, seems tiny and insignificant opposite the vast sweep of the new west roof. On its north flank is a taller, square viewing tower, the Regieturm (Control Tower), with three viewing balconies used by police, broadcasters and stadium officials. Linked to its rear, on stilts above the main concourse, is a typical 1950s' rectangular block whose north face carries a huge mosaic depicting various modes of sporting endeavour.

But there is one form of Hannoverian exercise of which visiting players need no reminder. To reach the pitch at the Niedersachsenstadion, the players emerge from dressing rooms under the Regieturm and descend through a long, perspex-covered stairway, down the bank to the running track below. Fine before the match, but enough to have one longing for Gelsenkirchen's escalator as one faces the long haul back at the end of ninety gruelling minutes.

BREMEN

WESERSTADION

On the banks of the River Weser, **SV Werder Bremen** play in a stadium which is well on its way to becoming an almost carbon copy of the Müngersdorfer Stadion in Cologne, even down to the design of its twin-mast floodlight gantries.

Bremen is the Federal Republic's oldest and now second largest port (after Hamburg), but Werder, who formed in 1899 and are named after the district, made little impact on the game until the 1960s. The Weserstadion opened in 1921 and for years was a typical municipal German venue, with a running track, three open sides and one main stand, behind which lay an open-air swimming pool and the river (which leads into the North Sea).

It has staged two internationals, v. Ireland in May 1939 and v. Malta in February 1980, the year the Weserstadion's modernisation programme began with the rebuilding of the main, south stand. There then followed several seasons of determined challenge for Werder's second Bundesliga title (the first was in 1965), which encouraged the city of Bremen to begin the second stage of remodelling. This involved the addition on two sides of a J-shaped all-seated, double-decker, cantilevered stand, behind the existing terracing on the west and north sides, which, with perfect timing, was completed just as Werder at last attained the championship, in 1988. The Weserstadion's capacity increased at this point from 31,000 (including 15,000 seats) to 40,000 (25,000 seats).

Eventually, the last remaining open terrace, at the east end, will be covered as the roof is completed, making the Weserstadion completely enclosed and thus a fully paid-up member of West Germany's already substantial number of international-class super-stadiums.

The Weserstadion cover-up continues. Note the Cologne-clone floodlights.

ALAIN SCHROEDER

HAMBURG

VOLKSPARKSTADION

Anyone who has tried to reach the Volksparkstadion by public transport might feel that the case for out-of-town super-stadiums has been somewhat overstated. Leaving the suburban train at Stellingen one can either get lost in an industrial estate, or trek doggedly under a grimy subway, along pathways, across a bridge then through some woods for a good twenty or thirty minutes before finding the stadium. It makes the walk to the Waldstadion in Frankfurt seem like popping out to the corner shop by comparison.

Furthermore, the Hamburg stadium is not even in Hamburg. It is in Altona, as separate from its neighbour as Colombes is from Paris or Solna from Stockholm.

Opened in September 1925 at the height of Germany's golden era of stadium construction, the Altona Stadium, as it was first called, had just one tiny stand holding 1874 seats, with wide open terracing for 40,000. Directly behind the east end terracing, three enormous open-air swimming pools were added in 1927. Düsseldorf, Berlin and several other German sports parks already had a similar layout, but Altona's trio of pools covered an area almost as large as a football pitch.

The stadium's first international came in October 1927, v. Norway, and in the next twelve years it became Germany's most used provincial venue (although still some way behind Berlin). Plans were drawn up to increase its capacity to 100,000, but war intervened, and from 1945–9 the stadium was commandeered by the occupying British forces. Remodelling work finally started in 1951, and then, as in Hannover, Munich and Leipzig, the stadium was the indirect beneficiary of Allied bombers, as rubble was ferried in from the ruins of Altona and nearby Eimsbüttel.

Now called the Volksparkstadion – the People's Park Stadium, it reopened on 12 July 1953, with an intercity representative match, Hamburg v. Birmingham. At the same time, Hamburg's senior club, **Hamburger Sport-Verein** (Sport Club), moved in from their old Rothenbaum ground, several kilometres eastwards near Hamburg's city centre. Rothenbaum was a charming, innocent little venue, with iron gates, a humble wooden stand and grassy terracing. Now called HSV Platz and used by the club's amateurs, it can still be seen, close to the Alster lake, by Hallerstrasse metro station.

Moving from Rothenbaum to the distant 75,000 capacity Volksparkstadion must have been a terrible wrench for both the club and its supporters, but it cannot be denied that the new stadium put Hamburg (rather than Altona) firmly on the football map. Since 1953 the Volksparkstadion has staged more internationals than any other West German stadium.

Similar in some repects to Hannover, HSV's new home was a large open bowl with one small cantilevered stand set back on the north side. Curiously, the uncovered lower tier of this side was sunk lower than the line of the remaining three tiers, and was thus bordered with retaining walls on either side.

From 1953 until 1974 there were no major changes apart from the addition of floodlights in 1961, first used for Hamburg's European Cup tie v. Burnley. Then, in preparation for the 1974 World Cup, when Hamburg staged three games, the open south side was covered with a cantilevered roof, again like Hannover, built onto the top of the banking. Cranked around the running track at each end, this new cover incorporates an odd little upper deck, along the rear wall, consisting of only six rows of seats. The installation of extra seats on the south side reduced the overall capacity from 71,000 to its present level of 61,351, including 28,561 seats. New leaning floodlight masts were also added. Bristling with lamps, they are shaped like modern telephone handsets, waiting to be picked up.

Nowadays the Volksparkstadion is more colourful than many a German super-stadium, if only because the crush barriers are painted in the club colours, red and white. The seats are pale green. Unusually, the players enter, à la Wembley, from a tunnel emerging from the open east end terrace, below the scoreboard. The dressing rooms actually back onto the enormous open-air pools directly behind, while further beyond lies the industrial area of Stellingen.

As one would hope for, after such a long trek, the rest of the stadium's surrounds are more appealing. There are large car parks for all those Volks in their Volkswagens, training pitches, a children's playground, and rambling groves of firs and pines all around. And while the main stand

The Volksparkstadion and open-air pools. But is out-of-town out-of-fashion?

houses a kindergarten, the open west terrace looks down on a cemetery. From the cradle to the grave, the Volksparkstadion has a place for everyone.

Also noteworthy is a blue tower on top of the main stand; nothing to do with football but a control point for what is called the DESY Electric Synchotron. This is some highly technical experiment which apparently sends current whizzing round a circuit tunnel built around the Volksparkstadion. Expect, therefore, an electric atmosphere at the stadium, which, who knows, might even be renamed the Volts Spark Stadium if the experiment is a success. On second thoughts, bringing the railway line a bit closer might be a more useful conservation of energy.

● The popularity in recent years of HSV's local rivals, **St. Pauli**, who were promoted to the First Division in 1988, speaks volumes for the fans' preference for smaller, traditional venues. St.Pauli's barely developed **Wilhelm Koch Stadion 'am Millerntor'** (known usually as 'am Millerntor') is the smallest venue to stage Bundesliga games for many years. It has no athletics track,

holds only 22,500 (of which 3500 are seated in one simple cantilevered stand), the other three sides are open terraces, and until recently there were not even any floodlights (and on the proud day St. Pauli were due to switch them on, for a match v. Bochum on 25 February 1989, the sun shone so brightly that no artificial light was needed!).

Bordering Hamburg's infamous Reeperbahn red-light district, 'am Millerntor' is overlooked by the massive, indestructible concrete bulk of the Hochhaus, a Second World War fortification, and attracts a colourful mixture of local leftists, sailors from the nearby port, Turkish *Gastarbeiters* (immigrant workers) and HSV exiles who grew tired of the trek to Stellingen.

Because 'am Millerntor' is central, and because everyone loves an underdog, in season 1988–9, St. Pauli's attendances averaged 20,848 – over 2500 more than the Bundesliga average and nearly 6000 more than even HSV's gates. The message is clear, not just to HSV but to clubs like Schalke. Big is not necessarily beautiful, and out-of-town may be going out-of-fashion.

WEST BERLIN

OLYMPIASTADION

Having started our survey of West German grounds at the Olympiastadion in Munich, we finish at the Olympiastadion in West Berlin. Hitler's infamous exploitation of the 1936 Olympics is well chronicled, yet had it not been for the First World War, Berlin would have hosted the games exactly twenty years earlier. In readiness for the 1916 games, architect Dr Otto March had designed the Deutsches Stadion on what was then the north edge of the Grünewald racecourse (which March also laid out). Opened in July 1913 by the Kaiser, March's arena, with its columns, porticoes and sculptures arranged in monumental symmetry, was sunk slightly below ground level so as not to obscure sight of the race track, and, uniquely, it had an open-air swimming pool cut into the shallow terracing, opposite the main stand.

War deprived Berlin of the 1916 games, Otto March died before the 32,000 capacity stadium was complete, and once the popular sports boom of the 1920s had begun – a period of intense stadium building all over Europe – the Deutsches Stadion was swiftly rendered obsolete, like a kitsch Hollywood filmset. Yet the sports facilities there were immensely popular; one foreign visitor called it 'the stadium that knows no rest'. However, the structure could not be enlarged upwards without disrupting viewing at the racecourse, and the city of Berlin's crippling financial crisis prevented further construction taking place anyway.

Despite this impasse, in 1931 Berlin won its second Olympic nomination (beating Barcelona), and by June 1933 the IOC had approved the plans of Werner March (Otto's son) for enlarging the Deutsches Stadion (also sometimes referred to as the Grünewald Stadium). But once the newly elected Hitler visited the site in October 1933 and saw its possibilities as a rallying point for German youth and sport, the Reich took over, while March's designs were, in some quarters, castigated as being 'culturally worthless, banal and unimaginative' (according to recent research on March's work by Thomas Schmidt). Since Berlin already had two other racecourses and the Grünewald was a loss-maker, Hitler ordered its closure and dedicated the site entirely to the Olympics. From that moment on, both the stadium and the 1936 Games became tools of Nazi propaganda.

'The Stadium must be erected by the Reich,' announced the Führer. 'When a nation has four million unemployed it must seek ways and means of creating work for them.' Hitler demanded the use of natural stone, not concrete, and a shifting of the old stadium's axis 150 metres eastwards, to provide one long vista from the main approach road. No expense was to be spared, and March was sent back to his drawing board, now under the direct command of Interior Minister Frick and Hitler's inexperienced but pet architect, Albert Speer.

March tried to circumvent Hitler's insistence on the use of limestone blocks for the stadium's surrounding pillars, instead of reinforced concrete – the in-vogue material, but was angrily overruled in October 1934. Thomas Schmidt writes of that period: 'Under the Nazi regime, natural stone symbolised "indomitable German strength and the enduring nature of the National Socialist ideology"'. March's work was thus to be clad in an 'ideological mantle', while he, apparently, 'never criticised the interference in his work and quietly abandoned the modern architectural concepts underlying his early designs'.

March was not the only one to be swept up in Hitler's great venture. During two years of building, 42 million Reichsmarks were spent on this symbol of German revival – seven times more than the 1931 estimate – as 2600 workers from 500 separate companies toiled to meet the deadline. Over 30,000 cubic metres of limestone, basalt, granite, marble and dolomite from all over Germany were brought in on 6000 railway wagons, while thousands of mature trees were transplanted from nearby woods. To increase capacity, the pitch level was excavated further to a depth of 12 metres, thus creating accommodation for 86,000 spectators (although 100,000 attended most Olympic events).

But the stadium was only part of Hitler's grand plan; a 131 hectare Reichssportfeld, including hockey, riding and swimming stadiums (the latter linked at right angles to the main stadium, instead of March's plan to build the pool at one end of the stadium), an open-air amphitheatre seating 20,000 (built on Hitler's insistence and now used,

Berlin's Olympiapark in 1936, with its amphitheatre (foreground), Maifeld, and swimming stadium (left of main stadium).

ironically, for rock concerts) and, linked to the west end of the stadium, the largely ceremonial Maifeld (May Field). This vast expanse of turf – the size of ten football pitches with open terracing on three sides – was intended for large displays and mass gatherings, such as when Mussolini addressed an estimated crowd of 900,000 Germans in 1937, in the pouring rain. (The Maifeld is now used exclusively by the British military for football and cricket, and for the Queen's annual birthday parade.)

In addition to the Reichssportfeld's sports facilities, a wide ceremonial piazza lined with flagpoles was laid down at the eastern approach of the stadium, leading to two 50 metre tall gate towers, between which were strung the five Olympic rings. Thus, a straight line carried the eye from the two gate towers to the stadium's two clock towers, at the opposite, west end, which in turn framed the bell tower of the Maifeld. This was totalitarian architecture on a grand scale.

The austere neoclassicism of the stadium itself is powerful too, but without beauty. Faced in grey, rough-hewn Franconian limestone with no

external relief or colour, it is ringed by square columns and surrounded by level paths and lawns. The interior is similarly lacking in colour or warmth, having plain brown bench seats on two tiers. At the west end, the upper tier breaks to provide a platform for the Olympic torch (which in 1936, for the first time, was powered by liquid propane gas). This gap, the Marathon Gate, through which the Maifeld's bell tower appears in the distance, is flanked by two square clock towers. The stop-clock on the North tower was, in 1936, the largest ever built. On the tower wall below are plaques listing the Berlin Olympic gold medallists, the name of Jesse Owens, USA, being prominent among them (Owens was the black athlete whose prowess upset the Nazi's theories of Aryan superiority). There are also relief profiles of both Otto and Werner March and of the IOC President in 1936, Baillet-Latour.

It was through the Marathon Gate, as the clock chimed 4 pm precisely, and to the accompaniment of Richard Wagner's 'March of Homage', that Hitler entered the stadium to open the Games on 1 August 1936. As cheers and Nazi salutes – many

GROUNDWORK

Austere neoclassicism in limestone – the stadium's upper concourse.

made by neutrals swept up in the hysteria – filled the stadium, Hitler made his way to the south side, where he took his seat alongside Hess, Frick and Field Marshal von Blomberg in the marble loggia. Other dignitaries entered from the southern approach via the so-called March-tunnel – hence the lack of a formal main entrance in the stadium façade – which actually had two levels, one for VIPs and one for athletes, which carried on below the west terrace to the swimming stadium and beyond.

The Olympiastadion may have set a million Nazi hearts aflutter, but many visiting football teams were not so impressed, especially when they discovered that between the dressing rooms and the pitch there were six flights of stairs. There was even a resting room near the tunnel, to allow players to catch their breaths before embarking on the long haul back to the dressing rooms, where, on arrival, each player was said to have been wrapped in a warm blanket by a member of the Hitler Youth.

On the south concourse above the Marchtunnel is now a plinth on which stands the stadium's original bell. This 16.5 ton monster was cast in Bochum in 1935 and transported (care of Hitler Youth, again) in triumphal procession to Berlin, where atop the bell tower it signalled the start and finish of the Games. When unearthed from the bombed ruins of the Maifeld – as late as 1956 - the bell was found, fittingly, to have a deep crack through the swastika on its rim, where is etched the motto, 'I summon the youth of the world.' They were summoned indeed, but not for sport.

Since repair work on the stadium site finished in 1965 there have been two additions. Firstly, floodlights were erected on four 88 metre high grey steel poles, set well back from the actual structure. (They were not the first lights at the stadium, however. For the 1936 Games, eight searchlights were used to illuminate such events as a baseball demonstration, a military tattoo and a mass-participation Festival Play, with inevitable Aryan nymphs et al.)

Secondly, for the 1974 World Cup, DM26 million was spent on renovation, half of which went towards the construction of two, rather controversial roofs.

Such is the stadium's sparse uniformity that for any roof to knit successfully with the existing structure would have required great sensitivity. Yet the eventual choice of tubular steel with transparent acrylic glass panels (as at Munich) could hardly have been less sympathetic to the original design. The covers sit uneasily above the seats like temporary scaffolding, and in addition to being expensive to maintain they provide little shelter, since the wind whistles through openings at the rear. March himself, who died in 1976, was said to have been less than delighted with these incongruous, ill-conceived appendages, but then he had grown accustomed to being overruled on the stadium's design.

Nowadays the Olympiastadion holds 76,006 all-seated, of which 29,145 are under the new covers, and it is used primarily by local Second Division clubs **Hertha BSC** and **Blau-Weiss 90**, both poorly supported by Bundesliga standards.

But whereas before 1945 Berlin was by far the most popular venue for internationals, since the war it has become just one of several venues on a wide circuit. True, it did stage three games in the 1974 World Cup, including the opening match, West Germany v. Chile, and a few days later East Germany's match, also v. Chile (very handy for all those DDR supporters wanting to nip over the Berlin Wall for the afternoon). It is also true that since 1985 the Olympiastadion has become the sole venue for West German Cup Finals.

But as the 1988 European Championships indi-

New roofs for the 1974 World Cup – Werner March was not amused.

SPORTING PICTURES (UK) LTD

cated, when Berlin was rejected as a venue because the Soviet Union refused to play there, the stadium will always struggle to become the mainstream international venue it would otherwise undoubtedly be, were it not for West Berlin's unique political status.

For many visitors the stadium is, instead, just another stop along the well-trodden tourist trail; a gaunt reminder of the reactionary forces unleashed under the Olympic banner in 1936, and a grim example of the style in which Germany's cities might have been remodelled, had Hitler and his henchman Speer survived to rebuild them according to their own architectural dogmas.

● Three other venues staged football in the 1936 Olympics, and all survive, by chance, in the Western sector. Near the Olympiastadion, West Berlin's second most important venue is the 16,300 capacity **Mommsen Stadion** (built in 1931 and home to **SC Charlottenburg** and **Tennis Borussia**). Within a few yards of the Wall, improvements are planned for the **Post-stadion**, a cavernous, earthy, crumbling bowl with tall floodlight pylons, currently used by **SC Union 06**. Also by the Wall is the original Hertha-BSC ground, **Am Gesundbrunnen**, now a training ground by the S-Bahn station of the same name.

YUGOSLAVIA

ZAGREB

STADION DINAMO

Since it was reorganised on Socialist principles after the war, Yugoslavian football has been dominated by four clubs, among them **Dinamo Zagreb** – pride of the Croatian Republic.

Situated in the Maksimir district, their stadium, once the home of prewar club HASK (Croatia Academic Sport Club – from whom Dinamo effectively took over in June 1945), is now modern, colourful and plastered in advertisements; a graphic example of how Croatia prospered under Tito's special brand of Socialism. Unlike their Eastern European namesakes, Dinamo are an independent professional outfit who own their stadium, even if it was a gift from the Croatian governor in 1950. (Tito himself, said to have been a Dinamo fan, might have had a say in this.)

As well as staging a handful of internationals

Zagreb – an example of how modern synthetic materials can give stadiums new life.

(most are held in Belgrade), the Dinamo Stadium's greatest moment of celebrity was as venue for the European Championships in June 1976, when it staged the semi-final, Czechoslovakia v. Holland, followed by the third place play-off, Yugoslavia v. Holland. At club level, meanwhile, Dinamo are the only Yugoslavian team to have won a major European honour, the Fairs Cup in 1967.

Since then the stadium, if not the team, has improved greatly. The east stand has an open, upper tier, like a leaning slab of concrete, decked cheerfully in yellow bucket seats, with a terrace in front where, as the graffiti testifies, Dinamo's 'Bad Blue Boys' gather. Backing onto this stand, but neatly incorporated into its structure, is another terrace, this one overlooking Dinamo's training pitch (as at Porto).

The south, or scoreboard end, has a curved upper tier of seating over the players' dressing rooms, while the north end is a bank of terracing, lined at the rear by the trees of Maksimir Park and Zoo. On this terrace stands a torch holder. This was put there for the 1987 World Student Games, an event for which, much to Dinamo's delight, the city council invested heavily in refurbishment work.

This principally involved the main, west stand, whose base – also slab-like on angled concrete supports – dates originally from 1956. But with a new translucent roof, braced from behind by vertical cables, and with its steelwork painted blue, it looks the very picture of hi-tech modernity. At one end there is even a discotheque and a terrace café. These facilities, plus the addition of a synthetic track, yellow seating and new offices under the stand, have helped transform the stadium into a bright, exciting venue with 35,000 seats in a total capacity of 55,900. And if only the new roof didn't leak, it would be even better.

GROUNDWORK

BELGRADE

STADION CRVENA ZVEZDA

They call it the Maracana, but in some ways it is better. For the sweeping bowl of the Crvena Zvezda – or Red Star – Stadium, is not only Yugoslavia's largest stadium but also the power-house of an ever developing commercial empire of offices, restaurants and duty-free shops. If tomorrow **FK Crvena Zvezda** stopped playing football, or any of their other seventeen sports, they would still have a tidy little business. Half their expenses are met by non-sporting activities already, and with plans to build a second office block that percentage will certainly rise. For a club in a nominally Socialist country, Red Star put some of their capitalist counterparts to shame.

They are rather successful on the pitch, too, as one learns in the club's reverential museum. Since being formed by students of Belgrade University in 1945, the Serbian club has won the championship sixteen times and the Marshall Tito Cup eleven times (up to 1988). They haven't missed a season in Europe since 1968 and their record gate of 96,070, for a European Cup Winners' Cup semi-final v. Ferencváros, is an all-time Yugoslav record. The stadium's capacity is actually a mite larger – 97,502, of which 27,502 are seated.

It even has a good address, the Topčider district of Belgrade being where all the best apartments and embassies are located.

There was first a stadium on this site in 1927, belonging to a moderately successful club called Jugoslavija. Being sunk into a natural dip in the hillside it was able to hold 40,000 without the need for additional structures. Red Star took it over in 1945 and built a simple cover on the west side, then in 1959, in order for a complete renovation to take place, they moved down the road to share with their near neighbours and deadly rivals, Partizan.

They returned, eventually, on 1 September 1963, to a stadium twice the size, it having been dug twice as deep. Floodlights were switched on for a friendly v. Benfica in September 1971, and the stadium then became the first outside Western Europe to stage either a European Cup Final (Ajax v. Juventus, in May 1973) or a European Cham-pionship Final (Czechoslovakia v. West Germany,

A pink glow at Red Star.
But is the pitch really that lush?

in June 1976). It also took over from Partizan's stadium as Yugoslavia's prime international venue.

In time, a high, dramatically cantilevered roof went up over the main stand, to be joined by a slightly lower roof over the remaining sides of the bowl. But even then the stadium structure still barely surfaced above ground level, as if it had sunk in quicksand.

Like the real Maracana, though spectacular from afar and impressive at first glance, the Red Star Stadium is actually quite basic when seen

Belgrade's answer to the Maracana. Red Star fans joke that the Partizan Stadium (above) is really their training ground.

close at hand. Inside the bowl the predominant tones are those of the grey roof, red steelwork, faded red seats, the pink-coloured paving stones which form the terracing, and the bright terra cotta of the new synthetic running track. There ought to be a lush looking pitch as well, for it was revealed before England's visit in November 1987

that the groundsman has a special green chemical for painting out the bare patches on his turf. Now there's an idea – 'Let the Serbs cure your herbs', a bottled miracle from the Red Star Corporation. That should earn these enterprising Serbians a dinar or two among the threadbare football grounds of Europe.

BELGRADE

STADION JNA

A five-minute stroll from Red Star's stadium brings us to the rather more straightlaced home of Belgrade's second major club, **Partizan**.

With a capacity of 47,509 (15,500 seated), the Jugoslovenska Narodna Armia (Yugoslav People's Army) Stadium is a plain, single-tiered open bowl, broken up only by a VIP viewing balcony and bands of black and white seating on both sides. Otherwise it is exactly what one might expect of a stadium built and owned by the army – efficient, orderly, colourless.

But that is to miss its real significance. Partizan were formed in 1945 and two years later won the

Double. In 1948 work had just begun on remodelling the stadium when in a nearby guardhouse in Topčider Park, Tito announced that Yugoslavia was jumping off the Soviet bandwagon to pursue its own path to Socialism.

And so while soldiers and youth brigades toiled at the stadium (and on houses, hospitals and schools, amid the ruins of Belgrade), the angry Russian bear growled menacingly from afar, leaving Yugoslavia to wonder what the dawn might bring.

It brought only empty threats, as we now know, and instead of confronting the Red Army, Partizan's players ended up challenging Red Star.

The JNA Stadium reopened in 1951 and apart from staging Partizan matches (even after they became independent of the army in 1963), it has had two major functions. Until the Red Star Stadium was renovated in 1963 it served as the national football stadium (though it still stages Cup Finals), and every year on 25 May it plays host to the Day of Youth celebrations, in which an ornamental baton, relayed by runners all over Yugoslavia, is ceremonially handed to the President. In the 1950s the stadium was also used as a popular open-air cinema.

Nowadays the structure seems quite spartan, but the setting, amid tree-lined, cobbled walkways, is pleasant enough; a tennis club behind one end, a domed church by the other. On the west side a ceremonial entrance leads up through parkland to the October Revolution Boulevard, where, in a museum complex dedicated to Tito, one can see the batons he received at the stadium.

But before we leave the JNA Stadium behind, there are plaques by the main entrance recalling two prewar members of the Yugoslav national team: Milutin Ivković, killed in 1943, and 'Boško' Petrović, who died as a fighter pilot during the Spanish Civil War, both in the fight against fascism. Two true partisans among many.

The JNA Stadium – home fans think it's great, but then they are rather Partizan. Red Star's empire lies just beyond the tower blocks.

GROUNDWORK

SPLIT

STADION POLJUD

And so, nearly 200 stadiums after setting out from Milan, our Grand Tour ends on the Adriatic coast of Dalmatia, at a stadium so beautiful that words can barely improve on the pictures. Like a glimmering pearl on an azure bay – you see, the pictures are better – the Poljud Stadium was opened by Tito for the Mediterranean Games on 15 September 1979 and is home to Yugoslavia's oldest football club, **Hajduk Split**. (The Hajduks were local bandits who fought against the Turkish Ottoman occupation.)

Poljud Stadium is characterised by two 'space-frame' roofs, shaped like quarter moons and wrapped majestically over each side of a sunken bowl, so that when seen from a distance they seem to float above the ground. Professor Boris Magaš, the stadium's award-winning Yugoslav architect, described the roof concept as 'a transparent vault of lace'.

The transparency derives from the use of translucent Lexan panelling, a polycarbonate developed by the American space programme, while the 'lace' is formed by a latticework of nearly 13,000 slender steel members, joined together by 3640 nodes. So complex are the geometrical patterns woven by these frames – which must withstand both earthquakes and high winds – that their West German designers reckoned it would have taken one man twenty-two years, making one calculation every fifteen seconds, to arrive at the same formula their computers managed in weeks.

The base of the stadium is also of technical note. The precast units which form the saddleback-shaped bowl – circular on the outside, elliptical around the track – are literally held in place by three high-tensile steel ropes tied around the upper perimeter. And because the Poljud area (formerly farmland and vineyards) is only 200 metres from the Adriatic shoreline and falls between views of the verdant Marjan peninsular to the south and the distant Zagora mountains in the north, it was vital for the stadium to maintain a low profile. The bowl and its ancillary buildings are therefore sunk below ground level or hidden behind landscaped mounds, with ramps leading

'A transparent vault of lace' – the diaphanous Poljud Stadium and indoor pool (left).

spectators inside the stadium from a peripheral concourse. (In this respect the Poljud was the precursor of both new World Cup stadiums in Turin and Bari.)

Next to the stadium is an extensive swimming complex, also built for the Mediterranean Games, which borders upon a serenely enclosed Franciscan Monastery. Less appealing is a line of utilitarian modern apartment blocks immediately behind the stadium's south curve. Unusually, there is no terracing at this end. Instead, in front of an electronic scoreboard is a fountain, flanked by shrub-covered banks and, this being modern Yugoslavia, two incongruous advertisements for American jeans. On the rear wall, on either side of the scoreboard, are painted Hajduk's haul of trophies (nine championships and eight Marshall Tito Cups).

Mention of the great man leads us to the main reception area, where there is a lift, installed especially for his visit to inaugurate the stadium. It has hardly been used since, while the lounge it leads to has been kept just as it was on that opening day. But Poljud's links with Tito did not end with his visit. Hajduk were in the 42nd minute of a game v. Red Star on 4 May 1980 when play was halted, and Hajduk's president announced that Tito had died. A stunned crowd of 50,000 stood weeping as the national anthem was played and the game abandoned.

Since those early days, Hajduk Split have dis-

YUGOSLAVIA

Split image – but do the Hajduks miss the Gasworks?

covered two drawbacks to using Poljud (also referred to as the Gradski – or City – Stadium).

Firstly, although the stadium was financed jointly by the Federal Government, the city of Split and the Croatian State Government, Hajduk have to pay for its maintenance, which is not cheap. Those Lexan panels, for example, must be regularly cleaned to prevent deterioration, and though the club, to raise funds, has built and rented out an 8,000 sq. metre commercial development nearby, and receive 50 per cent of all stadium advertising revenue, the costs are still a burden.

But the second problem goes deeper than money, and it is on this note that we end our story – the dilemma which so many clubs and their followers have faced throughout the century.

From their formation in 1911 until 1979, Hajduk played at a ground nicknamed 'Plinada' – the Gasworks. It held 28,000 at a pinch and was shoehorned into a district of narrow alleyways and residential streets, with the crowded balconies of tenement blocks providing a grandstand view on match days. The ground was primitive, it was cramped and, of course, it was home.

Plinada still exists. Now called Lenin Park, the pitch is used for rugby and the stand for storing produce of a fruit and vegetable market. But you still see the occasional old man staring in, lost in his memories; a scene we have encountered throughout our journey – in Turin, Bruges, Nantes, Elche and Schalke. All over Europe, the emotions are the same.

And then along came the Poljud Stadium, with its great beauty, its comfortable capacity of 51,700 (26,700 seated), its superb facilities, its sheer concrete logic. And suddenly the Hajduk fans could no longer reach out to their players. There was a running track in the way. The terraces were too distant to hear the swish of the netting as a goal was scored. A big crowd was no longer a throng, an average crowd seemed lost.

For this was a stadium, not a football ground. The Hajduks had been tamed, and are we not all Hajduks at heart?

BIBLIOGRAPHY

General
Encyclopedia of World Soccer: Richard Henshaw (New Republic Books, 1979)
European Football Yearbook: Ed. Mike Hammond (Facer Books, 1988)
Football Grounds of Great Britain: Simon Inglis (Collins Willow, 1987)
History of the World Cup: Brian Glanville (Faber and Faber, 1980)
Twentieth-Century Architecture: Ed. V.M. Lampugnani (Thames and Hudson, 1986)
World Club Football Directory: Ed. Keir Radnedge (Queen Anne Press, 1984)

Austria
Wiener Sportstätten: Friederike Stadlmann (Europa, 1986)

Belgium
RSC Anderlecht 1908–83: (Editions Gamma, 1983)

Finland
Suuri Areena: Helge Nygrén (Stadion-säätiö, 1988)

France
Allez les Verts: Dominique Grimault, Patrick Mahe (Editions Denoel, 1981)
Le Red Star: Guillaume Hanoteau (Editions Seghers, 1983)
Roger Taillibert – Recent Works: Marc Emery, René Huyghe (Métropolis, 1977)

Italy
ABC del Calcio 1988–9: (Casa Editrice Universo)
Almanacco Illustrato del Calcio 1989: (Edizioni Panini)
Impianti Sportivi: Cesare Mercandino (Gorlich Editore, 1966)

Hungary
75 Éves a Fradi-Pálya: Bela Nagy (1986)

Northern Ireland
Linfield 100 Years: Malcolm Brodie (1985)
The Story of Glentoran: Malcolm Brodie (1982)

Portugal
Sport Lisboa e Benfica, Fotobiografia: Rui Guedes (Publicações Dom Quixote, 1987)
História e Vida do Sporting Club de Portugal: Eduardo de Azevedo (CERC Lisbon)

Soviet Union
Sport in Soviet Society: James Riordan (Cambridge University Press, 1980)
Soviet Sport: James Riordan (Basil Blackwell, 1980)

Spain
Real Madrid, Historia de un gran club: Luis Miguel (1984)
Nuestro Estadio: Manuel Martínez (Elche, 1982)
Real Betis Balompié – 75 Years: Antonio Bustos (1983)
Sevilla FC 1905–80: Manuel Rodriguez, Antonio Somoza (1980)
Fútbol y franquismo: Duncan Shaw (Alianza, 1987)

Sweden
Twenty-five Fantastic Years – Ullevi: Bengt Hansson, Kurt Johannson (Fritid Göteberg, 1983)
Råsunda 50 Years: Svenska Fotbollfoerbundet (1987)
Stadium, 75 Years: Göran Löwgren (Stockholms Idrotts-förbund, 1987)

Switzerland
100 Jahre, Grasshopper-Club: Henry Eggenberger (1986)
Servette FC: Jacques Ducret (L'Age d'Homme, 1976)

Turkey
The Republic of Fenerbahçe: Yalçin Doğan (Tekin, 1989)

West Germany
Deutschlands Kampfbahnen: Dr Mar Ostrup (Berlin, 1928)
Sportbauten: Rudolf Ortner (Georg Callwey, 1953)

Yugoslavia
Crvena Zvezda 1945–85: Dragoslav Markovic (Yugoslovenska Revija, 1985)
Hadjuk Split 1911–81: Eterović, Reić and Vukašin (Slobodna Dalmacija, 1981)
Partizan 1945–70: Prosveta Beograd, 1970)

Periodicals
Acier, Stahl, Steel (Brussels)
ARCA (Milan)
Architect and Building News (London)
Architects Journal (London)
Architectural Design (London)
Architettura (Milan)
Arquitectura (Madrid)
BOUW (Holland)
Building Design (London)
Byggmästaren (Stockholm)
Casabella (Milan)
Concrete (London)
Construction Moderne (Paris)
Corriere della Sport (Milan)
Der Aufbau (Vienna)
Der Baumeister (Munich)
Design (London)
Don Balon (Madrid)
Foot Magazine (Brussels)
Informes de la Construccion (Madrid)
International Lighting Review (Holland)
L'Architecture d'Aujhourdhui (Paris)
La Repubblica (Rome)
Onze Magazine (Paris)
Plan (Dublin)
Spaziosport (Rome)
Sportecho (East Berlin)
Sport und Baderbauten (Düsseldorf)
Structural Engineer (London)
Voetbal International (The Hague)
WERK (Zurich)
When Saturday Comes (London)
World Soccer (London)

INDEX
OF
PLACE NAMES